Listen to what others are saying about TIME OFF!

"I wish I could be Mayor of San Francisco forever but even us politicos need a break once in awhile. *Time Off!* has given me a wealth of ideas for enjoying life after City Hall and the book beautifully represents San Francisco. It will greatly assist my staff and me in getting the most out of our leisure time."

~**Former Mayor of San Francisco, Willie L. Brown, Jr.**

"*Time Off!* is full of practical ideas and thoughtful medicine, delivered with a big, funny spoonful of sugar. I'm jealous—why does San Francisco get all the fun? Every city needs one of these! I'm rooting for The Leisure Team against The Workaholics in the Superbowl of real life.

~**John de Graaf, national coordinator, Take Back Your Time and co-author of** *Affluenza*

"*Time Off!* encourages you to take your leisure time seriously—to expand your mind and invest in friendships and family—the important things in life that no employer can ever take away. Take this book to heart and you'll someday start the story of losing your last job with this sentence: 'You know, that was the best thing that ever happened to me.'"

~**Ethan Watters, San Francisco writer, author of** *Urban Tribes: A Generation Redefines Friendship, Family and Commitment*

"With impressively researched lists detailing cheap happy hours, free art, and ways to stop feeling guilty about taking a giant loan from Mom and Dad, this exhaustive tome eloquently preaches the love of leisure and the importance of wise financial planning. Dean LaTourrette and Kristine Enea offer enticing suggestions for what to do with your extended free time."

~*SF Weekly*

"Authors Dean LaTourrette and Kristine Enea dissect all that's cheap, free, and otherwise beneficial for the unemployed, from the city's best happy hours to window-shopping to public pools to the science of a good garage sale."

~*The Wave Magazine*

"Forget the GNP, think of your own *personal* GNP: what is going to add to your life, bring you more joy and less stress? *Time Off!* is a great first step to getting your life on track, your priorities in place, and your panties (or boxers) out of a bunch! Whether you're employed or unemployed, this guide will improve the quality of your life."
     ~**Bridget Fonger, co-author of** *The Lazy Woman's Guide to Just About Everything*

"Hands down, the San Francisco Bay Area is one of the most brilliant playgrounds in the world, both natural and urban. Get off your duff and get out and enjoy it! And keep this book in your back pocket. It's a fantastic resource for the cost-conscious, the lifestyle-conscious, and the 'soul' conscious."
     ~**Susan MacTavish Best, founder and editor,** *Posthoc San Francisco* **(posthoc.com)**

"If you're not working (and really, who works anymore?), you may as well sit down with a good book. A good book about not working? Hell, that's even better."
     ~**Camper English, San Francisco writer and man-about-town**

"Leaving work behind to travel and reconnect with the spirit and core values has always been an essential part of my life and is what led to the creation of 'Mister SF.' For locals and travelers alike, San Francisco is an epicenter of joy and imagination. *Time Off!* is all about enjoying the city as San Franciscans do—with leisure as a top priority!"
     ~**Hank "Mister SF" Donat, San Francisco's "Heart of the City" columnist (MisterSF.com)**

"I wholeheartedly believe that leisure is critical for romantic success; in our hurry-up world, what could be more meaningful than slowing down to enjoy life with the person you love? Leisure Team has created an amazing resource, jam-packed with suggestions and inside tips... which makes it that much easier to have fun!"
     ~**Jennifer Jeffrey, writer, co-founder, "Sex and the Kitchen" (sexandthekitchen.com)**

"This book will make you want to quit your job."
     ~**Tom Haan, founder, Bojon.com (bojon.com)**

TiME OFF!

THE LEiSURE GUiDE

TO

SAN FRANCiSCO

Second Edition

TiME OFF!

THE LEiSURE GUiDE TO SAN FRANCiSCO

Second Edition

SFORBUST

DEAN LATOURRETTE
KRiSTiNE ENEA

leisure team
productions

Time Off! The Leisure Guide to San Francisco

Published by Leisure Team Productions.
First printing 2004; second edition printing 2007.

10   8   6   4   2   1   3   5   7   9

Distributed in the United States by Publishers Group West
Distributed in Canada by Publishers Group Canada

Publisher's Cataloging-In-Publication Data

LaTourrette, Dean.
   Time off! : the leisure guide to San Francisco / Dean LaTourrette, Kristine Enea ; edited by Ellen Clair Lamb. -- 2nd ed.

   p. : ill. ; cm. -- (Time off!)

   First edition had subtitle: the unemployed guide to San Francisco.
   Includes bibliographical references and index.
   ISBN-13: 978-0-9741084-1-4
   ISBN-10: 0-9741084-1-3

1. San Francisco (Calif.)--Guidebooks. 2. Leisure--California--San Francisco--Guidebooks. I. Enea, Kristine. II. Lamb, Ellen Clair. III. Title. IV. Title: Leisure guide to San Francisco

F869.S33 L38 2007
917.94/610454   2006908695

Edited by Ellen Clair Lamb, Jennifer Birch, Kate Williamson and Moira Bartel
Proofed by Sue LaTourrette and Kate Williamson
Cover and Illustration by Jamie Leap Designs
Additional Illustration by Sara Irvin and Kristine Enea
Layout by Kristine Enea and Christie Miller
Printed and bound in the United States by Malloy Incorporated

To order online, visit us at leisureteam.com. To talk leisure, debate leisure principles, or just complain about your job, e-mail us at info@leisureteam.com. For bulk orders, please e-mail your inquiry to orders@leisureteam.com.

*This book is dedicated to
all of San Francisco's leisure seekers.*

As a born contrarian, I've lived my life breaking the rules. While this is no surprise to those who know me well, it has seemed to surprise many in the often-conservative world of business. I built an entire hospitality management organization based not on what already existed in the industry, but based on a very personal belief that in the end, people want to enjoy and celebrate life. Our company name, Joie de Vivre ("Joy of Life") comes directly from this philosophy, as does our corporate mission statement, "Creating the opportunities to celebrate the joy of life."

Personal fulfillment, in my view, has always been about following your own path. What's rewarding to others, whether it's money, love, business success, family or any other measure of a person's satisfaction, isn't necessarily what's going to make you happy. As simple as that sounds, I'm always amazed at the number of people who try and measure their success and happiness based on the scorecards of others. Work or play, it's all about what makes *you* happy, not anybody else.

Leisure
It just so happens I'm in the business of leisure. While this might seem a paradox to some, I've never seen it as such. For one, my company provides what I believe to be vital services that aid people in enriching their travel and hospitality experiences, whether that be relaxing at a spa, dining at a comfortable restaurant, or staying at a hotel that somehow connects with their personal values.

From a personal perspective, I've also created a work role for myself that draws on my own natural strengths and passions, and an organization that's an extension of my personality. And that's about the most leisurely accomplishment I can imagine.

Time Off

Taking breaks from work has always been a priority for me. Is that a "rebel rule?" Unfortunately, in our society, time off seems to be a rebellious concept. It often takes a fair bit of courage to break away from the herd and carve out significant time away from work.

Since as far back as my undergrad days at Stanford, I always took the opportunity to take off and travel whenever the chance presented itself. But, American culture and its Protestant work ethic have somehow suggested that two weeks is all we have each year to experience the opportunity to "vacate." How does one experience magical places around the world like South Africa or the Amazon when your employer only gives you two weeks a year?

That's part of the reason Joie de Vivre offers all of its salaried employees a paid one-month sabbatical every three years. We have people visiting our hotels from all of over the world, so it's nice that our employees have enough vacation time to return the visit to some of these far-flung places around the world.

Sabbaticals have allowed me to rejuvenate and focus my business mind. In fact, some of my best entrepreneurial inspirations have come during vacations or personal periods of transition. I came up with the idea for the popular outdoor private bathtubs in the penthouse bamboo garden at Spa Vitale from my travels to Bali. Some of my favorite "modern meets Moorish" design ideas have come from my trips to Marrakesh, Morocco where I celebrated my 45th birthday with 65 friends in 2005. I don't know about you, but my busy life can be way too linear, so these crevices of time are when the light of inspiration is able to crack open my all-too-organized life.

Cultural Tourism

I've long been a proponent of the concept of cultural tourism. To me this essentially means connecting with a place in a manner that's "real," as cliché as that may sound. Think about what your most memorable travel experiences have been. I'm willing to bet they involved connecting with the people, the flavors, the sites, smells and sounds of a particular location. This didn't happen because you visited a particular tourist attraction or bought a souvenir—not that there's anything inherently wrong with that. It likely occurred because you somehow interacted with local people, and experienced a slice of their life. In short, you connected with the culture.

Time Off! The Leisure Guide to San Francisco not only makes the case for using breaks to renew and refresh, it also makes this cultural connection. Whether you're living in the San Francisco Bay Area or just visiting, it seeks to dig beneath the surface of where typical guidebooks live, and uncover the true culture and flavor of San Francisco. All at a leisurely pace, of course!

San Francisco

This city is truly a magical place, full of wonderful surprises, underground secrets, and hidden treasures. I fell in love with San Francisco when I first moved here in 1984, and I haven't left since. Its whimsical and creative nature is the perfect setting for me, as well as for my company Joie de Vivre. Our San Francisco hotels attempt to celebrate and contribute to this culture, by creating unique, theme-based hotels with distinct personalities such as cinema, art and literature, and rock 'n roll.

While hotels, restaurants and other amenities usually require a fair bit of money (and let's face it, around here it never hurts to have some extra pocket change), many of the wonderful experiences in San Francisco are available for little or no money—you just have to know where to look. *Time Off! The Leisure Guide to San Francisco* does a wonderful job of ferreting out these local experiences that money can't necessarily buy.

And speaking of money, mull over this little bit of wisdom: instead of running out and buying yourself that next "thing" that you think you need, consider instead using that money to buy yourself a little extra time. In the end, if need be, you can always go back and make some more money. But you can never go back and get that precious time back.

Chip Conley
Founder & CEO, Joie de Vivre Hospitality
Author, *The Rebel Rules: Daring to be Yourself in Business*
San Francisco Bon Vivant

TABLE OF CONTENTS

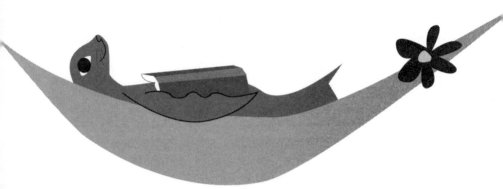

INTRODUCTION

WELCOME to the second edition of *Time Off! The Leisure Guide to San Francisco*, the ultimate guide to local leisure with a purpose. If you're picking this book up for the first time, then congratulations—we'd like to introduce you to the wonderful world of leisure. If you've already perused the first edition, then welcome back.

The first obvious change you'll notice is in the second edition's new title. Yes, we've updated that dubious "unemployed" word—you know, the one that so many had trouble with. We ourselves are big fans of unemployment in the broadest sense, but also realize that "unemployed" is an inescapably loaded term. We therefore changed it to "leisure," a word more reflective of the true spirit and content of the book. We begrudgingly concede—unemployment maintains a stigma that even we, the Leisure Team, with our far-reaching powers of leisure, cannot alter. So be it.

That being said, we've always intended the book to be the definitive leisure guide for locals, to live like tourists in their own town—as well as a unique guide for tourists, to play like locals in a foreign town. And that's whether you're fully employed and on vacation, taking an extended sabbatical, in a career transition, or fresh off an all-too-sudden layoff. It's all about taking time off and maximizing your leisure time, whether that's for one day or one year, at home or on the road.

Those of you who *are* in the unemployed ranks, do not fear—we haven't abandoned you! You'll still find plenty of information that will help smooth your transition, as well as inspiration to turn your *accidental sabbatical* into something positive and worth remembering.

WHAT'S NEW

So what's new for edition number two? First, we have an all-new, highly entertaining foreword written by local entrepreneur and titan of leisure, Chip Conley. Chip is founder and CEO of Joie de Vivre Hospitality, one of the most successful boutique hoteliers in California, if not the country. Chip certainly knows his leisure, and has built an entire organization around the concept of cultural tourism. With 17 properties under management in San Francisco alone (and likely more by the time you're reading this), he also knows and loves the City by the Bay.

Next, we've put together a new Chapter 1: The Art of Leisure, one we feel delves deeper and is even more reflective of our overall philosophy behind leisure and time off. Read this chapter, and ponder the role of leisure in your own life. The chapter sets the tone for the remainder of the book, and puts all the wonderful ideas throughout the text in proper perspective.

We've also updated many of the listings in Chapter 4: Rediscovering San Francisco, including the special sections: Fairs & Fests, Dining & Nightlife, and the Unemployed (now Leisure) Shopping Guide. We've added some new and entertaining Great Moments in Unemployment and San Francisco's Wild Characters. Beyond that, other changes are spread throughout the book, and include factual and editorial updates. In certain cases, whole sections were nixed because we didn't like the passages or didn't think they were as pertinent anymore, while new content was added as needed with each new discovery.

You'll notice some subtle modifications like different chapter titles, new Leisure Lingo entries, and some additional anecdotes here and there. Oh, and we've dropped the "www" from all website address-es—that's *so* 2003!

If you've read the book before (thank you!), you can skip ahead to the all-new Chapter 1: The Art of Leisure. We hope you continue to pass the book along to friends, visitors, and fellow leisure-seekers.

If you're reading *Time Off!* for the first time, do read on.

IT'S TIME FOR TIME OFF

Yes, you *can* take time off from work and still enjoy life. Your life *can* and *should* flourish while you're not slaving away at a job. You'll need to be smart with your finances and rid yourself of self-imposed "unemployment guilt"—then just embrace the wide open, captivating world of leisure around you!

Can you contribute to society when you are not working? Can you be fiscally responsible between jobs? Can taking time off transform you and everyone around you?

The simple answer to these questions is an unequivocal and resounding, "YES!" But the story doesn't stop there. *Time Off! The Leisure Guide to San Francisco* ventures well beyond the simple answer to tell you how you can make the most of your free time, whether that's a three-month sabbatical or an afternoon playing hooky. It's part philosophy, part "how to," and part guidebook. It hails the benefits of working less and playing more, explains how (and why) to take time off, and guides you to the best of San Francisco.

WHO THIS BOOK IS FOR

You don't have to be unemployed—at least in the conventional sense of the word—to read this book. San Francisco is an ideal stomping ground for anyone with any amount of free time.

If you *are* out of a job, you're now perfectly poised to discover a new town, or to rediscover your hometown. If you merely aspire to be unemployed, we hope to tip the scales in favor of gaining a new perspective on the familiar.

Maybe you have a job but it's part-time or project-based. If you're not into hustling 60 hours a week for The Man and would rather save some daylight hours for feeding your own soul, this book is for you too.

And if you're lucky enough to like your job, or have a secure job and want to keep it—well, what's wrong with playing a little hooky now and then, or establishing a healthier work-life balance? Even workaholics need a vacation day once in a while.

Whether you were "downsized" or are gainfully employed, living here or just visiting, this book will offer you hundreds of ideas on how to savor your free time in San Francisco.

By the way, you don't have to be a millionaire to live well here. If you have a few dollars saved, that's a good start. We'll share some ideas on how to manage your money to squeeze out another month or two of relaxing. If you don't, not to worry; you can find plenty of fun in this city without a big price tag and we'll tell you where.

Time Off! is all about enjoying San Francisco the way a local would and should, at a relaxed pace and without burning through piles of money.

WHAT IS TIME OFF?

America hardly embraces non-work time. Unlike cultures where downtime is an integral part of a balanced life, our culture dismisses any kind of time off as an anomaly, a tragedy for the unmotivated, or a gift for the spoiled. The stereotypes are miserable! But why should *non-employment* have such a bad rap?

The very fact that there's no good word for "not working by choice and loving it" hints at a greater societal ill—*over*-employment. Someone who slaves 60+ hours a week at work is not only accepted but revered. That's crazy!

So, forget the stigma. "Time off" means so much more than not working. In the broadest sense, it covers any down time at all, especially time not owed to an employer. In the best sense, it connotes a period of renewal, reflection and meandering creativity that produces original and lasting contributions to humanity. Even an unexpected layoff can lead to personal growth.

It's time to jettison the mindset that you're freeloading or unworthy if you're not contributing to the gross national product. The gross national product can't measure the value of the arts, volunteering, or any other low- or non-wage-earning activity. Ironically, too much time "producing" means not enough time to explore, create or invent—and without creativity or innovation, growth and prosperity disappear.

Time off doesn't have to be lengthy or formal. All it requires is a desire to transcend your daily obligations for a year, a month, or one savory afternoon. Time off can work wonders for your psyche when overwork has turned you into a psych-o (not to mention what it will do for the psyche of everyone around you!). So even if your non-employment was a surprise and you need a new job *right now*, strive to find the free time you need.

Rich or poor, famous or obscure, working or not—everyone needs time off. And everyone can get it.

LEISURE

"Time which one can spend as one pleases," says the Oxford English Dictionary. "Time free from the necessities of work," said Aristotle. Some scholars view leisure as a distinct period of time, to be enjoyed only as a luxury or by an elite leisure class; others see it more as goofing off. One thing's for sure, the daily grind is consuming too many hours these days to leave much room for leisure.

Many Americans believe that leisure awaits them only in retirement, but a growing number of us see leisure as something deeper—a

SAN FRANCISCO

Ah, San Francisco! A city that needs no introduction... or does it?

Most tourists have heard of the Golden Gate Bridge and cable cars, Fisherman's Wharf, Alcatraz—even the Great Earthquake of 1906. Fewer know San Francisco as "Baghdad by the Bay," a city that encompasses more than 800,000 residents in its 47 square miles and that served as the backdrop for such classic films as *The Maltese Falcon* and *Vertigo*.

History buffs know that Spanish colonists rechristened the small town of Yerba Buena after St. Francis on June 26, 1776, and that the United States won the city from Mexico in 1846. San Francisco's Spanish-language heritage endures in the present-day city motto, *"Oro en Paz, Fierro en Guerra"* (Gold in Peace, Iron in War). Serious San Franciscans can even name our City Colors, City Tree, City Flower, and City Bird. (City Bird? Find out in Chapter 4!) If any of this is news to you, maybe it's time to rediscover San Francisco!

The City has been the world's favorite tourist destination for decades. It has inspired immortals of literature, music and the arts, whose memories linger in place names such as Jack Kerouac Alley or Dashiell Hammett Street. San Francisco is famous for its tolerance and liberalism, welcoming those who would be outcasts elsewhere. It never stops inviting novelty, culture, and adventure. Financiers, entrepreneurs, strippers, hippies—all call San Francisco home.

San Francisco is all these things and more. It is a city that constantly reinvents itself, which is good news for you—tourist or local—as it means there are always new activities and culture to explore.

way of living life to the fullest, and closer to the heart. We see leisure as an attitude and a lifestyle, and it is the reckless pursuit of leisure in San Francisco that is the focus of this book.

FORMAT OF THE BOOK

Time Off! is divided into three parts: contemplating and preparing for leisure, making the most of your free time, and transitioning back to work.

Part One makes the case for taking a break, and lays out strategies for overcoming financial and psychological hurdles.

Part Two seeks to whet your appetite for San Francisco during your *leisure odyssey*, with recommendations for local sites and activities, events, dining & nightlife, and leisurely shopping. Besides rediscovering your hometown, you can travel, explore unemployment on the edge, boost your health and fitness, get to know your friends and family better, and volunteer.

Part Three focuses on "re-entry", be it pursuing higher education, finding more balance in job hunting, or incorporating more moments of leisure into a working world.

Spread throughout the book are celebrations of **Great Moments in Unemployment**. If you see an italicized term that you're not familiar with, edify yourself with our **Leisure Lingo** glossary in the back of the book.

Most of the sites, shops, and other resources we recommend are in San Francisco—except for a few irresistible ones within easy striking distance. Recommended resources are shown in bold as well as indexed alphabetically in the back; recommended reading is in the back too.

Time Off! The Leisure Guide to San Francisco is not a guide to job hunting, although we do share some unconventional means for landing one. It's not "San Francisco on the Cheap," although we *are* big fans of free fun. And it's not a traditional San Francisco guidebook, although we'll give you plenty of unconventional and intriguing information on the City.

It *is* full of ideas on making the most of your San Francisco sabbatical, whether that's part-time or full-time, one day or one year—all designed to enrich your time off journey and propel you forward into the wonderful world of leisure.

UPDATES

Although all of the information herein was current as of the publication date, it's always a good idea to double check to see if websites, phone numbers or any other information has changed. Please share your ideas or feedback by emailing us at info@leisureteam.com. We'll publish updates and other breaking news at leisureteam.com.

Finally, a caveat: in the weeks leading up to publishing this book, a funny thing happened. Indian summer arrived in earnest in San Francisco, and the City was blessed with day after day of brilliant weather. The surf at the coast turned on, and the allure of the waves grew powerful. Prime festival season (September-October) also kicked in, and it seemed that everywhere we turned there was some fabulous outdoor party, concert or festival to enjoy (see **Fairs & Fests** for details).

The point is we got a bit... distracted. On more than one occasion, we found ourselves jigging to live music or savoring an Oktoberfest beer in the sun, when we probably should have been at home editing and proofreading. In the end though, it somehow seemed insincere, even *irresponsible* that we should be denying ourselves these indulgences while wrapping up a book about taking time off.

So in the very remote chance you happen upon a typo or some minor mistake within these pages, please accept our humble apologies. Know that it was all done purely in the name of leisure. Enjoy!

PART ONE

CHARTING YOUR COURSE

CHAPTER 1
THE ART OF LEISURE

*Leisure, some degree of it, is necessary
to the health of every man's spirit.*

~ Harriet Martineau

ASK some people what they would do if they won the lottery and their answers mostly *sound* like leisure—shopping in exotic locations, driving fast cars to happening nightclubs, and basically living like a rock star. For others, "leisure" is a weekend time-share or a cookie-cutter vacation, or some other pre-packaged pricey getaway that's too short to truly refresh. Yet quick-fix vacations and lottery dreams that focus on the cost-intensive, media-driven image of leisure—with its misleading promise of sex appeal, status and fulfillment through spending—aren't particularly realistic or satisfying in the long run. In fact, they miss the mark completely.

Consider, for a moment, leisure as a grander concept, one more holistic in nature. Just imagine the feeling of having all the time and money in the world—even though you don't. The consumer-economy version of leisure is fine for what it is and at times can hit the spot as conveniently as an all-inclusive resort or a double latte, but true leisure has little to do with how much money you spend, and everything to do with how you spend your time.

Researchers confirm what we already know—most leisure takes place in and around the home, and what's most important to the majority of us are interactions with our loved ones and activities we've invested in. You don't need big bucks in order to get together with your family and friends, learn a musical instrument, or improve your basketball game. Just like love, many of your greatest moments will be experiences that money just can't buy.

While leisure doesn't depend on money, it *does* depend on time. It may sound like the same thing, but that's only because we're used to hearing the "time is money" mantra. Taking a break can be crucial if you find yourself needing a new direction or even needing to learn how to live.

Leisure means much more than just being out of the office. It means enjoying life and living richly. It means living life in balance, both at work and at play. With the right mindset, a little planning, and a healthy splash of creativity, leisure turns mere day-to-day existence into a life worth living.

WHAT IS LEISURE

Anthropologists have observed tribes that mix work and leisure across every aspect of life, but most societies sharply distinguish the two: work is what we must do, leisure is what we want to do. Scholars believe that leisure did not exist until we humans, as a species, were able to meet our basic survival needs.

Well, are we there yet? We're way beyond gathering our basic scratch yet our concept of leisure hasn't changed much since the times of the ancient Greeks when philosophers expounded that only the elite were entitled to downtime, often gained at others' expense. The Romans "democratized" leisure with the Circus Maximus but it turned out that "bread and circuses" was designed by the politicos to divert social protest and sedate the masses with entertainment. Today's mass entertainment diversions—television, shopping, video games—have the same potential for sedation: sapping energy from endeavors that can be more satisfying and significant, such as working on that fast ball with your kid or putting in your two cents at the city council meeting. After all, you have only so much room in your closet for "bargains" from the television shopping channels, don't you?

SIZE YOURSELF UP

You're not alone if you identify closely with your job or feel guilty when you're not working. Americans have always been wary of leisure.

Almost a hundred years ago, the German sociologist Max Weber identified the link between capitalism and the self-denying ethos of Protestantism, and dubbed it the *Protestant Work Ethic*. This conviction tells us that wasting time is evil and the grindstone clears the path to salvation. The concept of "nose to the grindstone" has been ingrained into the American psyche ever since.

Yet, the average American workplace runs rampant with depression, chronic fatigue and burnout. Most workers don't get the proverbial two-week vacation, much less use all the vacation days they do get. People are volunteering to get laid off just to get a break from the grind. Despite the evidence all around us, our culture continues to cling to the notion that material success symbolizes divine favor and that our purpose on earth is to work for *work's* sake.

What's wrong with this picture?

identity check

If any of these statements have passed your lips, take them as a sign to get yourself to Leisure School, pronto!

I'm not at the top of my game.
I can't balance work and family.
I never have enough time.
I am so tired I can't think straight.
I've become someone I don't like.

self-worth ≠ net worth

Self-worth does not equal net worth, promotion does not equal success, and life really isn't a competition to see who can climb highest on the corporate ladder.

you ≠ your job

Taking time off makes you no less smart, attractive, funny, kind, or any of the other things that define you. You're still the same person—maybe even a better person—if you're on sabbatical or under-employed. Saying no to more work allows you to renew relationships and become a better citizen of your community. Non-employment presents an ideal opportunity to rediscover your best self.

THE LEISURE COMMANDMENTS

Thou shalt enjoy at least one sustained period of unemployment during thy career.

Thou shalt switch careers to do something thou really enjoyest, even if it means taking a pay cut.

Thou shalt pursue one secret childhood dream without regard to status or the judgment of others.

Thou shalt party until dawn on at least one weeknight.

Thou shalt lounge around thy house in thy pajamas.

Thou shalt create, experiment, and ponder.

Thou shalt reconnect with thy community.

Thou shalt partake of the great outdoors.

Thou shalt travel and explore, beginning with thine own hometown.

Not enough downtime, that's what. Every hour of overtime is an hour that you don't spend playing, singing, dancing, learning, or enjoying the company of others. It's an hour that you're not spending on an experience that you choose purely for its own sake, whether or not anyone rewards you for it. All work and no play, as the saying goes, makes Jack a dull boy. Well, Jack needs mental space to create and grow. Jack needs a break.

If overwork has turned you into someone you don't like—you don't want to know yourself and no one else does either—take a deep breath and repeat this mantra: "I am not my job. I am *not* my job." Then remember that you can't reminisce with the friend you never had, you won't be telling fish tales about the adventure you never found, you can't enjoy the satisfaction of volunteer work that you never did. Trust us, you will not be on your deathbed wishing you had spent more time in the office. When you think in terms of what you might have lived or done, leisure becomes nothing less than crucial. The art of living will never be perfected without practicing the *Art of Leisure*.

LEISURE REDUX

When we say "leisure" we mean more than unoccupied time. We mean the freedom to pursue whatever activity it is that revitalizes you. If you lack autonomy in your day job, take matters into your own hands by launching your own business. If you're tired of navel-gazing, step outside yourself and volunteer to help others. Not happy with where you're at in life? Take off on a personal journey of self-discovery and contemplation. Got cabin fever? Feeling just plain lifeless? Hop on a jet plane and start a torrid international love affair.

GREAT MOMENTS IN UNEMPLOYMENT

GAME AFTER GAME AFTER GAME

During the Depression of the early 1930s, an unemployed salesman living in Pennsylvania developed a strange new board game while struggling with odd jobs to support his family. The inventor? Charles Darrow. The game? None other than Monopoly. Parker Brothers bought the rights to Monopoly in 1936, but Darrow shrewdly negotiated a royalty payment for every game sold. Darrow's entrepreneurial instinct and refusal to buckle despite being out of steady work made him a millionaire, the first game developer ever to have made as much money. • • • Unemployed Michael Wurstlin created the layout, design and logo for the iconic board game Trivial Pursuit. His payment? Five shares in the company. By 1986, those five shares were valued at two-and-a-half million dollars. • • • Alfred M. Butts, an unemployed architect looking to play a game that required equal amounts of skill and chance, created the predecessor to Scrabble in 1931. It would take until 1948 for him and his business partner to get the word out and begin manufacturing Scrabble in its modern form. The game has since become an international phenomenon—over 100 million sets have been sold in 121 countries—and early royalties to Butts allowed him to retire. Although Butts enjoyed playing the popular board game until his death in 1993, he wasn't a particularly good player. The reason? Por speling.

Leisure activities that demand intense attention and effort, such as taking an art class or playing a competitive game of racquetball, can provide the feeling of accomplishment and rigor that might be missing in your lackluster *McJob*. On the other hand, playing, relaxing, socializing, entertaining, taking in the sensual pleasures of life—activities that you choose for their own sake—can provide the release from mental or physical tension that overwork spawns.

We strongly support lounging around—in fact, it's one of our commandments. Moreover, downshifting while the world rushes around you is hardly unproductive. Research has repeatedly found that people who spend less time at the office are more productive than those who spend extra hours at work. Even pure loafing can relax the body and mind to a state where new ideas blitz you from all directions. Bring *that* creativity to the boardroom, why don't you?

Be it childlike and light or serious and competitive, as short-lived as an amiable conversation or intense enough to send you into that frame of mind where you're so absorbed in what you're doing, you don't think about anything else—leisure means doing what comes naturally, and engaging in intrinsically rewarding activities.

The best work is work you want to do; the best leisure involves a conscious decision to improve your life or at least your state of mind. Leisure and work can be one and the same if you choose what fulfills you and then pursue it for all you're worth—and that's *self*-worth, not net worth.

YOU'LL GET NOTHING AND LIKE IT

Out of 168 countries surveyed, a healthy number guarantee family-friendly benefits:	
Paid leave for new mothers	163
Paid leave for new fathers	45
Paid sick leave	139
Paid annual vacation leave	96
A maximum limit on the workweek	84
Paid time off for parents when children are sick	37
But the U.S. guarantees none of the above to any worker.	

WHO HAS LEISURE?

Workers around the world today have less free time than our ancestors did. In fact, no group enjoys less leisure than today's Americans. Ancient Romans, by contrast, designated over a hundred days a year "unlawful for judicial and political business" and medieval Europeans took off three to five months every year, including long vacations for Christmas and Easter and weeks-long "ales" to celebrate marriages, deaths, harvests and other special occasions. Pre-industrial societies might have been less wealthy but they were far more relaxed.

The year-round workweek is a relatively modern invention, introduced during the Industrial Revolution, which saw American work-hours balloon to nearly 80 per week. The workweek contracted through the Great Depression, but the end of the World War II created a new boom in the standard of living and consequently a new boom in the working hours required to achieve it. Between 1969 and 1987, the average employee added almost a month's worth of hours to the working-year. Most Americans today work more than 55 hours a week, not counting housework or childcare.

In Japan, a society that takes its work ethic to the extreme, the literal English translation for "I work for Nissan" is "I am Nissan." Never mind getting too caught up in your work—in Japan, apparently you *are* your work! Yet Americans now work longer than even the Japanese, by almost two weeks a year.

we're number one!
(but do we want to be?)

Americans have longer workweeks and less vacation time than workers in any other industrialized country, according to the United Nations' International Labour Organization.

American workers average almost 2,000 hours a year. This substantially exceeds the workweeks of industrial Europe: the British work 1,731 hours a year, the French 1,656, the famously industrious Germans only 1,560 hours, and those lucky Norwegians—1,399 hours.

The countries with workweeks most similar to ours are the developing nations—Sri Lanka, Thailand, Malaysia—where underpaid workers are scrambling to improve their quality of life.

We, on the other hand, have no such excuse. So much for "first world" evolution!

Long hours aren't America's only burden. Family-friendly work policies barely exist in the U.S., even though 61% of young families say they spend too much time at work. Today, fewer than half of Americans can take advantage of the 12 weeks of unpaid leave provided by the Family and Medical Leave Act of 1993. About a third of female employees earning less than $40,000 a year receive no paid vacation at all. The only bright spot is that American employers are more likely to offer flex-time than are employers in other advanced industrialized nations, although part-time workers generally don't receive pro-rated benefits.

wasted leisure time

Too often, the burned-out ooze home, spend four unproductive hours in front of the television, and drag themselves back to the office the next morning. Work becomes an escape from home and home an escape from work.

"I kept going for more money," former work-junkie Mary Mangold told us. "I got a really nice apartment, lived in a good neighborhood, bought designer clothes, with no energy to do anything. When I came home it was time to sleep. I might as well have been living in a closet."

This is not a minor problem. This is a tragedy, and the underlying syndrome has been dubbed *Wasted Leisure Time*. Inoculate yourself!

TIME KEEPS ON SLIPPING...

As unemployment has gone up, so has overwork. Survey respondents recently told Expedia.com that they'll be taking 10% less vacation than in the year past—they have too much work to get away. Many Americans take no more than a long weekend. Five years ago, all but 5% of U.S. companies offered at least some paid vacation. Today, almost 15% offer none. American employers offer the most miserly vacation allotment in the industrialized world—just 8.1 days off after one year on the job and 10.2 days after three years.

Yet, most Americans say they would trade money for more free time. It's not hard to see why. Email, instant messaging and cell-phone calls pervade our lives, nagging us at all hours with unfinished business. We hurry everywhere and begrudge anyone who intrudes into our space. The more we work, the less likely we are to eat dinner with our family, spend enough time with our pets or even vote. Our short vacations leave us more stressed-out than before, and we use up the rest of our paid time off taking "mental health days." The Chinese word for busy has two characters—one means heart and the other means killer—and indeed, the perpetual time crunch can cause weight gain, weight loss, insomnia or anxiety attacks. "I can see the difference between me and my co-workers," says Bob, a computer programmer who takes regular sabbaticals. "They have lots more gray hair."

wake up call

One survey in the U.K. (where workers log in more hours than anywhere else in the European Union) revealed that given an extra hour in the day in bed, most respondents would rather sleep than make love. Now that's just not right!

The laid-back Australians get four weeks a year guaranteed by law; Americans are guaranteed zilch, zero, the big goose egg.

And it's not even a golden goose egg. Overtime is now the norm, frequently without any extra pay. Subtract from your pay the costs of your commute, the professional clothes you have to buy, your lunches at the deli downtown, and the childcare bill you pay each week. Add to your work-hours the hours you spend every week getting ready for work, going to and from work, and then winding down after work. Divide one by the other. How much is your true hourly wage? Overwork doesn't benefit business, either. American business loses $300 billion a year in job stress-related costs, not including the billions spent replacing absent workers.

WHAT HAS HAPPENED TO LEISURE?

Working long hours and being plugged into the office at all times (cell phone implant, anyone?) blurs the division between work and personal time. Some people work longer hours on weekdays and try to squeeze in the rest of their life on Saturday and Sunday. But by Friday night the weekend warriors are so exhausted that it's all they can do to get ready for work again by Monday. Others toil away their whole youth in a misguided attempt to save their leisure for retirement. Somehow a gargantuan mortgage slips in, medical bills from a premature stress-related disease, college tuition for kids who you don't really even know, and you're too far in debt to retire in luxury like you planned. What kind of leisure savings account is that?

off-peak driving   Take regular breaks.

Use a headset.   TACKLE THE HARD STUFF FIRST.

Keep an overnight bag packed.   ten minutes a day

DoNotCall.org

SPEED DIAL   Plan your route.

☒ junkbusters.com   Clean up as you go.

Do it now.   You gotta ♥ clogs.

Make a list.

FREE YOUR TIME

One subject per email.   Freeze the leftovers.

Log on for a specific purpose.

Measure twice, cut only once.   no-phone zones

smartertravel.com   Be selective.   SCREEN CALLS.

Have a place for things.   Schedule downtime.

SPEED CLEANING   Prioritize.

Break a challenging task into small pieces.

Set goals.   Get rid of things you don't use.

Turn commute into exercise.   just one junk drawer

WE NEED MORE LEISURE!

We are bombarded with thousands of messages a day telling us first to spend, then to consume, then to spend again. We can't sustain that kind of consumption without then going to work, work, work to pay all the bills, and loans, and…and…. ENOUGH!!!!!!!!

Whew! The work-spend-consume cycle is *exhausting*. It's time to get Jane off that crazy train and onto the leisure locomotive.

If working too much causes all that harm, what happens when you get more leisure? Is it like playing a country song backwards—you get your dog back, you get your friends back…?

Yes! Leisure will bring you all that and more.

Playing and dabbling are not only hedonistic and relaxing, but can also generate new ideas. All the major arts and sciences, especially the humanities, developed from the creative use of leisure. Constructively used, free time leads to cultural, societal and individual enrichment, all crucial to the evolution of advanced society. Just take a look at the **Great Moments in Unemployment** throughout this book for some examples. Goofing around can be serendipitous, the source of accidental discovery and spontaneous invention.

Bill Coleman, a CEO who grew his software company to a billion-dollar run rate after just five years in business, shared one of his most important management secrets with us. "I ask all my employees to take off at least two weeks in a row each year," he told us. "I get my best ideas during time off, including the idea for this company." If it worked for him, it can work for you. Bring on the Art of Leisure!

Taking a "time out" can help you to re-create yourself after a lengthy tour of duty in corporate America. Working hard may or may not have swelled your bank account. It may or may not have advanced you up the proverbial ladder. But there is no maybe in the effect your tour has had on your family, your neighborhood, and your community. They want you back! The energy you have diverted toward work will be a tremendous gift when directed toward them.

Free time allows you to figure out who you are and how you relate to the people around you, whether they're former colleagues or family members, and to give more thought to where your efforts will be most productive in the long term. The skills you have learned in the workplace can be put to use in many other aspects of your life. Management and organizational skills can help you run a civic league, coach a softball team, even run for local office. Negotiating skills can help you start your own business, raise money for a local non-profit, or serve as a Big Brother or Big Sister.

Leisure isn't a luxury to squeeze in after taking care of your basic needs. Leisure *is* a basic need. You need to get away from it all and recharge yourself in order to handle life's many obligations.

LEISURE SCHOOL

If you're starting to burn out, you need to enroll in Leisure School!

The first lesson is all about attitude. Convince yourself that you truly need and deserve leisure, and that you and everyone around you will be better off for it. You're on your way to becoming an honor student once you begin to adopt this mindset, since leisure is as much a state of mind as it is a function of free time.

Freeing your time is important, though—one unhurried step at a time. Life is about making memories. Are most of your memories packaged in a gray cube and tagged with a sticky note?

Take this simple quiz: Have you taken a significant break from work in the last several years? Do you make yourself available by cell phone at all hours of the day? If you're looking for work, should you really spend every waking hour searching for a job?

If your answers are "yes," don't worry—this is the most enjoyable course of study that you'll ever take! Start small by remembering that you don't have to be "scheduled" every minute of the day. Decide which goals are most important and let the least-pressing ones go. Don't rush around just for speed's sake. Take a risk—unplug from the World Wide Web and get out to see the wide wonderful world! It's time to launch your very own *Leisure Odyssey*.

The rest of this book is full of ways to free up time and make the most of it. These ideas can work whether your sabbatical is by choice or circumstance; whether you're working full-time, part-time, or no-time.

Don't worry if you can't just snap your fingers and be leisurely. Remember, you're fighting the tide of culture and history, and change takes time (oh the irony). Leisure is a process that most of us need to adjust to slowly and in stages.

So get out your number two pencil and start taking notes—right after your siesta!

CHAPTER 2
ADJUSTING TO TIME OFF

*Leisure is the most challengingresponsibility
a man can be offered.*
~William Russell

I slip from workaholic to bum real easy.
~ Matthew Broderick

WELCOME to the world of leisure, where every day feels like Friday! We know a bit about you, simply because you're reading this book. You might be non-employed or thinking about taking the big non-employment plunge. Perhaps you've just been laid off from your job, and find yourself taking an *accidental sabbatical*—pausing to reassess your work and personal life, even though you weren't the one to initiate the sudden change in status. Or maybe you're completely burned-out at work and are conspiring to make the break and treat yourself to a well-earned hiatus. Finally, if you *are* happily employed, it could simply be time to add a little more "life" to the work-life balance.

Regardless of your situation, congratulations! Whether by design or circumstance, you've already taken a big step forward in freeing yourself from the culture of overwork, and for that we salute you. You may feel ill at ease with the concept of taking time off but that's perfectly normal in our work-centric society. Remember, just because you want or need to take a breather from the grind does not mean that you plan to never work again, or that you'll have any greater difficulty landing a job in the future. It does mean that until you're ready to work again—and work is ready for you—you can unwind, have fun, and make good use of your freedom. So put your watch away, chuck your PDA into a drawer, and learn to embrace a leisure lifestyle by launching your Leisure Odyssey—whether that's one afternoon or one year—guilt-free.

FREE YOUR MIND

Reactions

You hear countless stories about individuals who retire only to be bored out of their minds with no job or career to occupy their time. Erik's dad got laid off and decided to stay retired rather than find new work. He got so restless, he resorted to vacuuming his driveway—with the hose attachment! At the other end of the non-working spectrum, Drew Jordan of San Jose, California, suffered from strong bouts of guilt. "I hated being unemployed," he told us. "I felt a lot of guilt that my wife (and really most of the rest of the world) was off working away, and I was home in my pajamas screwing around on the Net."

Paydirt

Most of us only dream about what we would do if we didn't have to work. So why, when that wish is granted even temporarily, do we have difficulty seizing the moment? "Most of us have an innate love of security, even if we envy someone who doesn't have that as their main goal in life," says Hope Dlugozima, sabbatical expert and co-author of *Six Months Off.* "Doing things out of the norm is a really hard thing to do, even if philosophically you think you're in favor of it. It's like jumping off a cliff, and it's really hard to make that first jump.

"But once you do it," she adds, "it's exhilarating. Things start to fall into place, and all kinds of energies and drives you didn't even know you had, all of a sudden they're right there because you took that one big step first."

This holds true whether your break is planned or not. You're definitely not alone if you don't hit a groove right away, but sooner or later you'll learn to take downtime in stride.

Obstacles

Clearly, the health of your financial position is critical to your peace of mind, which is why we devote the entire next chapter to getting your money house in order. "I think it's really important that you can cover [a break from work] financially," says Tess Roering, a marketing executive who recently took a six-month break to travel and volunteer. "I think it would be extremely stressful to try and relax and enjoy the time if you didn't know how you were going to pay the rent."

Experts, however, say that it's usually *psychological* barriers that keep people from enjoying a break—or even taking one in the first place. "I just don't have the money," or "I'm not independently wealthy," or "That's nice for other people," are excuses you hear all the time. But the professionals say that financial obstacles typically exist as a *result* of mental constraints, not the other way around.

"People think that money is going to be the biggest problem in taking a sabbatical, but our findings were that it really isn't money," says Hope. "People can find their ways around money once they really start focusing on things. It's usually fear, more the sense that 'I just can't really do this,' 'this is too weird,' or 'I'm going to screw up my career going forward' that keeps people from doing it."

POST-EMPLOYMENT HOUSEKEEPING

Sometimes we forget how many personal benefits are covered by a full-time employer. Psychological challenges aside, non-working newbies should deal with several logistical issues right away. Leaving the employed world, even if for a short time, can trip up the unsuspecting neophyte. Here are a few tips to smooth your transition.

Severance

If you're unfortunate enough to have suffered a layoff, did you negotiate a severance package when you were hired? (Or in *Aspiring Retired* mode?) It might not be too late, either to start from scratch or to improve the one you have.

Your severance package should cover not only the severance amount but also things like benefit continuation, pro-rated bonus, and vesting of a portion of any stock or options—as well as spelling out the circumstances under which you'll be entitled to receive severance in the first place.

Get it in writing. Severance can occur after a takeover, a new boss, an economic downturn or any other job-changing event, and can be paid either as a lump sum or a salary continuation.

pink slip: fact or fiction?

Getting the "pink slip" has long been a euphemism for getting fired. The term is even in most dictionaries. But has anyone ever actually gotten one?

Traditional lore says that companies issued employee termination notices on pink slips of paper. At the Henry Ford Motor Company, managers reputedly placed slips of paper in workers' cubbyholes at the end of each day—white meant that their work was acceptable, pink meant that they were out the door.

Neither theory has been verified, according to **Snopes.com**, a popular website that researches urban legends.

Snopes reports that Peter Liebhold, a curator at the Smithsonian Institution's National Museum of American History, has searched for ten years to find an actual pink slip but so far hasn't found one.

So while the concept of "getting the pink slip" is very real to certain unlucky workers, the origins of the term remain a mystery.

Know Your Rights

Do you suspect you were unfairly laid off? **Nolo** (800-728-3555, nolo.com) has released the sixth edition of the popular book *Your Rights in the Workplace* by Barbara Kate Repa. Nolo offers a few nuggets of free legal advice on their website, too. Consulting either of these sources might help you size up whether your employer followed the rules when sizing down.

Direct Deposit

If your paycheck used to be deposited directly into your bank account, you may get socked with monthly fees once those direct deposits end (curses to fake-free-checking banks!). A quick phone call can let you know whether your bank will be charging you fees and whether you can avoid them by switching to a different type of account.

Health Insurance

Whether you are leaving of your own accord or are a victim of downsizing, parting ways with a full-time employer usually terminates your healthcare plan. Unless you're willing to roll the cosmic dice, you'll need insurance to protect yourself against major injury or illness, regardless of the duration of your break.

If you're leaving a company that offered a health insurance plan, you qualify for COBRA, the national program designed to ensure continued coverage for workers after they leave a company. Paying a monthly premium will guarantee you the same coverage you were receiving before you left, for up to 18 months after you leave. The rub? You have just a brief window of time to decide whether you want COBRA coverage. The good news is you can decide, retroactively, to enroll in the coverage up to 60 days after your company plan terminates. For tips on whether to elect COBRA or some other kind of insurance, see **Chapter 3**.

Stock Options

You may or may not have been offered stock options at your former job. If you were, you'll normally have a fixed amount of time to exercise vested, unexercised stock options after you leave a company, or forfeit them altogether.

For publicly traded stock, your decision is straightforward: if the current stock price is higher than your option "strike" price, exercise the options. You can either sell them all immediately and bank the profits; sell just enough to cover the cost of exercise (a partial-sale); or, if you can afford it, hold all the stock until you want to sell.

If the company is pre-IPO (Initial Public Offering), the choice is less obvious. To exercise the options, you'll have to cut your company a check with no immediate chance to recover any costs by selling. If the company never goes public, the stock could end up being worthless. Double-check your paperwork to verify how much time you'll have to decide. You may want to wait until the last

pink slip: fiction or fact?

The layoff stories we've heard involve methods a lot wackier than pink slips of paper.

Software veteran Andrew Riley's boss lured him to his favorite bar, and then laid him off between sips. Account manager Mary Mangold showed up one morning to find her desk cleared and her computer missing. "That was my first clue," she said, "that something wasn't quite right." And a whole group of high-tech employees who got canned in one fell swoop were then marched over to a table in the corner where the local newspaper offered them a special deal: half-price subscriptions for the recently unemployed.

Layoffs didn't take graphic designer Steve by surprise. He got tipped off that they were coming the next day, so he brought a disposable camera to work to document the scene. "I hid the camera under the table while the flash was warming up," he told us. "The shots didn't turn out too clear but they sure caused a stir." Management complained to no end that Steve was trying to "make a case"—for who knows what.

minute to see how the company is faring—particularly if you left as part of a large layoff!

Keep in mind that exercising stock options represents a taxable event, whether the company is publicly traded or privately held. That means you could have a substantial tax liability even before you sell. Your tax burden will depend on the fair market value of the stock on

BEFORE TURNING IN YOUR BADGE

If you're facing an impending layoff or have just plain had it with your job, take these important steps before you walk out the door:

• **Transfer Your Contacts.** Whether it's a pile of old business cards or a comprehensive database, your contact information could be the most important asset you leave work with. Back up this information so that you can access it once you're no longer with the company—provided, of course, that your employer's confidentiality policy allows you to do so.

• **Transfer Your Personal Files.** If you're like most workers, you have personal files mixed in with business files. Separate them out and take them with you. Security policies might apply here, especially if you're walking out the door with a box of documents. Discs will fit nicely into your pockets. You can also email stuff to a personal email address.

• **Set Up a Personal Email Account.** If you haven't already, get a personal email account and let friends and associates know before you leave that your contact information will change.

• **Settle All Financial Reimbursements.** If you can, have the company cut you a check for any money they owe you before you walk out that door. This includes salary, travel expenses, or any other reimbursable expenses you've incurred.

• **Don't Sign Anything!** Don't sign a parting agreement—including a severance package—that you're unsure about until you've had a chance to review it thoroughly. At a minimum, take it home with you to evaluate outside of your work environment. Better yet, have a lawyer look it over and advise you on how to proceed.

the date that the options are exercised and whether your options are qualified ("ISOs") or non-qualified ("NSOs"). You'll want to consult a tax adviser, preferably one who has experience with stock options (not all do). Remember to keep exact records of when you exercise your options, and how many shares you bought. For more on taxes, see **Chapter 3**.

Retirement Plans
If you had a 401(k) or some other retirement plan with your former employer, you might be forced to do something with the funds. Many plans or companies will continue to administer your retirement funds if they exceed a minimum threshold amount. Otherwise, you should consider rolling over the funds into an IRA to avoid early withdrawal penalties.

FIVE STEPS OF UNEMPLOYMENT GRIEVING
Ever heard of "The Five Stages of Grief" from Elisabeth Kübler-Ross's book, *On Death and Dying*, or seen the movie *All That Jazz*? If you feel like you're going through a similar mourning process, it's because you are. You're mourning your former employed self.

Those who find themselves suddenly out of work usually do go through some sort of grieving process to get over the shock of joblessness. The good news is, the unemployment grieving process has a much happier ending. It goes something like this:

1-Denial. Denial is fairly common for people who feel pressured to work constantly and feel unproductive if they're not. Some people lie to themselves; others experience such shame that even if they don't outright lie to family and friends, they conveniently fail to mention that they've quit or been laid off.

DENIAL
I'm not un-employed—I'm simply "between jobs."

ANGER
*That @&%$ employer! I never liked working there anyway. I hope that f****** organization goes under.*

2-Anger. Some people get angry about their predicament, lashing out at former employers, the economy, the government, or anyone else in range. Instead of embracing and enjoying time off, they expend a great deal of energy being mad at the world.

BARGAINING
I'll trade you half my old salary for my previous job.

3-Bargaining. Many try to bargain their way out of unemployment, either trying to hang on to their old job under less desirable circumstances or settling for a job that's beneath their abilities.

4-Depression. Depression afflicts the newly-unemployed more than any other emotion. Don't fall for it!

DEPRESSION
This sucks. I'll never find another job.

5-Acceptance. Acceptance is your goal if you want to get the most from your non-working time. It's a Zen mindset that will come fairly naturally when you've become versed in the Art of Leisure.

ACCEPTANCE
I'm at peace with my non-working status. Now, please pass the hookah.

DEALING WITH GUILT

Guilt is your enemy. Guilt stands between you and your happiness and could be your greatest obstacle in reaching time-off enlightenment. You must fight it off at all costs! We implore you, do not let it grab hold of your psyche; it can spoil an otherwise savory time of relaxation and self-fulfillment, and cause you to cut this precious time short.

Give yourself a break, both figuratively and literally. This is your time and your life. As long as you can maintain financial stability, you're entitled to do as you please. Transitional times are tough enough without assigning unnecessary and destructive blame.

AVOID THE COMPLEX

Guilt is one of the most common emotions associated with unemployment, says Rochelle Teising, psychotherapist, life coach, and co-founder of the San Francisco-based consulting group Success at Work. "It's really hard for people to see the gift in not working," she says, "because they often think that they've done something wrong. They don't let themselves enjoy the time off."

Many of her clients try to alleviate this guilt by immersing themselves in their job search, not allowing time for leisurely activities, and driving themselves crazy in the process. Don't let that be you!

Liberate yourself from the "must-work" mentality and instead of berating yourself for your current status, congratulate yourself. *Sit* for a while. Celebrate your standing in the non-working world!

THE UNEMPLOYMENT TIME-SPACE CONTINUUM

The *Unemployment Time-Space Continuum* is a loosely formed concept that goes something like this:

* You will be late.
* You will forget non-essential appointments.
* You will be transported to an alternate parallel universe where...this is okay.

Time becomes much more fluid when you're not working, and you'll find yourself on a completely different clock. Don't be alarmed if you're convinced it's Monday when it's really Tuesday. A severe case will have you thinking it's a weekend when it's not—lucky you! Just don't expect any sympathy from your working friends.

It's also normal that you won't make it to every appointment or task that you set for yourself. The reality is, you don't *have* to do anything— at least not in a work sense—and human nature tends to breed apathy in the absence of necessity.

Again: this is okay. Don't get overly upset or feel guilty, but do monitor your personal flake factor. Skipping out on your friends or colleagues is hardly anything to aspire to during a sabbatical.

SLOW DOWN, YOU MOVE TOO FAST

If you want to truly break away from a set schedule, try telling your friends and others ahead of time that you're going off the clock for a bit, and not to expect immediate responses from you, or your presence at every gathering. Remember, there's nothing wrong with taking a break from social obligations in addition to work obligations, especially if your goal is to slow down your pace of life.

Speaking of slowing down, there's something of a movement afoot in this country and around the world. Advocates call it the Slow Movement, but we prefer to call it the "move at your own pace" movement. Carl Honoré, recovered "speedaholic" and author of *In Praise of Slowness: How a Worldwide Movement Is Challenging the Cult of Speed*, went through his own personal transformation to arrive at a more leisurely pace. "I just couldn't slow down," he told us. "I was speed reading *The Cat in the Hat* to my son. Then, while reading a newspaper at an airport, I saw a series of books called *The One-Minute Bedtime Story*—which is an appalling idea, but I was like 'Great! That's what I need.' And that's when I saw the lightbulb. As a journalist, the first step is to write, so I started writing about it." Sounds like the write stuff to us, but we're sometimes a bit slow ourselves.

GETTING OFF THE GRID

No, we're not talking about saving on electricity, but the concept of "unplugging" from a number of modern life's communications and conveniences. Technology provides us with a fantastic array of devices that enable us to stay connected to people and places like never before. But this technology can come at a price: an over-stimulation of media and messages, and ever-accelerating demands on our time from an increasing number of people. We're not just talking about work, either. Between cell phones, email, instant messaging and text messaging, our social lives can become a rapid-fire succession of stress-inducing stimuli.

John de Graaf, a Seattle-based author and television producer, runs an advocacy group called **Take Back Your Time** (timeday.org), organized to fight overwork and what they call "time poverty." "Technology is playing a factor in making lives busier around the world," says de Graaf. "It's all the more necessary to find ways to protect people's time off because you're on this electronic leash all the time."

Consider cutting the cord on some or all of this technology for a set period of time. Trust us, it's extremely refreshing. If you're packing up and hitting the road during your break (see **Chapter 4**), you may have no choice, particularly if you're traveling to some far-flung corner of the world. But even if you're hanging out in your own community, give it a whirl and see how it goes. The peace of mind you gain from not answering your cell phone or email for a few weeks (do we hear a month, anyone?) can be enough to recharge your batteries—and that's *personal* batteries, not cell phone batteries.

"One of the most refreshing breaks I ever had was when my girlfriend and I took a vacation, but then ended up not going anywhere," Dane Larson told us. "We actually didn't plan it that way, but at the last minute we decided not to travel, yet didn't tell any of our friends. It became an adventure—no phones, no email, no responding to messages of any kind for over a week. We just cruised around town and did whatever we wanted, whenever we wanted."

AFTER THE HONEYMOON

If you're like most non-employed people, it's been a long time since you've had your weekdays free. After a few weeks of waking up with boundless energy for carefree, pure enjoyment (the *Unemployed Honeymoon*), you might start to wonder what retired people do with themselves. You run the risk of losing motivation, getting too much sleep and (doh!) actually watching daytime television. Here are better options.

daytime specials

Weekdays suddenly free? Challenge those parking tickets! Those who do are often rewarded just for showing up. Motor on over to the *San Francisco Department of Parking and Traffic (1380 Howard, 415-255-3900 for citations, ci.sf.ca.us/dpt).*

Any small claims you'd like to collect? A pesky misdemeanor or two to clear up? The *Superior Court of California, County of San Francisco (ci.sf.ca.us/courts)* can guide you through solving your "problem." Even jury duty might become a weekday "to do." You can't really say no to it now!

Have you heard? Runs to the DMV no longer take up an entire afternoon. Make medical appointments, dental appointments, or any other appointment that you'd normally have to squeeze into your lunch hour, and cross them all off of your list.

When you run out of your own errands, take care of your friends and neighbors: you'll score big-time brownie points, and make some serious deposits in the favor bank.

Personal Maintenance

Ever wish you had a personal assistant? Now you do—yourself. Spend some time on your personal life maintenance. And no, we're not talking about manicures, pedicures or bikini waxes (ouch!), but activities that hopefully go a little bit deeper than the skin.

Start with getting "stuff" done. Clean the closets. Shine your shoes. Alphabetize the spice rack if you've been wanting to. Everyone keeps a running tally of "nice to do's" that aren't urgent but can stack up like dishes in a sink. Checking them off of your list will clear your mind (or at least the table!) for more advanced leisure pursuits.

Rob DeWaters multitasked his job-search time in front of the computer by digitizing his entire CD collection and portions of his friends' collections. The fruits of his labor amounted to over 40 gigabytes of music files and paid huge dividends more than two years later when the iPod was introduced to the market. That's a lot of burning, ripping, and otherwise organizing your love for music. "Investing the time that otherwise would have been spent at work allowed me to pull this off while simultaneously looking for a new job," Rob told us. "Alan Greenspan has no idea how productive the computer has made me!" Try tackling *that* project while you're working full-time.

Setting Goals

Once you've come down from the initial euphoria of your freedom from work, you may want to set some goals for yourself. Wait a minute, set goals? Whoa, you say, I didn't take a sabbatical so I could set goals. If this sounds a bit ambitious, keep in mind that worthy non-work goals can range from such lofty pursuits as travel or reading as many classics as possible, to hanging a hammock in the backyard—seriously, it takes several steps!

The point is—and you've heard the saying before—time flies when you're having fun. Before you know it, you'll be facing the prospect of work again. So outline what you'd like to accomplish, as grandiose or as simple as it may be, and prioritize your leisure.

For more on goal setting and exploring new directions, see **Chapter 7**.

PREPARING FOR CHALLENGES
Talking To Your Family

Families can be a real challenge when it comes to not working. Consciously or unconsciously, most families expect financial and career success of their members, and don't see taking time off as a way of furthering either.

Are your parents on your case? Maybe they were raised in an era when unemployment carried even more of a stigma than it does today. To their generation, work was a large part of a person's identity and it was uncommon to leave a job without having a new one. For the most part, that generation didn't face the level of layoffs and employee turnover that characterize today's

preemptive strike

One non-employed gentleman we know took the bull by the horns, as had always been his secret yen (you'll see…).

He was so tired of fielding questions on what he was doing for work and his plans for the future that, in anticipation of a friend's wedding, he drafted a one-page personal fact sheet. The sheet mockingly explained that he had left his last job to "pursue other interests," including his "dream to someday be a rodeo clown."

He handed out copies at the beginning of the reception, forcing everyone in attendance to focus on other areas of interest in his life—whether they wanted to or not! While it might not have dramatically changed anyone's opinion of him, he did manage to score a date with a cute coed.

working environment. Constant change became a way of life toward the end of the baby boom—the U.S. Bureau of Labor Statistics reports that people born between 1957 and 1964 changed jobs an average of 10 times by the time they were 36 years old. It's a new type of generation gap, one that can leave you feeling like a disappointment to your parents.

Being married can also make time away from work more stressful. Many who are not working fear that their spouses will see them as lazy or inept. Whether real or imagined, this perception can create barriers, conflict and even resentment between partners. "There's the stigma of job loss to deal with—will your spouse think you're a failure? Your kids? Your parents even?" says Peter Hannah (changingforgood.com), a one-time victim of technology layoffs who now counsels others on the topic as a trained therapist.

GREAT MOMENTS IN UNEMPLOYMENT

TAKING THE PLUNGE
Dan Briody was an account executive for Purdom Public Relations, a small high-tech PR firm in San Francisco. In 1995, he informed his boss, Ned Purdom, that he was quitting his job and moving to Hawaii, with no plan and no job. His boss informed him he was committing career suicide. Briody's "career suicide" involved publishing the critically acclaimed bestseller *The Iron Triangle,* followed by *The Halliburton Agenda,* both about the Carlyle Group's business dealings with the Bin Laden family. Ned was then featured in Michael Moore's incendiary *Fahrenheit 9/11.* If this is suicide, sign us up!

"I personally shared more with my partner and less with my parents when I got laid off."

Add kids and your obligation to support them into the mix, and you could have a real disaster. "There may also be an internal drive to hide real-world problems from the kids, to try to insulate them," says Peter. "Kids are pretty wise though—the older ones figure things out, and the younger ones can sense that something is wrong."

Career counselor Rochelle Teising claims that communication within families is often poor during times of unemployment. Some of her clients who are laid off are so ashamed of losing their jobs that they keep it a secret! "The irony," says Rochelle, "is that these people need to connect with friends and family more than ever."

So, take your *family* to Leisure School! Explain to them your goals and intentions. Tell them why you're taking time off—even if it *is* largely to goof off. Your goal is to make them more comfortable with your non-employment, even if they don't necessarily agree with the concept, and to circumvent those awkward moments at the dinner table. For more about time off-in-the-family, see **Chapter 8**.

What To Say To Friends

Chances are, your friends will be more understanding than your family when it comes to taking time off. Ted Witt, a 35-year-old operations director, claimed that most of his friends were happy for him when he lost his job. "They knew I was miserable at work, and that I wanted to go and travel anyway," he says. "My parents, on the other hand, didn't quite see it the same way."

In many instances, though, even your true friends will think, "You should be working like me," or "When are you going to go out and get a job? *Coaster!*"

Don't let unemployment come between you and your friends; use it to re-connect. Not only will you have more flexibility but you'll be getting reacquainted with your non-work self—the self that your friends might have been missing. Eileen and Alexia had fallen out of touch after college but they picked up right where they left off after Alexia quit her demanding day-job. "Eileen's a mom whose free time is when her daughter's at school," Alexia told us, "so she's got a lot of good ideas about how to have fun during the day."

Being open with friends is the best way to combat any resentment. Without explanation, your friends could translate "not working" into "lazy" or "spoiled"—or both! They might jump to the conclusion that you have a large trust fund, for example, when in reality, you were smart with your money and saved. Or maybe you do have a leisure patron—offer to help find them one too! (See **Chapter 3** for tips on how.) Who knows, you might even convince one of them to join you on your Leisure Odyssey!

♪ ...Tell me why, I don't like Mondays--tell me why!

~Boomtown Rats
"I Don't Like Mondays"

Mondays

Conventional wisdom holds that Mondays are the toughest day of the week for the working set. Yet, Mondays can be strange for the non-working, too. Others go off to work, but not you. Your weekend simply continues.

Nearly all of the people we spoke with who used to work nine-to-five experienced some sort of anxiety around Mondays. "Sometimes it's the best day and sometimes it's the worst day," says Dave Casuto, a human resources coordinator who was unemployed for six months. "It's the worst day because everyone's going to work, and you feel kind of useless. It's the best day because on Sunday night, you get that instinctive pang about work the next day, until you realize, 'Oh yeah, I don't have to go to work tomorrow.'"

Fiona, a software executive who quit her job to travel for a year, says the first few Mondays were the weirdest. "I was so used to waking up early that for about a month after I quit, my internal alarm clock was still going off at 6am. I would wake up with all this restless energy that I didn't know what to do with. What on earth do people do before 6am besides go to work?" Undaunted, Fiona set to the task of re-learning how to sleep in. Ah, the perks of leisure!

Turn what could be the worst day of the week into the best. Make it your bonus day. Go to your favorite café and read a good book. Partake in your preferred workout. Do whatever it is you care to do, and set the tone—or the tune—for the rest of the week.

Having free Mondays is not only okay, it's cause for celebration. Embrace it! Revel in it! If you can conquer the Monday Blues, you'll be well on your way to reaching a higher time-off plateau.

CURES FOR THE BLUES

Being on sabbatical can open up new worlds of freedom for you. Or, you might find yourself sleeping too much, missing appointments and letting your laundry pile up.

Beware! While we are all in favor of moving a little to the right on the **Unemployment Time-Space Continuum** (see earlier in chapter), we do want you to *feel* like a million bucks, even if you don't actually have a million bucks.

Everyone's got a favorite cure for the blues. Working out is one. According to many experts, all forms of regular exercise combat depression, anxiety, stress, and sleeplessness through a massive release of the same chemicals in the brain that produce "runner's high" (see **Chapter 7** for fitness ideas). Taking responsibility for another living creature also works. "It's not for the faint of heart," Marsha Converse told us after getting a dog, "and it was a long-term commitment, but it got me out and about in the neighborhood every single day."

Rochelle Teising recommends music and dance, noting, "You cannot be depressed when you're dancing." Chinyan Wong changed her tune with new music. "I started listening to more classical music," she said. "My dad left his radio alarm clock in my bedroom which is set on the local classical station. It's actually a very gentle and soothing way to start the day."

And Rob DeWaters went to the beach once a week, weather permitting. "Seeing beautiful women in various forms of undress always had a way of keeping my spirits up," he quipped.

If you can't seem to break out of a funk, you might need some professional help. We can't make that call but mental health specialists can. They'll help you see the *Layoff Blues* for what they are—tired old tunes that you can do without.

"what do you do?"

??????

This all too familiar inquiry haunts the leisure seeker. Perhaps no other question is more indicative of our workaholic culture. It might come during a first meeting at a cocktail party or from an uncle at your brother's wedding but it always implies the same thing: what do you do for *work*?

The "what do you do" question clearly subscribes to the tired old work-as-identity doctrine, implying that working is the one and only way of "doing."

"It's funny, when people ask me what I do," said Tess Roering during an extended break from work. "I always just say 'nothing,' which takes people a little bit by surprise."

Next time someone asks what *you* do, whether you're working or not, try out the following responses to help turn the tables:

Play ignorant.
"About what?"

Tout your favorite hobby.
*"I climb mountains.
How about you?"*

Get philosophical.
*"I enjoy life.
And what do you do?"*

Holidays and Special Occasions

Ah yes, the holidays. If ever a time was rife with societal and familial pressures, this would be it. You should be working, you should be dating, you should be marrying, you should be having kids! Whatever you should be doing, you should be doing it doubly over the holidays, making November through January the most challenging months for the non-working set.

According to counselor Peter Hannah, there's also financial stress to contend with. "Christmas is a time where we want to give gifts, where we may feel we need to match the gifts others give us. It's definitely an easy time to feel 'poor' when finances are constrained."

If you can avoid succumbing to traditional pressures, however, the holidays can actually be the best time to not have a job. Think about the bright side—stress-free Christmas shopping! (Or *reverse* shopping, see **Chapter 4**.) Leslie Gonsalves, a recruiter who was out of work for four months beginning one November, savored the holiday season. While her friends could take off only an afternoon here and there, she could shop every day, enjoying the company of a different friend each time.

And beware of special occasions. Birthdays and weddings can unite you with extended relatives and friends who'll want to know what you're "up to" or will toss you the infamous, "What do you do?" Because holidays and special occasions can be such trying times, we recommend these tactics to minimize the damage:

Stay Out of the Corner

Watch for family traps like the inevitable two-on-one gang-up. The minute you sense the conversation at the dinner table turning against you, bob and weave, anticipate and avert. Change topics quickly, and deflect questions about your time off by asking your own questions in return.

> *Your mother:* So, are you even *looking* for a job?
> *You:* Mom, this cranberry sauce is fantastic. Did you make it from scratch?

Be Proactive

The best defense is a good offense. Being the initiator means you won't get caught off guard and sound defensive. Have stock answers ready for questions about your transitional time, and offer information to head off awkward lines of questioning. It's the "nothingness" that makes people uncomfortable.

> *Transitioning between careers, or thinking about it?*
> —I'm taking a class.
> —I'm doing some research.
>
> *No such ambitions?*
> —I'm exploring my creativity.
> —I'm writing my memoirs.

Know Your Allies

Know who will rush to your defense in tight situations. Your protectors are usually the people who know you best, and they can help fend off the work-centric attacker from advancing within your comfort zone. Defense in numbers is almost always more effective than a solitary defense. Unite with the Leisure Team!

Losing Friends from Work

One potential side effect of being job-free is losing your friends from work. You could be surprised to discover that your relationships with these people you spent so much time with were bound by the job and not much else. This realization can be unpleasant, particularly if much of your social life was wrapped around your workplace.

"I had a hard time filling the social void after I quit," Fiona told us. "I had spent so much time on the job that my non-work relationships had all but disappeared."

Be prepared to confront this issue by making an extra effort to keep in touch with former co-workers. This is your chance to put more energy into friendships outside of work, too. (See **Chapter 8** for ideas.)

Too Much Sleep

Sleeping too much can leave you drowsy all day and lead to depression. Try to get up on the early side and start your day with something physically active to get your blood pumping. There's no need to imitate the army (you know—getting more done before 9am than most people do all day) but there's nothing wrong with getting one thing done early—wash last night's beer mugs, maybe? At least take a shower!

The January Effect

January is to the year what Monday is to the week. The holidays are over. Vacations have ended. People have gone back to work. This can be unsettling for the aspiring leisure seeker.

Although Leslie Gonsalves enjoyed having time off during the holidays, the opposite was true once January rolled around. Low on funds and with potential employers back at work, she no longer had any excuse to put off her job search efforts.

Stand fast and do not waver, for yours is a mission of quality of life, not of logging in as many work hours as you can. January can be the month to use your flexible schedule to set personal goals and decide how you want to spend your free time for the rest of the year.

Tailor your New Year's resolutions to what you want to accomplish over the coming months: pledge to transition to a new career by taking classes or applying to graduate school, for example, or just resolve to enjoy your time off!

SURPRISE!

Don't worry, time off also brings plenty of pleasant surprises. Besides being able to catch up with old friends, you'll feel more relaxed and you'll probably become a kinder, gentler person. Your refreshed demeanor can lead to many other subtle benefits, such as improved restaurant service, better rapport with law enforcement officials ("You don't really need to write me that ticket, do you officer?"), and smiles from strangers on the street.

HOW MUCH TIME?

Wondering how long to stay off the work clock? That's easy—as long as possible! If you have financial stability, peace of mind, and a good story to go with it, you can justify almost any length of time away from work. Employers are gradually changing their attitudes about extended breaks and that's something we can all be glad for.

Jamie Alfaro, a human resources specialist and professional recruiter for the past ten years, says that the amount of time off employers view as "acceptable" depends on the circumstances. "In a challenging job market," Jamie says, "hiring managers wouldn't even question a candidate whose job search took a year or

top ten accomplishments of the recently non-employed

10 Ann Marsh, a writer going through a career transition, went on more than 100 dates in six months, and found her man!

9 John Donnewald saw his son off to kindergarten every day and performed a self-scribed song with his daughter's 7th grade chorus in front of a live audience—to a standing ovation!

8 Leslie Gonsalves got her carpets as "clean as they've ever been" by cleaning them for *three days straight*.

7 Steve Friedman, a former software VP, furnished his entire vacation house— with furniture he built by hand.

6 Anastasia Shilling moved to the central coast of California and became the local "chocolate fairy."

5 Cheryl Beck sold a couple of scripts to a children's TV show taping near her home—which might lead to a full-time job.

4 Dana Magenau, on a one-year trek around the world, climbed some of the world's highest peaks in Africa, South America, and Asia.

3 Dave Shefferman co-founded non-profit **One Brick** (onebrick.org), a volunteer organization that brought 21,476 volunteer hours to communities in 2005.

2 Nelson Hyde Chick wrote a novel; was awarded one patent and filed three more applications; and got a beagle, noting that people with dogs live three years longer, statistically speaking.

And the number one accomplishment of the recently non-employed...

[go on, flip the page!]

> **1** Marlo Sarmiento got hired as an independent contractor by his former employer for more money than he was making before he left, went scuba diving three or four days a week, completed his underwater photography portfolio, and won a photo contest sponsored by *Smithsonian Magazine.*
> **Congratulations, Marlo!**

more. In a red-hot economy, however, a candidate should have a very clear explanation for time off, and be able to talk intelligently about it."

In a stagnant economy, less than six months is almost self-explanatory. Between six months and a year, you should probably have a good story about why you haven't taken a job sooner.

Most employers consider travel a legitimate use of six months. Being able to afford your respite also sells well. Matt Green, a former software sales executive, says, "I always mentioned in interviews that I could afford to take time off. Once people heard that, they understood, and I also gained credibility that I had made a little money in my life."

After a year, according to most career experts, you'll be better off having either completed some kind of project or taken care of a medical or family situation. The bright side of taking a year off is that you'll be thoroughly rested for your next job. The challenge, if you simply enjoyed yourself while living off your savings, will be finding a compelling way to describe it.

THE PIGGY BANK

Did we mention savings? It's obviously a key factor. Don't give up too easily if you want to take a long leave but wonder whether it'll fly financially. Even if you have a financial goal beyond covering your cost of living—such as buying a house—set a minimum under which you won't let your savings drop, then enjoy yourself until then.

Whatever you decide, you will need to get a solid grip on your expenses—the fear of running low on cash or missing your financial goals can seriously bum your hiatus high. Read on for tips on how to cut costs, as well as generate some interim lounging lucre.

CHAPTER 3
FINANCE

Money frees you from doing things you dislike.
Since I dislike doing nearly everything, money is handy.
~ Groucho Marx

I have enough money to last me the rest of my life,
unless I buy something.
~ Jackie Mason

MONEY. Whether you can't get enough of it or think it's the root of all evil, probably no single factor troubles (or eases) the non-working mind more. It's no fun to be on a sabbatical and broke, so if you're going to take time off, you're going to need some money to do it—it's as simple as that.

In the best case scenario, financial planning for time off starts while you're still working. Saving money for a rainy day (or better yet, a sunny day!) is a critical step to enjoying your time. That said, a budget will come in handy whether or not you were able to plan ahead. The first section of this chapter, **Finance 101**, covers these topics.

In the worst case scenario, unemployment comes unexpectedly and sticks you in a financial bind. Don't panic. Even if you have just a small financial cushion, there are many ways to maximize your standard of living without a steady paycheck. You can scale back your discretionary expenses and, with a little more discipline, cut some of your fixed expenses too. You can even reduce your tax bill! If you have debt, you can deal with it proactively. **Finance 202** covers all of these ways to "play defense" and conserve your cash.

Finance 303 gets to the offense: bringing some funds your way. We include information on an array of funding sources—from severance packages and unemployment insurance to odd jobs—plus information on loans, grants, and proceeds from selling your things.

Be prepared—this is one looonnnnnng chapter. Give yourself plenty of time to digest it. It's dense, but it's important, so cancel all your plans and get your slide rule handy… No, not really, but if you need a break from the number crunching, sneak a peek at the fun stuff in **Part Two: The Leisure Odyssey.**

FiNANCE 101
PLANNING & BUDGETING

start with the little things, finish rich

Most financial advisors recommend stashing three to six months' salary in the bank to protect against the unexpected. How much do you have? How much will you need?

David Bach, a financial advisor and author of *Smart Couples Finish Rich*, told the Associated Press* that couples often stumble when the husband or wife loses a job. "They should be looking to cut their overhead 50 percent," Bach said. "But people don't do that. They cut back maybe by 5 percent, and the bills pile up."

Your sabbatical budget will depend on how long you want to take off and how you want to pass your time, especially if you want to travel. If you're currently not working, you'll need to know how long you can milk your savings. If you're a member of the *Aspiring Unemployed*, you'll want to know just how long you'll have to save up before you can cut loose.

See "Advice for the Long-Term Unemployed" by Eileen Alt Powell, AP Business Writer

Libraries are full of good books on personal financial planning. Check out *Living Well On Practically Nothing* by Edward Romney, *Life or Debt* by Stacy Johnson, or the out-of-print but still priceless *Blindsided: Financial Advice For The Suddenly Unemployed* by Edie Milligan (available used at Amazon.com). Any of these resources can help you get a handle on your current spending, and each offers ways to cut back.

Six Months Off by Hope Dlugozima, James Scott and David Sharp is an excellent guide to planning a sabbatical. "Plan three months ahead for every one month you plan to take off," Hope told us. "So six months off would be eighteen months ahead." Then figure out how much you need, divide by the number of months before you leave, and set aside that much each month. "It comes down to a mathematical equation."

Yes, budgeting is fairly straightforward—and kind of a snore. The good news is that the non-employed lifestyle costs less, so you'll be able to get by on fewer dollars than you usually spend. This begs the question: how much do you usually spend?

Start by journaling your expenses for a full month. Track every last dime you spend—on morning coffee, afternoon snacks, cab fares, movie tickets, non-network ATM fees, everything. Include your housing and utilities costs, and make sure you record those "invisible" debit card charges by saving your receipts and tallying them up later. Save your credit card receipts too, and if you carry a revolving balance, budget for your minimum monthly credit card payments.

An Excel or Quicken spreadsheet can help show you where your money goes. You might also experiment with one of the free online financial calculators found at bankrate.com. Finally, even though it's a pain (and sometimes painful to see), remember to balance your checkbook.

With your expenses laid out on the table, you should be able to figure out where you spend your money. If you're curious how you

THE LOCAL COST OF LIVING

In the first quarter of 2006, San Francisco was only a hair less expensive to live in than Manhattan, according to the ACCRA Composite Index. The Index found that San Francisco was 71% more expensive than the average of 300 selected metropolitan areas in the United States. Only utility expenses were below average. Housing costs were way, way above average, so it's no surprise that housing typically consumes such a large proportion of a San Franciscan's budget.

AVERAGE SPENDING PROPORTIONS*		
	Nationwide	**San Francisco**
Housing	30%	49%
Groceries	13%	11%
Healthcare	4%	3%
Utilities	9%	4%
Transportation	9%	6%
Other	35%	27%
TOTAL	100%	100%

*Approximate proportions, based on the spending proportions of the average American and on a 2006 cost of living index created by ACCRA (accra.org), now posted on various third party websites.

compare to "average," see the table below. Then for a chuckle, compare your cost of living in San Francisco to the cost on October 20, 1904, when the *San Francisco Chronicle* reported that a family of 4 could get by on $14 a week, and rent ran a whopping $7 to $17 for a small three-to four-room flat.

Separate the necessary expenses from the discretionary ones, which are usually the easiest to cut and make the biggest impact on your budget. But you can reduce even your fixed expenses, as we'll explain. Wouldn't you rather spend that money on entertainment? Make realistic decisions and then stick to your new budget.

Sabbaticals

All right, we won't be totally bohemian. Few would fault you for wanting to have income when you return from your time off adventure. If you have a job now and you'd like to keep it, consider negotiating for a sabbatical.

Gone are the days when the word "sabbatical" was used primarily to describe the wacky university professor who needs a year overseas to research the mating habits of the Australian wombat. Many traditional companies now offer paid and unpaid sabbaticals to their employees.

The Society for Human Resources Management's *2004 Benefits Survey Report* found that of U.S. companies with 500 employees or more, 8% offered paid sabbatical programs while 28% offered unpaid leave. In certain high-burnout

the roots of sabbaticals

The modern sabbatical has its roots in academia, where the concept of checking out of the classroom is commonplace. Those madcap professors are at least smart enough to have figured out a way to regularly ditch work and keep their jobs!

• • •

The origin of the word itself refers to taking a year off from planting crops once every seven years, to give the ground a chance to lie fallow and regenerate itself. This was before the concept of crop rotation, clearly.

• • •

Although it's taking them a while to come around, corporate America is beginning to grant its blessing to the notion of taking an extended break from the job. Consulting firm Accenture, for example, proposed a progressive sabbatical program called "FlexLeave." FlexLeave allowed certain employees to take up to 15 months off at 20% pay plus benefits, and guaranteed their jobs on return. While the program may have been created specifically as an alternative to layoffs, it represents the increasing flexibility employers are offering their employees.

industries such as law, high-tech and consulting, the numbers are significantly higher.

If your company doesn't offer a formal program, consider negotiating some type of custom leave of absence. Collaborate with your employer to create a win-win scenario: work extra hours before you leave, arrange to job-share, accept reduced pay, or take an unpaid leave.

Hope Dlugozima recommends workers have all their ducks in a row before negotiating. "In almost every company, there's already an example where people take sabbaticals: they're called maternity or paternity leaves... the companies have learned how to lose even key employees for three months, and everything's fine. Use that as an example."

FINANCE 202
HOW TO CUT YOUR PERSONAL BURN RATE

Think of yourself as a company, with revenues and expenses as well as operating cash. When you stop working, your monthly revenue probably drops close to zero. You'll have to cut your expenses to make your operating cash last—which might sound strangely familiar to those of you who have worked for a struggling startup! If you're working full or part time, maybe you just want to tighten the belt in order to increase your cash reserves. In any event, the most direct path is to reduce the cost of things you need, and cut the expenses you don't.

Alas, since some perks will have to get the axe, start with the small conveniences. Do you really need a cell phone *and* a landline? With call-waiting on both lines? Could you brew your own coffee instead of paying someone to brew it for you? Your nearest library branch probably has your favorite magazines and newspapers, so freeze or cancel your home subscriptions and spend some time amongst the book stacks instead. Consider putting your gym membership on hold too and get your exercise free by walking, biking, or running.

You get the idea. Each "convenience" charge may seem small on its own, but squandering two or three dollars here and there adds up over time. When you're feeling the pain of cutting back, call this truth to mind: every dollar of your savings that's spent on the luxury of convenience could be spent on extra time off instead.

FINANCE FUNDAMENTALS

$— **Pay off as much debt as you can**

$— **Build a cash reserve**

$— **Line up several sources of credit, in case you need emergency funds**

HOUSING

Running through half of the average San Francisco budget, housing is one area in which you can potentially save a bundle.

Reducing Rent

Are you a renter? Sixty-five percent of San Franciscans are. If you've lived in your place for a while, get up-to-date on what market rents are. They've gone down substantially as residential vacancies have gone up. "I moved to Alameda two years ago, at the height of the market," Claire Bannister, a legal assistant, told us. "Now I'm moving back. Rents in San Francisco are cheaper."

Many landlords have reduced rents when asked—some even *without* being asked. If your landlord isn't one of them, consider moving, especially if your place isn't subject to rent control (any place built after 1979 is exempt from the rules that put a cap on rent increases). With a large amount of vacant properties, you have a solid chance of finding one that's cheaper. Shaving even $100 off your $1,000/month rent could stretch your housing budget from nine months to ten. That's a full extra month of housing leisure!

there's no place like—*mom & dad's?*

When Mary Mangold realized that she was running out of savings, her bills were looming, and no jobs hovered on the horizon, she decided to move home.

"I was back in my old room with that ugly carpet and the horrible drapes that haven't changed in fifteen years," she said at the time. "I kept thinking, 'It's only going to last a month,' so I kept all my stuff in storage, but it's been over a year now and still counting."

The renter's market eventually rescued Mary; she's back in a one-bedroom apartment—at the same rent as she used to pay for a studio.

Lowering Your Mortgage Payment

If you're fortunate enough to own your home, is your monthly mortgage as low as it could be? Talk to a lender or mortgage broker, and see if you can save money by refinancing. There are a wide variety of flexible programs for borrowers, including adjustable rates and interest-only loans that might help with cash flow, at least in the near term. If you're really pressed for funds, you might also consider a cash-out refinance (see **Finance 303** for more details).

Moving Home With Mom and Dad

The drawbacks of moving back in with your parents are obvious: living under someone else's roof requires a sacrifice of a little independence and a lot of privacy. Still, more and more people are doing it.

If you're heading back to the nest yourself, prepare for some "casual" yet prying questions from your parents, particularly after you've spent a night out. Beware too of regressing to child-like and dependent behavior. Is your mom doing your laundry again? Your dad paying your phone bill? As well intentioned as they are, Mom and Dad can sap your drive to find work by making it too easy not to. You might want to keep track of any parental subsidies so you can pay them back later.

On the other hand, you might treasure the chance to spend quality time with your folks, especially if you've been living far away from them. "Moving back in was much to my mother's happiness," Mary confessed. "She never liked the idea of my moving away in the first place." Having someone to lean on financially might be just the break you need to stay afloat during your time off.

all i wanna do... is have some fun!

You might be in a real financial crisis. It would be simple to say, "Cut all discretionary expenses," but here's the problem: that's no fun. Now more than ever, you need a little fun.

Are you paying your mortgage with your credit card? Subsisting on rice and vegetables? Walking distances to rival Forrest Gump? If you don't see much humor in that, make sure you do find humor somewhere else.

Do not—repeat, do not—deprive yourself completely. Deprivation has a strange way of costing you extra in the long run.

Budget a monthly amount, small though it might be, for entertaining yourself. The investment you make in keeping up your spirits will surely pay off by keeping you motivated for other tasks—like resolving the crisis!

FOOD

Definitely one of the necessities of life.

Cooking at Home

Cooking at home can save you a lot of money. If this is not a new idea to you or you're already on your way to becoming a celebrity chef in your own right, guess who's coming for dinner?!

If you've had the inclination to cook but haven't had the time until now, this is the time to feed that desire (pun intended). At the extreme, someone who's used to having an expense account or in the habit of eating on the run might spend upwards of $1,000 a month on food. Eating every meal out, buying a couple of coffee drinks each day, and chipping in for cocktails with your friends can add up to a per diem of $50-plus, which might easily be as much as or more than your rent.

Shopping for your own food and cooking it at home can trim the fat from your food bill. See if you can match Marlo "The Balinese Gigolo" Sarmiento, who spent only $25 a week on food when he was in law school (see below). That's less than the tip you might leave for a single dinner at Rubicon. Now *that's* food for thought!

Budget Beveraging

Between mixed drinks, coffee drinks and bottled mystery waters, the beverages you consume can start consuming you, or at least your pocketbook. Save a few dollars through judicious imbibing.

It doesn't take heavy analysis to conclude that alcohol feeds you a lot of empty calories at a high expense. No need to teetotal—just par-

Food Budget Award Winner: THE BALINESE GIGOLO

Marlo Sarmiento ate on $25 a week by buying multi-purpose ingredients and catching his own fish. "Hey, if the people from the Mediterranean have been thriving on anchovy and sardines for millennia, why can't we?" he asks, noting that no license is required to fish off public piers like **Fort Point**. So if you're not too worried about the mercury levels in fish, go for it.

Marlo's weekly grocery bill included a $3 bag of rice, "not the Uncle Ben stuff," $4 on ground beef (or tofu), $2 on dry pasta, a $1 can of whole beans (pinto or kidney), $3 on fruit from Clement Street or Chinatown, $3 on onions & garlic, $3 on canned and fresh tomatoes, $2 on tortillas, $3 on cheese, and a buck on "miscellaneous" (spices, peppers).

With minimal investments in a crab net ($25), a rice cooker, a crock pot, and a cheap rod and reel set, Marlo enjoyed a varied diet of spaghetti with fresh seafood sauce, fish tacos & burritos, chili, and seafood stir fry, supplemented with fresh fruit "as needed."

take a little less, or start your happy hour at home. When you're out, learn to nurse a single mixed drink all night or explore your affinity for warm, a.k.a. long-life, beer. Think of it as a survival skill that could come in handy if you return to a job that includes frequent office parties: while others become loose-lipped after too many cocktails, you'll be a model of decorum, and all ears for taking in intriguing inside information. If one drink per night is a little under your normal quota, let your employed friends pick up a couple of rounds—you can always even things out at a later date.

"Unleaded" drinks can cost just as much as the juiced-up ones. Are you addicted to caffeine? Do you spend $10 a day, $300 a month on coffee drinks? You will have more energy, more money and probably better health if you drink water instead. Skip the energy water, electrolyte water and other fitness drinks and try tap water. Carry a water bottle even. San Francisco tap water has tested at the highest quality levels for many years, thanks to our clean water source at Hetch Hetchy. That's something any budget beverager can be glad for.

Oh, okay, okay. Buy some beer or wine for drinking at home—as long as you shop wisely for it. Try **Beverages & more!** (3455 Geary, 415-933-8494, bevmo.com) or **Trader Joe's** (555 Ninth Street Retail Center, 415-863-1292; 3 Masonic @ Geary, 415-346-9964, 401 Bay @ Mason, 351-1013).

Food Shopping

Even if you already cook at home, you can save more through judicious grocery shopping. How about farmers' markets? Meals were a group effort not so long ago, when households shared refrigerators and stoves, and communal food-buying is enjoying a renaissance today. Farmers' markets offer fresh produce, open-air shopping and a casual place to socialize with your neighbors and the people who grow your food—not to mention the samples! Find details on market hours and location in the **Leisure Shopping Guide**.

HEALTHCARE
Health Insurance

With healthcare costs on the rise and health insurance costs rising even faster, it might be time to consider whether you need all the HMO bells and whistles. If you're lucky enough to be in good health, look into "major medical" plans offered by providers such as Blue Cross of California, or HealthNet. These plans come with a high deductible—up to $5,000 a year—and you'll have to pay for incidental checkups and prescriptions yourself, but you'll have the peace of mind that you will not have to deplete your own savings or bankrupt your family should some major accident befall you. Individual major medical plans can cost as little as $100 a month for both medical and dental coverage.

medi-cal

Medi-Cal might be an option for those who are low on income—even temporarily. Medi-Cal's government-imposed fee schedule is also low, though, which makes some doctors reluctant to see Medi-Cal patients. In a bind, Medi-Cal patients may have to seek medical care from a hospital emergency room.

See the online newsletter published by *The Medi-Cal Policy Institute* in Oakland (*medi-cal.org*) for the latest Medi-Cal news.

COBRA

Continuing healthcare coverage through your former employer's plan falls at the other end of the cost spectrum. COBRA, or the Consolidated Omnibus Budget Reconciliation Act (simply rolls off the tongue, doesn't it?), is the federal law that allows you to stay insured through your former employer for up to 18 months. The bad news is that you'll have to pay the premiums yourself, and they're usually expensive. The good news is that you have 60 days to decide whether you want to enroll. Within that period, coverage is retroactive—if you get sick on day 59, you can activate COBRA and be covered that same day.

If you're confident that you'll have a new job and therefore new health benefits within two months, you might skip paying for COBRA. But if you're not so sure or if you're going to be traveling out of the country (yeah!), don't wait. It's also not a good idea to wait if you have any pre-existing conditions—a new insurer can refuse to cover treatment for that condition for up to a year if you can't prove that your coverage was continuous.

If you do elect for COBRA, you'll be legally entitled to health coverage through another company when your COBRA coverage expires, even if that same company refused to insure you before.

Community Health Clinics

San Francisco has at least twenty community health clinics. One of the more well known is the **Haight Ashbury Free Medi-**

cal Clinic (558 Clayton, 415-487-5632, hafci.org), founded in 1967 by Dr. David E. Smith on the premise that health care is a right, not a privilege. It offers primary health care as well as specialties, and welcomes everyone who walks through the door. While they can't treat emergencies like broken bones or severe bleeding, they can provide you with referrals and community resource information.

Other clinics include the **Castro-Mission Health Center** (3850 17th Street, 415-487-7500) and the **Chinatown Public Health Center** (1490 Mason, 415-364-7654). For a more complete list, check the Haight Ashbury Free Medical Clinic's site (hafci.org, click on "Links").

Staying Healthy

Various sources estimate that each dollar spent on prevention saves between three and seven dollars in treatment costs. Does that mean if you spent another $10 on prevention, you'd spend $20 to $60 less overall? That's how the math works, anyway. Yet prevention accounts for only three cents of each healthcare dollar spent in the United States. See if you can't save money by keeping yourself educated, preventing illness wherever you can, and staying in shape (see **Chapter 7**).

UTILITIES

Utility costs might not eat up a real big chunk of your budget but they can add up. So change a few habits and save a few bucks.

Shut off your cable subscription for awhile and watch TV at a friend's

---

low income *is* low income...

If you're not generating much income (a strong probability when you're unemployed), you might qualify for reduced rate programs for phone, gas and garbage.

The income cutoff for these programs was $19,600 in 2003 and is adjusted each year to reflect changes in the average cost of living. If you qualify at the beginning of the year but end up earning more than the income cutoff, you'll owe the difference between the regular rate and what you already paid.

• • •

PHONE
AT&T's ***Universal Lifeline Telephone Service*** (800-310-2355, att.com) provides basic phone service at a reduced rate ($5.34 per month in 2003). You have to attest in writing to your annual income level.

[still dialing...]

lllll [cont'd]

GAS & ELECTRIC

For qualifying households, the **PG&E CARE Program** (866-743-2273, pge.com/care) discounts the utility bill by 20%. Whether you're in the CARE program or not, PG&E can work out a payment schedule if you need more time to pay your bill. They'll also provide free energy education and weatherization to income-qualified customers. Call **PG&E Customer Service** (800-743-5000) for more details.

If you need one-time help to pay PG&E, contact the **Salvation Army** (800-933-9677) and ask about their **REACH** program: Relief for Energy Assistance through Community Help. When you're back in the green, you can help your neighbor by making a tax-deductible donation.

• • •

GARBAGE

Sunset Scavenger (415-330-1300) and **Golden Gate Disposal & Recycling** (415-626-4000) both offer certain households a 25% discount on basic garbage collection. Get an application by calling whichever collector serves your neighborhood.

instead, or offer to run a daytime errand for someone who's willing to tape your favorite show for you. Same goes for that new TiVo system. Save on your electricity bill by turning out the lights when you're not home. Turn off your computer when you're not using it. Avoid per-message text messaging charges on your cell phone by sending e-mails instead.

Live without a cell phone for a while, or think about how to combine it with your landline to better advantage. Most major mobile phone service providers offer plans that let you call long distance within their nationwide "network" at no extra charge. Make your long distance calls on the cell and all your local calls from home, or make long distance calls only when the rates are at their lowest. Or, as Jeffrey Yamaguchi, founder of workingfortheman.com suggests in Part 2 of his online "Laid Off 101" article: "Do the really smart thing and make your calls when you know people aren't going to be home. That way, people will return your calls and you'll escape long distance charges altogether."

More energy and water saving tips are available to members of **San Francisco Community Power** (2325 3rd St., Suite 344, 415-626-8723, sfpower.org). If your income is low, you can join for only $5 a year.

Internet Access—Wired

There are any number of places to log on around the City, which can help you stay in touch with e-mail pals or apply for jobs online (but only if you have to!). You can pay by the hour via wired terminals serviced by providers like **ZRNetService** (zrnetservice.com) and **SurfandSip** (surfandsip.com).

However, we prefer our rates a little cheaper, as in gratis; complimentary; on the house. Free wired access isn't prevalent in San Francisco but it does exist.

If 15-20 minutes will do ya, stop by the **Main Library** (100 Larkin, 415-557-4400, sfpl.org) or one of the cafés that offer brief access with a purchase. If you get lucky and no one's waiting, your briefly-free minutes can go on indefinitely.

Comp USA (750 Market, 415-743-2000) offers ten minutes of limited free wired access—be prepared to wait in line behind the local high schoolers.

And if you have the right purpose, you can log on at the **Kalmanovitz Medical Library** at UCSF (530 Parnassus at 3rd Avenue) for surfing related to the "missions of UCSF," or the **Foundation Center** (312 Sutter #606, 415-397-0902, fdncenter.org/sanfrancisco) if you're a non-profit or individual grant seeker.

Internet Access—Wireless

Wireless access, on the other hand, is easier to obtain for free. Where it's not free, it's generally less expensive—as low as $5 a day for drop-in usage or $20 a month for a remote subscription plan.

Nearly two dozen cafés currently share their wireless subscriptions with their customers at no charge, with new hot spots cropping up every day. But note that some will kick you out if you start using their wireless without buying anything. Other cafés host providers like **SurfandSip** (see above), **Deep Blue Wireless** (deepbluewireless.com), **Boingo** (boingo.com), or **T-Mobile** (at the ubiquitous Starbucks, tmobile.com).

The website 80211hotspots.com lists hundreds of SF cafes and hotels that offer wireless access (some free, some for a fee), and the truly intrepid can scout for signals elsewhere with the right equipment, or even share a wireless subscription with neighbors. This isn't necessarily legal, mind you; we're just saying it's been done. We promise, we won't tell Comcast.

Of course, by the time you read this, hunting high and low for free wireless service may be a thing of the past. In 2006, San Francisco's city government awarded Google and Earthlink a joint contract to provide wireless service for the entire city. The plan calls for Google

FREE WIRED CAFES

- *Emma's Coffee House*
  1901 Hayes @ Ashbury, 415-221-3378
- *Java Beach*
  1396 La Playa Street, 415-665-5282
- *Last Laugh*
  1551 Dolores Street, 415-824-5524
- *Luv a Java*
  1300 Dolores Street @ 26th, 415-401-6444

to provide a free service to everyone that's faster than dialup but slower than broadband, and for Earthlink to provide a faster fee-based service. But as of September 2006, City Hall and the companies were still hammering out the details, and the startup date is now sometime in 2007. On the next page are a few hotspot suggestions in case your blanket in Golden Gate Park isn't yet ready for online primetime.

TRANSPORTATION

In this expense category more than in others, saving money means spending time; the faster you want to get there, the more it'll cost. Slower paced travel does offer advantages beyond saving money though, such as getting outdoors to enjoy the City and even getting some exercise. You might help keep the air a little cleaner, too.

Drive Less

Gas is expensive. Insurance is expensive. Parking tickets—we won't even go there. Add in car payments and maintenance, and it becomes clear that giving up a private car could fund many extra months of leisure time. If you're really dedicated to cutting every cost and you have a car, sell it.

Does the mere thought of being without wheels give you the jitters? Then check out **City CarShare** (131 Steuart Street, Suite 205, 415-995-8588, citycarshare.org, and see "Sharing a Car" below) or talk to a friend or neighbor about sharing a car. With some advance planning and good communication, it's easy to create your own car-share plan.

FREE WIRELESS CAFES	
Cole Valley Café 701 Cole @ Waller, 415-668-5282	**H Café** 3801 17th Street, 415-487-1661
Jumpin' Java 139 Noe, 415-431-5282	**Mission Creek** 968 Valencia, 415-641-0888
Rockin' Java 1821 Haight, 415-831-8842	**Emma's Coffee House** 1901 Hayes, 415-221-3378
Muddy Waters 1304 Valencia, 415-647-7994	**Oakside Café** 1195 Oak, 415-437-1985
Notes from Underground Café 2399 Van Ness, 415-775-7638	**The Canvas Gallery** 1200 9th Avenue. 415-504-0060
Java Beach 1396 La Playa, 415-665-5282	**Sacred Grounds** 2095 Hayes, 415-387-3859
Central Coffee 1696 Hayes, 415-922-2008	**Bazaar Café** 5927 California, 415-831-5620
Ritual Coffee Roasters 1026 Valencia. 415-641-1024	**Velo Rouge Café** 798 Arguello, 415-752-7799
Progressive Grounds 400 Cortland, 415-282-6233	**Papa Toby's Revolution Cafe** 3248 22nd Street, 415-642-0474

Cab Less

Door-to-door service without the hassle of parking is hard to forego, especially on a wet, foggy day. But cabs are pricey, so if you're not late for an appointment and you don't need a cab for safety, try another form of transport—you might have a bit more time on your hands. As Natalia Lincoln, who was an unemployed dot-commer a few years ago, told Jeffrey Yamaguchi in "Laid Off 101—Part 2": "The main thing to realize when unemployed is that you're very time-rich and money-poor. If you get home a half-hour later on the train than in a cab, it really doesn't matter as much."

Use Public Transportation

You can get almost everywhere in the City on **MUNI** (415-673-6864, sfmuni.com). Call them for point-to-point routing assistance. For trips to the East Bay, **BART** (Bay Area Rapid Transit, 415-989-2278, bart.gov) can now get you as far as Pittsburg. It can also (finally!) take you to SFO. If you need to get to the South Bay, **Caltrain** (800-660-4287, 4th & Townsend, caltrain.com/caltrain) offers a pleasant ride and is almost always on time, and now has high-speed rail service that will get you to Palo Alto in about half an hour. Your best bet for getting to the North Bay is one of the dozens of bus lines operated by **Golden Gate Transit** (415-923-2000, goldengatetransit.org).

In addition to individual transit providers, a couple of online resources tie together the seemingly fragmented Bay Area travel network. The main one is **511.org** (511.org). Check out their site for comprehensive information on all of the Bay Area public transit options, including ferries, vans and shuttles. For really long-distance trips, call **Amtrak** (800-872-7245, amtrak.com) or **Greyhound** (800-231-2222, greyhound.com) and leave the driving to them.

SHARING A CAR

If you, like the average American, use your a car just a couple of hours a day, maybe you'd rather share a new lime green VW bug with 25 others instead. That's how many members share each of the vehicles maintained by *City CarShare* *(citycarshare.org)*, the nonprofit that launched its car-sharing program in San Francisco in March 2001.

The VWs and other models are parked at more than 20 San Francisco locations, or "pods," often in garage or lot spaces donated by the City. To use a car, you need only make a reservation online or via voice-activated phone line, then use your key fob to open the door and enable the ignition. An onboard computer automatically tracks your mileage and bills you monthly. If you need more gas, pay for it with the City CarShare gas card. Comprehensive insurance coverage is also included.

Makes sense, but does it make cents? Compare the fees to what you'd spend on your own car. Driving time with City CarShare—measured by reservation hours versus actual time on the road—runs $4 per hour and 44 cents a mile. Add to that a $30 application fee, a $10 monthly membership fee, and a $300 one-time, refundable damage deposit. If you decide you want to make the trade, you can apply online (if you're a minimum of 25 years old with a valid California Driver's License and at least three years' driving history, that is). Before you know it, you'll be zipping around looking like a green gumdrop yourself!

Bike More

Since you've got more time on your hands (and feet), why not use them to ride a bike instead of driving? You'll save money on gas, and the extra exercise will help keep you fit. The City has official bicycle lanes and plenty of great bike routes (see **Chapter 7** for details).

For longer journeys, you can combine a bike with other public transportation. The **Bikes-on-Muni** program (call 415-673-6864 for a brochure) equips buses on about ten MUNI lines with double bike racks. Cyclists must load and unload their own rides. Bikes are allowed on most ferries (at the captain's discretion), on BART during non-commute hours, and in Caltrain's designated bike car. To travel between Oakland and San Francisco during commute hours, you can catch a ride on the Caltrans Bay Bridge Bike Shuttle for only $1.00 each way. This shuttle leaves San Francisco from the **Transbay Terminal** (on Mission between 1st Street & Fremont) and Oakland from the **MacArthur BART Station** (555 40th Street, Oakland).

No bike? Find one on **Craigslist** (craigslist.org), where cheap bikes abound. You should have no problem securing a decent two-wheeler for about $50, and a good one for $100.

ditching your car

No, we're not talking about launching your old clunker off a cliff *Dukes of Hazzard*-style (not that that wouldn't that be really cool), but donating your tired old vehicle to charity (see "Taxes" later in chapter). Zillions of San Francisco non-profits will take it off your hands. Locate one of them or get assistance with the paperwork through *America's Car Donation Charities Center* (800-513-6560, *donateacar. com*).

Walk More

City planners take pride in the fact that, after Manhattan, San Francisco is the country's second most "dense" city, meaning that people can live, shop, and work without leaving their neighborhood. Pick one of SF's great commercial streets to explore (see the **Unemployed Shopping Guide**) and you might find that you can get all your errands done without the hassle of looking for parking, with the pleasure of strolling leisurely past store fronts instead.

OTHER

Not all of the expenses that fit into the "other" box are truly discretionary. Most dining and shopping are, though. Adopting frugal habits when it comes to entertainment and purchases will save you from having to cut them out completely.

Replace Expensive Outings With Activities That Are Free

No doubt, eating out fits nicely into a busy schedule and can also be fun. You can meet up with friends, have a bottle of nice wine, talk about how Masa's has real staying power in a city of fly-by-night Asian-Fusion-Americana-homestyle wanna-be's...

Or, if your life is now moving at a slower pace, you can entertain at home. Banish the image of chomping a bowl of cereal in the kitchen; morph that vision into a potluck dinner party with good friends, listening to music and drinking the bottle of fine wine that your friends brought (or the Two-Buck-Chuck that you bought at Trader Joe's!). Your friends will probably thank you for setting a low-cost trend. Plus, you'll have that much more incentive to keep your house clean.

As far as the music goes, before you go out and buy the latest Norah Jones CD, see if you can't borrow it from the library. Guess what? You can borrow cookbooks there too!

Throwing your own party is just one way to entertain yourself inexpensively. For evening events, look for house parties instead of bars. Skip concerts at Shoreline in favor of free music in Golden Gate Park. Want more frugal yet fun action? Find plenty of ideas in **Chapter 4** and **Fairs & Fests**.

Let Others Pay

San Franciscan Maureen Brown wasn't used to going on expensive outings after losing her job (especially after her savings were depleted to buy a house!) so when the bill came for a sushi dinner with an out-of-town friend, she told us she "looked at it and felt sick." Her friend offered to pay. "I said 'No, I'll pay,' but inside I was thinking, 'Oh god, yes, yes, please pay!'" And pay he did.

Don't be afraid to skip the suspense when your friends offer to pay. Just say, "Thanks, I'd appreciate that," and make a mental note to return the favor when you can. Same with Mom and Dad—if they want to treat you once in a while, let them.

Spend Less On What You Do Buy

What's that you say—no money to shop?

Well, for one, shopping doesn't necessarily mean buying. Two, you can't deprive yourself completely just because you might not have a stable income. Pick some lower priced items, such as music or books, and do a lot of looking before buying. Buy things on sale or second-hand. Go to garage sales (or sidewalk sales, or estate sales). Be aware of when you're shopping not for *things* but for instant gratification, and avoid major purchases for now—that's right, no plasma TV.

You can even out spartan living on the Friday after Thanksgiving, which was designated first by the British and then by the world as "**Buy Nothing Day**"—a day to either shop less and live more or to "conga against consumerism" (buynothingday .co.uk).

On the other days of the year, you can patronize the retailers listed in the **Leisure Shopping Guide**, who offer the best values on items in the unemployed budget. If you do find yourself needing a major appliance (a vacuum cleaner, say), look for places that offer refurbished appliances, which often come with a limited warranty. They can cost less than half as much as new ones.

DEALING WITH DEBT

If your unfortunate enough to be out of work—not by your own choosing—pressing financial burdens aren't much fun.

If you have debt but purchased unemployment protection insurance from your credit card carriers way back when, now would be a good time to file a claim. If your debt is still oppressive, you

simplicity in san francisco

The Simplicity Movement is alive and well in the Bay Area. Simple San Franciscans who want to learn from a guru can check out the work of **Cecile Andrews** (*cecileandrews.com*) or meet other simple folk at one of the **Simplicity Forums** (every fourth Monday evening at **Pacific Heights Swedenborgian Church**, 2107 Lyon) that Cecile used to moderate. The books published by the **Center for the New American Dream** (in Maryland, 301-891-3683, *newdream. org*) are good reads—*More Fun, Less Stuff* or *Simplicity for the Holidays* can each help lengthen the life span of an unemployed budget.

Even if you aren't looking to save money, shedding some luxuries and their maintenance gives you the one thing that a true leisure seeker can never get enough of—more free time.

might find **Nolo Press** (950 Parker Street, Berkeley, 510-704-2248, nolo. com) a valuable resource. Nolo publishes Robin Leonard's *Money Troubles: Legal Strategies to Cope with Your Debts*, among other self-help legal titles, plus they are just good friendly people who offer a 40% discount to those who buy books and software in their Berkeley retail outlet. Other organizations in the Bay Area can help you alleviate financial strains or avoid financial crisis altogether (see below for some leads).

Avoiding Debt

The easiest way to get out of debt is, of course, not to get into it in the first place. As obvious as this is, most Americans spend 10% more than they make, and then spend 14% of what they make servicing their debts. Servicing debt without generating income can be a juggling act, especially if you weren't expecting to be out of work. If you're under a mountain of financial liabilities, you're definitely not alone.

But you can't afford to be average when you're unemployed, so first and foremost, control your credit cards. Adopt some simple habits—pay card balances in full each month, setting aside enough money in your prospective budget to cover each purchase. If you must make a major purchase while you're unemployed, budget and save for it before you make it, not after. The **Consumer Credit Counseling Service of San Francisco** (595 Market St., 15th Floor, 800-777-PLAN, cccssf.org) can help you with debt management and other financial matters via phone, online, or at one of their many free or low-cost workshops. **Debtors Anonymous** (415-522-9099, debtorsanonymous.org) meets in San Francisco—to find out exactly where, check their NorCal website at ncdaweb.org.

mortgage mulligans

If you can present them with proof that you can pick up where they left off, the *Department of Social Services* might help you catch up with your mortgage and utility payments by making a one-time-only, lump sum payment to you or your lender (or utility company). Government grants issued through local charities can do the same. Each requires that you show you have no other funds available, including a second mortgage lender (if you own a home).

Reducing Debt—Consolidation

Consolidate your debts if you can. A home equity loan can be a great way to go as it can come with the added benefit of a tax write-off. Another option is to transfer high-interest rate card balances to lower-rate cards. The average American's credit card debt is $8,500. Letting a balance this big revolve can cost you a seven-course dinner at Jardinière every month, depending on your rate (and your taste in wine). This is lost money that could be going to paying down your debt (or enjoying a succulent foie gras washed down with a '97 Cab).

To do that most efficiently, focus on paying off the highest rate debt first. Make minimum payments on everything else until that entire loan is paid off. Then move to the next highest rate, and so on. If you have good timing, you can float debt with teaser rates, transferring balances from card to card. You could probably find more exciting ways to spend your time though, and the card companies will catch on after a while; plus, you can damage your credit rating by opening up too many new accounts. On the other hand, your credit rating might be the least of your concerns, in which case we'll just note that federal interest rates are near a 40-year low—which means that other interest rates are low too—and likely will be for a while.

Reducing Debt—Negotiation

Americans carry consumer debt like no others. In true American fashion, entrepreneurs have capitalized on this by creating companies and services to get people out of the very debt that other companies helped get them into.

Debt reduction service providers will negotiate with creditors on your behalf to try to reduce your debt to 55-60% of what you currently owe, but you'll have to give them a cut of what they save you. If you're a good negotiator, you might try calling your creditors directly and negotiating yourself.

Consumer credit counselors can also help you negotiate away some of your debt but unlike debt reduction servicers, credit counselors generally work for your *creditors*, not for you. If you decide to go this route, look for a non-profit agency such as the **Consumer Credit Counseling Service of San Francisco** (see previous page), which offers counseling for a sliding-scale fee.

Credit counseling has its pros and cons. Some lenders view it negatively, and won't lend to people who've recently used it. Other lenders are neutral; some even see it as a positive, figuring that you're at least

the negotiator

Marina Sarmiento highly recommends trying to strike a deal when you can't pay what you owe. "I've been out of work a bunch of times," says Marina. "At first, I couldn't pay my bills. Then I started negotiating with my creditors. I felt good about it. At least I was doing something."

Marina points out what the creditors know too: if they don't negotiate with you and you're forced to declare bankruptcy, they'll probably get just a small fraction of what you owe them. They also know that a collection lawsuit against you would be time-consuming and costly. Faced with these realities, savvy creditors will entertain reasonable offers. It's worth a shot!

taking a proactive approach instead of passively defaulting. The company that created the most widely used credit scoring formula ignores it; they discovered that consumers who use credit counseling are at no greater risk of default. Since credit counseling is not universally considered a negative (unlike bankruptcy), it might be something to explore.

Erasing Debt—Bankruptcy

You've probably heard that declaring bankruptcy can damage your credit rating—while you might solve some short-term financial problems, future landlords and lenders will be able to see "bankruptcy" on your credit report for up to ten years. But do you know all of your bankruptcy options? The bankruptcy code's Chapter 7, the "liquidation bankruptcy," (not to be confused with **Chapter 7** of *this* book, which is about Fitness and is a lot more fun!) allows debtors to walk away from their debts only after handing over all of their assets to a trustee, who will sell them and divide the proceeds among the creditors. The code's Chapter 13, however, the "wage earner plan," allows debtors to continue to own and operate a freelance consulting business. That could come in handy for the *self-unemployed*.

Find more free information online—from **WebLocator's** detailed comparison of the different types of consumer bankruptcy (weblocator.com, select "California" then "California Law Guide" then "Bankruptcy") to **FreeAdvice.com's** answers to such important questions as, "Can I go to jail for filing bankruptcy?" (the answer is no—see law.freeadvice.com under "Consumer Bankruptcy").

Consider your options carefully. If you need a lawyer, the **California State Bar** (180 Howard, 415-538-2000, calbar.ca.gov) can point you to several certified referral services. Although The State Bar cannot itself refer you to a lawyer, it *can* tell you whether the one you have found has the required bankruptcy specialty certification. The Bar Association of San Francisco (415-989-1616, sfbar.org) also has a lawyer referral program.

TAXES

Below, we pass on selected general tax information (found on official websites or from the experts we consulted) that seems—to our novice eyes—to be specific to the *unemployed, self-employed* or *self-unemployed* (see **Leisure Lingo**). We also point out a few local organizations that will gladly accept your charitable contributions, should making them be on your agenda. This information is certainly not exhaustive and it may have changed by the time you read this, so please confirm with the powers that be that you're doing everything right.

What's Taxable

You, like Odd Todd (read his story in **Finance 303**), might receive gifts or donations when you're unemployed, and you might be relieved to know that they are generally not taxable. Unemployment insurance payments are, however, and what's more, the Employment Development Department will report them to the IRS. The EDD will withhold federal taxes from your unemployment check, if you want, which can save you an unpleasant surprise at tax time. On the other hand, you can increase your cash flow now by planning to pay a lump sum later on.

Also taxable is all bartering "income" and self-employment income if you've earned more than $400 of it. Self-employment tax isn't easy to calculate—it's an "above the line" deduction and you'll owe higher-than-normal social security

the authorities

Both the ***Internal Revenue Service*** (IRS, 866-860-4259, *irs.gov*) and the ***Franchise Tax Board*** (FTB, 800-338-0505 or 916-845-7057, *ftb.ca.gov*) will answer your tax-related questions over the phone. Each provides downloadable forms and instructions on its website and makes them available in hard copy at most post offices.

TAX-AID (55 Second St., Suite 1400, 415-963-5133, *tax-aid.org*) connects low income individuals with attorneys and CPAs who will assist in preparing their tax returns.

As always, we recommend consulting professionals for individualized financial and legal advice.

and Medicare taxes, but then you can deduct them as business expenses.... Good luck with it!

What's Deductible

"Attend tax planning seminar" might not top your "to do" list but you might learn something worth your while. Some are even free! IRS Publication 501 discusses whether you should itemize your deductions but we won't here. We'll just point out that if you do want to itemize, save your receipts. Also worth investigating is whether you're eligible to deduct student loan interest—an "above the line" deduction that can adjust your income even if you don't itemize other deductions.

• **Job Search Expenses:** Tax attorney Heather Emigh explains, "If you're out of work and you're looking for new employment, you can deduct your job search expenses. For example, if you travel to New Orleans and apply for a job when you're there, you can deduct some of the meals, lodging, and travel expenses. The rules say you're supposed to divide your trip into that portion that was for pleasure and that portion that was to apply for the job, and you can deduct the job portion."

war story

A tax advisor who requests anonymity relates a tactic he's seen more than once—people deducting a portion of their expenses for every vacation they go on. As he tells it:

"They just get a local paper from the city where they're vacationing and when they get home, they mail a resume to one of the employers who advertised in that paper. They choose a 'high profile' employer like GM so they're sure to get a rejection letter. That letter, they assume, would serve as proof to the IRS—in the event of an audit—that they were actually looking for a job in that city."

• **Charitable Donations:** Gifts to tax-exempt charitable and religious groups might be deductible for you. Straight from the horse's mouth (a.k.a., the **IRS** website, irs.gov) is the following guideline: "The tax benefit for charitable contributions is only available for taxpayers who itemize deductions—about one-third of all filers. Those who take a standard deduction receive no additional tax benefit for their contributions." You can include only those contributions actually made during the calendar year. Ask for a receipt—you'll need a written acknowledgement from the charity for any single gift of $250 or more.

GOOD DEEDS THAT ARE ALSO GOOD DEALS

Year after year, you can donate to certain local charities and record your own assessed value on the blank receipt they provide. Worthy beneficiaries include *Goodwill* (1500 Mission, 415-575-2100, *sfgoodwill. org*), the *Salvation Army* (*salvationarmy.org*) and *Community Thrift* (623-625 Valencia, 415-861-4910), which will give the non-profit of your choice a percentage of the proceeds from selling your donated items. Note that Community Thrift can't accept personal computers or software.

Drop-Off Locations	
Goodwill	**Salvation Army**
1500 Mission	1500 Valencia, 415-643-8000
629 Hyde	1185 Sutter, 415-771-3818
2350 Noriega	Crissy Field
large item pickup 888-446-6394	

• **Business Expenses:** If you're self-employed or running your own business, you might be able to deduct certain business expenses, including a portion of what you spend to outfit a home office. Determining the right proportion can be tricky and you'll have to fill out an IRS Schedule C. If you travel and earn some money on your trip, you can deduct a portion of your travel expenses if you "actively" work (spend 500 hours/year or more) in the field that corresponds to your deduction. If you're a self-employed snowboarding instructor, for example, then you might be able to deduct snowboarding expenses from any money you earn as an instructor. Note that you can actively work in more than one field. If you're working as an independent contractor for someone else, you might be able to deduct certain non-reimbursed business expenses from your personal income.

Tax Credits

Whether or not you take deductions, you might be eligible for tax credits. While deductions can reduce your taxable income (which can in turn reduce your tax liability), credits reduce the amount of tax you owe dollar for dollar. In fact, some credits entitle you to a refund—even if you had no tax withheld and owe no tax! The Education Credit, the Earned Income Credit, and the California Renter's

Credit all come to mind but there might be others you can use. The standing caveat applies here—please do your own research. The **IRS** website (irs.gov) is a good place to start.

Deferring Taxes

Want more time to file your return? You can get up to six more months by filing two different forms. IRS Form 4868 (*Application for Automatic Extension of Time to File U.S. Individual Income Tax Return*) extends the deadline from April 15 to August 15—no reason needed—and IRS Form 8809 (*Request for Extension of Time to File Information Returns*) extends it again, from August 15 to October 15. On this second form, you *will* need to state your reason, such as, "Additional time is needed to file a complete and accurate tax return."

The catch is that these are extensions to file, not extensions to pay. If you owe any taxes, the *payment* is still due by April 15. You'll have to estimate your tax liability reasonably well and pay a sufficient percentage of what you actually end up owing (90% for federal, 80% for California) to avoid penalties.

FINANCE 303
STASHING SOME CASH

Whew! Budgets, bankruptcy, and taxes—if you're still with us, we salute you. Now it's time to get out of the red and into the black by bringing in some much-needed cash.

UNEMPLOYMENT INSURANCE

The joint federal-state Unemployment Insurance Program, or "UI" for short, provides weekly payments to workers who lose their job "through no fault of their own." "Fault" is, of course, a subjective term but depending on your circumstances, you may be eligible for UI even if you quit your job or were fired. You can't apply for benefits until you are actually unemployed, even if you know you're about to get laid off, but you can apply if you're working part-time. While some part-time workers will be eligible for benefits, most self-employed workers will not. For an individualized assessment, contact California's **Employment Development Department** (800-300-5616, edd.ca.gov).

Filing a Claim

You can file a claim or an extension day or night if you file online or by mail, or during business hours by phone. Have your social security number handy plus the name, address, and phone number of your last employer. It will take the EDD about two weeks from the time your initial claim is filed to assess your eligibility for benefits, so file as quickly as you can. You must file your claim by Friday to get credit for that week.

odd todd, odd job

Check out one investigation of a guy you might have heard of: Todd M. Rosenberg, better known as "Odd Todd" of online fame. Rosenberg made $9,000 in cybertips from his animated cartoon, "Laid Off: A Day in the Life," at *oddtodd.com*. The trouble was, Rosenberg was also receiving unemployment benefits and the combination did not go over well with the New York State Department of Labor—at least initially.

The unemployed are generally not supposed to collect unemployment and earn money at the same time. They are supposed to be actively looking for work, not "kicking it on a couch, answering e-mails or drawing cartoons or getting interviewed on television about being unemployed."* It's also true, however, that the unemployed are generally allowed to accept donations. Luckily for Rosenberg, New York put his tips in that category and agreed that he didn't have to repay any benefits. Score one for the unemployed guy!

*See "Making Unemployment Work (Sort Of)"
by Leslie Eaton, Home Front,
February 24, 2002*

The EDD maintains an automated phone system (also at 800-300-5616) through which you can check on the status of an expected payment. To do so, you'll need to use this same system to create a PIN number. If you're eligible, benefits will start with the effective date of your claim, which will be the Sunday before the date your claim was filed. All claims have a one week waiting period, which is not a paid week and doesn't start until the claim is filed.

Maintaining Eligibility

Establishing your initial eligibility is just the first step. To continue to get paid, you'll have to maintain eligibility, which means that you must be "able to work," be "actively looking for work," and be "willing to accept a suitable job." You'll also have to mail in a completed and signed "Continued Claim Certification" every two weeks; a new form will arrive with each check. Regular benefits can last up to 26 weeks, although if statewide economic conditions justify a state or federal "extension of benefits" program, this period can stretch—up to 65 weeks in recent years.

Benefit Amounts

How much you'll receive each week depends on how much you earned during a "base period" year, which starts about 16 months before your claim is filed. Work and earnings from another state can be used to establish a claim. The maximum weekly benefit was $450 in 2006.

Special Programs

Claims are generally valid for one year after you've filed. Because the benefit amount can't change within that year, you might get stuck with an obsolete rate if you file towards the end of the year. Recognizing this, many people who are laid off in December wait until January to file their claims.

Enter the special programs approved by California or the Feds from time to time, such as retroactive benefits increases, backdating, and extended benefits. While each individual program is designed to fatten your check, you might need a Ph.D in math to figure out how they all intersect.

Fortunately, the EDD can tell you what's on the table at the moment and help you figure out whether you should apply. Keep in mind that the EDD might suspend your benefits while it completes its research and that electing to backdate could change your payout amount.

Going Out of Town

The EDD mails claim forms to your home address and requires your signature on each one. To be eligible for benefits, therefore, you (technically) need to be at home and actively looking for work (read: not traveling). Unfortunately, this means that if you travel even to pursue a professional opportunity, you might disqualify yourself for that time period's benefits—unless you can verify the purpose of your trip to the EDD's satisfaction. The silver lining is that if benefits are disallowed for any given time period, they are deferred, not lost altogether, until you're eligible again.

a traveler's run at fooling the EDD

San Franciscan James Trudy (name changed) was laid off from his job as an architect, which coincided nicely with a pre-planned six-month trip around the world. He successfully filed for unemployment insurance following his layoff and decided to try and keep the ball rolling during his trip.

He had his address with the EDD changed to a friend's address, and had his friend forge his signature and send back the claim forms when they arrived. For bank deposits, he left deposit slips and addressed envelopes to his financial institution. The plan worked fine for several months, until the EDD randomly scheduled a phone interview to check on James' progress in "looking for work." As he wasn't available for the interview and unable to respond otherwise, his benefits were discontinued.

UI and Moonlighting

Not that any San Franciscans *would* cheat, but off-the-record surveys show that plenty of otherwise honest citizens earn cash on the side while collecting UI. Beware—the EDD is onto this and will try to ensnare you with the help of those calling their **Fraud Tip Hot Line** (800-229-6297).

If you're contemplating collecting a little "extra" unemployment insurance, you should know that falsifying unemployment claims may subject you to (at the very least) repaying all of your ill-gotten gains.

LEISURE LOANS

Depending on the circumstances, the concept of a "leisure loan" can be a good one: borrow money to fund more time off. This is not to say that we encourage you to accumulate large amounts of debt. But if the timing is right for you to take some time to yourself, yet you don't have the cash reserves, a small loan to support your leisure may be just what the financial doctor ordered. Particularly in a low interest rate environment, borrowing money to fund leisure can be a savvy investment in your well-being.

Leisure loans can come in many forms, including personal loans from family or friends, a home equity loan if you're a home owner, or even a margin loan if you maintain an equity portfolio. Unfortunately, we were unable to find any banks out there that offered loans specifically with the intent to "fund leisure." We therefore call upon

THE BANK OF MOM & DAD

Without significant assets such as a house or stocks, you might find that a loan from the Bank of Mom & Dad is the easiest to obtain, and carries the best interest rate (0% financing, anyone?). But any family loan comes with its own unique costs, usually in the form of unsolicited opinions and parental "guidance."

Some of you will find those hidden costs prohibitive. Others will reject the familial borrowing notion straight away out of pride. Be wary of "pride," however; it often represents little more than a false sense of obligation based on societally-imposed expectations.

our nation's financial institutions: offer leisure loans as an investment in the balance and health of the American worker!

Home Equity Loans

If you're a home owner, a home equity loan may be a relatively secure way to borrow. As the name implies, these loans borrow against the value of your house. Home equity loans are usually available at lower rates than margin debt, and to the extent house values are more stable than stock values, your home will be a less risky asset to borrow against. Again, as with any borrowing situation, weigh the debt to equity ratio—in this case, compare the amount of the loan to the total value of the house, and consider total equity built up as well. The last thing you need is to jeopardize your home simply for a little extra cash.

Margin Loans

If you own a portfolio of stocks, why would you borrow against those very equities when you could sell them?

Well, for starters, if the markets are down, selling could net you a very poor price. You might be better off taking a short-term loan, then repaying it by selling when stock prices are higher. Brokerage houses make it very easy to borrow money; most offer checks that draw on automatically margined funds when written.

Neil Brown, Oakland-based CFA and financial services consultant, recom-

cash out mortgage

If you own a home and have built up some equity, refinancing might get you more than a lower rate or better terms. It might get you cash back—just like at the grocery store! With a "cash out" mortgage, you can pay off your existing first mortgage and have cash left over, up to the entire value of the equity in your home.

As appealing as that sounds, cash outs can be risky business. Around two-thirds of homeowners refinancing today are borrowing at least five percent more than they already owed, and using more than half of that cash to straighten out their bills, up from 30% just a couple of years ago.

In the words of one savvy San Francisco home owner, "It's really attractive to think you can refi and put some cash in your pocket. For some people, this might be more than they make in, say, six months—so the unemployed might find this attractive. But you really do not affect your monthly payments much, and you do not pay off your house any quicker."

mends that stockholding *leisure seekers* not borrow more than 20% of their total holdings, although the exact percentage would depend greatly on the composition of the portfolio. If you own only volatile equities such as small technology issues, for example, you probably shouldn't borrow against them at all.

Brown further cautions:

> *Margin borrowing should never become an addictive panacea for the chronic leisure seeker. Essentially, you are borrowing against the future earnings of your portfolio. At some point you will need to pay off the margin debt you have incurred with capital gains from the sale of winning positions, dividends, and/or interest earned from your investment portfolio (or if your portfolio goes nowhere, then cash from other sources). The worst words an equity borrower could ever hear are 'margin call.'*

RAIDING YOUR RETIREMENT FUND

Explore all your other options before you raid your nest egg. Look for more ways to cut expenses; reduce your debt as much as you can; even use a teaser-rate credit card to "borrow" money before you turn to your retirement fund.

If you're really in a bind, however, and you have an Individual Retirement Account ("IRA"), you can make an early withdrawal. Beware: you'll be subject to a 10% tax penalty, plus lose the real tax benefits of a retirement account.

Are there ways to avoid the penalty? Yes, a couple. You can withdraw up to $10,000 to buy your first home, or withdraw any amount to pay for "qualified higher education expenses." You'll owe ordinary income tax on these withdrawals, of course, but at least your tax hit will be in a year when you've probably received little other income.

If you have a 401(k), roll it over into an IRA, because you can't make an early withdrawal from a 401(k) without proving "undue hardship," and that's unduly hard. According to tax attorney Heather Emigh, "You have to write a letter to the IRS (it's not a form) and explain your situation—you're about to get evicted from your apartment, you can't afford to eat, and you can't find a job anywhere. If you can throw in some medical problems and/or starving kids, that would work even better." As if being unmonied weren't hardship enough!

Note, however, this small perk for the unemployed: the jobless can take money out of any qualified retirement plan, including an IRA, a 401(k), or 403(c), to pay for health insurance premiums.

SHOW ME THE MONEY

It's been said that free money is the best kind of money, although "free" is usually open to interpretation. Even as a gift, money rarely comes without strings attached. Still, you *can* find alternative sources of funding to finance time off.

Patronage

Explorers and artists of eras past were supported by the rich, powerful and royal. Famous sponsors flocked to Galileo, for example, and Shakespeare wrote some of his greatest plays and poems under the haven of patronage. Where are today's patrons?

Scholarships and grants are modern forms of patronage. Corporations are probably the single biggest patrons today, sponsoring such far-flung endeavors as science, athletics, and travel. How do you think the America's Cup yachting race with its multi-million dollar high-tech boats fills its sails? It may be a competition famous for its billionaire boys' club, but the America's Cup rakes in hundreds of millions of sponsorship dollars from corporations as well.

Coming out of graduate school, Internet and television producer Erik Olsen scored a sweet scholarship through the Rotary Club of Seattle, allowing him to travel and "work" in Chile for an entire year. His part of the bargain? Report back to the Rotaries on what he learned and tell them about his experiences—which, among other things, included meeting infamous Chilean dictator Augusto Pinochet.

The time-honored yet controversial concept of having a "sugar daddy" or "sugar momma" fund your leisure won't appeal to some, but its attractions have certainly withstood the test of time. Many a grand project has been funded through the "sweetness" of loved ones over the years. We're not here to pass judgment, only to present another option...

Such as explaining to your relatives or wealthy friends the concept of "patronage." Enlighten them as to how many great artists and philosophers have made world-changing contributions this way! Your modern leisure patron may come in the form of a rich uncle, a corporation, or perhaps even a government grant.

Regardless of where you find your funds, remember to share the leisure!

Grants and Scholarships

Scholarship and grant money (see **Chapter 10**) is often geared towards funding education—but not always. Numerous programs fund

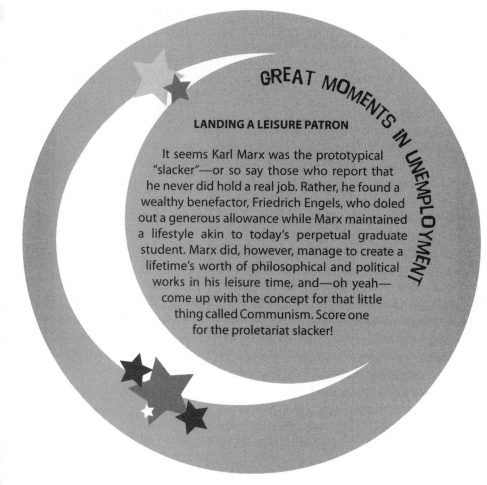

GREAT MOMENTS IN UNEMPLOYMENT

LANDING A LEISURE PATRON

It seems Karl Marx was the prototypical "slacker"—or so say those who report that he never did hold a real job. Rather, he found a wealthy benefactor, Friedrich Engels, who doled out a generous allowance while Marx maintained a lifestyle akin to today's perpetual graduate student. Marx did, however, manage to create a lifetime's worth of philosophical and political works in his leisure time, and—oh yeah—come up with the concept for that little thing called Communism. Score one for the proletariat slacker!

other goals in areas such as business, healthcare, or the delightfully nebulous "personal" category (we like! we like!).

An entire industry, not all of it ethical, exists to help you locate this money. Beware of get-rich-quick spins and advance-fee Internet offers unless you can verify the integrity of the organization another way.

Instead, see the book *Finding Funding: The Comprehensive Guide to Grant Writing* by Daniel M. Barber, which is, in fact, a comprehensive guide to finding grant money. You might also have luck with *I'll Grant You That* by local authors and teachers Jim Burke and Carol Ann Prater.

Another resource is **The Foundation Center** (312 Sutter #606, 415-397-0902, fdncenter.org/sanfrancisco), a San Francisco organization whose mission is "to support and improve philanthropy by promoting public understanding of the field and helping grant seekers succeed." Sounds good to us! Their free library and computer center houses an extensive grant database.

Do you have something more specific in mind? There are yet more sources that can help. The book *Six Months Off* includes information on grant money specifically geared towards sabbaticals. Writers and aspiring scribes should seek out the essential *Grants and Awards Available to American Writers* by John Morrone, Victoria Vinton, and Anna Jardine. Artists should look to the **California Arts Council** (800-201-6201, cac.ca.gov).

dream money

Live the dream on someone else's dime with these choice scholarships and grants:

Rockefeller Foundation's Bellagio Study and Conference Center (rockfound.org)
Nestled in a small town on the shores of Lago di Como in Northern Italy, the Bellagio Center provides a tranquil setting to create alongside other artists and scholars.

Rotary International Ambassadorial Scholarship (rotary.org)
Let Rotary International appoint you cultural ambassador to the world. All you have to do is make a report on what you learned.

Fulbright Scholarship (fulbrightonline.org)
The Fulbright is for any U.S. citizen with an undergrad degree and a desire to study, teach, or conduct business or research abroad.

Professional Development Fellowship (iie.org)
This fellowship funds three to seven months of study and research in Eastern Europe or the former Soviet Union. A monthly living stipend in addition to travel and study costs makes this a prized program.

bartering

If you have a useful talent or skill, consider bartering your services to others (no, we're not talking about anything sleazy!). If you're a photographer, for example, offer your work for trade-in-kind. You could get more in trade than you would in cash, and end up with a needed product or service.

If you're operating on a limited budget, perhaps bartering for a nice dinner out is just the ticket to spark your taste buds as well as your social life. So go on, make a deal!

SELLING YOUR STUFF

Offline

One of the smartest ways to shop isn't shopping at all. It's more like "reverse shopping"—trading or selling your used records, books or clothes for cash or store credit. "Buy-sell-trade" stores (see listings in the **Leisure Shopping Guide**) will turn them over at a fair price, just as fair as the prices you'll pay for any used goods you buy there.

A word of warning: it can be humbling indeed to have some 16-year-old sprite pass harsh judgment on your clothing, or reject every single one of your used CDs—not that this has ever happened to us! For best results, tailor your wares to the venue, and present them clean, pressed, and on hangers.

Online

The Internet has become a grand virtual marketplace for buying and selling "stuff." This represents a boon to the leisure seeker because it offers a way to raise cash quickly by simply selling your junk. "People love junk," says Eddie Foronda, an experienced seller. "You can quote me on that." Thanks Eddie—we just did.

eBay (ebay.com), and the culture that has emerged from it, is at the center of this magnificent bazaar, where everything is for sale. In fact, as Adam Cohen talked about with *Book Magazine*, "the number of… users [of the more than 40 million users registered on eBay] who have quit their jobs and are now making a living solely as eBay traders is now measured in the hundreds of thousands."

Choose some non-essential items (furniture, sporting goods, and electronics are in particularly high demand) and put them up for auction to see what you can get for them. You'll have to arrange for payment and shipping of course, but this is pretty straightforward. Be honest, or buyers will use eBay's feedback system to ding you. "At first it doesn't seem like feedback is a big deal, but it's the biggest thing ever," Super Sale Eddie says. "Even if you have 1,000 transactions and only one negative, people will look at the negative to see what it says." To support your local cybermarket, the site to see is **Craigslist** (craigslist.org) and its sale/wanted section.

Garage Sales, Flea Markets, Swap Meets

Garage or moving sales, if they're well-advertised, can pay off not only in money (no matter what the state of your finances), but also in reclaimed space in your closets and cupboards. Other people actually want your cast-offs—imagine that!

In addition to the typical places to list your garage sale, try posting flyers at a local college, especially in late summer. Don't forget your favorite café or pub, and sending a mass e-mail to your friends wouldn't hurt either. The point is, get the word out. Also important is not to advertise too early. For a Saturday sale, post to Craig's List ("no need to advertise in the paper," says sale maven Foronda) on Thursday, and don't let anyone show up early except your friends. On the other hand, be prepared to get bought out before your sale begins. "Some people just want the whole shebang, to see what they can get," Eddie has found. If you get an early request like this, entertain it. Be ready for business on time, with your wares tagged, plenty of change available, and some peppy music playing. Finally, sell cheap.

Flea markets and swap meets present a more consolidated market. First-timers should arrive early with their "mystery truckloads." For locations, see the **Leisure Shopping Guide**.

ODD JOBS

Willie Brown might not be hiring anymore, but you can find your own odd job in the classifieds of the *Chronicle*, *Bay Guardian*, or Craig's List. Some of those listings are downright wacky—serious *McJobs*!

You can also register with one of San Francisco's general temporary placement agencies, such as **Advanced Employment Services** (760 Market, Suite 1046, 415-989-1188, advancedemployment.com) or the **Certified Employment Group** (111 Pine, Suite 1200, 415-433-3600, certifiedemployment.com), or look for one that specializes in placement in your field, such as **Semper International** (785 Market, Suite 710, 415-974-1078, printstaff.com) for print, copy and digital professionals.

You must have an unusual skill or two. Let people know that you're available for services like small business bookkeeping, freelance photography, bodywork, whatever. Put on your marketing hat and get creative! Better still, look around, see what people need, then figure out how to get it to them. Services like tutoring, yard work, house sitting, and housecleaning (we like "Spouses Do Houses") are always in demand.

Bartending and waiting tables might be reliable standbys in other cities, but you'll face stiff competition for those jobs in this food and drink town. On the other hand, San Francisco does have almost 4,000 restaurants, so someone's bound to have an opening.

Actors and extras earn $100-500 per day. And don't forget—there's always "*consulting!*" (See **Leisure Lingo**.)

SHORT-TERM GIGS?

Just to jolt your brain cells, consider these job titles:

• tutor ($27-$80 an hour) • substitute teacher •
• personal assistant (to anyone who's always so busy!) •
• junior college professor (if you happen to have a master's degree) •
• child sitter • pet sitter (same thing? $20-$35 per night) •
• day trader • Amway/Mary Kay/Tupperware representative •
• house painter • handyman • launderer •
• tour guide (create a tour of your own!) •

subbing

If you're after the big bucks and don't have nerves of steel, forget about substitute teaching, advises full-time classroom teacher Alayne Brand. "The sub jobs range anywhere from a highly enjoyable experience to possibly being the worst day in your whole life," she says. But if you can live with an erratic schedule, love working with the City's youth and want to be more visible in the school setting, go ahead and launch the five-month process of testing and documentation.

You'll need a bachelor's degree from a U.S. college, passing scores on the CBEST (California Basic Skills Test, $41, given seven times a year), fingerprinting, negative results on a TB test ($20) and a $100 cashier's check just to get the paperwork to apply to the *San Francisco Unified School District* (555 Franklin, 415-241-6101, *sfusd.edu*). If you survive the lengthy interview process and complete training and more paperwork, you can pay another $55 to receive your 30-Day Substitute Credential.

Don't worry too much about the "30-Day" part—if you land a longer-term position, the district will be able to bend the rules for you, if they like you. In fact, becoming liked and well-known at a couple of schools is the best way to get consistent, steady work. "A good, reliable sub is a gold mine," Alayne says. "You will be called almost daily if teachers like you and the students get their work done when you are in the classroom."

Although you won't receive employment benefits, you can earn between $121-200 per day subbing, sometimes more for long-term positions. If the lengthy and cumbersome application process discourages you, look into a district outside the City, where the hiring cycles are shorter.

If you'd prefer higher pay, consider attending the year of school you'll need for full-time work. Alayne did, and has found the intangible rewards amazing. "I have never for a moment regretted going into teaching," she says. "And it gets better each year."

For general information about teaching in California, check with:
California Commission on Teacher Credentialing
Sacramento
916-445-7254
ctc.ca.gov

HOW TO MAKE A BUCK

	How To Get The Job	How Much $$$
Balloon Maker	Buy some balloons and a dual air pump and set yourself up amidst the tourists and other street performers at Fisherman's Wharf, or contact **Balloonabilities** (800-350-8947, *balloonabilities.com*), a balloon-maker placement agency. Training is provided!	Up to $100 in tips during a 3-hour shift at Chevy's—more if you're supernaturally entertaining.
Day Labor Program	Have skills in child care, gardening, painting, janitorial work… the list goes on. Bring your desire to fuel this worker-run organization. (17th Street & Potrero, *sfdaylabor.org*)	Workers receive 100% of all wages—from $12-$15/hr—plus meals, health care, classes in English and computers, and job-safety training.
Sperm or Egg Donor	Must be male or female. Sperm donors must be 21-35 with a high school diploma. Call **Pacific Reproductive Services** (444 De Haro, Suite 222, 415-487-2288, *pacrepro.com*) for more information on sperm. Eggs are a lot more involved (hence the handsome compensation). You must be 21-29, be willing to receive injections and be available for the full donor cycle, about three months.	For millions of sperm, $100 once or twice a week for a year. For one egg (or more, if the fertility drugs do their thing), $3,500-$5,000 plus expenses.
Blood Donor	Must be human, at least 17 years old (or 16 with permission from your parents), weigh 110 pounds or more and be in good health. Don't do drugs or have AIDS, cancer, hepatitis or organ failure. For more information, check *bloodcenters.org*.	No dollars, but you will get a mini-physical (blood pressure, temperature, iron level and blood type), plus you can save a life without even going to med school!
Focus Groups	Ever wonder why a great movie like "The Shawshank Redemption" had such a weak name? The producers forgot to run a focus group, that's why. Bring your opinion and be an otherwise run-of-the-mill consumer, and you're in. Check *silentway.com/tips/sf/focus.html*.	$50-$150 for a one- or two-hour session.

WithOut Making A Career

How To Get The Job	How Much $$$	
The website says you need to be currently employed in your field. "Yes," says MB, "they *say* that you have to be working in your field, but I was indeed already laid off, as were many other teachers. They really have to say that to maintain reputability." Request application info online. 185 Berry, China Basin Landing Lobby 3, 800-448-6775 *universityofphoenix.com*	$800 per five-week course. The trick is to leverage your investment in prep time by teaching the same course repeatedly.	**Lecturer, University of Phoenix**
Desire to have "girl" in your job title. Selling and acting ability also helps, as does a fun and carefree attitude. You'll need a valid California Seller's Permit, which is free. You must be 21 or older. Try **Peachy's Puffs** (415-553-4415, *peachyspuffs.com*).	You pay a $25 security deposit. They provide your costume. Income will be, on average, $50-180 for a five-hour shift. Perks can include free admission to concerts at the Warfield!	**Cigarette & Candy Girl**
Be qualified for and willing to run the full course of a given study. Find UCSF program qualifications at *ucsf.edu* under "Research," then "Clinical Trials Seeking Volunteers." You can also find calls for research volunteers on **Craigslist** in the "Jobs" column under "et cetera jobs."	Payment ranges wildly, from fringe benefits only, to $1200 for completion of an antibiotic study involving seven I.V. doses, a bronchoscopy and five days in the hospital.	**Medical Research Studies**
Be aggressive; you'll be competing with a lot of seasoned walkers. Still, the pet industry *is* growing by 700% a year...	$9-$14/dog, 6-8 dogs/walk, 3-4 walks/day. That adds up to $2240 a week for a walker who's fully booked. Not bad, not bad at all.	**Dogwalker**
You probably know if you have a knack for helping other people get organized. Learn more about creating order from chaos from the San Francisco Bay Area Chapter of the **National Association of Professional Organizers** (*napo-sfba.org*).	Full-time or part-time available. Expect to earn between $10-$30/hr as a total "newbie," $30-$50 with some background (in office or project management, say), and $50-$70 if you've been in law or nursing. Experts command up to $150/hr.	**Professional Organizer**

PART TWO
THE LEISURE ODYSSEY

CHAPTER 4
REDISCOVERING SAN FRANCISCO

*One's destination is never a place but rather
a new way of looking at things.*

~Henry Miller

THINK you know your own town? You might be surprised. Did you know, for instance, that Lombard is *not* actually San Francisco's crookedest street? Vermont Street in Potrero Hill beats it, based on a complex calculation incorporating bends per yard combined with grade and angle. What's more, it has better views!

Do you know what the highest point in San Francisco is? (Hint: it's a trick question). While tourists might claim Twin Peaks (902 feet) and locals Mount Davidson (925 feet), the highest actual point by a longshot is the top of Sutro Tower, at 1800 feet above sea level. Incidentally, the tower itself is also the tallest structure in the City at 977 feet, surpassing the Transamerica Pyramid by over 100 feet.

The tall and short of it is, spend your non-working hours discovering SF's true highlights, as well as soaking up the culture and ambience that make living here or visiting so great. Rest assured that our City's boundless opportunities for urban adventure and exploration will entertain you whether a tourist or a local. "There's a reason why everyone moves here," says sabbatical veteran Mary Mangold. "This is such a great city. Have as much fun as you can." Words to live by!

BECOME AN EXPERT ON YOUR OWN TOWN

San Francisco has always been proud of its distinctive character—and with good reason. Among our City's quirky claims to fame: we gave birth to the modern-day strip club (thank you, Carol Doda!), North Beach bathtubs served as LSD factories in the 1960s and '70s, and the Church of Satan was founded in the Richmond district. What local wouldn't be pleased to regale visitors with factoids like that?

With extra time on your hands, now's your chance to stock up your trivia drawer. San Francisco may not be quite as volatile as it once was, but it still houses an eclectic mix of personalities and goings-on, both above and below board, and they all await your rediscovery.

History and Trivia

Let's start with the original locals. The Ohlone Indians occupied what is now the San Francisco peninsula from about 10,000 years ago until the Europeans began displacing them in the late 18th century. The Ohlone were actually a collection of different tribes spread throughout the greater Bay Area. Like many modern-day San Franciscans, these tribes were nomadic and, by most accounts, lived very much in harmony with their natural environs. They clearly understood the concept of leisure, as they lived completely in the present, and enjoyed in abundance what the land provided.

Enter the Spaniards, who must have seen all this good living as a threat to their hard-working, Catholic way of life. These "civilized" settlers responded by attempting to enslave and convert the leisurely "heathens" to Christianity. To speed things up, they founded **Mission Dolores** (3321 16th Street) in 1776, marking the beginnings of modern-day San Francisco. That same year, the Presidio was formally established as a Spanish military outpost, and the early stages of a town began forming.

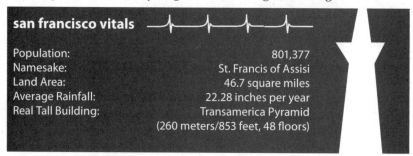

san francisco vitals

Population:	801,377
Namesake:	St. Francis of Assisi
Land Area:	46.7 square miles
Average Rainfall:	22.28 inches per year
Real Tall Building:	Transamerica Pyramid
	(260 meters/853 feet, 48 floors)

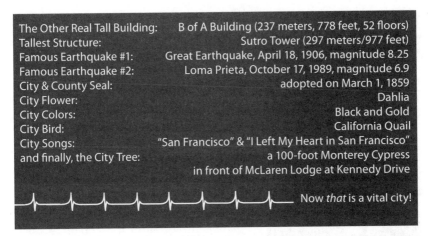

The Other Real Tall Building:	B of A Building (237 meters, 778 feet, 52 floors)
Tallest Structure:	Sutro Tower (297 meters/977 feet)
Famous Earthquake #1:	Great Earthquake, April 18, 1906, magnitude 8.25
Famous Earthquake #2:	Loma Prieta, October 17, 1989, magnitude 6.9
City & County Seal:	adopted on March 1, 1859
City Flower:	Dahlia
City Colors:	Black and Gold
City Bird:	California Quail
City Songs:	"San Francisco" & "I Left My Heart in San Francisco"
and finally, the City Tree:	a 100-foot Monterey Cypress in front of McLaren Lodge at Kennedy Drive

Now *that* is a vital city!

When Mexico won independence from Spain in the early 1800s, San Francisco returned to Mexican rule. But Californians were then an independent mix of Mexicans, Americans, native Americans, and Spaniards, who didn't exactly heed Mexico's head honcho.

Things really started cooking in 1846 with the outbreak of the Mexican-American War. San Francisco (then a small village known as Yerba Buena) officially passed from Mexican to American hands, and held its first municipal elections. In 1847, the town name was formally changed from Yerba Buena to San Francisco, after St. Francis of Assisi—and if you have any doubts about taking time off, note that our patron saint was also unemployed!

The discovery of gold on the American River in 1848 led to a temporary mass exodus from the City to the foothills of the Sierra Nevada. Soon after, however, San Francisco's population skyrocketed, soaring from 800 or so at the beginning of 1848 to an estimated 100,000 by the end of 1849. Most newbies arrived by sea, including thousands of immigrants from South America, the South Pacific, and Europe, as well as Americans from the Eastern United States.

Gambling, prostitution, and other assorted vices took root in the wake of gold fever, transporting the City into the heyday of the Barbary Coast, a seedy old waterfront area rife with crime. The **San Francisco Museum and Historical Society** (sfhistory. org) offers a historical walk of the area (barbarycoasttrail.org) for those wishing to delve into the underbelly of the City's past; the Barbary Coast is marked by a series of bronze medallions set in the sidewalks.

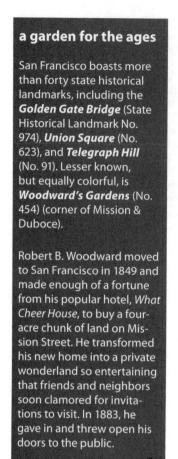

a garden for the ages

San Francisco boasts more than forty state historical landmarks, including the **Golden Gate Bridge** (State Historical Landmark No. 974), **Union Square** (No. 623), and **Telegraph Hill** (No. 91). Lesser known, but equally colorful, is **Woodward's Gardens** (No. 454) (corner of Mission & Duboce).

Robert B. Woodward moved to San Francisco in 1849 and made enough of a fortune from his popular hotel, *What Cheer House*, to buy a four-acre chunk of land on Mission Street. He transformed his new home into a private wonderland so entertaining that friends and neighbors soon clamored for invitations to visit. In 1883, he gave in and threw open his doors to the public.

more...

In 1872, the *San Francisco Real Estate Circular* arrogantly claimed, "San Francisco is in very little more danger of a disastrous earthquake than the Eastern States of being flooded by an overflow of the Atlantic Ocean," and "San Francisco is in less danger from fire than any city of the East." Oops. Not only did the Great Earthquake rock the City's world in 1906, but the more destructive Great Fire was the seventh and worst in a series of Great Fires.

The completion of the Panama Canal in 1914 gave San Francisco the perfect excuse to throw a big-ass party—and invite the whole world. They did so with great fanfare at the Panama-Pacific International Exposition, spending more than $100 million to build 625 acres of lavish palaces, gardens, and other wonderlands. The legacy of this hugely ambitious undertaking remains the better part of the City's Marina district, including the Palace of Fine Arts, Crissy Field, the Marina Green, and most of the land along the northern waterfront.

The year 1939 was a blockbuster as well. San Francisco hosted the Golden Gate International Exposition (otherwise known as the World's Fair) on the newly created Treasure Island, to celebrate—among other things—the recent completion of the Golden Gate and Bay Bridges.

The beats emerged in the '50s, and formed a literary culture in the City that remains to this day. Joe DiMaggio and Marilyn Monroe wed at City Hall—and there was the odd earthquake or two. Speaking of turbulence, the '60s and '70s brought tumultuous times to the City, with the emergence of pop music, drugs, youth culture, and activism, encapsulated by the Summer of Love in 1969. They also saw the rise of a politically active gay community, led by Supervisor Harvey Milk, who was assassinated along with Mayor George Moscone in 1978.

The outbreak of the AIDS epidemic dominated the 1980s. San Francisco became (and remains) a focal point in the treatment and politics surrounding the disease. A decade later, dot-com fever raged through city streets as wildly as the Great Earthquake and Fire, and ultimately might have left just as much destruction in its wake. The tremors from the "bubble burst" are still being felt today.

Whew! That's a lot of action in a relatively short time period. Interested historians can study up on SF history at the **Virtual Museum of the City of San Francisco** (sfmuseum.org), a superb site that would make most librarians proud. If you're looking for a more current perspective, introduce yourself to **Mister SF** (mistersf.com), and let him guide you through our fine city. Mister SF (columnist Hank Donat) has painstakingly scoured the streets of San Francisco, so you don't have to.

SAN FRANCISCO BACTERIA IS SPECIAL

Why is the uniquely tangy taste of San Francisco Sourdough impossible to cook up anywhere else? Because special types of the two most important ingredients grow here and only here: *Saccharomyces exiguus* (yeast), and *Lactobacillus sanfrancisco* (bacteria).

The yeast culture is something you can now buy in specialty shops around the country, but the bacteria (fortunately?) are not. This means that, unless you expose your fine loaf to our home-grown Bay Area bacilli, the flavor will always come out different. See "Get Baked" in **Dining & Nightlife** for more on the Bay Area's baking culture.

...cont'd

Known as the "Barnum of the West," Woodward strove to provide ordinary folks with "Education, Recreation and Amusement." His gardens were a West Coast superlative in several respects: its largest and most comprehensive zoo, its first aquarium, and its largest rollerskating rink. Its attractions included ostriches, camels, and Japanese roosters with 25-foot tail-feathers; crystals, precious stones, and petrified fossils; hot-air balloon rides; and a 5000-seat octagon concert pavilion. For years running, it was San Francisco's most popular resort.

Woodward's land was split into 39 parcels after his death. Only one hint remains of what was: a gourmet restaurant of the same name.

Woodward's Garden
1700 Mission
415-621-7122

San Francisco's Wild Characters: Then and Now

The City by the Bay has long been home to crazy characters and personalities, from the highly eccentric "Emperor Norton" in the Gold Rush era, to "high priest" Timothy Leary in the 1960s, to former Mayor Willie Lewis Brown—love him or hate him—spearheading city politics from 1996-2003.

Although famous-folk sightings in San Francisco might be running a bit thin (where have you gone, Nicolas Cage and Wynona Ryder?), today's local luminaries are nonetheless approachable. You might, for example, find yourself pedaling the stationary bike next to Danny Glover at USF's **Koret Center** (see **Chapter 7**), or enjoying an Irish coffee next to Sean Penn or Francis Ford Coppola at **Tosca** in North Beach (242 Columbus, 415-986-9651). And hey, George (Lucas, of course) is finally in town, bringing a portion of his Lucasfilm empire to the Presidio. Surely *that* will boost the wattage of the City's star power!

SAN FRANCISCO'S WILD CHARACTERS

Sally Stanford (1903-1982) ★ THEN

Former Mayor Willie L. Brown, Jr. (born 1934) ★ NOW

Sally, as in the song "I Wonder What's Become of Sally," and Stanford, as in the university (she liked the football team), became SF's most famous madam in the 1930s and '40s, operating brothels in Russian Hill, Nob Hill, and the Tenderloin. Her clientele included a who's who of City elite, and her one-time 1144 Pine Street address was known far and wide to taxi drivers and police alike. Despite her reckless youth, Sally grew to achieve popular mainstream status in both society and politics, giving up the "biz" in 1949 to move to Sausalito, where she opened the **Valhalla Restaurant**, which had a long run before its recent sale. Her election to the Sausalito city council in 1972, and mayor in 1976, earned her the nationwide moniker, "Madam Mayor."

"Da Mayor," or former Mayor Willie Brown, was undeniably a character in office, from his fetish for feathered hats and Armani suits to his infamous junkets to San Francisco sister cities with attractive assistants in tow (for a complete list of sister cities, see **Chapter 5** under "International Travel"). He certainly shook things up in a city that for many years was suffering from political gridlock, managing to make things happen where others could not. Put simply, Willie Brown in office made San Francisco more interesting.

CINEMA SAN FRANCISCO

San Francisco has been a player in the movies since the beginnings of the industry itself. Although the majority of California's film production has long since moved south to Los Angeles, the City has fostered scores of notable filmmakers—Francis Ford Coppola, George Lucas, Kathryn Bigelow, Clint Eastwood, and Alfred Hitchcock among them—and has served as the studio backdrop to an abundance of celebrated films over the years.

Many of these films use San Francisco's distinct culture and topography as key plot and character elements, from the Mission Dolores setting of Hitchcock's psychologically twisted *Vertigo*, to the drag-queen undertones of Robin Williams' character in *Mrs. Doubtfire*.

The good news is that film culture in the City has been undergoing a small renaissance in recent years. George Lucas has moved Lucasfilm headquarters to the new Letterman Digital Arts Center in the Presidio. The Roxie, Red Vic, Balboa (see listings below) and other independent theaters have not only survived, but have thrived through community support and creative partnerships. The completely revamped **San Francisco Film Commission** (City Hall, Room 473, 415-554-6241, sfgov.org/film), led by new executive director Stefanie Coyote (yes, Peter's wife) is striving to bring film production back to the City. The **San Francisco International Film Festival** (415-561-5000, sfiff.org) has found

the san francisco international film festival (sfiff.org)

Every Spring for 49 years and counting, San Francisco has hosted the increasingly popular two-week San Francisco International Film Festival. While star-gazing in the VIP rooms at the opening and closing night galas can be a hoot (Peter Coyote and Delroy Lindo are regulars), the films take center stage.

The festival has been given a much-needed boost with the arrival of new Film Society executive director Graham Leggat, who brings big-city festival experience from the Film Society of Lincoln Center in New York, An expert programming staff brings more than 200 independent documentaries and films from 40+ countries to the screens at the *Kabuki 8 Theatre*, now the *Sundance Kabuki* (1881 Post, 415-922-4262), which serves as ground zero for the festival; the illustrious *Castro Theatre* (429 Castro, 415-621-6120); and two out-of-area venues. Some of the best screenings are scheduled for weekday matinees—perfect for those living off the clock!

Find more film festivals listed in *Fairs & Fests*.

SAN FRANCISCO'S WILD CHARACTERS

O.J. Simpson (born 1947)

"The Juice" grew up in Potrero Hill before attending high school at Galileo in the Marina and junior college at City College of San Francisco. He went on to achieve college football fame at USC and pro fame with the Buffalo Bills and 49ers before succumbing to the allure of Hollywood. And, well, you probably know the rest of the story from there.

new zeal and is quickly growing in size and stature. Heck, even Robby Redford is getting in on the action, with Sundance Cinemas snatching up the Kabuki 8 Theatre. When was the last time you heard of an independent theater buying out a large chain location?

So get out there and take in a flick at your local theater—single screen or multiplex, independent or blockbuster. Fire up that DVD player. Explore the cinematic world of San Francisco!

Essential Viewing

Scott Trimble, a location manager and scout who manages **Film in America** (filminamerica.com/PacificNorthwest/NCA/SanFrancisco), maintains a comprehensive list of the great films of San Francisco dating all the way back to 1880! Although his personal "can't miss" list includes some obscure flicks, such as *The Lady From Shanghai* (1948) and *Star Trek IV: The Voyage Home* (1986), he goes with *Vertigo* (1958) and *Bullitt* (1968) as "probably the most common films associated with San Francisco, the former for its picturesque views of the City and the latter for its famous car chase." We couldn't agree more, so after plenty of popcorn and soda, we chose eight more flicks for a top ten listing of San Francisco movie magic.

The Maltese Falcon
starring Humphrey Bogart, 1941
A film noir classic. Bogart stars as detective Sam Spade, with an office in downtown San Francisco at Sutter & Montgomery. Scenery highlights include a shiny new Bay Bridge, and the Ferry Building downtown.

Vertigo
starring James Stewart, 1958
Hitchcock loved San Francisco and Northern California, and it shows in this twisted and strange thriller. He throws in at least a handful of

City landmarks: Mission Dolores, Fort Point, the Palace of the Legion of Honor, the Palace of Fine Arts, and Ernie's Restaurant at 847 Montgomery (reportedly one of Hitchcock's favorite drinking holes, but unfortunately no longer in existence).

Bullitt
starring Steve McQueen, 1968

By all counts a great film, and one of Steve McQueen's best. Not only does it feature one of the most famous car chase scenes ever (see sidebar this page), but it shows off some of the best of SF, including a beautiful home at 2700 Vallejo in Pacific Heights (still there), the Mark Hopkins Hotel, Grace Cathedral, and the Marina.

Dirty Harry
starring Clint Eastwood, 1971

Hometown boy Clint Eastwood (born in San Francisco in 1930) does his city proud in his Dirty Harry movies, with perhaps more on-location City shooting (of both the film and the gun variety!) than in any film before or after. The original story is, predictably, the best, but there are five in the series, spanning from 1971 to 1988 (in order): *Dirty Harry, Magnum Force, The Enforcer, Sudden Impact*, and *The Dead Pool*.

cops & chase scenes

For some unknown reason, San Francisco has had a film and television obsession with cops. Street cops, private detectives, homicide investigators, undercover narcotics, you name it—it's been done here. All this, in a city that's not particularly known for its crime, or even its police force. And for every cop movie or show, there is, of course, a cool chase scene, where the City transforms into a spectacular racecourse for chasing bad guys.

The fixation began when Bogart played "Sam Spade" in *The Maltese Falcon*, but the "SF cop" was immortalized forever in the 1970s TV crime drama *The Streets of San Francisco*, starring Michael Douglas and Karl Malden. Douglas returned to his City cop roots in 1992, in the saucy thriller *Basic Instinct*.

Other notable local cop portrayals include *Vertigo* (retired cop), *Dirty Harry* (five films total), *48 Hours, Jade, The Rock* (FBI), and the recent *Nash Bridges* (TV series). As for riveting chase scenes? While *Streets* and *Nash Bridges* offered them up weekly, top honors go to McQueen and his Mustang in *Bullitt*, followed closely by *The Dead Pool* (Dirty Harry), *Jade*, and *The Rock*.

For more information, go to filmamerica.com/PacificNorthwest/NCA/SanFrancisco.

matinee price, please

Whatever happened to the good old-fashioned weekday matinee—has it gone the way of the drive-in? Almost, but not quite. A few "mats" survive (that's theater lingo), split between the indies and the multiplexes. But a matinee is a matinee, and once you're plunked down in a dark theatre smack-dab in the middle of the day, you won't notice your surroundings.

Your best movie bargain about town is at the *Balboa Theater* (p. 102). You won't necessarily see first-run blockbusters here, but matinees are only $6 every day of the week. You even get in free on your birthday—how cool is that? Kung Fu fans will like the nearby *4 Star* (2200 Clement, 415-666-3488, 4starmovietheatre. net), which also screens $6.50 matinees Monday–Friday before 4pm and weekends before 2pm.

The Castro Theatre (next page) offers $6 matinees the first show of every day, which is usually early afternoon. The *Red Vic* (p. 102) and *The Roxie* (p. 102) offer matinee prices on Wednesday, Saturday and Sunday: just $6 and $5 a pop, respectively.

 *[next reel...]*

48 Hours
starring Nick Nolte, Eddie Murphy, 1982

Okay, so this movie is less "classic" than some of the others. But Nolte and Murphy are at the top of their games, and an exciting bus chase scene shows us just how fast Muni *could* run if it had its act together.

Pacific Heights
starring Michael Keaton, 1990

Pacific Heights, Potrero Hill, what's the difference? As long as you've got a beautifully renovated Victorian, downtown city views, and a psycho tenant who's protected under a liberal San Francisco rent ordinance, you can't go wrong.

Basic Instinct
starring Michael Douglas, 1992

Michael Douglas and Sharon Stone in a sexually charged, kinky love/murder mystery—are you kidding? Dynamite stuff. Add to that a multimillion dollar Pacific Heights mansion, plus a quintessential San Francisco chase scene where Douglas ends up swimming in the Bay, and this one will be a repeat rental.

Mrs. Doubtfire
starring Robin Williams, 1993

The authors personally witnessed the filming of this movie in 1992, and have to admit that Robin Williams looked pretty good in a dress! Excellent location shooting in Pac Heights and North Beach, along with Robin Williams at his best, make this a worthy rental.

The Rock
starring Nicolas Cage, 1996

Nicolas Cage flexes his muscle and Sean Connery grows hair extensions. Ouch! Still, *The Rock* does rock, from opening bell through to final knockout punch. Plus, it has one of the best modern car chase scenes ever (we're starting to think the City was designed for them), culminating in a spectacular local crowd-pleaser: a Department of Parking & Traffic three-wheeler gets blown sky high!

The Game
starring Michael Douglas, 1997

[...cont'd]

Finally, you'll find mats in the multiplexes: at the **AMC Van Ness 14** (1000 Van Ness, 415-922-4262) for $8 before 6pm Monday-Thursday, and before 4pm Friday-Sunday and holidays, and at the **AMC Loews Metreon 15** (101 4th Street, 415-369-6200), same owner, same price and schedule. The two AMC theatres also offer something called A.M. Cinema for those early risers—$6 shows before noon Friday-Sunday and holidays.

You just can't get Michael Douglas out of the streets of San Francisco, can you? Douglas is back in the City in *The Game*, and remarkably this time he's not a cop! Instead, he plays an uptight businessman whose brother (Sean Penn) gets him mixed up in a mind bender of a treasure hunt around San Francisco. Two stellar actors with strong SF ties combine with fine on-location shooting throughout the City, plus Douglas manages to plunge a car into the Bay... once again.

The Dark Rooms

A disturbing trend is sprawling across the Bay Area and the nation: multiplexes are consuming the classic, single-screen theatre that projects character in addition to first-rate movies. That said, the good news locally is that the independents are giving the multiplexes a run for their money, and several have recently avoided this inauspicious fate.

The Castro Theatre (429 Castro @ Market, 415-621-6120, thecastrotheatre.com) is the granddaddy of all independent cinema in San Francisco. If you haven't been to this grand palace, sat under the dramatic, mandala-like ceiling, and listened to the mighty Wurlitzer organ introduce a film, you have yet to truly experience the movies in the City.

But the Castro isn't the only show in town. Other notable single-screens in San Francisco include:

The Balboa Theater (3630 Balboa, 415-221-8184, thebalboatheater.com)
The Bridge (3010 Geary, 415-267-4893)
Regal's Vogue Theater (3290 Sacramento, 415-221-8183)
Clay Theatre (2261 Fillmore, 415-267-4893)
United Artists Metro (2055 Union, 415-931-1685)

If funky art-house is your style, check out the **Red Vic Movie House** (1727 Haight, 415-668-3994, redvicmoviehouse.com), where the draw is the atmosphere and unusual films, not the screen or sound quality. **The Roxie** (3117 16th Street, 415-863-1087, roxie.com) is a Mission district independent with plenty of moxie. The theatre has recently undergone extensive renovations as part of a new non-profit partnership between Roxie Cinema and New College of California.

For more on the culture of neighborhood theatres in San Francisco, view the **San Francisco Neighborhood Theater Foundation** website (sfntf.org).

THE BEST THINGS TO DO FOR FREE IN SAN FRANCISCO

The City by the Bay presents endless opportunities for free fun. This is by no means an exhaustive list of gratis excursions—just (in our opinion) some of the best.

Take a Walk through Crissy Field

(crissyfield.org)

The new Crissy Field national park and recreation area, on the northern edge of the Presidio, is a gem. Opened in 2001, the newly created park is a combination of marshland, walking paths, sand dunes, and bay-front beaches. Start out at the Crissy Field Center on the southeast side of the park—equal parts museum, education center, and café/bookstore—and work your way west along the pathways. Walk all the way out to Fort Point, in the shadow of the Golden Gate Bridge, and watch the surfers and boats whisk by. The cozy **Warming Hut** (Building 983, Presidio, 415-561-3040) café and bookstore on the waterfront makes an excellent pit stop. Amble back along the water and witness some of the best sailboarding and kiteboarding in the world.

Bike across the Golden Gate Bridge

Grab your mountain bike for a spin across the most beautiful bridge in the most beautiful city in the world. It never gets boring; the splendor of the scenery never wanes. Stop mid-way across and take in the City skyline, Alcatraz, and Angel Island on the Bay side, the Marin Headlands and the vast Pacific blue to the west. As a bonus, continue on the north side to the top of the Marin Headlands, where you can look back towards the Bridge with the City in the background—one of the most breathtaking vistas in the country, if not the world (see **Chapter 7** for more bike ride ideas).

Explore Sigmund Stern Grove

(Sloat & 19th Avenue, sterngrove.org)

Once home to the infamous Trocadero, a hotel and compound that was known as a raucous hideaway for the rich and elite at the turn of the century, Stern Grove is now a true jewel in the Sunset. Bound by Sloat Boulevard to the south, Wawona Street to the north, 19th Avenue to the east and 34th Avenue to the west, "The Grove," together with Pine Lake, comprises some 63 acres of beautiful tree-lined recreation space. It comes complete with hiking trails, lawn bowling greens, croquet courts, golf putting greens, tennis courts, and horseshoe pits (see **Chapter 7** for more on fitness in The Grove). A well-equipped children's playground will keep the tykes smiling, too. As for the Trocadero? The original structure is still there, and although a bit tamer than in years past, it's still available for rent for social functions.

Stern Grove is said to be ten degrees warmer than the rest of the City, due to its wind-blocking eucalyptus trees—although we're prepared to dispute that claim! It certainly *is* warmer than the surrounding Sunset, particularly on windy, foggy days.

What's more, the trees and sloping terrain form a natural amphitheatre, which some dub "nature's music box." The **Stern Grove Festival** has become famous for its eclectic (and free) summertime concerts.

SAN FRANCISCO'S WILD CHARACTERS ☆ Shanghai Kelly (19th century, dates unknown)

THEN

Perhaps a bit mythologized over the years, Shanghai Kelly was nonetheless a colorful personality from the Barbary Coast days. What we do know is this: James "Shanghai" Kelly, a fiery red-bearded character, owned a boarding house on either Pacific or Broadway, and later ran a saloon called the Boston House at Davis & Chamber. From there, the line between fact and fiction starts to blur.

Kelly was reportedly involved in the practice of "shanghaiing," or kidnapping unsuspecting young souls and shipping them off to sea as crewmen on international voyages. Legend has him utilizing various deceits to capture his prey, including trapdoors in his saloon, drugged-up drinks, and opium-laced cigars made in Chinatown.

The most infamous tale has Kelly throwing himself a blowout "birthday" bash aboard a steamer on the Bay: inviting all on the waterfront for a night of free booze and revelry, then serving them drug-poisoned drinks—which were slurped up with pleasure. Kelly then unloaded his cargo of passed-out men onto three ships waiting outside the Golden Gate, collecting a tidy sum in return.

NOW

Good thing no such fate awaits you at *today's* bar!
Shanghai Kelly's
2064 Polk @ Broadway
415-771-3300

They are one of the best freebies in the City, so bring a picnic lunch, and be sure to arrive early for the best seating. Tip: You can reserve picnic table seating for up to six people by calling the **Recreation & Park Department** (415-831-5500) at 9am the Monday before each concert. Have your speed dialer ready. Go to sterngrove.org or see **Fairs & Fests** for the full scoop.

Spend an Afternoon in Golden Gate Park

Golden Gate Park is one of the world's greatest urban refuges. At 1,013 acres, it's the single largest man-made urban park in the U.S., larger even than New York's Central Park. Unlike Central Park, however, it remains a relatively safe place to visit.

Built in 1870 from little more than sand dunes, Golden Gate Park has nine lakes and more than a million trees within its borders. The park's diversity is nothing short of astonishing, home to (in no particular order): buffalo, soccer fields, fly-casting ponds, windmills, arboretums, Japanese gardens, museums, amphitheaters, golf courses, tennis courts, archery ranges, lawn bowling greens, pétanque courts, handball courts, horseshoe games, hiking trails, biking paths, skating areas, merry-go-rounds, baseball fields, softball fields, polo fields, and boating lakes. Take your pick of activities or locations, or simply bring a blanket and relax in a grassy meadow. For details on how to use the park as your very own gym, see **Chapter 7**.

ANCHOR'S AWAY!

Although the building itself dates back to 1896, the brewery now known as ***Anchor Brewing Company*** (1705 Mariposa, 415-863-8350, anchorbrewing.com) was purchased by Fritz Maytag (yes, *the* Maytag's) in the 1960s, a transaction that marked the beginning of the modern microbrewing movement. Today's free plant tour begins with a lesson in ingredients, brewing methods for steam beer, porter, and ales—and the company's colorful history.

You'll generally need to book your reservations at least a month in advance, although you *could* tag along with a group of regulars. "We went every Friday when I got laid off," Mary Mangold told us, "and compared notes on how to fill out the unemployment forms."

We'll drink to that!

One of the best new freebies in the park is at the recently completed (and spectacular) **de Young Museum** (50 Hagiwara Tea Garden near 8th Avenue, 415-863-3330, thinker.org/deyoung). The museum's unique tower, with it's 360 degree views of the City, is free for visitors—no need to pay the museum entrance fee, just enter through the main entrance and head to the right towards the tower. You can also stroll the grounds outside the building, and marvel at the unique architecture, the space ship-like structure towering within the surrounding eucalyptus trees.

THE PERFECTLY FREE—AND LEISURELY—DAY

10am	City Guides walking tour
12 noon	picnic lunch @ Fort Mason, free Ghirardelli chocolate for dessert
1pm	Anchor Brewing Company tour
3pm	always-free museum
5pm	happy hour with free food
8pm	free outdoor cinema... or after-dinner nap if you're tuckered out!
10pm	no-cover dancing

Start your day with a walking tour led by **City Guides** (415-557-4266, sfcityguides.com). We like the year-round "Bawdy & Naughty" tour of the former Barbary Coast that meets at the east end of Maiden Lane, but take your pick from the hundreds of different walks they offer.

We'll call it a free lunch if you paid for it yesterday—or if you'll gladly pay Tuesday. Stop by the **Ghirardelli Chocolate Factory** (Ghirardelli Square, 900 Northpoint) to snag a free chocolate sample for dessert before you tote a picnic lunch over to the grassy expanse at nearby **Fort Mason** (corner of Marina & Buchanan).

Drinking as entertainment? You bet, as long as it's free and comes with education in hops, barley, and other parts of the beer-making process. **Anchor Brewing Company** (1705 Mariposa, 415-863-8350, anchorbrewing.com) hosts a 90-minute brewery tour every weekday at the company's Potrero Hill facility, which culminates in—you guessed it—ample tasting at the end of the tour.

If you're game for a bite of brain candy, albeit a bit tipsy, seek out one of the more obscure and always-free museums, such as at the

Federal Reserve Bank of San Francisco (101 Market, 415-974-2000, frbsf.org) where you can brush up on your macro economic theory— it's actually quite cool, honest! Or sail on down to the always-free **National Maritime Museum** (Aquatic Park, end of Polk Street, maritime. org) and cruise through San Francisco's storied maritime history.

Continuing the brewski theme from earlier, hit a bar that serves free food during happy hour. San Francisco is elusive in this department, so do check ahead, but the latest word on the street is you'll find gratis grub (and good drink specials) at **The Last Supper Club** (119 Valencia, 415-695-1199, lastsupperclubsf.com) from 5-7pm, at **Sugar** (377 Hayes, 415-255-7144, sugarloungesf.com) weekdays from 4:30-7pm, and a free gourmet pizza with the purchase of two drinks at the upscale **Palio d' Asti** (640 Sacramento, 415-395-9800, paliodasti.com) from 4-7pm. For more happy hour recommendations, see **Dining & Nightlife**. Eat up, free grub!

SAN FRANCISCO'S MILD ☆ AND PROGRESSIVE ☆ CHARACTER * Mayor Gavin Newsom (born 1967) *

After winning a tight runoff election with rival Matt Gonzalez at the end of 2003, it didn't take Newsom long to win over the hearts and minds of most San Franciscans, including many Gonzalez supporters. Since taking office, his approval ratings have hovered in the 80 percent range, making him one of the most popular elected officials in the country. His controversial decision to issue same-sex marriage licenses at City Hall in 2004, despite political and legal opposition, gained him international notoriety as a political progressive, as well as made him an instant hero within the LGBT community. Citywide proposals and programs such as Care Not Cash, Universal San Francisco Healthcare, and Project Homeless Connect have only served to bolster his popularity. Once painted as a rich, slick politician who would only cater to the City's wealthy, Newsom has spent a surprising amount of time and effort with the City's underprivileged neighborhoods, changing his once "Greasy Gavin" image to... dare we say it... "Gracious Gavin."

If you like free flicks (and really, who doesn't?), take in an outdoor film put on by the **San Francisco Neighborhood Theater Foundation** (sfntf.org). They screen free films on miscellaneous Saturday nights during May-October at Union Square, Washington Square Park and Dolores Park—see their website for the schedule. And Dolores Park has proven popular enough to generate its own outdoor movie movement, **Dolores Park Movie Night** (doloresparkmovie.org), which screens the second Thursday during the months April-October.

Cap off the night in your boogie shoes at **Holy Cow** (see **Dining & Nightlife**), where there's "never a cover, always a party." Or if it's a weekday and you're in a bit more of a hipster mood, try grooving to the DJs across the alley at **Wish** (1539 Folsom, 415-278-9474).

NINE TO FIVE

Nine to five? No, we're not talking about work (or the Dolly Parton movie), but about creative ways to occupy yourself during standard

WE'LL SEE YOU IN COURT

Step inside a courtroom and see justice in action. Some trials are downright fascinating! If you get a doozy, hey, it's not jury duty—step out at any time, or join the jury member who nods off during closing arguments.

Decide for yourself whether the lower courts erred when you hear the appeals at the *United States Court of Appeals for the Ninth Circuit* (95 7th Street, 415-556-9800, *ca9.uscourts.gov*). When the court is not in session here, take a public tour of the courthouse instead (on certain Tuesdays at 1pm—call ahead, 415-556-9945, meet in front of the museum near the Seventh & Mission entrance).

The *California Supreme Court* (Earl Warren Building, 350 McAllister, 415-865-7000, *courtinfo.ca.gov/courts/supreme*) convenes for a good chunk of the year near the Civic Center, and *Small Claims Court* (Civic Center Courthouse, 400 McAllister, Room 103, 415-551-4000) is just across the street. Remember, no lawyers are allowed in Small Claims Court, which makes for some juicy if not always well-reasoned debates. Then again, lawyers aren't always the most logical creatures themselves...

"business hours" Monday through Friday, while you're not working. You won't be able to enjoy these daytime activities once you go back to work—at least not very easily. So don't waste your day watching a soap opera, go out and create one of your own!

Wild Characters:
GOOD RIDDANCE!

James Jones (1931–1978)

The story of Jim Jones and the People's Temple is one of the darkest chapters of San Francisco history. Jones brought the headquarters of the infamous Temple to 1859 Geary Boulevard (now a post office) in the City's Fillmore district in 1971. The charismatic leader immediately established himself as a political power broker, ingratiating himself with California politicos Art Agnos, then-Governor Jerry Brown, and Willie Brown, among others. Indeed, Jones was said to have delivered Mayor George Moscone's victory in 1975 (amid allegations that the People's Temple committed voter fraud). Mayor Moscone later rewarded Jones with an official post: running San Francisco's Housing Commission.

Tragedy struck in November of 1978, when Bay Area Congressman Leo Ryan, with then-aid Jackie Speier (now a state senator), led an investigative mission to Georgetown, Guyana, seeking the compound where Jones and his followers had been living for over a year. Ryan and several reporters were gunned down at a Guyana airfield trying to rescue defectors. Later that same day, Jones ordered his congregation of roughly 1,000 to drink cyanide-laced Kool-Aid in the largest mass suicide in modern history.

Ride Alongs

Always hankered to jump on the back of a screaming red fire engine? Citizens can hitch a ride with the **San Francisco Fire Department** (HQ: 698 2nd Street, 415-558-3200, 415-558-3403 for ride alongs). Although they reserve the right to limit the activities depending on the dangers involved, SFFD does accept informal ride along requests on a case-by-case basis. Be sure to make your "case" a special one.

Or, hitch a ride with local law enforcement. It's an eye-opener—really! You may spend more time drinking coffee than chasing bad guys but no matter. The SFPD knows good coffee (no diners and donuts for these folks).

The SFPD doesn't have a formal ride along program so call the **Citizens' Police Academy** (415-401-4701, sfgov.org/police, under "Citizens' Academy") and say you're looking for a ride along. The inside word is that you can also arrange one informally through a friend on the force. If their request for you to ride is approved, you can tag along for four hours of their eight hour shift.

If you really get into all this police stuff, check out the full Citizens' Academy program, detailed in **Chapter 10**.

Brain Candy

Miss the intellectual stimulation of office life? Never fear. Stimulation for the brainy and outspoken is in no short supply in San Francisco.

The "Alerts" section of the weekly **San Francisco Bay Guardian** (135 Mississippi, 415-255-3100, sfbg.com), both in print and online, lists political events, lectures and community meetings, most of which are free. San Franciscans will protest anything. Find out how and where to join in.

Want to absorb valuable information that could help you change careers? Stop by an industry conference. Most are free for non-exhibitors. You can walk the floor, visit different vendors, people watch, and learn a ton—about what, of course, depends on the convention.

All events at the **Main Library** (100 Larkin @ Grove, 415-557-4400) are free, from internet classes to children's book readings. Pick up a Calendar of Events at the front information desk.

The **Moscone Center** (747 Howard, 415-974-4000, moscone.com) is the City's primary venue for big exhibitions. The annual **Macworld** (macworldexpo.com) in January is a local favorite: listen to Steve Jobs preach the Mac gospel and munch on all the latest Apple goodies.

Getting Political

The idea of a democracy is that the people rule—but with everyone working so much, who has the energy?

You do. Whatever issue you're passionate about, now is the perfect time to get involved in SF's longstanding activist culture.

Many political organizations dealing with hot issues would love to have an intelligent, energetic volunteer like you. Start at *the* site for City politicos—**The Usual Suspects** (sfusualsuspects.com, check out "Political Links" under "Resources"). There you'll find info on a host of local organizations, elected officials, and media outlets.

An easy place to start is to voice your opinion about rent control or the homeless at City Hall. The Board of Supervisors' weekly meetings are open to the public, every Tuesday at 2pm. The agenda and schedule of special meetings are posted at sfgov.org. Need a better understanding of city government structure before you go? Docent

what do we want? to protest!

The history of organized political protest in San Francisco dates back at least 150 years, to an 1852 "indignation meeting" at **Portsmouth Plaza**, held to block the city council from purchasing the Jenny Lind Theatre and using it as the City's first city hall. The demonstrators failed.

Lost causes of modern times include:

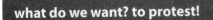

- the 1969 cry that the shape of the Transamerica Pyramid "won't fit in the City."

- Jim Jones' march of 600 people across Golden Gate Bridge to call attention to the need for—get this—suicide barriers.

- Margo St. James' founding of COYOTE (Call Off Your Old Tired Ethics), a prostitutes' rights organization.

- The 2003 anti-war protest against the pending invasion of Iraq, which saw some 200,000 folks make their voices heard.

Win or lose, activist citizens will always feel at home in San Francisco, where former KFOG DJ Scoop Nissen used to say, "If you don't like the news, go out and make some of your own."

led tours of **City Hall** (415-554-4933) are free. Sign in at the City Hall Docent Tour Kiosk on the Main Floor for this 45-60 minute tour, offered at 10am, noon and 2pm during the week (except on Mondays) and at 12:30pm on Saturdays. Groups of eight or more should call for a reservation.

If you're going to get political, be sure you're registered to vote. Contact the **Department of Elections** (415-554-4411, sfgov.org/election) to get yourself all squared away.

TV or Radio Show Audience

Does all that civic stuff have you snoring? Then tune in to the great American pastime—TV. Only this time, get off the couch and into a

GET REAL

Ever thought about trying out for a reality television show? While not for everyone, reality shows offer fantastic perks, and in many cases some serious prize dough. Oh, and unless your employer is amazingly sympathetic, you'll need an open work schedule to partake.

San Francisco has produced it's share of home-grown "real" stars, beginning all the way back in 1994 with MTV's *The Real World: San Francisco* and that infamous antagonizing character, "Puck." In 2003, Andrew Firestone, tire and wine heir, swept women off their feet as the handsome star of the third installment of ABC's *The Bachelor*.

More recently in 2006, at the other end of the aristocratic spectrum, Bay Area film prodigy and worldly denizen Tyler MacNiven and friend BJ Averell starred in and won the ninth edition of CBS' *The Amazing Race*. Known affectionately as "Team Hippie," the duo instantly won over fans with their irreverent humor and positive attitudes. Said Tyler after the race, "BJ and I approached each country with wide eyes and enthusiasm and a huge spirit of adventure. There's so much in this world. We might as well take advantage of as much as we can and give back as much as we can and that's important. That's how it all works." Sounds like a leisurely mindset to us, especially considering the free-spirited pair won a cool $1 million!

To keep close tabs on reality show casting calls, check these sites out in real time: *realitytvcastingcall.com* and *realitywanted.com*.

live studio audience. Okay, so there aren't a *lot* of television studios in the Bay Area—you'd have to hop down to LA or out to NYC for the best selection—but there *are* a few random ones to look into.

If quiz shows and kids are an appeal, you can explore **Bay Area Quiz Kids** (1250 San Carlos Avenue, 2nd Floor, San Carlos, 650-637-1936, pentv.org), where the audience reportedly "plays an important role in the show and is on television often," so there you go.

KQED Public Broadcasting (2601 Mariposa, 415-864-2000, kqed.org) doesn't have studio audience facilities, but they do offer free tours of their production facilities, which are pretty cool. Call their main number and ask for KQED Tours to arrange a group visit.

LIGHTS, CAMERA, ACTION!

According to Edward Guthman, film critic for the **San Francisco Chronicle,** finding work as an extra isn't hard. You don't have to be an actor or a member of the Screen Actors' Guild, just look like a "real person" (we know, this is difficult for some of us). Keep in mind that the work isn't glamorous—the hours are long, there's a lot of sitting around, and you have to take orders all day. That said, getting behind the scenes can be a lot of fun.

To be an extra, you have to either answer a film company's "open call" or go through a casting company. Try out your act with one of the following:

★ **Beau Bonneau Casting** (84 1st Street, 415-346-2278, *beaubonneaucasting.com*) uses the SF Casting Network to procure extras. Their website explains how the whole process works.

★ **Nancy Hayes Casting** (400 Treat, Ste. E, 415-558-1675, *hayescasting.com*) maintains an impressive list of projects.

★ **Laura Folger Casting** (2245 17th Avenue, 415-664-3072). You'll need to pay a small registration fee, and supply a recent photo (clothes on, please).

For a comprehensive list of local casting resources, try out **Bay Area Casting News** (*bayareacasting.com*).

all filler, no killer

Although many of his proclaimed exploits have since been proven myths, Anton LaVey *was* the founder and High Priest of the Church of Satan—and that certainly counts for something.

His celebrity status during the '60s and '70s was based in large part on a self-created legend, a very clever PR campaign, and his ability to snow both the media and his "disciples." *The Satanic Bible*, authored by LaVey and the guiding work for the Church, was largely plagiarized from various sources, and was originally conceived as a commercial vehicle by Avalon Books.

Still, LaVey did manage to attract a loyal following, including Jayne Mansfield and Sammy Davis Jr., and many an SF notable attended satanic rituals at his notorious "Black House" at 6114 California Street—where he kept a pet lion chained in the back yard.

To get behind the camera, peer into **Artists' Television Access** (992 Valencia, 415-824-3890, atasite.org), whose mission is "to bring the tools of the mass media within reach." They provide cheap access to audio-visual equipment for artists, as well as a venue for a wacky mix of events. Suffice it to say you're bound to see performances here the likes of which you've never seen before. Check their website for a complete calendar.

Access SF (1720 Market, 415-575-4949, accesssf.org) is the local public access channel (local Cable Channel 29), and a hip one at that. The org has been growing quickly since their founding in 1999, and serves as a particularly good resource for non-profits.

Movie or TV Extra

Looking for an opportunity to claim your 15 minutes of fame? Or just interested in blowing off an afternoon and meeting some stars? Movies and television programs are constantly filming in San Francisco; you just need to know where to find them. They always need extras, hangers-on, groupies, or whatever you'd care to label yourself.

The **San Francisco Film Commission** (City Hall, Room 473, 415-554-6241, sfgov.org/film) will be able to tell you what movies are being filmed in the City at the moment. It pays to be extra nice to them on the phone.

During a break between high-tech jobs, Russian Hill resident Joe Parente worked as an extra on the film *Bedazzled*. Although he calls the film itself "very forgettable," he felt it was still a great experience. "In addition to a couple of crowd scenes, I was also chosen to play a San Francisco Policeman in full uniform. I had the opportunity to meet Brendan Fraser, and I think—think—Elizabeth Hurley actually checked me out when I was in my uniform!" Joe could've sold his story to the tabloids, he says, but he chose instead to respect Liz's privacy. He received $71 for eleven hours of work. Woo-hoo! Drinks on Joe!

Get On a Boat!

With water in just about every direction, the San Francisco Bay Area is a boater's dream. So how can you enjoy the waterways of the Bay if you're not a yacht-owning tycoon? Start by hitting up those rich friends! But if boat-owning compadres are in short supply, you'll have to get a little more resourceful.

If you just want to soak up some nautical history, try touring the **S.S. Jeremiah O'Brien** (Pier 45, 415-544-0100, ssjeremiahobrien.org) in the heart of Fisherman's Wharf. It's a little touristy, but will set you back only seven of your leisure bucks. The people watching alone is worth the price of admission. While you're down there, jump aboard one of the **Blue and Gold Fleet** (Pier 41, 415-705-5555, blueandgoldfleet.com) and ferry over to Sausalito or Tiburon.

For a bigger adventure, rent a Boston Whaler from **Bay Adventures** (85 Liberty Ship Way, Sausalito, 415-331-0444, sfbayadventures.com). This is one of those rare activities you feel like you

shouldn't be able to do: cruise a small motorboat anywhere you want in the Bay—under the Golden Gate Bridge, along the Marin Headlands, or around Angel and Alcatraz islands—for $75 to $125 an hour. It's spectacular! Boating experience is "required," but as long as you can start the motor, steer in forward or reverse, and dock the boat, you'll be fine. Be sure to consult the experts before setting out for info on tides, currents, and hazards.

Want to leave the motor behind and sail your way across the Bay? Start by visiting the **SFSailing** website (sfsailing.com), chock full of incredibly useful information on local sailing. The site's original and most useful purpose is to connect skippers with potential mates. That's right—you too can crew! The best part is, you don't even need any experience. Many captains actually seek out rookie crew members, so they can teach them the "right" way to sail. Of course, if you are an experienced sailor, there are skippers looking for you, too. The website's "crew" lists include Racing, Bay Cruising, Ocean Cruising, and Pick-up, and it also has a skippers list.

Local yacht clubs post crew opportunities on their bulletin boards too. The most buttoned-up of the bunch is the **St. Francis Yacht Club** (on the Marina waterfront, 415-563-6363, stfyc.com). Not far behind is

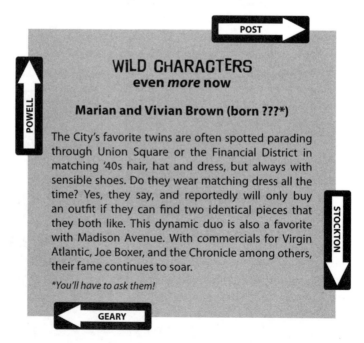

POST

POWELL

WILD CHARACTERS
even *more* now

Marian and Vivian Brown (born ???*)

The City's favorite twins are often spotted parading through Union Square or the Financial District in matching '40s hair, hat and dress, but always with sensible shoes. Do they wear matching dress all the time? Yes, they say, and reportedly will only buy an outfit if they can find two identical pieces that they both like. This dynamic duo is also a favorite with Madison Avenue. With commercials for Virgin Atlantic, Joe Boxer, and the Chronicle among others, their fame continues to soar.

*You'll have to ask them!

STOCKTON

GEARY

the North Bay's **San Francisco Yacht Club** (98 Beach Road, Belvedere, 415-435-9133, sfyc.org). Both are blue blazer-type clubs, so wear your finest duds when you drop by.

Care for some formal instruction before putting out to sea? **SFSailing** (see above) lists companies that offer lessons in the Bay Area. Most are pretty pricey. A much less expensive alternative is **Sailing Education Adventures** (Fort Mason Center, Building E, Room 235, 415-775-8779, sailsea.org), a non-profit membership organization "dedicated to promoting sailing through competitively priced instruction and related educational and social activities." They offer reasonably priced adult lessons, boat rentals, a children's sailing camp, and volunteer opportunities (which may make your boat rentals that much cheaper). An annual membership costs $65 for individuals, $85 for families. It entitles you to benefits including eight free group sails per month—which by themselves are worth more than the price of membership.

BE A TOURIST IN YOUR OWN TOWN

If you've lived in the Bay Area for any length of time, you've no doubt visited tourist traps that are dull, cheesy, overpriced, or all of the above. So why bother? Because our City is full of treasures that are often taken for granted by all-too-jaded residents, places that are special whether you're a tourist from Des Moines or a fourth generation San Franciscan.

Make it your duty as a local to stay up-to-date on the City—or at least as up-to-date as the tourists are. Pick up your very own tourist packet at the **San Francisco Visitor Information Center** (Hallidie Plaza, 900 Market @ Powell, 415-391-2000, onlyinsanfrancisco.com). The packet includes coupons and a guide to discount shopping (which is available at major hotels, too. For more stores, see the **Leisure Shopping Guide**). Check the end of this chapter for other references that are good for tourists and great for locals. But you won't likely need your tourist packet to reconnect with these SF essentials.

Golden Gate Bridge

Ah yes, the Bridge. An obvious choice, but it's always attractive. Drive it, bike it, walk it—crawl it for all we care! Just take it all in.

Look up and imagine climbing one of the two towers, which crazed Berkeley students did, by the way, back in the '60s. Look down and imagine (morbid as it may be) plummeting to the frigid water below, as an estimated 25 people do each year. As graceful as it is, the Golden

THE ORIGINAL "LOCALS" ON THE ROCK

No one knows exactly how long ago the Ohlone Indians first landed at Alcatraz Island, only that they used it to isolate and ostracize those who had violated tribal law. (Sound familiar?) European settlers took it, along with the rest of San Francisco, from the Ohlone in the late 1700s.

In 1969, however, long after Alcatraz had closed its doors as a federal penitentiary, a group of Indians led by the charismatic Richard Oakes occupied the island and symbolically claimed it for the Indian people. The group remained there for almost two full years before the federal government moved in and removed them. Although the land never did officially return to the Indian people, the occupation is credited with giving birth to the modern Indian self-determination movement.

Gate Bridge holds the dubious distinction of being the number one suicide location in the world. Or maybe it's *because* of its beauty—experts believe that even the suicidal are partial to aesthetics. On a happier note, the Coast Guard reports that the number of deaths in recent years has decreased dramatically due to increased patrolling. Do everyone a favor—stay on the bridge while enjoying it.

Alcatraz
Blue & Gold Fleet: 415-705-5555, nps.gov/alcatraz
Never been to "The Rock?" Shame on you! This is one San Francisco landmark that is as intriguing as it is spooky. It's managed by the GGN-RA and the National Park Service, and they've done a wonderful job at preserving and re-creating the different historical incarnations of the island: prison, military installation, Indian reservation, and nature preserve. The Cell House recorded audio tour is guaranteed to raise the hair on the back of your neck. Don't get sold out—buy your ticket online ahead of time. (blueandgoldfleet.com or alcatrazcruises.com). Save a few clams by going in the (warmer) off-season—before July 1.

Cable Cars
sfcablecar.com
Sure, a cable car travels slow and you can no longer hop on and off it at will but Andrew Hallidie's invention is still a great way to roll. Pick

up the California Street line from downtown and ride up to Nob Hill, then transfer to the Powell-Hyde line and ride down to Fisherman's Wharf. Other good places to catch a ride without waiting in line: top of Lombard Street (Lombard & Hyde) or at California and Van Ness. Best perk for locals: no $3 fare if you have a MUNI Fast Pass. Visit the **Cable Car Barn & Powerhouse** (1201 Mason) for a direct line into the history and the mechanical inner-workings of the cars.

Ferry to Tiburon
Blue & Gold Fleet: 415-705-5555,
blueandgoldfleet.com
Just being out on the San Francisco Bay is breathtaking enough. But boat across to the pleasant town of Tiburon, with its wonderful waterfront restaurants and spectacular City views, and you can almost fathom why Bay Area houses are the most expensive in the nation. Stop off at **Sam's** (27 Main Street, Tiburon, 415-435-4527, samscafe. com) and suck down a Sam's Smoothie (fully leaded) out on the deck and you'll swear you're in heaven. As a bonus, continue on the ferry to Angel Island for great hiking, biking, and picnicking (see **Chapter 7**).

Palace of Fine Arts and The Exploratorium
Originally conceived for the 1915 Panama-Pacific International Exposition by architect Bernard R. Maybeck, this strangely situated, seemingly out of place work of neo-Roman architecture is undeniably appealing. The Palace was reconstructed with modern materials in 1966 and, in 1969, a quirky new science and technology museum called **The Exploratorium** (3601 Lyon, 415-397-5673, exploratorium.edu) opened its doors to the public. According to the museum's own mission statement, "The Exploratorium was conceived to communicate a conviction that nature and people can be both understandable and full of newly discovered magic." We're down with that!

Union Square
Post, Stockton, Geary & Powell Streets
We know, we know, Union Square is crowded, jam-packed with tourists, and appears to be little more than a giant shopping mall. But trust us, it *is* cool if you know where to look, and you'll find just about any mainstream retail store you might need, if shopping is indeed your

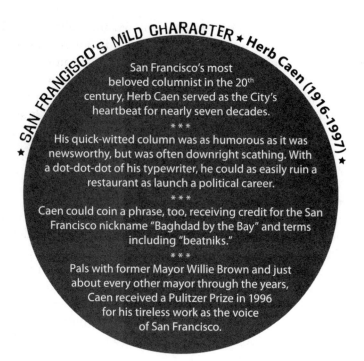

SAN FRANCISCO'S MILD CHARACTER ★ Herb Caen (1916–1997)

San Francisco's most beloved columnist in the 20th century, Herb Caen served as the City's heartbeat for nearly seven decades.

* * *

His quick-witted column was as humorous as it was newsworthy, but was often downright scathing. With a dot-dot-dot of his typewriter, he could as easily ruin a restaurant as launch a political career.

* * *

Caen could coin a phrase, too, receiving credit for the San Francisco nickname "Baghdad by the Bay" and terms including "beatniks."

* * *

Pals with former Mayor Willie Brown and just about every other mayor through the years, Caen received a Pulitzer Prize in 1996 for his tireless work as the voice of San Francisco.

bag. It's also a great place to people watch—you're bound to make some new international friends among the throngs of sightseers who flock here from all over the globe.

Park at the **Sutter-Stockton Garage** (444 Stockton @ Post), one of the cheapest downtown. If you happen to stumble into the **E&O Trading Company** (314 Sutter, 415-693-0303, eotrading.com) on the way out of the garage, all the better. E & O houses a delicious Asian restaurant and brewpub rolled into one. Sounds a-okay to us!

Upscale retailers Macy's, Saks Fifth Avenue, Tiffany's, and Neiman Marcus anchor the square (look for the prominent neon signs). Say what you will about the prices, these establishments are nonetheless elegant. Neiman's internal architecture alone makes it worth a visit.

If you feel like splurging, lunch with the Pacific Heights ladies in Neiman's fourth floor **Rotunda Restaurant** (150 Stockton, 415-362-4777).

Zip across the square to the **Westin St. Francis Hotel** (335 Powell, 415-397-7000) and into their great glass elevators to zoom up 31 floors for a panoramic eastward view.

To get off the main drag, take a stroll down the tranquil **Maiden Lane** (off Stockton between Post & Geary), formerly "Morton Street," one of the

City's most notorious alleys for crime and prostitution. The street is now much more pedestrian—literally—during the day, with a variety of cafés, boutiques, and galleries nestled into its semi-chic single block.

Architecture buffs shouldn't miss the **Xanadu Tribal Art Gallery** (140 Maiden Lane, 415-392-9999)—its 1948 brick structure is the only Frank Lloyd Wright building in San Francisco.

THE ANIMAL KINGDOM

A surprising number of creatures—human and otherwise—mill about the Bay Area. Some are caged; others are just making their way out in the world.

Free Zoo Day

Zoos aren't for everyone, sometimes not even the animals. The **San Francisco Zoo** (1 Zoo Road @ Sloat & Great Highway), 415-753-7080, sfzoo.org), for example, hardly served as a model of animal care—until recently.

Thanks to a large infusion of new funds, the Zoo has been imbued with new life and a welcome change in philosophy: it's now a "conservation zoo" that focuses on preservation and education. So far, the upshots have included new facilities for visitors, a new Lemur Forest in a large outdoor setting, and the creation of a multi-species African wildlife roaming exhibit. Parents and their kids should enjoy the expanded Children's Zoo.

Mark your calendar: the first Wednesday of every month is free; otherwise you're looking at $11 admission ($9 for City residents).

connemara's escape

San Francisco sported numerous horse racetracks and even a few dog tracks back at the turn of the 20th century. According to Raymond H. Clary, who wrote *The Making of Golden Gate Park*, an independent-minded greyhound named Connemara decided he'd had enough of chasing mechanical rabbits.

After crossing the finish line of a race he'd won at a track in Ingleside, Connemara just kept on running, eventually all the way to Sutro Forest, near present-day UCSF. There he took up residence and became the leader of a pack of wild dogs who regularly terrorized cats, chickens, pigs, and even took out a few peacocks in Golden Gate Park. The valuable greyhound was never recaptured, preferring instead to live a life of leisure in the wilds of San Francisco.

A model of freedom for us all!

SAN FRANCISCO'S WILD CHARACTERS ★ Alma Spreckels (1881-1968) ★

An early model for the strong woman, "Big Alma" was equal parts beautiful, outrageous, provocative, and stubborn. Born on a farm in the Sunset district, she married wealthy sugar magnate Adolph Spreckels and proceeded to shake up San Francisco society with her liberated views. She gave them views of the scenic kind, too—inspired by the French Pavilion at the 1915 Panama Pacific International Exposition, she and her husband recreated the landmark by building the *Palace of the Legion of Honor* (100 34th Avenue, 415-863-3330, *famsf.org*). Alma was fervently involved with causes supporting war efforts during the two world wars. She posed for the risqué statue (still there) in Union Square, invented the garage sale (so they say), and at age 57(!) chartered a plane and eloped with a cowboy. A famous Alma one-liner: "I'd rather be an old man's darling than a young man's slave." You go, girl!

Whale Watching

The Bay Area coastline is ideally situated for viewing the gray whale in its annual migration from arctic waters to Baja breeding grounds. December through May is the season, and the **Oceanic Society** (415-474-3385, oceanic-society.org, then "Whale Watch") is the vessel.

Day trips from SF cost $75 per person Fridays, and $78 per person on weekends. San Francisco departures, however, are the most expensive and lengthy (six hours). If an entire day on a rocking and rolling diesel powered boat sounds a little much for you (several locals we spoke with found that it was), try driving north to **Bodega Bay** where trips cost $45 or south to **Half Moon Bay**, where trips run $34 to $38. Trips from both locations last about three hours.

Bird Watching

Point Reyes National Seashore (nps.gov/pore) is the preeminent bird-watching venue within easy striking distance from San Francisco (see **Chapter 5** for more). Its amazing selection of land and sea birds will satisfy beginner and expert birders alike.

Just south of Point Reyes is the **Bolinas Lagoon**, long a top destination for coastal bird-watchers. **Audubon Canyon Ranch** (egret.org) manages the nearby Bolinas Lagoon Preserve as well as the Bouverie Preserve in Sonoma, which is home to over 130 species of birds and to 350 species of wildflowers.

But you don't have to leave home to find birds. Plenty of land birds and waterfowl can be sighted in **Golden Gate Park**, and the **Marin Headlands** within the **Golden Gate National Recreation Area** (nps.gov/goga) is the perfect place to view raptors, particularly in September and October.

LiONS & TOGARE & BABOONS—OH MY!

In one of the more bizarre tales involving a lion, a Satanist, and a baboon, an SF Zoo director was severely beaten by apes in 1968, and left bloody and unconscious in the ape cage.

It all started with a pet lion named Togare, who was owned by the notorious Satanist Anton LaVey, founder and leader of the Church of Satan. Togare was living at LaVey's infamous "Black House" in the Richmond until the City responded to neighbors' complaints by passing an ordinance banning lions in private homes. Togare was banished to the San Francisco Zoo. For reasons unknown, the zoo director took an extreme dislike to Togare and eventually had him shipped to Lion Country Safari in Southern California, never giving LaVey a chance to say goodbye.

This is where the story gets weird. Being a Satanist and all, LaVey was predictably angry. He supposedly channeled his anger into a curse, to be delivered through the Zoo's Egyptian crystal baboon. Not long after, when the zoo director wandered into their cage, the normally docile apes (led by a certain baboon) launched a vicious attack, brutally clawing and beating the director.

The moral? Damned if we know. But it sure does make for a good *tail.*

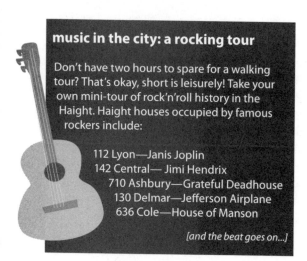

music in the city: a rocking tour

Don't have two hours to spare for a walking tour? That's okay, short is leisurely! Take your own mini-tour of rock'n'roll history in the Haight. Haight houses occupied by famous rockers include:

112 Lyon—Janis Joplin
142 Central— Jimi Hendrix
710 Ashbury—Grateful Deadhouse
130 Delmar—Jefferson Airplane
636 Cole—House of Manson

[and the beat goes on...]

Bison, Peacocks and Other Fauna in Golden Gate Park

Not all of the animals who have made Golden Gate Park their home still live there, as the park's flora and fauna are ever-changing. But over the years, the park has hosted a zoo's-worth: wild peacocks, turtles, ducks, herons, hawks (and plenty of other birds), weasels, rabbits, snakes, quail, fox, feral cats—even grizzly bears! (They were in cages. Don't ask.) Did we mention the bison paddock? As Jurassic as it sounds, it's really quite docile, amounting to nothing more than a few grazing buffalo in a fenced in area. Fun? That depends. Just knowing they're there might be enough to float your boat.

Sea Lions at Pier 39

pier39restaurants.com/cam.htm

Yes, they smell. Yes, they're lazy. But are there any creatures more leisurely than those lounging lions (of the sea variety) that have made Pier 39 their own retirement community? Ray-catching and napping seem to be their prime daytime activities.

We suppose some of them have to go out and catch fish from time to time, but you wouldn't know it by watching them. Witness the alpha males staking their "docks," knocking others into the water, or the pups who can't quite find room to sun-tan—and keep falling into the drink! Watching the frolic may be one of the few good reasons to toss yourself into the mêlée that is Fisherman's Wharf.

People Watching

People are animals. Watch them and you'll see!

The males of the species bask in the sun at "Dolores Beach"—the affectionate nickname for the City-facing slope of **Dolores Park** (20th Street @ Church)—stretching out, preening, and trying to attract a mate. Many females, meanwhile, can be observed in their own native habitat: the shopping mall. The food court in the pit of **San Francisco Center** (865 Market @ 5th Street) places observers in prime position to analyze the bags-in to bags-out ratio as shoppers enter and exit the mall via the underground Powell Street BART station.

Human athleticism, competition and aggression are all on display during the Nordstrom Half-Yearly Sale. Doh! We *meant* to say in amateur sports and games. We suggest **Police League Soccer Games** at the fields in Golden Gate Park near Ocean Beach, or pickup basketball in the Panhandle, for the best combination of testosterone and colorful language.

Fisherman's Wharf features a crazy combination of indigenous and nomadic humans. Kick back on a bench near the audience for any street performer or balloon-folding clown at **Pier 39** to watch the circus unfold amongst high concentrations of non-natives. Another 80,000 migratory humans arrive by sea each year to the **Port of San Francisco** on twenty ships making an average of 45 calls.

Your study of human behavior can only come in handy once you're back in the workforce. How do you think Machiavelli got so good at politics? Haight Street, downtown at lunch hour, North Beach on a weekday afternoon, hotel lobbies and the airport—each provides a fine vantage point for observing humans in action. It's free, it's leisurely, and it can even further your career by helping you better understand your future boss or co-worker.

[...and the beat goes on]

Round out this short survey by sharing your knowledge of our native musicians with your friends, or anyone else who happens to be hanging out in Buena Vista Park:

- *Chris Isaak*—still lives in his humble Sunset district home, oft mistaken for Elvis

- *Jerry Garcia*—dropped out of Balboa High School in the City's Excelsior district; joined the Army and was stationed in the Presidio—but was dishonorably discharged; dropped "in" to form The Grateful Dead and lived in the infamous Deadhouse in Haight-Ashbury

- *Carlos Santana*—moved from Tijuana to the Mission district at the tender age of 13, met Bill Graham, played Woodstock...and the rest, as the say, is history.

- *Joan Baez*—graduated from Palo Alto High School, has perhaps participated in more protests and civil disobedience than any other musician in history

A final tidbit: the Beatles played their last live concert at (then-named) Candlestick Park on August 29, 1966—an odd choice of venue for the Fab Four!

EXPLORING THE NEIGHBORHOODS

Everyone knows about Hunter's Point. Setting foot in it will lead to immediate death by gunfire (won't it?). The truth is, you're probably safer in Hunter's Point than in a cross-walk on Van Ness: for every murder in San Francisco, four pedestrians are killed by cars. Venture out that way and not only will you return alive, but you might stumble onto a find you would never have expected. A quirky café, perhaps, or a cool artist studio.

Anne Tesler (name changed) thought the time had come to check out Treasure Island. Little did she know that she'd picked the 25th Anniversary of the Treasure Island Museum as the day of her first visit. "I spent the whole afternoon there," she told us, "soaking up the incredible views of the City and exploring the museum. I even caught a short but fascinating old movie on the making of the Bay Bridge."

Even the tamest of neighborhoods harbors secrets. Peter Stein enjoyed them so much that he created an entire PBS series, *Neighborhoods: The Hidden Cities of San Francisco*. With time on your hands, explore a neighborhood you thought you knew, or choose a new neighborhood and poke around. Let us know what you find!

Neighborhood	Find
Bernal Heights	Locals have long known what we shall now proclaim: Bernal is cool—really cool. The area is as neighborhoody as they come, from colorful cafés such as **Liberty Café** (410 Cortland, 415-695-8777) and **Progressive Grounds** (400 Cortland, 415-282-6233), to eclectic eateries like affordable **Emmy's Spaghetti Shack** (3355 Mission, 415-206-2086, see Dining & Nightlife) or the more upscale **Blue Plate** (3218 Mission, 415-282-6777). But one of the best finds is atop the windswept Bernal Hill, which boasts some of the most spectacular views of the City, and where dogs can truly run amok.
Alamo Square	Surely you've seen the postcard: a block of Victorian row houses (a.k.a., **Painted Ladies**) set against the San Francisco skyline. Now go see them for yourself—on Steiner between Grove & Hayes. See if you can track down the shoe garden by the groundskeepers' shed while you're up there.
Pacific Heights	The **Spreckels Mansion** (2080 Washington @ Octavia), now Danielle Steel's house, was built in 1913 to be San Francisco's largest mansion. The house has 99 rooms. Yipes! That's gotta be some utility bill.

Neighborhood	Find
Financial District	Just to prove it *is* all about money, the Financial District proudly presents you with the ***Museum of Money*** (in the basement of the Union Bank of California, 400 California) *and* the ***Federal Reserve Bank of San Francisco*** (101 Market, 415-974-2000, frbsf.org), where the tours are free but the pallets of shrink-wrapped cash are not.
Hunter's Point	Everyone (including ourselves) gives Anchor Brewing Company and its free tours a lot of attention, and rightly so. But for a true underground microbrewery experience at the City's second largest brewery (about 1/10 the size of Anchor), slosh on over to ***Speakeasy*** (1195 Evans, Ste. A, 415-642-3371, goodbeer.com) on a Friday afternoon. Call ahead to sample some savory suds, arguably the best damn beer in San Francisco.
Russian Hill	First track down the skinny ***Macondray Lane*** (off Leavenworth between Jones & Taylor), then amble over its stone pathway to the wooden ***Taylor Street Steps***, on display in the PBS miniseries based on Armistead Maupin's *Tales of the City*.
Telegraph Hill	The ***Wild Parrots of Telegraph Hill*** have been captured—on celluloid, in a movie of that same name. Are they escaped pets? Did they arrive via steamer from Africa? No one seems to know.
Chinatown	A statue of the ***Goddess of Democracy*** presides over the heart of Chinatown in what is now known as ***Portsmouth Square Park*** (Kearny between Clay & Washington), formerly known as ***Portsmouth Plaza*** (State Historical Landmark No. 119). As a plaza, the site saw a lot of action, including Sam Brannan's 1848 announcement of "gold in them thar hills" and California's first celebration of admission to the Union in 1850.

Street Murals

Guiding yourself on a tour of the City's street murals is another aesthetically pleasing way to get to know new places.

Mona Caron drew the **Duboce Bikeway Mural** (Duboce between Church & Market, Duboce Triangle area) in 1998, simply to spruce up the 360-foot stretch of roadway closed to cars but well-traveled by bikes and pedestrians. You can catch a glimpse of it from the south-facing windows of the N-Judah as you enter or exit the Market Street tunnel, but the colors are much more vibrant when you're up close and personal.

It took a whole cadre of muralists and "aerosol artists" led by muralist Ray Patlan to liven up **Balmy Alley** (Balmy Street between 24th & 25th Streets, parallel to Harrison & Treat, in the Mission). The outdoor gallery now features a mural on every building, wall, and garage door on the block, about thirty in all.

While it *is* the densest, Balmy Alley is but one of dozens and dozens of open-air museums in the Mission. No one is better-versed in them than the docents at the **Precita Eyes Mural Arts Center** (2981 24th Street, 415-285-2287, precitaeyes.org), a nonprofit mural-arts association that teaches mural-making and hosts numerous year-round tours via bus, bike or foot. Care to learn the history of murals? Precita Eyes' slide show will take you back 4,000 years to the murals of Egypt. If your style is more urban contemporary, commission one of their artists to decorate your home or office walls.

Walking Tours

Like so many cities in Europe, San Francisco was made for walking. Sure, there are hills (43 named hills, in fact), and thus some really steep streets (the steepest blocks are Filbert between Hyde & Leavenworth, and 22nd Street between Church and Vicksburg, both 31.5% gradient).

But you'll steer around them all on the "Bawdy & Naughty" walking tour, covering only two flat blocks after leaving from the eastern Maiden Lane Gate. Explore the lives and "loves" of legendary parlor madams such as Belle Cora, Sally Stanford and Ah Toy starting at 11am on the first three Mondays of the month. Quite a topic that early in the day!

The non-profit **San Francisco City Guides** (100 Larkin, 415-557-4266, sfcityguides.org) is supported by more than 200 volunteers working under the auspices of the San Francisco Public Library, and hosts 125 free walking tours, plus an excellent web guide to the City. The **Visitor Information Center** (see "Best Resources for Locals" p. 138) includes the City Guides' *Free Walking Tours* pamphlet in their tourist packet.

NATURE IN THE CITY

San Francisco maintains a surprisingly large amount of open space for its small size. Blessed with the country's largest urban park and plenty of undeveloped, leftover military land, the City by the Bay boasts arguably the most beautiful recreation land of any city in the U.S. If you can't find yourself a favorite outdoor stomping ground here, then maybe urban nature just isn't your habitat.

Parks

San Francisco has made parks a priority since Golden Gate Park's founding in 1870. Its 230 "official" parks comprise roughly 3,500 acres, or nearly 12% of the total area within City limits—and we're going to list each one! Just kidding, only the best for you.

Land's End

El Camino del Mar near 32nd Avenue, or Point Lobos @ 48th Avenue

Land's End, the rugged and scenic stretch of coastline at the very northwest tip of the San Francisco peninsula, affords panoramic seascapes from both its hidden beach and its hiking trail. The trail can be entered from the west (near Point Lobos Avenue/Geary @ 48th Avenue) or the east (along El Camino del Mar near the California Palace of the Legion of Honor) and is a relatively easy two-mile walk. At the west end, follow the paths that lead down to the ocean, and you'll find yourself on a craggy, semi-private stretch of beach, perfect for some mid-week solitude.

site of the first U.S. dynamite factory

What must be one of the City's shortest lived business ventures (even by dot-com measures) has been memorialized in history for at least 60 times longer than it was in existence: the gunpowder and dynamite factory at what is now Glen Canyon Park (State Historical Landmark No. 1002).

The Giant Powder Company began America's first commercial manufacturing of dynamite on March 19, 1868. Just over twenty months later, the business ended with a bang: the factory exploded.

The obliteration of all of its buildings and even the surrounding fencing came to be known as the Glen Canyon or Rock Gulch explosion.

Sutro Park

48th Avenue @ Point Lobos

Just across from the Point Lobos entrance to Land's End lies another oft-overlooked gem of a park with primo vistas: Sutro Park. Ocean Beach resident Pete Reich claims it's a personal favorite. "It's one of the best parks and views in the City, especially when the sun is shining on the western edge of the world." Park at the lot down at Kelly's Cove and walk up and around Point Lobos and the Cliff House,

more parks to ferret out

• *Buena Vista Park* wooded and wild • *McLaren Park* 75 picnic tables, many private • *Michelangelo Playground* a North Beach oasis • *Visitacion Valley Greenway* formerly fenced parcels become garden spaces • *Who Hei Yuen Park* first new Chinatown park since the '50s • *Precita Park* cleaned-up and green • *South Park* ceded back to the homeless by short-lived startups • *St. Mary's Square* not just a garage • *Pioneer Park* hey, it's the space around Coit Tower! • Continue your research by parking your browser at the *Neighborhood Parks Council* (sfneighborhoodparks.org), a park advocacy group.

stopping at the **Camera Obscura** (aka "Giant Camera," giantcamera. com) for a 360 degree view along the way. Continue up and around the road and Sutro Park will be on your right. Strolling along the park's edge offers commanding views of Ocean Beach to the south, Seal Rocks to the west, and the Golden Gate Bridge and Marin Headlands to the north. Says Pete, "Climb the fortress and harken the days when Spanish explorers sailed galleons in and out of the Golden Gate."

Glen Canyon Park
Bosworth @ O'Shaughnessy
Yes, there *are* true canyon lands in San Francisco, as this hidden oasis in Glen Park attests. Although not a huge space, it comes complete with a running creek, cool rock outcroppings, and a decent but short hiking trail. Dog walkers and nature enthusiasts will be happy here. Beware of the poison oak!

Huntington Park
Mason & California, top of Nob Hill
This urban park rests auspiciously atop prestigious Nob Hill, while Grace Cathedral, The Fairmont, and "The Mark" (Mark Hopkins Hotel) watch over it like patrician aunts and uncles. Nap on one of its sunny park benches, dream of playing Parcheesi at the haughty Pacific Union Club next door, and ponder the mindset of Charles Crocker when he surrounded his neighbor with a 40-foot tall fence to "encourage" him to sell Crocker his property. And just think—you can enjoy all this gentried splendor *without* having to be a railroad baron!

The Presidio

415-561-4323, nps.gov/prsf

This former military base bordered by the Pacific Ocean, Lyon Street, West Pacific Avenue and the Bay is now a 1,480-acre public park with miles of hiking and biking trails, beaches, picnic sites, abandoned military barracks, artillery batteries, an army museum, and other assorted sites—even a pet cemetery and at least one major office development. **Fort Point** guards the foot of the Golden Gate Bridge. Find maps, books and other useful intelligence daily between 9am and 5pm at **The Presidio Visitors Center** (415-561-4323, temporarily located in the Officers' Club, Moraga & Graham).

Fort Funston

Skyline/Highway 35 near John Muir Drive
415-561-4323, nps.gov/goga/fofu/index.htm

Long a favored destination for dog walkers, Fort Funston and its surrounding turf invite cliff-hugging hikes, lost hours surveying the Pacific, and scampers down an uncrowded stretch of beach (chasing your pooch no doubt). Or leave Fido at home and just laze the afternoon away watching the hang-gliders launch off the glider port and then float along the coast.

Agua Vista Park

Mission Bay, next to Kelly's Mission Rock

Deep in the heart of Mission Bay lies a park you've probably never heard of: Agua Vista Park. Its specialty is ship repair. A little industrial, perhaps, but you can watch, listen, and learn. Then head over to **The Ramp** next door (855 China Basin, 415-621-2378) for a cheeseburger and a beer. You'll swear it's 1950 all over again.

Douglass Park & Playground

1100 Douglass @ 26th Street, Noe Valley, 415-695-5017

Tucked away in a corner of Noe Valley, Douglass Park is small and unassuming, dog- and kid-friendly. Its thrill du jour is a tall cement slide that's fun for grownups and kids alike. Sweet! For maximum speed, bring your own cardboard and sprinkle a little sand on the slide before you push off. Watch out for the infamous park mud during the wintertime.

For More on Parks

Not enough park info here for you? Then you could use another friend. Good thing then there's **San Francisco Parks Trust** (sfpt.org, use "Links & Resources"), where you can find all the rec-savvy friends a guy or gal could ever need. The City's official site is not a bad match-maker, either: **Recreation & Park Department** (sfgov.org, click on "City Agencies" and then "Recreation and Park Department").

BEACHES

You won't find the cast from *Baywatch* here (nor David Hasselhoff, thank god), but San Francisco has coastline galore—some of it urban, other stretches delightfully removed from the hustle of the City. A heads up: the beaches are typically cold. Very cold. You'll need multiple layers to stay warm, sometimes even your winter parka.

Baker Beach

off Lincoln near 25th Avenue, nps.gov/prsf/places/bakerbch.htm

Catch San Francisco's premier sunbathing beach on a warm day and you may never want to leave the City again. This mile-long stretch of sand starts just west of the Golden Gate Bridge and sweeps along the Presidio towards the Seacliff neighborhood. The closer you get to the bridge (to the north), the less clothing you'll spot on your fellow bathers. The north end is also a popular gay beach. Solid swimmers can take a dip in the frigid water but should mind the wicked cross-currents and undertow, as well as the fact that San Francisco's only recorded great white shark attack occurred here in 1959—just 50 yards offshore.

China Beach

Seacliff & 28th Avenue

Just west of Baker Beach lies its baby sister, China. This small strip of sand, tucked into the walls of the Lincoln Park cliffs, is ideal for families and picnickers. It's probably the best beach in San Francisco for swimming—which isn't saying much, as it's still very cold water and bathers need to mind the sometimes-strong currents. But lifeguards are on duty (hey, is that Mitch Buchannon?) during the summer months to help the occasional swimmer in trouble.

NAPPING, RAYS & READING

Where to Soak Up Some Vitamin D	Reading Factor	Sun Factor	Nap Factor
Lafayette Park (Sacramento @ Laguna)	good	excellent, stay west	good, so long as you're not on the side with the dog run
Kalmanovitz Library (UCSF, Parnassus @ 3rd Avenue)	excellent	poor, but incredible views of the Golden Gate	superior, but beware: the comfy leather chairs have been known to elicit heavy snoring
Main Library Outdoor Reading Room (100 Larkin, 6th floor)	excellent	superior, and no wind at all	poor, unless you're comfortable snoozing on a cement bench
Your Car (really!) Park up at **Mount Davidson**, the highest natural point in SF, or down at the **Marina Green**	excellent, lots of peace and quiet (provided your windows roll up)	totally at your discretion	depends on your cruiser
Washington Square Park (Columbus @ Union)	moderate	excellent	no good, possible for only the most tourist-inured
Dolores Park	good	excellent, stay on the west bank for wind block	good, but watch for dogs and the occasional pickup line

strybing arboretum

What the **Strybing Arboretum** (9th Avenue @ Lincoln, 415-661-5191, *strybing.org*) lacks in name recognition, it more than makes up for in spectacular flora.

A delightful backdrop for the average visitor, Strybing is a dream come true for the horticulturist, bursting with 70 acres of extravagant plants and flowers. It's a feast for all five of your senses. (You've had flower salads, haven't you?)

On your way out, stop by the quaint **Strybing Botanical Bookstore** to brush up on your knowledge of plants.

North Beach
neighborhood in northeast corner of the City

Okay, so it's not actually a beach—it's not even on the water anymore! But it once *was* waterfront, before landfill set in, and it remains one of the coolest neighborhoods in San Francisco. If you need to lay out, go bag some rays in **Washington Square Park**.

South Beach
Waterfront south of Bay Bridge

It ain't Miami, and South ain't any more of a beach than North, but the thriving waterfront neighborhood of South Beach features **AT&T** (formerly SBC/Pac Bell) **Park**, numerous new restaurants and bars, and the best weather in the City. Imagine laying out your beach towel between the ship docks and stripping down to your swimsuit without freezing!

Ocean Beach
(Great Highway from Point Lobos to Sloat, in the Sunset)

Ideal for running, biking, or exercising the dog (on a leash in most places), Ocean Beach is a massive natural playground spanning about four miles of western San Francisco. If you can handle the often-foggy conditions, you'll delight in this vastly underutilized recreational space. Don't count on swimming here, however, as waves can reach as high as 40 feet during the winter, and rip currents and rumbling whitewater constantly surge through the lineup.

Ocean Beach is *the* place in San Francisco to see the sun set. (They don't call it the Sunset district for nothing!) Even when the fog is in, the distant sky often magically clears just in time to watch a golden orb slip below the horizon. Grab a beach chair and a few beers (hide the glass bottles, they're not allowed), plant yourself somewhere along the spacious sand dunes, and savor a perfectly leisurely moment.

SECRET STAIRWAYS AND SPECTACULAR VIEWS

Vulcan Street Steps

(off 17th Street between Ord & Levant, Upper Market)
Serene and lined with pines, Vulcan Street ascends the southern slope of the Buena Vista hill. Look out over the Mission, and keep an eye out for paving stones from the area's original streets.

San Francisco Art Institute

(800 Chestnut, 415-749-4567)
Not only can you admire a Diego Riviera mural inside the Art Insitute, you can enjoy a fine, inexpensive lunch during the week. Then step onto the rooftop deck for a vista that extends past Coit Tower to Oakland.

Pemberton Stairway

(from Clayton & Corbett to the top of Corona Heights)
The renovated and redesigned upper section between Villa and Graystone Terraces and their accompanying gardens are the pride of Twin Peaks. Aficionados describe the views on the way up as "showstopping."

Harry Stairs

(Harry Street, from Laidley to Beacon in Glen Park)
This climb starts in Glen Park and summits at the bottom of Billy Goat Hill in Diamond Heights. If you're vertigo-free, take a peak back over your shoulder on the way up for sweeping views of Treasure Island. If you'd rather face forward, try to catch a glimpse of the charming cottages amidst the forest-like greenery. The stairs are mostly wooden, with a handrail.

16th Avenue Tiled Steps

(16th Avenue @ Moraga, tiledsteps.org)
Inspired by the Santa Teresa Steps in Rio de Janeiro, the 16th Avenue Tiled Steps were completed in 2005 and are a spectacular addition to the Golden Gate Heights neighborhood. The giant stair mosaic comprises 163 steps and panels that were constructed by hundreds of neighbors. Enjoy the colorful combination of animal, bird and fish tiles as you ascend the stairs, but don't forget to turn around at the top and take in the dramatic vistas of Ocean Beach and the Pacific Ocean.

MUSEUMS & ART GALLERIES

Ah yes, culture. We could all use a healthy dose of it, *n'est-ce pas?* Although San Francisco's art scene languished a bit in the late '90s, it's enjoying a refreshing renaissance now, with small galleries and studios sprouting up to fill the void left by collapsed startups. You can almost hear a collective sigh of relief blowing across the City. Add to that a thriving large-museum scene, and it all equates to a fine time to get yourself cultured.

Free Museum Days

Admission is free on the first Wednesday of every month at many San Francisco museums, including the **Exploratorium**, the **Academy of Sciences**, and all of the museums at Fort Mason. Other free museum days include the first Tuesday of every month for **SFMOMA** and the **Asian Art Museum**, the first Thursday of every month for the **Center for the Arts** at Yerba Buena Gardens, and every Tuesday for

san francisco's wild characters ✰ HARRY DENTON *(just turned 21!)*

Everybody in the City loves a party, and Harry is usually in the middle of it all. A local entrepreneur extraordinaire, Harry launched **Harry's on Fillmore** (now "Harry's Bar," 2020 Fillmore, 415-921-1000) in 1986, and his "guests" there are still partying hard (even though it's under new ownership).

He's since opened numerous other nightspots, including Southside, Harry Denton's, the **Starlight Room** (atop the **Sir Francis Drake Hotel**, 450 Powell @ Sutter, 415-395-8595), and **Rouge** (1500 Broadway @ Polk, 415-346-7683).

Harry's philanthropic contributions over the years have been legendary, as have his crazy antics. Through it all, he's managed to maintain his sense of humor and fundamental love of a great party. "Delusions of grandeur make me feel a lot better about myself," Harry says. He said it; we didn't!

the **Legion of Honor**. Remember, a museum outing makes for an impressive date, and you don't need to spend a lot of money. No excuses!

MUSEUMS	
free first wed every month except as noted	**always free**
de Young Museum (50 Hagiwara Tea Garden near 8th Avenue, 415.863.3330, thinker.org/deyoung).	***National Maritime Museum*** (Aquatic Park, end of Polk Street *maritime.org*) open daily, 10am-5pm
California Academy of Sciences (Steinhart Aquarium, Natural History Museum, Morrison Planetarium; 875 Howard, 415-321-8000, calacademy.org; temporary home while constructing new Golden Gate Park facility, to open in 2008)	***Mission Dolores*** (3321 16th Street, 415-621-8203, missiondolores.org) free *but* $2 donation expected open daily, 7:30am-5pm
Asian Art Museum (200 Larkin, 415-581-3500, asianart.org)) free first *Tuesday* of every month $5 every Thursday after 5pm	***Federal Reserve Bank of San Francisco*** (101 Market, 415-974-2000, frbsf.org)
Museum of Modern Art (151 415-357-4000, sfmoma.org) free first *Tuesday* of every month half price every *Thursday* 6pm-9pm	***The Virtual Museum of the City of San Francisco*** (sfmuseum.org)
Mexican Museum ***Museo Ital-Americano*** ***MOMA Artists Gallery*** ***African-American Historical & Cultural Society*** (all located in Fort Mason)	***Chinese Cultural Center of San Francisco*** (750 Kearny, 3rd Floor, 415-986-1822, *c-c-c.org*) Tues-Sat, 10am-4pm
Museum of Craft & Folk Art (51 Yerba Buena, 415-227-4888, mocfa.org)	***North Beach Museum*** (in Eureka Bank, 1435 Stockton, 2nd Floor, 415-391-6210) Mon-Thu, 9am-4pm; Fri 9am-6pm

MUSEUMS

free first wed every month except as noted	always free
San Francisco Museum of Craft+Design (550 Sutter, 415-773-0303, sfmcd.com) free first *Thursday* evening of every month from 5pm-7pm	**Cable Car Barn & Powerhouse** (1201 Mason , sfcablecar.com) open daily, 10am-6pm summer 10am-5pm winter (Oct 1-March 31)
Exploratorium (3601 Lyon, 415-397-5673, exploratoriaum.edu)	**Chinese Historical Society of America** (965 Clay, 415-391-1188, chsa.org) Thu-Fri, 12pm-5pm Sat-Sun, 12-4pm
Cartoon Art Museum (655 Mission, 415-227-8666, cartoonart.org) first *Tuesday* of every month "Pay What You Wish Day"	**Fire Department Museum** (655 Presidio, 415-558-3546) Thu-Sun, 1pm-4pm
Yerba Buena Center for the Arts (701 Mission, 415-978-2787, ybca.org) free first *Tuesday* of every month	**San Francisco Botanical Garden at Strybing Arboretum** (9th Avenue @ Lincoln, sfbotanicalgarden.org) Mon-Fri, 8am-4:30pm Sat-Sun, 10pm-5pm
Legion of Honor 415-750-3600 (Lincoln Park, near 34th Avenue and Clement 415-863-3330, thinker.org/legion) free first Tuesday of every month	**Wells Fargo History Museum** (420 Montgomery , 415-396-2619, wellsfargohistory.com/museums/sfmuseum.html) Mon-Fri, 9am-5pm

Celebrating the Arts

While the arts in San Francisco may have suffered temporarily in the shadow of dot-com business mania, creative communities in the City have come bounding back with a flourish. True, they might never have left, but presently the creative arts are enjoying much improved funding, focus and popularity.

This is all wonderful news for you, the leisurely art seeker. For example, ever wondered—just what *does* go on inside all of those South of Market live-work lofts, anyway?

FREE CONCERTS, PLAYS, AND DANCE

Sausalito Friday Night Summer Concerts
Escape the city fog and bike, ferry, or drive over to Sausalito for free concerts every Friday during the summer.

Shakespeare in the Park
September brings the San Francisco Shakespeare Festival, which is free on weekends. Take a blanket and picnic basket and enjoy (with luck) the Indian summer weather.

Free Noontime Concerts and Dance
Yerba Buena Gardens are alive with the sound of music all summer long.

Stern Grove Festival
The summer concert series at Stern Grove is the stuff of legends, and one of the best San Francisco freebies around. Every Sunday at noon from June-August, the Grove plays host to an eclectic array of music, from jazz to hip-hop to rock n' roll (see p. 103 for more on Stern Grove).

Finding an answer starts with the **San Francisco Bay Area Gallery Guide** (1369 Fulton, 415-921-1600), a bimonthly publication listing the City's current art shows. To get on their mailing list, send them a self-addressed, stamped envelope (ZIP is 94117). You can also pick up a guide at the **San Francisco Visitor Information Center** (at the cable car turnaround; find full contact info on p. 148).

San Francisco Open Studios (934 Brannan, 415-861-9838, sfopenstudios.com) is the oldest and largest open studio program in the country. Every October weekend each year, artists from throughout the City open their workspaces to the general public, enabling the artists to gain exposure and sell their artwork, and allowing the public to meet and interact with the artists.

Don't miss the annual **Spring Open Studio** (415-387-5936, springopenstudio.com) presented by the Artists of Hunters Point Shipyard. Each spring, usually in May, the Shipyard artists open their studios to you, the general public. An added bonus: Spring Open Studio marks one of only two times per year the general public is allowed to roam the former U.S. Naval shipyard.

SAN FRANCISCO'S WILD CHARACTERS NOW: Lawrence Ferlinghetti (born 1919)

Lawrence Ferlinghetti landed in SF in the 1950s and soon defined what it meant to be a liberal and literary activist. His City Lights Bookstore and publishing house fast became the focal point for the beat generation and the City's intellectuals. In 1956, he was arrested on obscenity charges for publishing Allen Ginsberg's *Howl*. The trial that followed drew national attention as a landmark First Amendment case, and further cemented Ferlinghetti's reputation as a leader in alternative publishing. Lucky for writers and book buyers, he was acquitted. In addition to promoting local talent, Ferlinghetti has published many of his own articles, poems, and books over the years, winning numerous literary awards. At age 84, he remains prolific as a writer and lecturer, and up until just recently wrote a regular column for the *San Francisco Chronicle*.

The **Artists Guild** (601 Van Ness #E3-140, 415-835-0610, artistsguildsf.com) was founded to exhibit artists' work at outdoor venues across San Francisco. Often these are park sites such as Washington Square, the Marina Green, or Huntington Park. The Guild maintains a monthly exhibit schedule on its website, if you'd like to plan your art viewing for the month.

Looking for something to do on a Thursday night? **First Thursdays** are a running series of after-hour gallery showings sponsored by the **San Francisco Art Dealers Association** (sfada.com). They happen on—you guessed it, the first Thursday of every month, usually from 6-9pm (although times are fluid). Participating galleries are located primarily downtown, and several even welcome visitors with complimentary wine and hors d'oeuvres.

The **San Francisco Art Institute** (800 Chestnut, 415-771-7020, sfai. edu) serves as a nucleus for exhibitions and public programs, most of which are free. Heck, their website alone is worthy of a tour, and will lead you to a world of physical exhibits.

At any hour and for no admission, you can study up on the fine works of art displayed in the online version of the **San Francisco Airport**

Museums (650-821-6700, sfoarts.org). Surf through eclectic and unexpected displays with themes drawn from science, history, design, and anthropology, or assess the new spaces created by the Airport's latest $3 billion expansion: a huge beast replete with moving sidewalks.

LEISURELY ENTERTAINMENT

You'll find plenty of food- and drink-based entertainment rolled into our special section, **Dining & Nightlife**. But for offbeat entertainment at little or no cost, where you won't need to tip the maitre d' or spring for a pricey round of drinks, read on right here.

The Spoken Word

Book and literary readings are usually free and, depending on the topic, can double as groovy social events. San Francisco maintains its literary tradition through a strong network of independent bookstores, as well as a series of ongoing literary events.

A FESTIVAL FOR THE ARTS

Springing up seemingly overnight, *ArtSFest* (artsfest. org) is a non-profit organization and annual festival that aims to "cultivate the next generation of the arts in the San Francisco Bay Area." Their programs include the ambitious ArtSFest put on each May, a four-week art extravaganza that spans a wide variety of art forms, including visual arts, performance arts, film, dance, education, music, and numerous others. While the events vary in price range from free to pricey, most fall in the affordable category and some even offer a sliding scale on admission.

Alas, one of the truly great independent bookstores has closed—we will miss you, **A Clean Well-Lighted Place for Books**! Despite the void, **Stacey's Booksellers** (581 Market, 415-421-4687, staceys.com), **Book Passage** (1 Ferry Plaza, 415-835-1020 in SF, 51 Tamal Vista Blvd. in Corte Madera, bookpassage.com) and now **Cody's** with its new Union Square locale (2 Stockton, 415-773-0444 in SF, 1730 Fourth Street, 510-559-9500 in Berkeley, codysbooks.com) host more readings

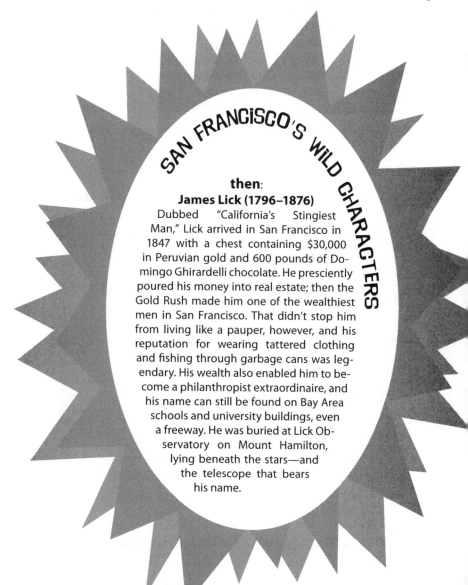

SAN FRANCISCO'S WILD CHARACTERS

then:
James Lick (1796–1876)
Dubbed "California's Stingiest Man," Lick arrived in San Francisco in 1847 with a chest containing $30,000 in Peruvian gold and 600 pounds of Domingo Ghirardelli chocolate. He presciently poured his money into real estate; then the Gold Rush made him one of the wealthiest men in San Francisco. That didn't stop him from living like a pauper, however, and his reputation for wearing tattered clothing and fishing through garbage cans was legendary. His wealth also enabled him to become a philanthropist extraordinaire, and his name can still be found on Bay Area schools and university buildings, even a freeway. He was buried at Lick Observatory on Mount Hamilton, lying beneath the stars—and the telescope that bears his name.

ALL THE LIT THAT'S FIT TO SHAKE

If you ever questioned the strength of San Francisco's modern literary scene, you need look no further than the growth and popularity of the City's newest and hippest literary festival, **Litquake** (litquake. org). Founded in 2002 by local writers Jack Boulware and Jane Ganahl, the annual fest has taken on Herculean proportions (at least in literary terms), now featuring over 300 authors over nine days during the month of October. The wordy event culminates with the ever-popular LitCrawl, which stumbles its way down Valencia Street in the Mission on Saturday night, and is "designed for those who like their literature served neat, on the rocks or with a water back." We'll drink (and read) to that!

than anywhere else in the City, hands down. You can try your luck by just stopping by, or check their sites for current schedules. The **Booksmith** (1644 Haight, 415-863-8688, booksmith.com) and the famed **City Lights Books** (261 Columbus, 415-362-8193, citylights.com) are also both excellent venues and regular stops on the author's tour.

If the bookstore environment doesn't exactly get your blood pumping, look into one of the more social venues. You can get your dose of Glenfiddich while listening to renowned authors at the proudly-literary **Edinburgh Castle Pub** (950 Geary, 415-885-4074, castlenews.com), where Scottish author Irvine Welsh premiered his work Trainspotting in 1996—as a play. The **Café Niebaum-Coppola** in North Beach (916 Kearny, 415-291-1700, cafecoppola.com) plays host to literary events but keeps it a bit hush-hush. Call them for details.

Discover even more artistic and literary venues at the excellent site by **SF Station** (sfstation.com, click on "Literary Arts Calendar"). Another solid resource is **Artist Resource** (artistresource.org, under "Writers Events"), which promotes and highlights the visual arts as well as the written word.

Ongoing literary events that will keep the creative juices flowing include the free and popular **Grotto events** (sfgrotto.org), put together by the increasingly famous writers' coop. The Grotto acquired new digs near Southpark (490 Second Street, 2nd Floor), and their events are evolving to match their new space. Sign up for their monthly newsletter to keep abreast of the latest. **Porchlight** (porchlightsf.com) is a colorful storytelling series that's currently hosted at **Café du Nord** (2170 Market, 415-861-5016, cafedunord.com), normally on the third Monday of each month. For more information, e-mail info@porchlightsf.com.

Theatre

There's a reason people think of the theatre as a rich person's activity. Hurray for **TIX Bay Area** (theatrebayarea.org under "TIX Bay Area"), Theatre Bay Area's half-price, same-day ticket program. Buy tickets starting at noon for a performance that same night, in person only, at the **TIX Pavilion** (in Union Square on Powell between Geary & Post).

You can also find reasonably-priced seats at the **American Conservatory Theatre** (405 Geary, 415-749-2228, act-sfbay.org), a performance and education-oriented theatre group. Second balcony seats run for $15 on weeknights, $19 on weekends, and as little as $8 on special preview nights. Call for details.

Ballet, Opera and Symphony

The ballet is not just for Pacific Heights limo riders anymore. The **San Francisco Ballet** (455 Franklin, 415-861-5600/415-865-2000 for tickets, sfballet.org), in its campaign to attract a younger, broader audience, now offers advanced-order balcony seats for as little as $8 for weekday performances, $10 for weekends.

There are two ways to get significantly discounted tickets for the **San Francisco Opera** (301 Van Ness, 415-861-4008/415-864-3330 box office, sfopera.com). You can stand in line for one of the two hundred $10 standing room tickets offered the day of each performance (cash only, one ticket per person). Tickets go on sale at 10am the day of the performance. Or—if you've still got a valid student ID (hold on to that City College card!)—you can buy any available ticket through the "student rush tickets" program. These tickets go on sale at the box office at 11am the day of a performance, and you can call ahead to check if tickets will be available. Balcony side seats are regularly $24 during the week, $26 on Fridays and weekends. Rather leave those little jeweled binoculars at home? You can hear live opera every Saturday for a song (the price of a cup of coffee) at **Caffe Trieste** (609 Vallejo, 415-392-6739, caffetrieste.com)

Getting in at a discount to hear the **San Francisco Symphony** (Davies Symphony Hall, 201 Van Ness, 415-864-6000 box office, sfsymphony.org) is a tougher nugget to crack. Select shows offer "center terrace seats" (seats that are sometimes occupied by a chorus just behind the stage), at $15-20 apiece. One hundred of these tickets are sold for non-chorus performances. Student rush tickets are also available for $20 each on the day of a performance. Call the student rush hotline at 415-503-5577 for the skinny.

AND DON'T CALL IT "FRISCO!"
Joshua A. Norton (1819-1880)

San Francisco's original **WILD CHARACTER** and the City's only monarch (sort of), "Emperor Norton," as he was fondly known to San Franciscans, arrived in San Francisco via South Africa in 1849 with $40,000 in his pocket and a screw loose in his noggin. He made the first of his many bizarre declarations ten years later, by proclaiming himself the Emperor of the United States.

The City press loved him, and published his outlandish proclamations and "decrees" on a regular basis, as well as making up a few of their own and attributing them to Norton. In addition to proclaiming himself the Emperor, Norton also declared himself "Protector of Mexico," decreed that the United States be dissolved and the Democratic and Republican political parties abolished, and demanded that a suspension bridge be built between Oakland Point and Goat (Yerba Buena) Island, and then on to San Francisco. He later ordered the arrest of the Board of Supervisors for ignoring all of his decrees. But the government body didn't hold a grudge: in 2004, North Beach Supervisor Aaron Peskin tried to have the Bay Bridge named after Norton.

"The Emperor" was adamant about the correct usage of the City name, saying, "Whoever after due and proper warning shall be heard to utter the abominable word 'Frisco,' which has no linguistic or other warrant, shall be deemed guilty of a High Misdemeanor." Penalty for noncompliance was $25.

So say what you will about our City, but—*don't* call it "Frisco!"

Open Rehearsals and Ushering

Many arts organizations will allow a limited audience for a dress rehearsal, or will occasionally advertise an "open" rehearsal. If you're interested in a particular show, don't be shy. Call and ask. If the director balks, mention that you are unemployed.

Ushering is another way to enjoy performances for free. Wear white on the top and black on the bottom, and you're nearly there. Once your job is done, you can relax, and enjoy whatever show you're ushering for free.

The **San Francisco Choral Society** (West Portal, 415-566-8425, sfchoral.org) welcomes volunteer ushers at any of their four annual concerts; many other choral groups do as well. Most of the 300+ volunteer ushers registered with **Cal Performances Volunteer Usher Program** (510-643-6710, cpinfo.berkeley.edu) stuff programs or tear

AT&T (SBC/PacBell) Park

While the name seems to change yearly (we know, blasphemy), even the skeptical have been won over by this urban baseball stadium. Ben Marcus, a self-proclaimed Giants fanatic, recently spent the better part of a summer going to games there. "Pac Bell [now AT&T] Park is the best-designed public facility I have ever seen," he says. "It's clean, convenient, safe, and somehow manages to be intimate for 40,000 people. Whoever designed and built the thing should be dipped in gold."

Ben funded his Club-Level tickets ($40–$65 a pop) through a combination of unemployment insurance and freelance writing gigs, but he also likes View Reserve seats ($18) on the first-base side for a great mix of game and Bay views. Bleacher seats and standing room only tickets are $10.

Other fans enjoy the game for free underneath the **Levi's Landing**. "If the crowd thickens," says stadium tour guide Steve Yung, "the Giants might ask those in front to clear the way every third inning or so." Otherwise, linger with the rest of the knot hole gang as long as you like, or invite yourself onto one of the various watercrafts (rowboats/kayaks/surfboards) floating the afternoon away in **McCovey Cove**, chasing down Barry Bonds' home run balls.

tickets at Zellerbach Hall, but a couple of the luckier ones caught one of Mikhail Baryshnikov's last performances at San Francisco's War Memorial Opera House. Call ahead to find out the exact schedule, and you might find yourself rubbing elbows with the theatre elite, or at least taking their tickets.

THE LEISURE SEEKER'S DAY OFF

No day could be leisurely enough without sleeping in. Thus, our ideal morning schedule goes something like: 7am—sleep. 8am—sleep. 9am—sleep. 10:30am—rise only if unavoidable. Kick around all morning—read, cook, have sex, whatever—then think about food.

The **Ferry Plaza Farmers' Market** (see the **Unemployed Shopping Guide**), where food quality is high but so sometimes are the prices, is now open four days a week and makes a great place to buy fresh fixings for dinner. The Alemany Farmers' Market (Alemany Blvd. near Bayshore Blvd., sfgov.org/alemany), the granddaddy of all farmers markets in California, is open only on Saturdays but, is far cheaper if you're trying to stretch a buck. With Union Square just two MUNI stops away from the Ferry Plaza, you can swing by after shopping to the **TIX Pavilion** to buy half-price tickets for an evening of live theatre (see "Theatre" p. 144).

If baseball's in season, spend the afternoon at a day game at AT&T (formerly Pac Bell) **Park**. Next, catch the N-Judah (it stops just outside of the park) for convenient transport across town to the beach. You can even sightsee a bit on the way (see "Street Murals" p. 127).

If your day off is a non-game day, catch the N-Judah from the Powell Street Station instead and disembark at Carl & Stanyan, then trot down to **Avenue Cyclery** (756 Stanyan, 415-387-3155) to rent a bike. The ride from there out to **Ocean Beach** is a leisurely one and the roll along the Great Highway sends you from the **Cliff House** (in its fifth incarnation) at the north end to the **San Francisco Zoo** at the south.

The luck of the Irish-Americans is with you as you ramble on into the Irish-run **Java Beach** (1396 Judah @ La Playa) with their tasty hot subs and beer specials throughout the week. Soak up the late afternoon sun on their outdoor patio, and/or pedal down to the **Park Chalet** (1000 Great Highway @ Ocean Beach) for a microbrew.

Drop the bike off afterward if you need to, go home and take a nap, then cook up dinner. Then you're off to the theatre. Enjoy the show!

BEST RESOURCES FOR LOCALS
(OR FOR TOURISTS TO LIVE LIKE LOCALS)

San Francisco Visitor Information Center
(Hallidie Plaza, 900 Market @ Powell, 415-391-2000, onlyinsanfrancisco.com)

Books
- *Lonely Planet San Francisco* (5th Edition, 2006)
- *Time Out San Francisco* (6th Edition, 2006)
- *Not For Tourists Guide to San Francisco* (2006)

Newspapers and Magazines
- *7x7 Magazine* (7x7mag.com)
- *The Examiner* (free daily, examiner.com)
- *SF Weekly* (free weekly, sfweekly.com)
- *San Francisco Bay Guardian* (free weekly, sfbg.com)
- *San Francisco Chronicle Datebook* (Sundays, sfgate.com)
- *San Francisco Magazine* (sanfran.com)

Web
- **Citysearch San Francisco** (sanfrancisco.citysearch.com)
- **San Francisco Parks Trust** (sfpt.org)
- **Mister SF** (mistersf.com)
- **SF Station** (sfstation.com)
- **San Francisco Bay Area Transportation Information** (511.org)
- **San Francisco City Guides** (sfcityguides.org)
- **San Francisco City Website** (sfgov.org)
- **Virtual Museum of the City of San Francisco** (sfmuseum.org)
- **Yelp** (yelp.com)

FAIRS & FESTS

SAN Francisco is nothing short of remarkable when it comes hosting events. Free concerts in Golden Gate Park for one hundred thousand-plus music fans? Check. A parade where the mayor waves alongside a float celebrating semi-naked bikers in butt-less chaps? Check. Civic Center plaza and City Hall jammed with fifty thousand costume-clad, techno-thumping freaksters? Absolutely. With more than one hundred major fests every year, how does the City pull it off? We have no idea. But when SF rolls out the welcome wagon for the funkiest, wackiest, most eclectic collection of jamborees on the planet, all we know is that we're all better off for it.

With only the highest regard for the other fabulous fiestas hosted here each year, we highlight three that simply scream "San Francisco!"

Only in San Francisco #1
BAY TO BREAKERS
3rd Sunday in May, 415-359-2800, *baytobreakers.com*

The Bay to Breakers race is one of the best and most peculiarly San Francisco events of the year. Why? For starters, picture an 8'x10' "boat" stuffed with kegs, rolling the entire 12K course offering "Free beer to naked people!" Then count all the thirsty nude runners taking advantage of the handout even as they are trudging up the Hayes Street Hill—and that's just the tame action. The largest foot race in the world steers more than 80,000 costumed and, uh, un-costumed racers from the corner of Howard & Spear to the breakers of Ocean Beach, hurling flour tortillas all the way. The fastest finish is just over thirty minutes, with the Back of the Pack pedestrians reaching the checkered flag as late as noon (4 hours after the starting gun) and centipedes falling somewhere in between. Pre-race prep includes group exercise sessions, energy drinks, a pasta feed, and an oxygen bar. Don't miss the post-race Footstock festival at the Polo Field for live music, food and drinks, and even massage.

STREET FAIRS

THIS WAY ➤

San Francisco neighborhoods come alive each summer with the smell of roasted garlic, the reverberation of jazz and rock music, the fresh flow of draft beer, sometimes even the slapping of chapped leather on bare skin! Yes, the street fair tradition is a good one, and whether you're a button-up type looking to show off the latest summer fashions or a biker boy looking for a leather buddy, you'll find a fair to fit your needs. They bounce and jig their way through summertime weekends, and admission is free to all. See next page for details.

ANNUAL FESTIVALS

San Francisco Festivals are all about celebrating a particular culture, whether it's ethnic, vocational, culinary, or sexual. The important thing is they go on and on, all year 'round! Unlike at the street fairs, admission is not always free, but you'll always find food, revelry, and assorted entertainment.

If it's a celebration of food you're after, you can't go wrong at the **Crab Festival**, encompassing the whole month of February. Whether you prefer your local Dungeness in cioppino or freshly cracked with a little oil and vinegar, at your favorite restaurant or on a bay cruise, you'll eat your fill during this series of events. Most are ticketed, but the Walk on the Wharf is free—organized by the **San Francisco Convention & Visitors Bureau** (201 3rd Street, Suite 900, 415-391-2000).

On the other end of the flavor spectrum is the **Ghirardelli Square Chocolate Festival** (900 Northpoint, 415-775-5500, ghirardellisq.com) in early September. Not much to explain about this one. Bring the kids, save your appetite for the sundae eating contest and content yourself in knowing that proceeds benefit Project Open Hand.

The kids can also join you at the straightforwardly-named **Street Performers' Festival** (415-705-5500, pier39.com) at Pier 39 in August, which features comedians, jugglers, unicyclists, and slack ropewalkers, among other "carni" delights.

the street	the action
Howard (*May*)	How weird! (Get it?) The amazing array of performance art at this South of Market fair includes butoh, belly dance, circus acts and stilt walkers. (415-933-8132, *howweird.org*)
Union (June)	A "see and be seen" affair in the Marina. Enjoy art, live music (classical and jazz) from two stages, a waiters' race and a kiddie area. (800-310-6563, *unionstreetfestival.com*)
Haight (June)	Hearken to the insistent Haight Street murmur of "Buds? Buds?" as you pass the face painters or either of the two live music stages. (415-863-3489, *haightstreetfair.org*)
Fillmore (July)	It's a jazz festival, really, with three stages of continuous jazz and other live music. (510-232-5030, *hartmannstudios.com*)
Dore (July)	Only Folsom Street wears more leather. This "Up Your Alley" fair features human masters and servants, raises bucks for charity and is quickly becoming as popular as its older brother, the Folsom Street Fair. (by SMMILE, 415-861-3247, *folsomstreetfair.org/alley*)
Third (August)	More music and family activities at this party in the developing stretch of the Bayview/Hunters Point district, benefiting community youth. (by MM&Associates, 510-237-5393)
Nihonmachi (August)	Lion dancers, Taiko drummers and children's events fete Japanese culture. (Japantown, 415-771-9861, *nihonmachistreetfair.org*)
Polk (September)	Basic and straightforward—music, arts & crafts, and multi-cultural cuisine—but the dancing in front of the swing stages keeps it be-boppin'. (415-383-3470)
Folsom (September)	It's the largest and the leathery-est. Adults only, please! Celebrates alternative lifestyles. All proceeds benefit local charities. (by SMMILE, 415-861-3247, *folsomstreetfair.org*)
Castro (October)	Dance, performances, and community groups help raise funds to benefit AIDS charities. (415-841-1824, *castrostreetfair.org*)

the dateline

Here's the whole *Fairs & Fests* shebang, with events listed by month.

For exact dates, check with the experts:

• *San Francisco Visitor Information Center*
Hallidie Plaza
900 Market @ Powell
415-391-2000
onlyinsanfrancisco.com

• *Festivals.com*
festivals.com
a wonderful party resource

• *Pier 39 Marina*
pier39marina.com
for events at Pier 39

• • •

january

Berlin and Beyond Film Festival

San Francisco International Art Expo

East-West Shrine Game

AMA Supercross Series

Sports and Boat Show

Mochi-Making for Japanese New Year

Anniversary of the Sea Lions' Arrival

Martin Luther King, Jr.'s Birthday

CULTURAL FESTIVALS

This assortment of cultural events doesn't capture *all* of SF's ethnicities, but if you make it to each of them, you'll have made a healthy beginning.

Kick the year off Slavic-style at the mid-February **Russian Festival** (Richmond District, russiancentersf.com). Celebrate the renewal of spring two months later at the **Cherry Blossom Festival** (Japantown Center; call SF Visitor Information Center for more into, 415-391-2000), which runs for two consecutive weekends in mid-April.

Pay homage to all that is Korean with the **Min-Sok Festival** (by the Intercultural Institute of California and Korean Center, Inc., 415-441-1881, koreannet.org) in mid-May, centered around a forum of Korean Studies Scholars.

Grab a whole handful of cultures in June at the nationally-acclaimed **Ethnic Dance Festival** (Fort Mason Center, Building D, 415-474-3914, worldartswest.org), which claims bragging rights as "one of the largest events of its kind in the country featuring real people, real dances and real music of Northern California communities." Herald Filipino culture—with more dancing—in early June at the **Fiesta Filipina** (Civic Center Plaza; call SF Visitor Information Center for more info, 415-391-2000).

The summer solstice wouldn't be complete without the flavors of Italy at the nation's oldest urban street fair—the mid-June **North Beach Festival** (Grant & Green, sfnorthbeach.org).

The **Juneteenth Festival** (at Kimball Park, bounded by Geary, Steiner, O'Farrell & Fillmore, juneteenth.com) celebrates June 19, 1863, the day African-Americans in the deep South learned of the Emancipation Proclamation.

Commemorate the French revolution on July 14th, **Bastille Day**, in the French Quarter near Union Square. Immerse yourself in Pacific Islanders' culture at the **Aloha Festival** (Parade Grounds in the Presidio, 415-281-0221, pica-org.org) in August, and in early September, head to Chinatown for the **Autumn Moon Festival** (Grant between California & Pacific, 415-982-6306, moonfestival.org).

Round out the year in honor of Latin American cultures. Celebrate art and independence at **Vivas Las Americas!** (Pier 39, 415-705-5500, pier39.com) and the **Latino Summer Fiesta** (Mission District and Civic Center Plaza, check latinbayarea.com under "Events"), both in mid-September, then join the candlelight processions through the Mission for **Día de los Muertos** (from 24th Street & Bryant to the altar at Garfield Square in Balmy Alley) on All Souls' Day, November 2nd.

CARNAVAL

Decide for yourself whether to bring your family to any of the many ethnic festivals throughout the year, but please, bring just your naughty adult self to *Carnaval* (Harrison between 16th & 22nd Streets, 415-920-0125 or 415-826-1401, *carnavalsf.com*).

Why San Francisco's version of Mardi Gras is held in late May and not on the days before Lent will remain a mystery to all but those who issue event permits, but no matter—it's one of the City's largest annual public events, featuring exotic dancers and pan-Latin jazz, salsa and samba. If it's got a beat, you can bet someone scantily clad will be dancing to it.

ALL THE WORLD'S ON STAGE

Art emerges organically at the **Exit The-atre** (156 Eddy) in September, as the producers of the **San Francisco Fringe Festival** (415-931-1094, sffringe.org) present nearly 300 performances of shows they have never seen before. Performers don't even have to audition (or sleep with anyone) to get their names in lights. All they have to do is be one of the first fifty applicants to meet the festival deadline. Really.

Artists from around the world take the stage for this non-juried and completely uncensored celebration of theater, sometimes with remarkable results. Kaliyuga Arts' *Beauty* toured internationally after premiering at Fringe in 1994. Although quality ranges from the up-and-coming to the just-plain-out-there, even a flop won't set you back more than $9.

Who says theater is dead?

FILM FESTIVALS

San Francisco is fast rising as a focal point for film festivals. The **San Francisco International Film Festival** (see next page) in late April is the City's largest and probably the most well known, but you can find movies to suit your own taste almost any other week of the year.

⊛ *Berlin and Beyond Film Festival*
January, Castro Theatre
415-263-8760
goethe.de/sanfrancisco

⊛ *San Francisco Independent Film Festival*
February, various locations
415-820-3907 or 415-421-TIXS
sfindie.com

⊕ *Tiburon International Film Festival*
March, location TBA
415-381-4123, *tiburonfilmfestival.com*

⊕ *San Francisco International Asian American Film Festival*
March, Castro and Kabuki Theatres
415-863-0814 x809, *naatanet.org*

⊕ *San Francisco International Film Festival*
April, Kabuki, Castro and other theaters
415-561-5000 or 415-931-FILM, *sffs.org*

⊕ *Urban Kidz Film Festival*
May, 762 Fulton
415-346-0199 or 800-965-4827, *ukff.org*

⊕ *San Francisco Black Film Festival*
June, Delancey Street Theater
415-771-9271 or 415-346-0199, *sfbff.org*

⊕ *San Francisco International Lesbian and Gay Film Festival*
June, Castro Theater
415-703-8650, *frameline.org*

⊕ *San Francisco Jewish Film Festival*
July, Castro Theater
415-978-2787/tickets and 415-621-0556/info, *sfjff.org*

⊕ *San Francisco Arab Film Festival*
October, 2 Plaza Avenue
415-564-1100, *aff.org*

⊕ *American Indian Film Festival*
November, Palace of Fine Arts Theater
415-554-0525, *aifisf.com*

⊕ *Film Arts Festival of Independent Cinema*
November, various venues
415-552-3456, *filmarts.org*

PARADES

Everyone loves a parade, especially tall people who can see over the heads of those who showed up early.

SF hosts a world-class marching spectacle almost every month. February's is the **Chinese New Year Parade** (2nd & Market to Columbus, 415-982-3071, chineseparade.com) which starts in early evening and caps three weeks of celebration that include a flower fair, the Miss Chinatown USA Pageant, and the Chinatown Community Street Fair.

The annual **St. Patrick's Day Parade** (2nd & Market to Civic Center, 415-675-9885) is in March, as it should be, and April's parades are several: **St. Stupid's** (Embarcadero Plaza to Washington Square), sponsored by The First Church of the Last Laugh on April Fool's Day; the **Cherry Blossom Parade** (at the Civic Center), which closes the Cherry Blossom Festival; and the **Easter Parade and Festival** (Union Street, 415-441-7055).

Cinco de Mayo (parade on Mission Street, festival in Civic Center Plaza, latinbayarea.com under "Events") highlights Mexican and Central American art and culture, and the **Gay Pride Parade** unites the queer community in late June. Parade season cedes to the street fairs until about October, when Italians, including Columbus, are feted on—where else?—Columbus Avenue, in the **Italian Heritage Parade** (Fisherman's Wharf & North Beach, sfcolumbusday.org). Two November parades wrap up the season just in time for Christmas: the **Veterans Day Parade** on Market Street, and the **Union Street Fantasy of Lights** ceremony and parade at the end of the month.

Only In San Francisco #2
GAY PRIDE PARADE
Market Street from the Embarcadero to the Civic Center
late June, 415-864-FREE, *sfpride.org*

A genuine slice of San Francisco, the Gay Pride Parade is for humans in all forms, as reflected in the event's official name: Lesbian/Gay/ Bisexual/Transgender Pride Parade.

It's très political, attracting speakers from around the world and a host of groups carrying banners, as well as famous hosts (including Nancy Sinatra, Sir Ian McKellen, Sharon Gless, and Margaret Cho), the formerly-named **Dykes on Bikes** (who now ride under the much-watered-down, litigation-required handle of "San Francisco Women's Motorcycle Contingent"), the **Sisters of Perpetual Indulgence** (*thesisters.org*), the cross-dressed, and the undressed.

The weekend-long event officially kicks off with a Fag Friday party at the **Endup** (*fagfridays.com*). It continues with Pink Saturday and on Sunday consumes the entire Civic Center area during the post-parade festival, with a main stage and nine side stages.

Five hundred rainbow flags fly from lampposts the entire length of Market Street. The crowd numbered nearly one million in 2006 and attendance shows no signs of waning. Viva la Rainbow!

OCEANS OF FUN

No matter how cold the water is, plenty happens offshore in this town, especially when sailing season begins on **Opening Day on the Bay** (Pier 39, 415-435-9133, picya.org) at the end of April. Boats and fireworks abound at the **Fourth of July Waterfront Festival** (Pier 39 & Fisherman's Wharf, 415-705-5500, pier39.com), and in very late August, the **Tall Ships Festival** (sailsanfrancisco.org) hosts crews from all over the world. October brings sonic booms and combustion of a different kind, when the U.S. Navy's Blue Angels push aeronautics to the limits to close out **Fleet Week** (Embarcadero & Fisherman's Wharf, 415-979-4000, airshownetwork.com). Early December brings **Christmas at Sea** (Hyde Street Pier, 415-561-6662, maritime.org), when children board the historic *Balclutha* to 'fess up to Santa.

BIG HUGE PARTIES

As far as we can tell, if you can't have fun at one of these parties, you'd better hang up your lampshade for good. Ticket prices can hit three digits, so it'll be up to you to make it money well spent.

"Money" is in fact the operative word at the biennial May's-end **Black & White Ball** (Civic Center & other venues, 415-864-6000, bwball.com). Thousands of Bay Area elite and want-to-be glams congregate at the B&W, the City's biggest black-tie block party.

Come September, there's love in the air as the funky and freaky pump up the beats and groove to serious electronic music at the **San Francisco LoveFest** (sflovefest.org). The dance music festival goes down over several days at various venues, culminating with a giant parade and party at Civic Center plaza.

Pump up the volume again for the trio of raucous affairs in October. To get the most out of **Oktoberfest By the Bay** (Fort Mason Center, Festival Pavilion, 888-746-7522, oktoberfestbythebay. com), wear your lederhosen and swim with the tide of traditional folk dancers, yodelers, nonstop German music, and (naturally) stein after stein of beer.

If you're still tipsy a few days later, that's okay—what better state of mind for enjoying an **Exotic Erotic Ball** (Cow Palace, 415-567-BALL, exoticeroticball.com), once in October, again on New Year's Eve. They're the largest adult indoor masquerades in the world, with truly outrageous costumes and nudity galore. Wait, maybe we're confusing it with **Halloween in the Castro**... No matter, the description applies equally to each.

tunes & giant jam sessions

the music	why it's better than a CD
Jewish Music Festival (March) various locations San Francisco and East Bay 510-848-0237 brjcc.org	Have you ever heard klezmer music? (Have you ever even heard *of* klezmer music?) It's a trip. Makes for an ambitious first date.
KFOG KaBoom! (mid-May) Piers 30 & 32 415-995-6930 kfog.com	This free all-day concert sports three bands and plenty of food, and closes after dark with a state-of-the-art, rivaling-fourth-of-July fireworks show, synchronized to a KFOG soundtrack.
Stern Grove Festival (June, July, August) 19th Avenue & Sloat 415-252-6252 sterngrove.org	More than a music festival, the Sunday afternoon symphonic, ballet, Cuban dance, and even hula shows are free all summer long.
North Beach Jazz Festival (early August) throughout North Beach 415-252-8773 nbjazzfest.com	If sipping wine to a groovy vibe is your scene, you'll dig this annual fest.
San Francisco Blues Festival (late September) Great Meadow @ Fort Mason 415-979-5588 sfblues.com	The blues greats turn out for the oldest blues festival in America.
Hardly Strictly Bluegrass (early October) Speedway Meadow, in Golden Gate Park hardlystrictlybluegrass.com	This kickin' three-day festival has become one of the best of the year, and it's all free— generously underwritten by local bluegrass fanatic Warren Hellman. Thank you Warren!
San Francisco Jazz Festival (late October) locations throughout SF 415-788-7353 800-850-7353 (outside CA) sfjazz.org	One of San Francisco's biggest and best music festivals features numerous well-known jazz musicians, yet generally operates below the radar. Smooth moves for smooth grooves.

Only In San Francisco #3
HALLOWEEN IN THE CASTRO
October 31st, intersection of Market & Castro

While the City almost lost its famed Halloween hoedown in 2006 due to concerns over increasing crowd problems, it appears cooler heads (and cross dressers) have prevailed—the party rolls on.

You'll find drag queens in brilliant gowns, feathers galore (think headdresses and boas), tall hats and wigs—even a rubber catsuit here and there amidst the 300,000-person sea of humanity swimming down Castro Street.

Considering that the crowd can be packed like sardines, the atmosphere remains festive and friendly. Beware the balconies, though. It's better to be at the house party that spills onto one of them than it is to be walking underneath. Keep an eye out too for the hunks in hot pants and a little naughtiness. It's all quintessential San Francisco.

SPORTS AND CARS

January's **East-West Shrine Game** (AT&T Park, 925-762-2277 tickets, 650-372-9300 info, shrinegame.com) is the prestigious groundbreaker of all of the university all-star football games, featuring America's best college seniors and benefiting the North American Shriners Hospitals for Children.

Same venue, January or February, is the **AMA Supercross Series** (AT&T Park, 415-478-2277 tickets, 415-972-1800 info, sxgp.com), a race of the world's fastest and toughest track motorcycle riders. A third highlight is April's **Opening Day for the San Francisco Giants** (AT&T Park, 800-544-2687 tickets, 415-972-2000 info, sfgiants.com).

Change gears—automatic or manual—at two car exhibits: from the time-tested and classic at the **Classic Car Show at Fisherman's Wharf** (February, Pier 45, 415-621-0500, sfmodelaclub.org), to the latest and greatest at the **San Francisco International Automobile Show** (November, Moscone Center, 415-331-4406, moscone.com).

AREN'T THERE
COWS AT THE COW PALACE?

Yes indeed, at least once a year at the *Grand National Rodeo, Horse and Stock Show* (415-404-4111, *grandnationalrodeo.com*) in late October. Then the heroic staff works like the dickens to get the giant barn-like structure smelling pretty in time for the *Great Dickens Christmas Fair* (415-392-4400, *dickensfair.com*), running each weekend between Thanksgiving and Christmas.

The *Sports and Boat Show* (805-389-3339, *sfboatshow.com*) hits the palace in January, and the *Flower & Garden Show* (415-771-6909, 800-829-9751, *gardenshow.com*) arrives in March, but it's the pre-Labor Day "greatest show on earth" that promises to bring out the kid in all of us: the *Ringling Brothers and Barnum & Bailey Circus* (415-478-BASS for tickets, *cowpalace.com*).

ARTS, CRAFTS & CRYSTALS

For a city that isn't known as particularly craftsy, San Francisco sure has a lot of crafts fairs. And those crystals! They're for sale at Fort Mason at least four times a year (Feb., June, Oct., Nov.) at **The Great San Francisco Crystal Fair** (Fort Mason Center, 415-383-7837, crystalfair.com) and again in August at the **Golden Gateway to Gems** (contact the Gem & Mineral Society for current location: 415-564-4230, sfgms.org).

The purely arts festivals are also plentiful. Start with February's **San Francisco Tribal, Folk & Textiles Arts Show** (Fort Mason Center, Festival Pavilion, 310-455-2886, caskeylees.com).

May brings the **San Francisco Youth Arts Festival** (at Zeum, Yerba Buena Gardens, 415-750-8630, sfyouthartsfestival.org), which showcases the artwork and music of San Francisco students in grades K-12. Participation and attendance for all Youth Arts events are free.

Jaunt across the Golden Gate in late August for the fine arts, music and food of the **Sausalito Art Festival** (415-331-3757, sausalitoartfest.org), then round out the year at the **San Francisco Arts Festival** (Bill Graham Civic Auditorium, Grove between Larkin & Polk) in October. With more than 15,000 original works, the San Francisco show is one of California's largest.

CRAFTS FAIRS

It's the subject of heated debate: what is "craft" and what is "art"? Decide for yourself at one of these bazaars of wearable art, home furnishings, ceramics, jewelry, stoneware bowls, silk scarves, and patterned quilts. Did we forget to mention the gourmet food? It would hardly qualify as a San Francisco event without it.

Contemporary Crafts Market (March)
Fort Mason Center, Festival Pavilion, 415-995-4925, *craftsource.org*

ACC Craft Show (August)
Fort Mason Center, 800-836-3470, *craftcouncil.org*

Harvest Festival and Christmas Crafts Market (November)
Concourse Exhibition Center, 635 8th Street, 415-447-3205
harvestfestival.com

KPFA Crafts Fair (December)
Concourse Exhibition Center, 635 8th Street, 510-848-6767, *kpfa.org*

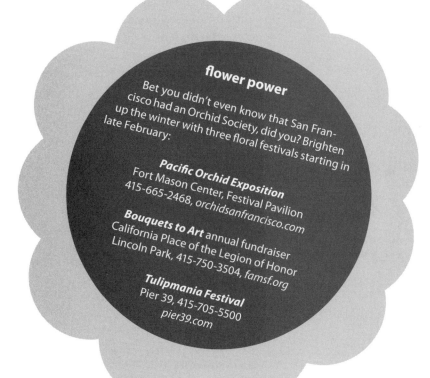

flower power

Bet you didn't even know that San Francisco had an Orchid Society, did you? Brighten up the winter with three floral festivals starting in late February:

Pacific Orchid Exposition
Fort Mason Center, Festival Pavilion
415-665-2468, *orchidsanfrancisco.com*

Bouquets to Art annual fundraiser
California Place of the Legion of Honor
Lincoln Park, 415-750-3504, *famsf.org*

Tulipmania Festival
Pier 39, 415-705-5500
pier39.com

OTHER COOL EVENTS
In A Category All Their Own

How's your herring? Ask any of the hundreds of sea lions basking on Pier 39's K-Dock at the **Anniversary of the Sea Lions' Arrival at Pier 39** (January 19th, 415-705-5500, pier39.com). Declared a "Watchable Wildlife" viewing area by the California Watchable Wildlife Project, this is where humans gape and sea lions honk, but there is noooooo feeding allowed.

Change your tune to "Happy Birthday" the next day as you're riding the **Freedom Train** (chartered by the Dr. Martin Luther King, Jr. Association of the Santa Clara Valley; for info, contact CalTrain, 800-660-4287, caltrain.com) up from the peninsula to march over to **Dr. Martin Luther King Jr.'s Birthday Celebration** (January 20th, Bill Graham Civic Auditorium and Yerba Buena Gardens, 510-268-3777).

Bookworms unite every other year at the California **Antiquarian Book Fair** (February, Concourse Exhibition Center, 415-551-5190, sfbookfair.com), the world's largest rare book fair. Convene again at **Books by the Bay** (mid-July, Yerba Buena Gardens, Mission @ 4th Street, booksbythebay.com), a celebration of independent bookselling with panels, signings and plenty of local literary stars.

Your experience of all that is officially San Franciscan just won't be complete until you attend the **Day of the Accordion** (June, The Cannery, 2801 Leavenworth, 415-771-3112, thecannery. com), a celebration of San Francisco's official musical instrument (don't ask) and an afternoon of Cajun, zydeco, conjunto, polka, and Parisian music. Doesn't ring your bell? Then how about the **Cable Car Bell-Ringing Competition** (July, Union Square Plaza; contact MUNI for info, 415-673-6864, sfmuni.com), where seasoned Muni operators vie for top honors, drawing on melodic as well as oral abilities.

You'll either laugh your guts out or throw Bronx cheers at the stand-ups of the decades-old **Comedy Day** (a Sunday afternoon in late summer, Golden Gate Park, Sharon Meadow, comedyday.com). No charge for the bellyache!

It's the same gratis entrance fee for spectators at the Northern California/International championship **Dragon Boat Races** and festival (September, North of Lake Merced at Skyline & Harding Road, cdba. org). Witness this ancient yet vibrant team sport at its best, where boats are decorated with dragon heads and tails, drummers don costumes and goofy hats, and the paddling rhythm keeps pace with the beats on a cedar and rawhide drum on the bow.

Less ancient but still vintage, American and European wares go on display at the **International Vintage Poster Fair** (September, Fort Mason Center, 800-856-8069, posterfair.com), the oldest and largest event of its kind in the world. For Halloween, you can peruse the pumpkins and parade around with the rest of the spooky crew at **Pumpkin Pandemonium** (October, Pier 39, pier39.com, 415-705-5500).

Traditional Irish and Scottish live music and dancing feet sound out at the **Celtic Christmas at the Cannery** during the first three weekends of December, while Santa comes to town nearby at **Ghirardelli Square's Jollyday Fair**. Not wintry enough for you? Then dash through the (indoor) snow at the **Metreon Center Winterland** (4th Street & Mission), which screens children's movies every December Saturday morning. Round out the holiday season at the hands-on **Mochi Making Ceremony** in Japantown, where the Masters of the Mochi demonstrate how to pound sweet rice into a gooey mass inside a hollow tree stump "bowl." You then get to try your own hand using mochi-pounding poles the size of a baseball bat. The yummy gum is rounded into balls, coated with soybean-sugar sauce and consumed as candy as a part of the traditional Japanese New Year celebration.

december

Skip the post-Thanksgiving shopping rush and get lit instead. No, not stinking drunk—lit up like a Christmas tree! Lighting ceremonies abound in November. They are beautiful to witness, for pagan and Christian folk alike. In rough chronological order, the electricity flows thus: first at the **Embarcadero Center** (415-772-0734), where a late afternoon holiday fair leads up to the flipping of the switch on 17,000-odd bulbs that outline four skyscrapers against the night sky for the rest of the holiday season. The celebration includes fireworks, music, and an ice skating show in honor of the official opening of the rink. Then **Pier 39** (415-705-5500, *pier39.com*) turns it on with a day of face painting, street performers and magic tricks, closing with the illumination of 2,500 lights on a 65-foot tree. The ceremony at **Yerba Buena Center** (in the **Esplanade Gardens**) includes entertainment, cocoa, cookies, and magic. **Ghirardelli Square** (415-775-5500, *ghirardellisq.com*) lights up the waterfront with a 50-foot tree, trimmed with Ghirardelli Chocolate and ribbons, and provides entertainment, caroling, dancing, and a visit from Mr. and Mrs. Santa Claus. **Fisherman's Wharf** lights a 50-foot tree at Taylor & Jefferson. Breakfast with Santa at Pier 39, then carol along the waterfront. Free motorized cable car rides, too! Finally, the **Recreation & Park Department** lights the Official City Tree, a magnificent Monterey Cypress, in front of the **McLaren Lodge** (Oak & Stanyan).

let there be light!

DINING & NIGHTLIFE

EAT, drink, and be merry, right? Well, right—but also, if you're a leisure seeker, watch your budget, connect with your community, and keep it real. It's about value, which includes but doesn't always mean bargains. You'll find value in a variety of price ranges and places, whether you're operating on $30 a day or $300 a day, a Mission tattoo artist or a Marina yuppie.

In this updated edition of Dining & Nightlife, as usual we were faced with a daunting range of choices, and our Leisure Surveys yet again turned up responses as broad and diverse as the City's culinary and cocktail scenes themselves.

San Francisco is a Mecca for all things gourmet—arguably the greatest in the world (bring it on New York and Paris!). You'll have no shortage of alternatives here for food, libations, and everything in between. Once again, we made our selections using the following four criteria:

      1—Value for the money
      2—Connection with the community
      3—Uniqueness or "funkiness factor"
      4—Positive vibe and other "intangibles"

If a pick from the first edition remained worthy, we kept it in. If we found something new and cool, we added it. And if an establishment faltered (shame on you)... or a bartender or waiter just really pissed us off (kidding), well then we 86ed 'em!

This section is not an exhaustive laundry list of restaurants and nightlife—there are numerous guidebooks for that. Rather, we feel the businesses listed here all provide something unique and special that adds to the culture in the City by the Bay. Okay we'll admit it: we think they're all very leisurely. And none of them paid us in cash or in kind to be here.

You won't necessarily agree with all our selections, but that's okay—you're not supposed to. Check it out for yourself. We think these locales all make the world, or at least our community, a better place to be. Either that, or they've just got really awesome noodles. Enjoy!

EATING OUT

Eating out on a limited budget can be a challenge, but fortunately San Francisco has a plethora of excellent lower-priced dining options. Restaurants recommended here range from spartan to upscale, and we've included some unusual categories in hopes of inspiring you to try something different, cuisine or otherwise. There's a variety of food-types for the most diverse of palates.

What they all share is exceptional value, so munch away!

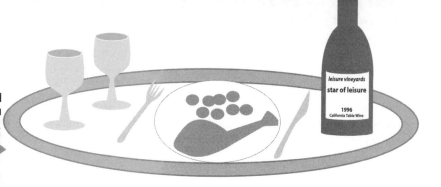

leisure vineyards
star of leisure

1996
California Table Wine

Five Cheap Restaurants You'll *Want* to Eat At

If you're operating on a limited budget, you want to know the bargain restaurants. The problem is, you want them to be good, not just cheap. Everyone has their favorite "cheap eats" joint—SF is full of them—but these five rise above the pack.

⍦ *Shalimar* (532 Jones, Tenderloin, 415-928-0333)

Good, cheap Pakistani cuisine in a sketchy section of the Tenderloin. Go for the food, not the atmosphere. You can eat comfortably here for $5, and like a king for $10.

⍦⍦ *Osha Thai Noodle Café* (696 Geary, Tenderloin, 415-673-2368)

The original restaurant in the burgeoning Osha Thai empire (there are two other, more upscale locations in the Mission and SOMA), this Tenderloin diamond in the rough has great, spicy Thai food and a hip scene. Added bonus: it's open until 1am Sunday-Thursday, and 3am Friday and Saturday to satisfy your late-night cravings.

♉♉♉ PPQ (Pho Phu Quoc) *(1816 Irving, The Sunset, 415-661-8869; 2332 Clement, The Richmond, 415-386-8266)*
PPQ is an insider's delight: inexpensive Vietnamese cuisine with great noodles, clay pot dishes, and curries. The lights may be a little bright, but hey—no one's complaining.

♉♉ Hard Knox Café *(2526 3rd Street, Potrero Hill/Dogpatch, 415-648-3770)*
An Asian-owned soul food joint? If that doesn't say "San Francisco," we're not sure what does. But Hard Knox rocks, as its many dedicated devotees will attest. While this is no place for vegans or dieters, it is the place if you want scrumptious cornbread, collared greens, mac n' cheese, fried chicken and the like. You'll rarely spend much more than $10 here, and you'll likely bring tomorrow's lunch home with you in a to-go box.

♉ Red's Java House *(Pier 30, South Beach, 415-777-5626)*
Enjoy burgers, dogs, and beers on the water at this San Francisco institution. Best enjoyed outdoors on a sunny day, but beware of the feisty pigeons. A burger and a Bud will run you $4. Daytime only.

Five Best Value Restaurants
These aren't the cheapest in town, but give serious bang for the buck:

Chow *(215 Church, the Castro, 415-552-2469)*
Park Chow *(1240 9th Avenue, Inner Sunset, 415-665-9912)*
Perhaps the best value to be had in a San Francisco sit-down restaurant. You simply get a lot for your money here: good food and drink, nice atmosphere, and an extraordinarily friendly staff.

---

fine dining value

If you're willing to roll the dice on some fancy food, "enroll" yourself in a gourmet dining experience at the **California Culinary Academy's Carême Room** (625 Polk, 415-292-8229 for reservations, *baychef.com*), where you can get four-star cuisine at two-star prices. Students prepare the food, and the extravagant buffets served on Thursdays and Fridays are the usually the best value ($27 for lunch, $38 for dinner). Food quality can be sporadic, depending on who's cooking, but they aim to please—don't miss dessert!

For a more tried-and-true meal, try **Metro Cafe** (311 Divisadero, 415-552-0903, *metrocafesf.net*), which serves a fixed-price three-course homestyle French dinner for $15 Monday-Thursday, or Friday and Saturday 5:30pm-6:30pm. Bring your own wine and pay the $10 corkage fee if you can't eat your food dry. Metro offers outdoor patio dining and is open seven nights a week, and for weekend brunch.

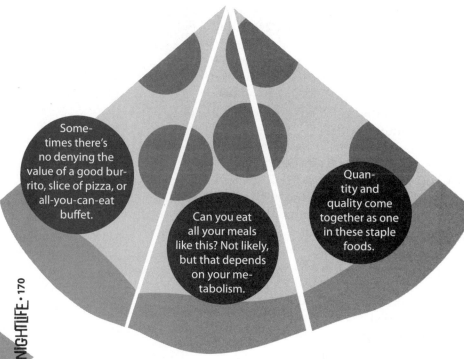

Sometimes there's no denying the value of a good burrito, slice of pizza, or all-you-can-eat buffet.

Can you eat all your meals like this? Not likely, but that depends on your metabolism.

Quantity and quality come together as one in these staple foods.

❚❚ *Eric's Restaurant* (1500 Church, Noe Valley, 415-282-0919)
Excellent Chinese cuisine comes with a California twist at this Noe Valley institution. Also try Eric's sister restaurant **Eliza's** (1457 18th Street, 415-648-9999 in Potrero Hill; 2877 California, 415-621-4819 in Pacific Heights), where the menu is curiously similar, but the décor decidedly different.

❚❚❚ *Cha Cha Cha* (1801 Haight, Haight-Ashbury, 415-386-7670;
2327 Mission, the Mission, 415-648-0504)
Long a popular choice for groups and big nights out, this Caribbean tapas joint is crowded, festive, and a good value. One word: sangria.

❚❚∨ *Nick's Crispy Tacos* (1500 Broadway, Russian Hill, 415-409-8226)
"Authentic" Mexican, "unauthentic" Mexican... does it really matter? Get your hiney down to Nick's, and order a couple of tacos "Nick's Way" (*the* way) and a bottle of Bohemia, and you'll find yourself in crispy taco heaven. Feeling a bit friskier? Their margies are good too.

Emmy's Spaghetti Shack
(18 Virginia, Bernal Heights, 415-206-2086)

If you've found yourself cocktailing through the dinner hours in the outer Mission, a plate of Emmy's spaghetti and meatballs can be a welcome reprieve. Of course, there's far more than spaghetti on the menu—this place puts the "F" in funk so you'll make fast friends here. Serving until midnight, it makes for a good one-two time off combo with **El Rio** (see "Chez San Francisco!") just down the street.

STAPLES OF THE UNEMPLOYED

The Slice
Pizza hasn't traditionally been one of San Francisco's specialties, taking a back seat to the slices in New York, Chicago, and other points east. Nevertheless, San Francisco is showing some encouraging signs in the "za" department, be it New York style, Chicago deep dish, gourmet or even traditional Neapolitan style. We were forced to seriously upgrade our picks from our previous edition, with several newcomers added to the list.

Little Star Pizza
846 Divisadero, Western Addition, 415-441-1118

A star is born in San Francisco pizza, and its name is Little Star. Their deep dish is to die for (trust us—try the Little Star pizza), but their thin crust is equally as good. And cool? Enough so that all those "NoPa" hip-no-philes should be satisfied. Those wishing to take it over the top ("wafer thin," anyone?) can finish with a slice of their homemade cheesecake.

---

all-you-can-eat buffets

Always a way to "pack in" value, buffets offer the hungry diner quantity for the money. Just don't expect to take home a doggy bag! Then again, stranger things have happened.

Bring your appetite and a friend or two and check out the buffet bars at these generous establishments:

Coriya Hot Pot City
852 Clement
The Richmond
415-387-7888

Not only is Coriya all-you-can-eat all the time, but it's cook-your-own-food as well!

The cuisine is a combination of Japanese shabu shabu and Korean barbecue. The fun of preparing your food at your own table makes this a great bargain date joint.

Cost per person at lunchtime (before 4pm) is $12.99, $14.99 afterwards, and that buys you sodas and desserts, too.

[mangia! mangia!...]

[...seconds, anyone?]

Funny how every single Indian restaurant offers a buffet lunch—or does it just seem that way? The food all goes down easy so we're not complaining. A couple of joints to stock up at are:

Star India
3721 Geary
Inner Richmond
415-668-4466

Lunch buffet costs $8.65, and is served from 11am-3:30pm. Decent Indian food comes in large quantity.

...

India Palace Restaurant
1740 Fillmore
Western Addition
415-567-7789,
indiapalacesf.com

India Palace offers a solid buffet lineup of Indian classics, oddly also for $8.65 a pop—available all day/night. They also deliver, and you can even order online.

[keep eating...]

Goat Hill Pizza
300 Connecticut, Potrero Hill, 415-641-1440
Goat Hill serves savory pies in a festive atmosphere frequented by post-victory co-ed softball teams. It's spacious and great for groups. Check out their Monday night, all-you-can-eat pizza extravaganza (see sidebar next page).

Za Pizza
1919 Hyde, Russian Hill, 415-771-3100
Speaking of "za," we find Za a perennial favorite among tipsy Russian Hill revelers.

Pauline's Pizza
260 Valencia, The Mission, 415-552-2050
Pauline's enters into the gourmet pizza arena—in fact, they even have tablecloths! Please don't let that deter you, as the pizza is scrumptious, however you might want to forego that accompanying brew-ha-ha here for a nice glass of vino.

Pizzeria Delfina
3611 18th Street, The Mission, 415-437-6800
Pauline's has some competition in the Gucci pizza department, and stiff at that. Highly touted Delfina has opened a pizzeria next door to their flagship restaurant in the Mission, and the Neapolitan-style pies are delicious—yet surprisingly affordable.

Giorgio's Pizzeria
151 Clement, The Richmond, 415-668-1266
This classic Clement Street pizzeria serves quality pies in a fun, family-style atmosphere. They do everything pretty well here—including stellar service—for a very reasonable price.

What, no Indian pizza? Well, okay, if you insist. We really like **Zante** (3489 Mission, 415-821-3949). Just the thing for showing the out-of-towners something new and delicious, and their food goes great with beer.

The Burrito

Atop the budget food chain, so to speak, the "little burro" actually has a fascinating history, both in San Francisco and beyond. Its origins can be traced back to our friends the Aztecs who, when the Spaniards first arrived in Mexico in the 1500s, were already pounding out corn tortillas of various sizes, and filling them up with meat and beans. But it wasn't until the Europeans brought the gift of wheat that the flour tortilla was added to the mix, enabling the more modern, gut-busting versions so prevalent today.

San Francisco's first burrito migrated up from the deserts of Southern California during the gold rush era, but it wasn't until 1961 that the first actual retail burrito was sold, reportedly from a corner grocery store at 2399 Folsom Street named **El Faro**—a burrito shop to this day.

According to the hilarious and extremely well-researched website, **Burritoeater.com**, burritos have supplanted chowder in a sourdough bread bowl as the signature food in present-day San Francisco. With over 150 taquerias within city limits, we're hardly going to argue.

In fact, given that the website painstakingly rates virtually every burrito factory in town based on a comprehensive, 13-criteria, 10-mustache rating scale (mustache?), as well as the fact that none of our selections from the first edition even made their *top 20*, let alone their top 5, we concede. They know more about the little burro locally than we ever could hope (or want) to know. That said, they were kind enough to provide us with their picks, along with Burritoeater.com master Charles Hodgkins' colorful commentary on each:

Taqueria San Francisco
2794 24th Street, The Mission, 415-641-1770
Hallmarks of Taqueria San Francisco's bulging burritos include ruthlessly grilled tortillas, scads of melted jack cheese, infernal spice (upon request), onion/pepper-pelted pico de gallo, and a wealth of tasty meats for all the carnivores. It's a neighborhood spot short on pretense and long on friendly service, with tuba-pop on the jukebox, and mighty delicious slabs. Anyone with a sliced avocado fixation may never want to leave.

Papalote
3409 24th Street, The Mission, 415-970-8815
Mechanically consistent and committed to top-shelf ingredients, Papalote has become a quietly infallible kingpin of the Mission's vaunted taqueria scene. It's slightly off the beaten path, family operated, and pretty much a sure thing every time. The modest-sized shop has gathered a loyal following in recent years, and is equally at ease serving everyone from steak lovers to vegans. Their signature chipotle salsa is available in to-go jars—the safe money says you'll want to take one with you. Breakfast is also available.

Tacos El Tonayense
Harrison @ 22nd Street, The Mission
This kitchen on wheels—part of an expanding army of Tonayense trucks crowding Mission District curbs—delivers some of the most hellacious burritowork on city turf. Sharply seasoned chicken, flecks galore of ground red pepper, and an elixir-like sauce are staple elements at this all-star slabwagon. Find someplace in the neighborhood to park yourself—a corner tavern, a stranger's front stoop, any number of hair salons—and enjoy your moderately priced food-blimp in comfort, because it's take-out only.

Taqueria El Castillito
136 Church, The Castro, 415-621-3428
With their signature, flaky-grilled tortillas and perfectly melted cheese sent straight from some intergalactic fromage-nirvana, the

Little Castle's dungeon of deliciousness rarely disappoints. It's tough to go wrong at any El Castillito, but public opinion seems to favor this location over the three others in town. Their ordinary chips are more than offset by a fusillade of extraordinary salsas, and their marinated, powerfully tangy al pastor (barbecued pork) is a meat for the ages. Breakfast is available, and they're open late.

LEAVE 'EM TO THE TOURISTS

Postrio
545 Post, Union Square, 415-776-7825
Long gone the way of Wolfgang Puck's now-franchised food empire, Postrio is expensive, impersonal, and lacks character.

Tonga Room & Hurricane Bar
950 Mason, Fairmont Hotel, Nob Hill, 415-772-5278
A strange combination of old-money San Francisco and tropical kitsch, this high-end tiki bar used to be a hoot. But these days, the service is abysmal (you'd be bitter, too, if you had to work at a "Pirates of the Caribbean" bar every night), and their "legendary" happy hour, from 5-7pm, is less than legendary, costing $7 per plate plus a one-drink minimum ($8-10 bucks) for below average food.

Beach Chalet
1000 Great Highway @ Ocean Beach, 415-386-8439
The Beach Chalet is loaded with potential: across the street from the beach, at the edge of Golden Gate Park, beautiful views of the sun setting over the ocean, an on-site microbrewery. Unfortunately, that potential gets hopelessly squashed by over-inflated prices, below average fare (including the beer), and horrible service. The Park Chalet in back gets kudos for its amazing indoor-outdoor space, but still suffers from some of the same ills. Locals pray for improvement.

House of Nanking
919 Kearny, Chinatown, 415-421-1429
Long known as an inexpensive staple on the edge of Chinatown, locals gave up on this place years ago as it became too crowded, too impersonal, and the food quality suffered. Come to think of it, was the food ever that good here?

Fisherman's Grotto
2847 Taylor, Suite 9, Fisherman's Wharf, 415-673-7025
Crowded, expensive, and noisy, with below average food, and located in the heart of the worst tourist trap in town. Need we say more?

El Burrito Express
1812 Divisadero, Western Addition,
415-776-4246

Solving pi may seem like a piece of cake after you've cracked the code of El Burrito Express' sprawling menu, but the reward of enjoying one of their swashbuckling slabs will make it worth your effort. Anti-environmentalists will appreciate the free Styrofoam plate presented directly under every burrito eaten on-premise, and slab size is never an issue here. Though it's a tiny space, their satellite location on Taraval Street in the Sunset is every bit this shop's equal. Both are closed on Sundays, a day of dietary rest.

CHEZ SAN FRANCISCO!

San Francisco is quirky, period. One way to explore its unusual side is through some of the restaurants and bars you're not likely to find anywhere else.

AsiaSF
201 9th Street, SOMA, 415-255-2742
asiasf.com

Exotic might be a tame word to describe the scene here. Gender illusion meets hip cocktail lounge meets sexy burlesque show. A true San Francisco original!

El Rio
3158 Mission, Outer Mission, 415-282-3325
elriosf.com

Forget happy hours, how about happy days? In addition to being a downright wacky, diverse bar-o-fun, El Rio also represents pure bar value. A recent calendar check of their deliciously irreverent website revealed the following: Dollar Day on Mondays, with $1 "Natty Lights" and $2 well drinks; Totally Fabulous Happy Hours Monday-Friday 5-9pm with all pints and well drinks for $2.50; free oysters on the half-shell on Fridays at 5:30pm (sharp!); Salsa Sundays from 3pm and after, an $8 cover gets you salsa classes, live music and a free BBQ! (See "Spice Up The Week" later in chapter)

Beach Blanket Babylon
Club Fugazi, 678 Green, North Beach, 415-421-4222, beachblanketbabylon.com
There's no food here, but this remains one of the most original shows around, and continues to re-invent itself year after year. Debuting all the way back in 1974 at the Savoy Tivoli, BBB is the longest running hit musical revue in theatre history. While it's on the must-see list for tourists, locals also need to get their hineys down to the Club Fugazi and check it out.

C. Bobby's Owl Tree
601 Post Street, Tenderloin, 415-776-9344, theowltree.com
San Francisco institution C. Bobby's Owl Tree is as quirky as it gets. We're talking taxidermic owls, Chex mix with wet-naps, a jukebox that plays Hall & Oates, shag rug, dancing girls on the walls and the greatest curmudgeon bartender in town—C. Bobby himself.

Tommy's Mexican Restaurant
5929 Geary, Richmond, 415-387-4747
Tommy's is hailed as the "epicenter of the tequila revolution," and claims to

timeless joints

Buena Vista Café
2765 Hyde
Fisherman's Wharf
415-474-5044

A bit touristy, but they pour some two thousand Irish Coffees here a day.

•••

Vesuvio
255 Columbus Avenue
North Beach
415-362-3370

A classic, bohemian favorite from the '50s that still thrives today. Write your leisure memoirs here during your sabbatical.

•••

Gold Dust Lounge
247 Powell
Union Square
415-397-1695

Mingle with the tourists (heck, you're on vacation too!) and listen to live jazz seven days a week at this relic.

the san francisco crepe mafia

Scattered throughout San Francisco are a string of extremely successful "creperies," establishments marked by inventive menus, colorful chalkboard art, and of course scrumptious crepes. These aren't your typical, foo-foo French crepes, either, but hearty, internationalized versions that span a wide range of delicious flavors and ingredients. Oddly, although independently owned (a few share the same ownership and thus the same name), all the restaurants have suspiciously similar menus and interior décor, right down to the chalkboard art. A mere coincidence? We think not. But we're not complaining, as the portions are big, the prices reasonable, and the food hits the spot—particularly the morning after a big night out.

Crepes On Cole
100 Carl, Cole Valley
415-664-1800

Crepe n' Coffee
2821 California
Pacific Heights
415-776-8866

The Crepe House:
1755 Polk, Nob Hill
415-441-2421
429 Gough, Hayes Valley
415-863-2422
597 Post, Nob Hill
415-351-2423

pour more 100% agave tequila than any bar or restaurant in the nation. We're not going to argue, and margaritas at this colorful neighborhood haunt are top-notch. Has celebrity bartender Julio Bermejo gotten too big for his britches? Perhaps. But day in and day out, he continues to deliver the gospel of quality tequila, and for that we can all be thankful. Go for the margies, not the food or service. Still, after a few rounds, their Mexican fare turns wholly functional, and you'll hardly notice the confused fleet of waiters attempting to hustle you through your meal.

THE WAY-BACK MACHINE

These aren't necessarily the cheapest eateries and bars about town, but with them come history, tradition, and plenty of character. Step out of the 21st century and commune with the famous San Franciscans who sought leisure in days of yore.

Tosca Café in North Beach
242 Columbus, 415-986-9651

Tosca is all that a leisurely time off hangout should be: friendly, eclectic, diverse, cozy, and oozing with character. The local film crowd hangs there, plus the jukebox plays nothing but opera! It may have gained a little too much notoriety for its own good in recent years, leading to a slight tourist infusion (believe us, we realize we're adding to the exposure with this very listing), but it all still seems to work. Bohemians, stars, tourists, and plain old folk blend well in this colorful European style-bandit.

Balboa Cafe *in the Marina*
3199 Fillmore, 415-921-3944

This is one bar and restaurant that transcends old and new. First opened in 1913, it remains popular with old-timers as well as young Marina singles on the prowl. The authors can personally attest to this but that's all we're saying. A lesser-known fact about the Balboa is that the restaurant is particularly good (locals rave about the burgers) and very reasonably priced. Leisure ruffians beware: the bartenders double as bouncers and can be seen hopping the bar with lightning speed at the first sign of trouble.

Tadich Grill *in the Financial District*
240 California, 415-391-1849

As the oldest of the oldies, Tadich is steeped in folklore. If you really want to bone up on its history, read the book, *Tadich Grill: The Story of San Francisco's Oldest Restaurant*. Sit at the bar with a stiff cocktail and soak up the Gold Rush era nostalgia or enjoy a boozy seafood lunch and mingle with Financial District types taking a break from the office.

Crepevine:
624 Irving, Inner Sunset
415-681-5858
2301 Fillmore, Pacific Heights
415-922-0102
216 Church, The Castro
415-431-4646

Squat & Gobble:
237 Fillmore, Lower Haight
415-487-0551
1428 Haight, Upper Haight
415-864-8484
3600-16th Street, The Castro
415-552-2125
1 West Portal, West Portal
415-665-9900
2263 Chestnut, The Marina
415-441-2200

The Saloon *in North Beach*
1232 Grant, 415-989-7666

The Saloon is dubbed the oldest operating bar in San Francisco, dating back to 1861. Originally known as Wagner's beer hall, this legendary blues dive packs a wallop, with live music every night of the week—a good place to go when you don't have to get up for work the next day, if you catch our drift. Leave your good shoes at home.

Little Shamrock *in Inner Sunset*
807 Lincoln, 415-661-0060

Opened in 1893 primarily as a restaurant and watering hole for workers in Golden Gate Park, they call the Little Shamrock the second oldest operating bar in San Francisco. Ponder how people used to travel here by train on their way out to the beach as you take a leisurely draw off a smooth Guinness or Murphy's—as long as the smell of stale beer doesn't put you off, that is.

Elixir
3200 16th Street, The Mission, 415-552-1633
Hold on a second—Elixir (formerly Jack's Elixir Bar) in the Mission claims to have found evidence of a saloon at their locale that dates back to 1858. While others mull over the oldest-bar-in-San-Francisco controversy, we'll opt instead to enjoy their popular five-hour happy hour from 3-8pm on weekdays, when drafts and well drinks are $1 off, and Bud Light drafts are $2.

NIGHT OWL EATING
San Francisco can be a challenge for late night eats—a frustrating attribute to say the least, especially if you're inclined to stay out late on a school night. If you don't have anywhere to be the next morning (and there's a good chance you don't), your evening may be just getting started around 10pm. But if you haven't made up your dinner mind by then, you'll often find yourself SOL (and we don't mean "Sorry Or Lost"). Never fear; these digs allow you to dine into the wee hours.

Brazen Head *(3166 Buchanan, Cow Hollow, 415-921-7600)*
Now this is what we're talking about. For 23 years, the Brazen Head has quietly served great food until 1am every night of the week. Darkened windows and cozy booths make it *the* place for that discreet affair. Add to that a classic, old-school bar, and you may be hitting up this hideaway at midnight several nights a week.

Liverpool Lil's *(2942 Lyon, Cow Hollow, 415-921-6664)*
Ah yes, Liverpool Lil's, a San Francisco classic if ever there was one. This dark and exceptionally friendly pub/upscale restaurant combo is a renowned, low-key place to hang. You're just as likely to run into Gavin Newsom here as you are Jerry Springer, and the kitchen stays open until 1am Tuesday-Saturday, 11pm Sunday & Mondays.

Globe Restaurant *(290 Pacific, Financial District, 415-391-4132)*
With a kitchen that stays open until 1am and a dynamic California cuisine menu, Globe is a favorite with restaurant insiders. That's always a good sign for professional and amateur foodies alike.

GET BAKED

The San Francisco Bay Area has a serious bread baking tradition, from the Boudin family's introduction of world-famous San Francisco sourdough during the Gold Rush era, to the hippy-dippy Cheese Board Collective in Berkeley formed in the '60s, to the modern-day phenomenon that is Tartine Bakery in SF. What can we say? Artisan bread making (and eating) is leisurely!

Acme Bread

(2730 9th Street, Berkeley, 510-843-2978, Ferry Building, Finanical District, 415-288-2978)

A spin off from Berkeley's Chez Panisse family, Acme has a reputation for creating some of the finest bread in the country. Indeed, for many it is the gold standard by which all other bakeries are measured.

Bay Bread

(Boulangerie Bay Bread, 2325 Pine, Pacific Heights, 415-440-0356, baybread.com)

What originally was intended to be a small wholesale operation on Pine Street back in 1999 has exploded into six boulangeries and seven restaurants around town. At the heart of it all, however, is master baker Pascal Rigo, and his passion for making fabulous organic breads in the French tradition.

Cheese Board Collective

(1504 Shattuck Avenue, Berkeley, 510-549-3183, cheeseboardcollective.coop)

Born in the bloom of late-1960s Berkeley, the Cheese Board is a classic—one of the last true coop businesses. Needless to say, their baked breads and pastries are out of this world. Naturally, pizza has followed, and they've created the Cheeseboard Pizza Collective. Groovy. Oh, and don't forget the cheese—they sell dozens of different cheeses from near and far, at high prices and low.

Tartine Bakery

(600 Guerrero, The Mission, 415-487-2600, tartinebakery.com)

Yes, it's true, devotees are fanatical about Tartine, and you'll often find yourself lined up out the door. But its reputation is well-deserved, with insanely good bread, and pastries and sweets that have been known to make people weep. Seriously.

Arizmendi Bakery

(1331 9th Avenue, Inner Sunset, 415-566-3117, arizmendibakery.org)

Formed as a coop in the spirit of the Cheese Board, Arizmendi first debuted in Oakland and then, to the City's benefit, created a separately owned collective in the Inner Sunset. In addition to the bread, locals rave about the cheese rolls and pizza.

Tsunami *(1306 Fulton, Western Addition, 415-567-7664)*

Late night sushi cravers, rejoice! The City's hippest new sushi haunt rocks and rolls until midnight Monday-Wednesday, and until 1am Thursday-Saturday, while the creative sake bar stays open until 2am daily (closed Sundays). Kampai!

Harry's Bar *(2020 Fillmore, Pacific Heights, 415-921-1000)*

This Fillmore Street classic has quietly reinvented itself over the past few years, raising the bar back to its former glory under original owner-operator Harry Denton. Lesser known is the fact that they serve solid grilled fare until 1am every night of the week, including one of the City's better burgers for $7 bucks a pop.

NOPA *(560 Divisadero, Western Addition, 415-864-8643)*

A stellar addition to the culinary scene in the Western Addition (sorry, we're not buying the real estate-driven moniker NoPa, i.e. North Panhandle), and for that matter the entire city. This restaurant delivers the goods, from its exceptional, mostly organic menu, to its well-crafted, inventive cocktails, to a staff that knows and celebrates the entire dining experience. Oh, all that and they serve food until 1am seven days a week, in a town where it's hard to find yourself a bad burger after 10pm.

Steps of Rome *(348 Columbus, North Beach, 415-397-0435)*

In fine Euro fashion, the Steps of Rome serves food at all hours. The food is good, not great, but you can grab breakfast first thing in the morning and dinner or a snack until 2am during the week—3am on weekends. A perfect place to bleed off that midweek bar crawl, if for no reason other than that you can.

CAFES OF THE CITY

The café is the unofficial home of the leisure seeker. If offers a connection point to your community (or, at a minimum, gets you out of the house), and loitering is encouraged—at least in most coffeehouses.

San Francisco maintains a strong café culture, with ample options varying by neighborhood, style, and ambience. Go in the morning and take pleasure in watching others scramble to work while you relax the morning away. Find one you like and make it your hangout, or pick a different one to visit each week, creating your own personal tour. For a comprehensive look at local cafés, see the beautifully published *The Cafes of San Francisco*, from TCB-Cafe Publishing.

In this second edition, we've once again included our favorites, with several exciting new additions making the list. Good coffee and community orientation are a given. Beyond that, we've again rated them for other important features: (1) loitering friendliness, (2) conduciveness to work (the laptop factor), (3) pleasure orientation (i.e. entertainment and ambience), and (4) uniqueness or funkiness. The "overall" rating is not an average, but a highly subjective score based on a certain je ne sais quoi. Venues are listed by alphabetically-ordered neighborhood.

'hood/café	why it's a good place to spend time off	rankings					
		Overall	Loiter	Work	Pleasure	Funkiness
Bernal Heights **Progressive Grounds** (400 Cortland, 415-282-6233)	A sun-dappled weekend in Bernal Heights almost requires a stop at Progressive Grounds' back patio. Great sandwiches, coffee, Mitchell's ice cream and a warm atmosphere make this quintessential San Francisco café.	5	5	4	4	5
The Castro **Philz Coffee** (3901 18th Street, 415-552-8378; original location: 3101 24th Street, 415-282-9155)	If hand-brewed, turkish-style coffee with real cream and a mint leaf topper is your idea of perfection, make the trip to Philz and meet the man behind the bean—you'll never drink coffee the same way again. While the Mission location offers better lounging, the Castro locale is a fine new addition to the 'hood.	4	3	2	4	5
Cole Valley **Reverie** (848 Cole, 415-242-0200)	An excellent, community-oriented café with a back patio, soft music and a mean latte. The fountain in the back is sure to soothe the most frayed of nerves, and if you loiter long enough you're likely to run into local luminary Craig Newmark of Craigslist fame.	5	4	3	5	4
Hayes Valley **Blue Bottle Coffee Company** (315 Linden @ Gough, Wholesale: 510-653-3394, bluebottlecoffee.net)	Although not much of a retail café, we just couldn't leave Blue Bottle out. Operating out of what amounts to a garage in a Hayes Valley alleyway, this mostly wholesale coffee company makes a strong bid for the best coffee in town, perhaps the country. Coffee geeks gush about the macchiatos, cappuccinos, and oh-so-smoothe lattes.	5	1	1	5	5

'hood/café	why it's a good place to spend time off	rankings				
		O	L	W	P	F
Hayes Valley **Momi Toby's Revolution Café & Art Bar** (528 Laguna, 415-626-1508)	Weathered wood, rustic décor and a good selection of coffee, tea and wine will make for a languid morning or afternoon at this bohemian Hayes Valley locale. You could spend hours here doing crossword puzzles or reading the paper at a tucked-away table, but don't forget to check out the ever-changing original artwork on the walls.	4	5	2	3	5
Inner Richmond (Lone Mountain) **Velo Rouge Cafe** (798 Arguello, 415-752-7799, velorougecafe.com)	The Red Bike puts the "C" back into community, with kick-ass java, creative lunches and an oh-so-welcoming vibe. Nice south-facing patio seating is out front, and there's free wireless internet to boot. Owner Meg is the grooviest and lives in the 'hood—she'll make you feel right at home.	4	5	4	4	3
Inner Sunset **The Canvas Gallery** (1200 9th Avenue, 415-504-0070, thecanvasgallery.com)	A cultural hub in the Inner Sunset, The Canvas is an excellent "working" location at all hours of the day. It comes complete with free wireless Internet access and doubles as a hip evening destination with music and various artist events.	5	5	5	4	4
The Marina **The Grove** (2250 Chestnut, 415-474-4843; 2016 Fillmore, 415-474-1419)	*The* café and daytime hangout in the Marina, The Grove is the place to go to see and be seen, and not for the diversity of the people. A good locale to get you out of the home "office." Also check out their other location at Fillmore & Pine.	3	3	4	4	2
The Mission **Que Tal** (1005 Guerrero St. 415-282-8855)	One of the last hidden gems of the Mission café scene, where you can also work quietly for hours on end. Visting Que Tal not only gets you excellent coffee and exquisitely prepared fruit plates, but also a chance to hang out with the nicest baristas in town, who always remember your name.	4	4	5	3	3

'hood/café	why it's a good place to spend time off	O	L	W	P	F
				rankings		
Noe Valley **Martha Brothers** (1551 Church, 415-648-1166; multiple locations)* *Rankings apply to Church Street location	A hometown success story, this family-run coffeehouse has several locations. 24th Street is the original, but the nearby Church and Duncan site is the best, with more space for lounging the day away. Arguably the best-tasting coffee in the City.	4	5	3	4	3
North Beach **Caffe Trieste** (609 Vallejo, 415-392-6739, caffetrieste. com)	This North Beach institution is San Francisco's original bohemian café. Reputedly the first espresso house on the west coast, Trieste is old Italy meets beat poet meets screenwriter (Francis Ford Coppola supposedly wrote the screenplay for *The Godfather* here). For all its notoriety, it still manages to retain its Old World charm.	5	5	1	5	5
Outer Sunset **Java Beach** (1396 La Playa, 415-665-5282)	Known for its great location, eclectic patrons, and convivial staff, this beachside café is a popular hangout at any time of the day. With good coffee, quality sub sandwiches and beer on tap, you may never want to leave. Comfy couches, a nice outside patio and free wireless complete the scene.	4	5	3	4	4
Pacific Heights **Peet's Coffee & Tea** (2197 Fillmore, 415-563-9930)	A coffeehouse chain, yes, but Peet's is homegrown in the Bay Area. The coffee is second to none (hey, it's Peet's), and its Fillmore street location is one of the chain's best.	3	3	2	4	2
Potrero Hill **Farley's Coffeehouse** (1315 18th Street, 415-648-1545)	Farley's may be the best neighborhood coffeehouse in San Francisco. It has it all: great coffee, tea, and other assorted beverages; a diverse, friendly clientele; indoor/outdoor seating with great views; and an extensive magazine selection—a true home away from home, and a great place to hang.	5	5	3	5	5

'hood/café	why it's a good place to spend time off	rankings				
		O	L	W	P	F
Potrero Hill **Atlas Café** (3049 20th Street, 415-648-1047)	Atlas makes an ideal place to nurse a beer on a Monday afternoon, with a diverse crowd and a spacious backyard patio. Look into the Sunday all-you-can-eat barbecue during the summertime.	4	5	2	4	5
Richmond **Bazaar Café** (5927 California, 415-831-5620, bazaarcafe.com)	An oasis in a cold, foggy stretch of the City, Bazaar's cozy atmosphere will keep you coming back. For those occasional sunny days, it boasts a protected back patio to chill on. It also hosts open mic nights for both musicians and comedians, writers' events, and even has released its own compilation CD. Need we say more?	5	5	3	4	5
Russian Hill **Nook** (1500 Hyde, 415-447-4100, cafenook.com)	Located on the quiet side of Russian Hill, Nook is a fine edition to the 'hood, delivering stellar coffee and yummy food (including a diverse sandwich menu), all done with a warm, neighborhood feel. Free Wi-Fi during the week also makes it a good mobile work spot.	4	4	4	4	3
Western Addition **Café Abir** (1300 Fulton, 415-567-7654)	A culturally diverse Arabic café that's popular with students and artists, and qualifies as an "any time of day" café. There's an adjoining magazine and smoke shop, and south-facing sidewalk seating on Fulton Street. Beware the water bowl for the dogs trotting home from nearby Alamo Square Park—and guard your muffin!	4	5	3	4	4
Western Addition **Central Coffee** (1696 Hayes, 415-922-2008)	This community-based coffeehouse is short on space but long on friendliness and great food. Park in one of their comfy red booths, work on your laptop with free wireless access, and groove to their eclectic music selection, chosen and directed by the staff.	4	5	3	4	4

Nocturnal crawls are great benefits for those not tied to a set schedule (read: don't have to get up for work in the morning). And with over 10,000 locales to wet your whistle, you won't have any difficulty finding yourself a good watering hole. Most nighttime events do, however, require some money, so be forewarned: nightlife can be a quick drain on the budget. But then again, when else will you be free to stay out until 3am on a school night? Pick your spots, and take advantage.

THE DIVIEST BARS (That You'll Still Want To Go To)

These salty dogs are short on appearances and long on, well, salt. Suffice it to say, there are a lot of dives in San Francisco, a sign of urban vitality if there ever was one. If you're looking to stretch your dollar a bit, keep these on your short list. Approach each establishment with caution depending on your individual tolerance level.

Our selection criteria? Extremely scientific: 1) Must be open on Monday nights—not only open, but thriving; 2) Bonus points given for attracting daytime clientele; 3) Extra bonus points given for a sign out front with a martini glass; 4) Super extra bonus points given if that sign is neon (see box on p. 190).

Zeitgeist (199 Valencia, the Mission, 415-255-7505)

No martini sign here but this is by far the best biker bar in the City—and by "biker" we mean primarily bicycles (this is San Francisco after all). If you're not the bike messenger type, consider acting the part when walking through the door. A great backyard deck and barbecue area highlight this rugged haunt.

Ha-Ra Club (875 Geary, Tenderloin, 415-673-3148)

The 'Loin is pretty much built on dive bars, and the Ha-Ra Club rises above (or sinks below) the pack. They offer, in their own words, "cheap cocktails served up low-end style." That more or less sums it up. Coax the bartender back inside to pour you a drink if he's out on a smoking break.

The Buccaneer (2155 Polk, Russian Hill, 415-673-8023)

Any bar with a name like this ought to live up to its reputation, and The Buccaneer certainly has the feel of a drunken Spanish galley. Happy hour pitchers of beer from 5-8pm daily are only $8–10. Hang on to your dinner as this ship rocks and rolls through the night.

Mauna Loa *(3009 Fillmore, Cow Hollow, 415-563-5137)*
Maybe not the roughest bar on this list, but a dive relative to its surroundings. A tropical oasis it ain't, but it does reek of, uh, character. One longtime bartender there recommends hitting it on weeknights to limit the "fraternity factor," and to wear your drinking shoes. Trust us, you don't want to ask.

500 Club *(500 Guerrero, The Mission, 415-861-2500)*
A rough-around-the-edges neighborhood bar that serves drink specials at all hours. This dive is all about drinking, in most cases quite heavily so those put off by disorderly conduct and raucous behavior best stay away. They run an extended happy hour Monday-Thursday from 3-7pm, plus different specials at on various nights, usually just when you want (and need) them.

The 540 Club *(formerly Max's 540) (540 Clement, The Richmond, 415-752-7276)*
Is the 540 Club really worth 40 more than the 500 Club? Ponder this (if you must), but don't let the hot pigtailed bartender playing Yo La Tengo and Pavement distract you from Chimay on tap and cheap PBR.

THE MARINA DIVE CRAWL?

A little known fact: Chestnut Street, in the upscale and wealthy Marina, has an above average ratio of dive bars—strange but true. Tucked in between Pottery Barn, Gap, and Noah's Bagels are some downright serious drinking establishments, but they are dwindling—get them while you can.

Starting on the western end and traveling east, begin your tour with **Delaney's** (2241 Chestnut). Consider ingratiating yourself with the locals by buying a round of drinks. Next up, stop by and say hi to Sulley at (Donahue's) **Marina Lounge** (2138 Chestnut, 415-922-1475), a locals' favorite. Further down the road, saddle on up to the **Horseshoe Tavern** (2024 Chestnut, 415-346-1430) for a cocktail and to shoot some stick.

If you're still standing at this point, there's nothing like finishing off a divey evening with some good old fashioned drunken karaoke. Sing your heart out at the nearby **Silver Cloud**, just off the Chestnut stroll (1994 Lombard @ Webster, 415-922-1977).

pink martini, anyone?

In our romps around the City, we found numerous bars with pink neon martini glass signs, a sign of a true dive if there ever was one. While you wouldn't want to frequent all of them, here are a few you might. Coat up the stomach, and join us for a little rabble rousing.

Murio's Trophy Room (1811 Haight, Upper Haight, 415-752-2971)
What exactly is a trophy room? We're not sure, but it seems to work. Anything goes at this diverse watering hole. Tattoo artists meet students meet freaks meet hipsters. Word to the wise: steer clear of those inclined to brawl here as the night wears on.

Il Pirata (2007 16th Street, Potrero Hill, 415-626-2626)
"The Pirate" is run by the same family that used to manage Bottom of the Hill. Part watering hole, part hipster hangout, Il Pirata is a lot of things. But dive bar drinking is what it does best. You can listen to quality live and DJ music most nights of the week. Bonus: the really cool mermaid mural to stare at in your drunken stupor.

Delirium (3139 16th Street, the Mission, 415-552-5525)
"Service for the sick" rests adjacent to the pink martini glass on the sign out front. Just what the doctor ordered? Perhaps. A replacement for the beloved Albion, Delirium does its predecessor proud with a no-frills, strong-cocktail approach. Bonus: happy hour from 4-7pm every day means $1 off all draft beer—except Chimay (bastards!).

Nestled among a slew of Vietnamese and Thai restaurants, The 540 Club gets you foosball, sexy lighting and a great sidewalk table for those rare warm evenings.

The Phone Booth *(1398 South Van Ness, The Mission, 415-648-4683)*
Always crowded and still smoky, The Phone Booth attracts hipsters, lesbians and the jukebox crowd to its tiny space. Drink Tecate out of the can and muscle your way through the crowd to the pool table. Definitely off the beaten Mission path.

BEST DAYTIME DRINKING

Drink the afternoon away? Sure, why not? Try your favorite pub during the daytime. You'll get to meet the bartender, which almost always leads to free drinks. While any old place would probably do, choose a locale where you'll likely have some unemployed company:

Pier 23
Pier 23, the Embarcadero, 415-362-5125, pier23cafe.com
Where would San Francisco be without Pier 23? Probably a little less drunk on a Friday afternoon, that's where. This waterfront special has likely housed more outdoor daytime drinking over the last ten years than any other establishment in the City. If you want to keep it going, they also bust out quality live music later in the evenings.

The Ramp
855 China Basin, in China Basin, 415-621-2378
This is the City's other great outdoor drinking establishment on the waterfront—tucked away in innocuous China Basin. While Pier 23 may resemble a frat party, the Ramp (at least during daytime hours) maintains a far mellower vibe. Catch one of the frequent steel drum bands there during the summertime, and you'll likely begin plotting a boat escape to the Caribbean.

Park Chalet *(1000 Great Highway @ Ocean Beach, 415-386-8439)*
On a clear sunny day, there may be no better place to be in San Francisco than in a reclined chair on the back lawn of the Park Chalet, sipping on a frosty lager. Then again, if you have an aversion to groovy live music and a mellow vibe, it might not be for you. Surfers and tourists co-mingle at this by-the-beach destination.

chinatown triple whammy

From the **Buddha Bar** (901 Grant, 415-362-1792) to **Li Po** (916 Grant, 415-982-0072) to the **Bow Bow Cocktail Lounge** (1155 Grant, 415-421-6730)—this trio of dives packs a worthy triple punch (you *will* feel the blows) and is a great tour to truck the out-of-towners on when you tire of sifting through trinkets or negotiating firecracker purchases. The Buddha Bar is the most hilarious of the three and features constant shouting in multiple languages and some top-notch peoplewatching.

Harrington's Bar & Grill
245 Front, Financial District, 415-392-7595

Harrington's is what it is, and that is the real deal—a hearty, authentic, hard-drinking Irish pub and restaurant. Is it day or night? Do you care? Probably not, but your Financial District friends might if you meet them at this dark, dingy classic for lunch.

The Irish Bank
10 Mark Lane @ Bush, Financial District, 415-788-7152, theirishbank.com

This raucous pub achieves Irish authenticity, at least in the drinking sense. Many a worker and non-worker alike have lost their way in the halls of the Bank, only to emerge hours later wondering who turned off all the lights. A favorite for happy hour and after work (or non-work!).

Anchor Brewing Company
1705 Mariposa, China Basin, 415-863-8350, anchorbrewing.com

We've mentioned it before (see **Chapter 4** under "The Perfectly Free Day") but it *is* free. And it *is* good beer. Not only that, but it requires you to drink during the day. Enough said!

BEST HAPPY HOURS

Happy hours have returned with gusto to San Francisco, which is indeed good news. A clever leisure seeker can find some real bargains here, and well beyond standard happy hour times.

As bars and their drink specials are constantly changing, we did a fair bit of revamping for this edition of *Time Off!*. Be sure to check ahead to ensure any deals are still current.

Doc's Clock

2575 Mission, The Mission, 415-824-3627

We're ecstatic to add the venerable Doc's Clock to the happy hour mix. By all standards, this is an outstanding, no-nonsense bar. The fact that they host a happy hour from 6pm-9pm every day with $1 PBR, $3 drafts and well drinks, and $4 Chimay (yes, you read that right) only deepens our respect.

John Colins

90 Natoma, SOMA, 415-543-2277

While its drink specials are admirable (from 5-7pm $3 draft, imports, micro-brews and well drinks, $2 domestics), what sets John Colins apart is that it's a cool, casual bar downtown in a sea of overpriced, stuffy haunts. It's the perfect after-work spot for those who are way beyond "dressing for success."

Bar 821

821 Divisadero, Western Addition

There are two reasons Bar 821 made our coveted list of happy hours: $3 Chimay from 5-7pm, and $3 Chimay from 5-7pm. Did we mention the $3 Chimay? Seriously, it's a cool neighborhood hangout and all their happy hour beers are $3, which also usually includes Hoegarden and some other good Belgians. Sweet.

Jade

650 Gough, Hayes Valley, 415-869-1900

We searched long and hard for an up-scale cocktail lounge with a decent happy hour, and finally found it at Jade. The space is smooth and comfortable, and it looks exactly like the type of place

[sure, fill 'er up...]

•••

Hobson's Choice
1601 Haight, Upper Haight
415-621-5859

Swig some rum punch at this graduate school hang-out, and order some food to match from the nearby ***Asqew Grill*** (1607 Haight, Upper Haight, 415-701-9301)—you can order from the Hobson bar and eat it on-site.

•••

The Bell Tower
1900 Polk, Russian Hill
415-567-9596

A great, sassy neighborhood stop. Owner Barbara will be in full support of your work break, and will likely contribute to your hangover to boot. Dinner is grand, but later in the evening the Bell becomes a serious drinking establishment.

•••

Horseshoe Tavern
2024 Chestnut, The Marina
415-346-1430

"The Shoe" is an island of sanity in a sea of striped button-down shirts and too much makeup. The bartend-ers rock, and make everyone feel right at home, while mixing some serious drinks.

[some more?...]

that will run you $8-10 per cocktail. But during weekday happy hours from 5-7:30pm, draft beers, well drinks, and certain specialty cocktails are all only two bucks! One of the best values in "hip" we've come across.

San Francisco Brewing Company
155 Columbus, North Beach, 415-434-3344, sfbrewing.com

It's not clear why, but this brewpub on a busy Columbus block in North Beach is often overlooked. Maybe it's because with all the mayhem of North Beach, a brewpub just isn't the first thing that comes to mind. Whatever the reason, it doesn't really matter—San Francisco Brewing Company delivers, and their happy hour is hard to beat. Every night of the week from 4-6pm and then again from midnight-1am, 10 oz. beer is a $1.50 and pints are only $2.75. Tip: try the Emperor Norton Lager for a brew with authentic San Francisco character (see "And Don't Call It 'Frisco!'" in **Chapter 4**).

Sugar
377 Hayes, Hayes Valley, 415-255-7144, sugarloungesf.com

This hip new Hayes Valley lounge hosts one of the best happy hours around—good, alternating drink specials on their creative cocktails along with free food, which ranges from chicken skewers to veggie platters. Let's just hope they keep it going! Runs weekdays 4:30-7pm.

Kennedy's Irish Pub & Curry House
1040 Columbus, North Beach, 415-441-8855, kennedyscurryhouse.com

Irish pub and curry house in one? You bet, and drink specials galore. Happy hour runs from 4-8pm and 11-11:30pm daily at this raucous pub, and is highlighted by two dollar Guinness and Beamish. Five bucks gets you a pitcher of Pabst Blue Ribbon all day or night, all the time.

 Club Waziema

543 Divisadero, Western Addition,
415-346-6641

Waza–who? This is another quality neighborhood joint that fits like a glove, serving beer, wine, and… Ethiopian food—what else? Their Monday-Saturday happy hour from 6-8pm features $2.50 drafts and $4 glasses of wine. No more free food, but they do have all-you-can-eat veggie dishes for $6.50 from 6-10:30pm.

Wish

1539 Folsom, SOMA, 415-278-9474

Running 5-8pm on weekdays, happy hour here means $2 beers (all of 'em) and $3 well drinks. One could hardly wish for more.

*Special thanks to local happy hour expert Marcus Ronaldi (marcusronaldi. com) once again for his input on this section.

BEST TUNES FOR THE BUCK

While these stages don't see the biggest, most heavily promoted shows, they get a surprising number of quality acts, from underground local musicians to big name artists. Depending on the type of show, the cover charge generally will leave you enough money to buy a round of drinks for your friends.

♪ Bottom of the Hill

1233 17th Street, Potrero Hill, 415-621-4455
bottomofthehill.com

This club consistently manages to book the best up-and-coming indie rock bands before they become famous, from the Beastie Boys to Bad Religion, Joan Jett to Juliana Hatfield, Kid Rock to Korn. Ticket prices vary depending on the band, but average $8-10 for most shows. A back patio provides a much-needed safety valve on crowded nights, and their all-you-can-eat BBQ plus live show on Sundays is the stuff of legends.

♪ Amoeba Music

1855 Haight, Upper Haight, 415-831-1200, amoebamusic.com

Save for the occasional unfortunate booking (uh, Pete Yorn?), Amoeba Music does a great job of bringing in emerging rock acts to play free in-store shows. As of late, lucky customers have seen Calexico and The Raconteurs. Get there early—these shows are packed.

♪ Cafe du Nord

2170 Market, the Castro, 415-861-5016, cafedunord.com

This speakeasy holdover is a downright cool, swanky place to hang out. The live music is all over the map, from jazz to hip-hop to German punk, and tickets usually cost around $10.

♪ Noe Valley Ministry

1021 Sanchez, Noe Valley, 415-282-2317
noevalleymusicseries.com

This venue is, as the name asserts, a ministry, located on an unassuming block of tranquil Noe Valley. As a "house of prayer and community," the ministry puts on an innovative music series that includes Bay Area and international performers. Folk is probably the most common, but the ministry has been host to virtually all types of music, as well as comedians and other performers. Concerts are usually on Saturday nights, and entry typically costs $15-20.

♪ Elbo Room

647 Valencia, the Mission, 415-552-7788, elbo.com

Long a staple in the live music scene in San Francisco, the Elbo Room delivers a non-pretentious vibe with bands most nights of the week. Like the Last Day Saloon, the club splits into a cool bar downstairs, and dance-friendly music upstairs. Reggae, rock, Latin, and hip-hop will all be heard here, as well as many other types of music. Tickets usually go for $5-10.

♪ Edinburgh Castle

950 Geary, 'Loin, 415-885-4074
castlenews.com

We weren't quite sure where to list this eclectic haunt, as it's part live music venue, part dive, part theatre—and part just good old-fashioned kickin' bar. You're equally likely to hear live music as a literary reading here. Cover charges are all over the map (the bar says they let the bands decide) but generally range from free to $10.

DANCE AND LATE NIGHT

When it's time to kick it up a notch and roll on into the evening, these venues will escort you on up 'round midnight.

No-Cover Dance

Get your groove on without fronting any cash and with a tad more intimacy than at your average mega club.

Blondie's Bar & No Grill

540 Valencia, the Mission, 415-864-2419, blondiesbar.com

Okay, we lied—there's a small cover here on weekends. But with 16 oz. martinis, you'll earn it back quickly on drink value, not to mention booty shaking on the dance floor.

Holy Cow

1535 Folsom, SOMA, 415-621-6087, theholycow.com

Sure, it might be a sweaty barn, but it don't cost nothin'! This San Francisco rite of passage is all about having fun. How can you go wrong with a motto like "never ever a cover"?

Wish

1539 Folsom, SOMA, 415-278-9474, wishsf.com

Wish is a lounge first and a dance venue second, but the music is so damn good, dancing seems to happen naturally.

Little Baobab

3388 19th Street, The Mission, 415-643-3558, bissapbaobab.com

Right, so Baobab also can charge a cover, but it's normally $3 or less, and this place brings it big-time. Get loose to eclectic world beats at this small and thumpin' venue.

¡Viva Salsa!

We can't quite put our fingers on it, but there's something quite leisurely about salsa dancing. It's just so…zesty. San Francisco has a surprisingly strong salsa scene, and in many cases it's happening in places you wouldn't suspect.

Salsa in San Francisco begins (and sometimes ends) with Salsa Sundays at **El Rio** (3158 Mission, Outer Mission, 415-282-3325, elriosf.com; also see "Chez San Francisco!"). Every Sunday afternoon in the Outer

Mission, the dance floor at El Rio pulses to the rhythm of live salsa music and couples of every background imaginable gyrate and spin their way to bliss. The cover is $8 (which includes a BBQ), the doors open at 3pm, and a dance class for beginners is given at 3:15pm. That's pretty much all you need to know.

When you've graduated to more advanced dance, the place to go is **Roccapulco** (3140 Mission, Outer Mission, 415-648-6611, roccapulco. com), which is just down the street from El Rio. Hot Latino dancers tear up the dance floor here—particularly on weekends—and lessons early on Friday and Saturday night are included in the cover charge.

Café Cocomo (650 Indiana, Potrero Hill, 415-824-6910, cafe cocomo.com) hosts steamy salsa on Monday, Thursday, and Saturday nights. Beginner and (two separate lessons) are offered at 7:30pm and 8:30pm respectively on Monday nights for $7.

Other notable salsa scenes include **Glas Kat (Ay Karamba)** (520 4th Street, SOMA, 415-495-6620, glaskat.com) on Tuesday nights with live music and lessons; **Elbo Room** (see "Best Tunes") on Thursday nights with live music; **El Valenciano** (1153 Valencia, The Mission, 415- 826-9561) on Friday nights with lessons; **The Ramp** (855 China Basin, China Basin, 415-621-2378) on Saturday afternoons, complete with an outdoor barbecue (summer only), and **El Rincon** (2700 16th Street, The Mission, 415-437-9240).

Karaoke

What sabbatical would be complete without a dose of karaoke tomfoolery? In addition to the traditional standbys, we've added some wacky venues to the list for this edition. We're not embarrassed to say it: we like to make fools of ourselves in front of others. Here's where you can too.

The Mint
1942 Market, the Castro, 415-626-4726, themint.net

The Mint is ground zero for karaoke in San Francisco. Top singers combine with drunken first-timers and everyone has fun.

Silver Cloud
1994 Lombard @ Webster, 415-922-1977
(see "The Marina Dive Crawl?" p. 179)
The Marina's answer to karaoke has caught on quickly, and crooners pack the joint most nights.

Do Re Mi Music Studio
1604 Post, Japantown, 415-771-8884
Do Re Mi is a traditional karaoke studio with private rooms for groups, and it stays open into the wee hours. There's no alcohol served here, and they no longer let you bring your own—so you have to be a little more... discreet (if you hear what we're singin').

Bow Bow Cocktail Lounge
1155 Grant, Chinatown, 415-421-6730
(see "Chinatown Triple Whammy")
Bark it out at Bow Bow, a Chinatown dive where the singing is so awful, patrons might not even notice how bad your own crooning is.

Encore Karaoke Lounge
1550 California, Nob Hill, 415-775-0442,
encorekaraokesf.com
The owners here encourage you to drink. In fact, they insist on it or ask you to move along. It's just as well—do you really want to be performing on stage sober?

STAYING OUT REALLY LATE

Keep it going into the wee hours of the morning at these hip places where you can keep on dancing long past last call.

---

miscellaneous fun

Ploy II Thai Cuisine
1770 Haight
Upper Haight
415-387-9224

Tucked away above Haight Street (2nd Floor), Ploy Thai provides a pleasant reprieve from the hustle and bustle of the Haight. Score a table by the window, order their $5 lunch special, and behold the colorful antics on the street below.

•••

Kan Zaman
1793 Haight
Upper Haight
415-751-9656

Enjoy nightly belly dancing, hookah pipes, and inexpensive cuisine at this delightful Middle Eastern eatery. Great for groups, but go early or prepare to wait.

•••

Make-Out Room
3225 22nd Street
the Mission
415-647-2888

A diverse crowd spices up this all-purpose bar, good for drinking, lounging, or dancing. There's live music and events from time to time, so best to call ahead. Drink Pabst Blue Ribbon for $1 during happy hour, 6-8pm Monday-Thursday.

[could you possibly have any *more* fun?...]

Rickshaw Stop
155 Fell, Hayes Valley
415-861-2011

We heart Rickshaw! It's a stylish, unassuming bar... it's an intimate live music venue...it's a value-oriented happy hour spot. They even have decent noshing fare. A rare place that's able to bring diverse elements together.

•••

Puerto Alegre
546 Valencia, The Mission
415-255-8201

If it's party-starting time in the Mission, Puerto Alegre is an inexpensive way to rev up, with strong margaritas and starchy Mexican food.

The Endup
401 6th Street, SOMA, 415-357-0827
theendup.com

In a town that generally goes to bed early, the Endup is the pillar of late-night debauchery. It's one of the few places that never really closes on the weekends, save for a few hours early Sunday when everyone stops to check their pulse. The Endup is, for lack of a better word, an institution. If you're going to let it all hang out while you're not owing time to an employer, this is the place to do it. Party on.

Pink
2925 16th Street, The Mission, 415-431-8889, pinksf.com

As a smaller, more intimate late-night club, Pink is an excellent place to dance to DJ music if you don't want that big club feel. Closing time depends on what's on tap for the evening, but generally hovers between 2 and 4am.

Ruby Skye
420 Mason, Tenderloin, 415-693-0777, rubyskye.com

Ruby Sky is what it is, and that's a large, slick club just off Union Square. While it might not be for all tastes, the venue interior is beautiful turn of the century Victorian, and they do host top-notch DJs and live performances.

Mighty
119 Utah, Potrero Hill, 415-762-0151, mighty119.com

This underground club has fast become the go-to locale for the funky and the freaky to get their groove on late into the night (and well into the morning). Top DJs from Black Rock City to the UK mix their beats here, much to the delight of late-night revelers.

THE
LEISURE SHOPPING GUIDE

SHOPPING while non-employed? Absolutely! True, the more you spend, the shorter your leisure, but trading a few bucks for some choice bargains is still a wise move. Books, music, and clothes to carouse in are all key ingredients of quality free time.

This shopping guide will help your dollars go the distance at a time when you need them to stretch, with tips on:

- where to swap your tired old things for what you really want
- secrets of veteran garage sale shoppers and cutting-edge online auctioneers
- finding good deals
- savoring the window-shopping experience
- transforming buying into recreation

No need to bust the piggy bank or surrender to impulse when you're shopping. Be selective. Keep a higher purpose in mind—lengthy leisure time—and you can resist the forces urging you to overspend.

You might also want to consider some alternatives for getting new things. Consider hosting a party with your same-gender friends to exchange clothes you never wear—your friend may have great duds that he or she just never loved, but you do. Then you can bag the leftovers and bring them to a consignment shop or a charity. Same goes for music—a "burn a mix CD" exchange party can get you great new sounds scot-free, and deepen your friendships at the same time!

buy • sell • trade

There is almost no reason to buy new things in San Francisco. How many people do you know who have moved out of this city or sold off their stuff in a fit of reinvention? This means that some of the best places to buy are also places where you can sell or trade items you're ready to part with. Music, books and clothing stores top this list. With a little scouting, you can find many others, like sports equipment or furniture. Just don't buy back your own stuff!

Music is vital to the soul. Treat yourself to some fresh tunes now and again, especially if you can acquire them by trading in songs you've grown tired of.

Amoeba Music (1855 Haight, 415-831-1200, amoebamusic.com) is the prime dealer for recycled tunes. Prices are based on the title and condition of your submission—with the biggest bucks paid for what's rare, popular and in mint condition—and you'll get 20% more in trade than in cash.

Buying at Amoeba is as much fun as selling. Their selection of new and used music is the largest in the City—in fact, they're the largest indie record store in the country—and you can easily kill an afternoon perusing the stacks. The San Francisco store has some listening stations; sadly, the **Berkeley Amoeba** (2455 Telegraph Avenue, 510-549-1125) lacks them. Meanwhile, enjoy free in-store performances

vinyl

Want to drop a request with your favorite DJ in a place where you can hear yourself think? Shop where the DJ's shop—in the Lower Haight. No less than five stores within three blocks (and one more just off the block) sell old-fashioned vinyl. From east to west, the spinners start at **Rooky Ricardo's** (448 Haight, 415-864-7526), which hosts a record swap the first Sunday of each month. Find more of the twelve-inch discs at:

Tweekin' Records 593 Haight 415-626-6995

Groove Merchant 687 Haight 415-252-5766

Jack's Record Cellar 254 Scott 415-431-3047

(check their website for the schedule or join the Amoeba Music Newsletter), the $1 bin, and the special "used" CDs: never-been-played copies dropped off by promoters.

Recycled Records (1377 Haight, 415-626-4075) also buys and sells used vinyl and CDs. Ditto for **Open Mind** (342 Divisadero, 415-621-2244), **Streetlight Records** (2350 Market, 415-282-8000; 3979 24th Street, 415-282-3550) and the punked-out **Mission Records** (2263 Mission, 415-285-1550), which occasionally hosts afternoon shows in the back room.

READ IT AGAIN, SAM

Those versed in the art of leisure have been known to read, read, then read some more, and when they're done, trade in those tomes for something new. Here are your stops if the library lets you down.

If **Green Apple Books** (506 Clement, 415-387-2272, greenapplebooks. com) didn't invent the buy-sell-trade concept, they're certainly among the foremost experts, after logging more than 35 years in the biz.

If you'd rather sell to **Russian Hill Bookstore** (2234 Polk, 415-929-0997), call first to confirm when the buyer will be in, and bring your art, history, or religion titles.

West Portal Books (111 West Portal, 415-731-5291) buys, sells, and trades, and is open every day. Bookmonger (2411 Clement, 415-397-2332) sells used books, paperbacks, and magazines.

Final stop on the circuit: **Phoenix Books & Records** (3850 24th Street, 415-821-3477), trading in art and out of print, literary and new titles. Cash and trade are offered here and at sister store **Dog Eared Books** (900 Valencia, 415-282-1901, dogearedbooks.com).

SHAVE AND A HAIRCUT

Lucky for the budget-conscious that Gene Hays at *Mes Amis* (193 Franklin, 415-558-7118) offers an affordable salon haircut—$55 for men, $60 for women—for a quality do. "People are tired of dropping $80 at other salons, so they come to me," Gene says.

Hip haircuts can be had for even cheaper if you're willing to live on the razor's edge by volunteering to be a hair model. *Blade Runners Hair Studio* (1792 Haight, 415-751-1723, bladerunnersstudio.com) shears human guinea pigs for $15 instead of $60 to $70. You'll need an appointment on a Monday afternoon.

HOT OFF THE PRESSES

Craving that new-book smell? Spend wisely: search behemoth Amazon. com first—then check these stores. They probably cost more, but a visit doubles as a shopping trip and a leisure destination, and they've got unique offerings.

• *City Lights Books* in North Beach (261 Columbus, 415-362-8193, citylights.com). Founded in 1953 by Peter Martin and beat poet Lawrence Ferlinghetti, City Lights has supported local writers for 50 years. Best for: world literature, small presses, zines, poetry or SF history.

• *Borderlands Books* (866 Valencia, 415-824-8203, borderlands-books.com). Serious book lovers run this place and they've been known to invite their artist friends over to create on site all day. Only for: science fiction, fantasy, horror.

• *Different Light* (489 Castro, 415-431-0891) A a part Castro history, Different Light has books, readings, and performances. Best for: LGBT titles.

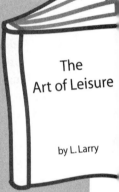

The
Art of Leisure

by L. Larry

DUDS TRADERS

Although clothing traders can be found throughout the City, upper Haight Street is the duds-trading epicenter.

Sell or swap at **Crossroads Trading Company** (1519 Haight, 415-355-0555; 1901 Fillmore, 415-775-8885; 2123 Market, 415-552-8743, crossroadstrading.com). You'll earn 35% of retail when you sell, and 50% when you trade. Ask about consignment, if that's the kind of transaction you'd prefer. **Buffalo Exchange** (1555 Haight, 415-431-7733; buffaloexchange.com) works much the same way, and they buy all day, with an eye towards vintage, punk and retro.

Wasteland (1660 Haight, 415-863-3150) or **Held Over** (1543 Haight, 415-864-0818) are other well-worn options, but your clothes had better be hip! To offload a more conservative wardrobe, try **Good Byes** (3483 Sacramento, 415-674-0151; 3464 Sacramento, 415-346-6388; goodbyessf. com), which sells clean and pressed clothing on consignment. You'll need to check back within 60 days to see if your finery has moved.

Discount Designs

Variously known as the warehouse district or the garment district, the large block South of Market between Brannan & Bryant, 2nd & 3rd Streets contains countless designer clothing outlets:

- Find $5 racks at the **Georgiou Outlet** (925 Bryant, 415-554-0150).

- Shop **Jeremy's** (2 South Park, 415-882-4929) if you absolutely must attend the Black and White Ball (see **Fairs & Fests**). They discount designer finery up to 50%.

Other Outlet Stores

Manufacturers' outlet stores can't advertise what they sell, but here's a hint: it's the same garb as at their retail stores, only it costs less. Some goods are new but slightly damaged, others are overstock or discontinued, but all of the leisure goods are covered and then some. Expect an odd cornucopia at awesome prices, although shopping fan Kelli Elliott advises, "It helps to know comparison pricing ahead of time."

Discount shopping guides are available at most major hotels, as are publications such as *The San Francisco Guide, Where,* and *Quickguide* that offer coupons and discounts. Or, if you'd like to take a shortcut, shop the **Nordstrom Rack** (555 9th Street, 415-934-1211).

If you don't find what you want within City limits, try the outlet malls: **Marina Square** (Marina Boulevard East exit off of I-880 in Oakland/San Leandro), **Petaluma Village Factory Outlets** (Petaluma Boulevard North, Old Redwood Highway exit off of US-101 in Petaluma, 707-778-9300), **Great Mall Of The Bay Area** (447 Great Mall Parkway in Milpitas, Montague Expressway exit off of Hwy 237, I-680, I-880 or US-101, 408-956-2033, 800-MALL-BAY), or the **Outlets at Gilroy** (Lleavesley Road exit off of US-101 in Gilroy, 408-842-3729, 800-866-5900).

Off-Price Clothes

A true shopper loves a bargain. For new clothes at fair prices, try:

- *Ross Dress for Less, 799 Market, 415-957-9222, four more San Francisco locations, see rossstores.com*

- *Old Navy Flagship, 801 Market, 415-344-0376; Potrero Center, 2300 16th Street, 415-255-6814, oldnavy.com*

- *Loehmann's, 222 Sutter, 415-982-3215*

- **Marshall's,** *901 Market, 415-974-5368*
- **Burlington Coat Factory,** *899 Howard, 415-495-7234*
- **Shoe Pavilion,** *899 Howard, Suite 101, 415-974-1821*
  three more San Francisco locations, see shoepavilion.com

Used Clothes

Vintage, pre-owned and pre-antiqued clothes can be not only washed by the pound, but bought by the pound—or the bagful.

The *Dollar Stretcher* newsletter reports one shopper's "bag sale" score: "I saw a woman stuff two wedding dresses in a bag. She told her friend, 'My daughter is getting married and if she does not like either of them I will just sell them at my garage sale for $20 each.'" The shopper's cost? A mere $4!

Fill your own sack for $8 a pound at **Clothes Contact** (473 Valencia, 415-621-3212)—only slightly pricier than wash and fold! Smile pretty at the clerks; sometimes they'll give you an even greater discount. For more, hit the City's other used-clothing mecca: The Haight. The first-in-the-phonebook **Aaardvark's** (that's right, three a's) Odd Ark

---

TIPS FROM THE VETERANS

To get the best pickings of a flea market or sidewalk sale, forget about breakfast. Most "early birds" hit an 8am garage sale closer to 7am, and some of the best flea market loot doesn't even make it off the flatbed! Take the opposite approach if your definition of success means getting the lowest price. Most sellers don't want a shred of that stuff going back into their house, so they slash prices or even give things away at the end of the day.

More tips from the experts:

- Plan a route if you want to hit more than one sale.
- Be reasonable and respectful in bargaining, but don't be afraid to offer a price lower than what's marked.
- Carry money in small bills. Garage sellers will love you for it, plus it will be a lot easier to use the "I've only got $5" tactic if you don't yank a 20-spot out of your pocket.
- Ask to plug in anything electronic to make sure it works before you pay for it.
- If you're looking for something large, make sure you have the means to lug it home.

(1501 Haight, 415-621-3141) specializes in denim, leather and crazy polyester shirts & dresses.

MORE RETAIL ALTERNATIVES

With time on your side, you can afford to wait for sales at garages and sidewalks. "There's a whole science to it," says shopper Eileen Sendrey, who bought a perfectly good laser printer at a garage sale for $10. "You're looking for people who really do want to clear out their closets. Every now and then you'll hit a total jackpot."

After you check the "garage & moving sales" section of **Craigslist**, track down the freebie paper, *Classified Flea Market*, or the *Chronicle* classifieds (online at sfgate.com/classifieds under "garage sales"). Then scout out signs on the street on the weekend. "I learned to judge the quality of a sale by the quality of the sign," says Eileen. "If it's just a cardboard sign with an arrow, chances are it's a junky sale. If it's an estate sale, however, you don't want to miss it."

If flea markets are more your bag (circus?), check out your options at fleamarketguide.com. On Sundays, the **Alemany Farmers' Market** becomes the **Alemany Flea Market** (100 Alemany, 415-647-9423). The **San Francisco Flea Market** (1651 Mission) runs all weekend. Weekends are good for swapping too, at the **Geneva Swap Meet** (at Geneva Drive-In near the Cow Palace, Daly City).

How about auctions? Join the mailing list of **A1 Auction Service** (a1auctionservice.com) for announcements of their live auctions, as well as instructions on how to hold your own auction—even a sound sample of the vocal skill peculiar to auctioneers: "chanting."

Skip The "Buying" Part
Sample Music For Free

A wealth of music is still available for download off the Internet, despite the crackdown. Dave Casuto suggests checking out new music at the listening stations at music stores like **Virgin Megastore** (2 Stockton @ Market, 415-397-4525, virgin.com/megastores/usa). "It's really rewarding, and it's free!" Find more listening stations at **Borders** (400 Post, 415-399-1633; Stonestown, 415-731-0665, bordersstores.com) or

---

pre•shopping

There's no reason to put your cultural education on freeze frame just because you don't have a lot of disposable income. Purchase alternatives (no, we're not talking about the five-finger discount) will keep your fingers snappin' and your head buzzin' with the most up-to-date music and literature, plus enable you to suss out your sporting goods before paying full retail price.

Tower Records (2525 Jones, 415-885-0500; 2280 Market, 415-621-0588 records, 415-255-5920 video; Stonestown Mall, 3205 20th Avenue, 2nd floor, 415-681-2001, towerrecords.com).

Borrow Your Sports Gear

Particularly if you're trying a new sport, borrow what you need from friends before you buy new gear. You'll get a much better idea of what you want if and when you decide to get your own stuff. And who knows, you may decide you don't even like the sport that much.

Go To The Library

Be it for books, magazines, video, or audio, "shopping" at the library can offer you choices you never knew existed (like the 1962 *Dolphin Guide to San Francisco*). The newly renovated **San Francisco Main Library** (100 Larkin, 415-557-4400, sfpl.org) near the Civic Center is open seven days a week, and boasts beautiful architecture as well as pleasant places to read. Patronize any of the 25 local library branches—visit the website to find one near you.

Thrifty Fillmore Street

Amidst tony home furnishing (read: furniture) and designer clothing stores, you'll find no less than six pre-owned goods dealers among the **Fillmore Street Shops** (fillmoreshop.com, a subset of sfbayshop. com):

- **Next-To-New Shop**
  (run by the Junior League)
  2226 Fillmore, 415-567-1627
  Peddles fine clothing and even some used couture.

SECONDHAND PRIZE PURCHASES

Jane shopped a garage sale and found a clean, intact and nearly-new 9'x12' area rug for only $10!

The worktable that Serafina bought at Busvan's going-out-of-business closeout sale cost only $5!

Foronda shopped at Goodwill and found a bag for his new laptop for 1/10th of what he would have paid even at a discount office supplies store. It was a perfect fit!

SHOPPING ONLINE

Spot a garage sale item that's peanuts to you but would be a treasure to someone else? Don't be afraid to buy it now and then sell it online. Shop for new and used goods using online auction and community sites like **Craigslist** (craigslist.org), one of the most efficient ways to buy or sell just about anything you need. And don't forget, Craigslist offers a space to post free things, which is great for books, art supplies and lawn-care items.

The larger **eBay** (ebay.com) is a good place to shop for bargains as well as auction off your goods. EBay's little sister, half.com (half.com), markets others' used goods to you at substantial discounts. Amazon.com (amazon.com) sells much more than books, these days—scroll to the Bottom of the Page for special one-day deals on all sorts of stuff.

(Thrifty Fillmore Street cont'd)

- **Repeat Performance**
(run by the San Francisco Symphony)
2436 Fillmore, 415-563-3123

- **Victorian House Thrift Shop**
2033 Fillmore, 415-567-3478
Benefits the California Pacific Medical Center.

- **Goodwill**
1700 Fillmore, 415-441-2159
Sells all clothes and furniture at 50% off during occasional half-price Wednesday Sales.

- **Departures from the Past**
2028 Fillmore, 415-885-3377

- **Seconds To Go**
2252 Fillmore, 415-563-7806

FOOD, GLORIOUS FOOD

All that bargain-hunting can sure work up an appetite! After you've studied the food-shopping techniques from the **Finance** chapter, put them to use at these fine food establishments, or just grow your own! (See "Grow Your Own" on p. 212)

Grocery Stores

Trader Joe's (555 9th Street Retail Center, 415-863-1292; 3 Masonic @ Geary, 415-346-9964; 401 Bay, 415-351-1013, traderjoes.com) is a good place to start. TJ's is all about good deals on food, which they extend by buying in large volume directly from suppliers and saving space, and therefore rent, with those funky check-out stands.

If you have the storage space, **Costco** (450 10th Street, 415-626-4388, costco.com) is great for bulk purchases—your savings should cover the $45 annual membership fee.

Leave some room in your pantry for the 20-lb. bag of rice, available at any of the Chinese groceries on Clement Street. Clement Street is likewise a great place to find inexpensive fresh produce. For live birds and fish, head to Stockton Street in Chinatown.

Food Co-Ops

Food cooperatives often buy food in bulk, saving money for members who take turns with food pickups, deliveries and other tasks. Unfortunately, we could find only two within city limits.

The first, **Other Avenues Community Food Store** (3930 Judah, 415-661-7475) is an Outer Sunset consumer cooperative with a mostly volunteer staff. The other, the **Rainbow Grocery Cooperative** (1745 Folsom, 415-863-0620, rainbowgrocery.org), has its own spin on the co-op concept: because its workers, rather than its shoppers, own and operate the business, you must apply for a job and be hired and then go through the rigors of their membership process to have a voice in decision making. Their food is organic and largely locally produced.

Farmers' Markets

Of the more than 3,000 farmers' markets in the state, San Francisco's **Ferry Plaza Farmers' Market** (One Ferry Plaza Building, Market & Embarcadero, 415-291-3276, ferryplazafarmersmarket.com) is one of the best, but also one of the most expensive. This market attracts more than 60 farmers even in the winter off-season, and more than 100 between April and November. Highlights include premium fruits and vegetables, plus a Saturday chef's program in summer that features live demonstrations from trendy local chefs, complete with samples for the audience. It's open on Tuesdays (10am-2pm), Thursdays (4pm-6pm, spring and fall only) and Saturdays (8am-2pm), plus there's a garden market on Sundays (10am-2pm, spring and fall only). Permanent foodie shops (including Acme Bread, Cowgirl Creamery and Scharffen Berger Chocolate) are inside.

The **Alemany Farmers' Market** (100 Alemany, 415-647-9423) is another San

furniture

Sprinkled along hectic and non-descript Van Ness Avenue are a series of furniture retailers. Some are uber chic and not exactly for the budget conscious. But mixed in between the Scandinavian sleek and ultra-modern are some real bargains.

If you need some furniture accessories—and if you can weather the lack of customer service—you can find unbelievable deals (such as a night stand for $15 or a sofa bed for $95) on used furniture from luxury hotels at *National Furniture Liquidators* (1110 Van Ness, 415-775-9999; 2301 Mission, 415-643-8888).

Francisco landmark and a much cheaper deal, if less organic. It's been operating in its current location since 1947. Sicilian immigrant John Brucato, the "father of the Alemany Market," took on the grocery lobby and won in order to launch the forerunner of this market during World War II. You can now shop there on Saturdays from dawn to mid-afternoon (6am-2pm). In addition to vegetables, it also has a fish market, live poultry, eggs, honey, olive oil and other staples.

If Wednesdays (7am-5:30pm) or Sundays (7am-5pm) are your shopping days, head to the **Heart of the City** at Civic Center Plaza (Market between 7th and 8th Streets, 415-558-9455).

Grow Your Own

Crags Court, Michelangelo, White Crane Springs, Potrero del Sol and Hooker Alley. No, they're not new restaurants, they're San Francisco community gardens—places where neighbors get together to make use of even the smallest patch of vacant land to grow their own.

Anyone can start a community garden, sometimes known as a "pea patch." For more information, call the **San Francisco Recreation and Parks Department** at (415) 581-2541

Even if you live in a yardless apartment, you can grow herbs in a window box. You could find one at a garage sale, or build one yourself. If you're lucky enough to have a yard, you can take an afternoon or two to plant a garden, and be grazing on fresh homegrown tomatoes and lettuce soon after that.

Dependable sources for seeds, dirt, and other supplies, including grown plants, are the **Sloat Garden Centers** (2700 Sloat, 415-566-4415; 327 3rd Avenue, 415-752-1614) and **Three Bees Nursery** (1921 Clement, 415-387-5608).

Of course, if you're being a smart and thrifty leisure-seeking gardener, you'll want to bone up on seed sharing, which is the novel idea of getting seeds from your fellow gardeners and sharing your own seeds with them. Are you buying organic produce right now? Keep the seeds! You can plant them in your own yard, or use them as a trade good. And remember: people give away dirt, mulch, and other gardening essentials away for free—check Craigslist.

SHOPPING AS RECREATION

Feeling the urge to create? Project stores such as the **Terra Mia Decorative Art Studio** (1314 Castro, 415-642-9911, terramia.net)—the original glaze-your-own ceramics store in Northern California—are good places to wile away some hours and leave with a relatively functional piece of art, in proportion to your skill level, of course.

The do-it-yourself theme can apply to clothes as well as dishes if you've got the knack and a workable sewing machine. Find fabulous discounts on fabric and notions at:

- *Fabrix,* 101 Clement, 415-221-4111

- *Fabric Outlet,* 2109 Mission, 415-552-4525

- *Discount Fabrics,* 1432 Haight, 415-621-5584; 2315 Irving, 415-564-7333; *warehouse & largest retail location:* 525 4th Street, 415-495-5337

beading

If your goal is to get a necklace for less, you probably won't save much money by beading it yourself, but if you size it up in terms of entertainment, you'll see that it's a much better value per hour than most movies. Six hours spent beading can be a valuable lesson in delayed gratification. You'll wind up with something personalized, to boot.

First, raid garage sales and cannibalize broken necklaces from your own jewelry box. If you gotta shop, *Surprise Party!* (1900-A Fillmore, 415-771-8550) carries beads, shells, and small Chinese antiques. . The stock at *General Bead* (637 Minna, 415-255-2323) fills two entire floors, yet perhaps the most gorgeous imported stones reside in the bins of the *Bead Store* (417 Castro, 415-861-7332).

Start with something simple if you need a refresher, like curtains or a duvet cover. Heck, sew two sheets together and get your duvet cover that way. Find them at the **Linen Factory Outlet** (1001 Clement @ 11th Avenue, 415-221-8598).

Maybe you're the craftier type. Scrounge up a project for yourself at **Scroungers' Center for Reusable Art** Parts (SCRAP) (801 Toland, entrance on Newcomb, 415-647-1746, scrap-sf.org), where the selection of paper, cloth, metal, wood, and glass bits changes daily, depending on what's been donated. Most parts are dirt cheap. **Pearl Arts and Crafts** (969 Market, 415-357-1400) might lead you to an artsy creation as well. We'd be remiss if we didn't add **FLAX Art & Design** (1699 Market, 415-552-2355, flaxart.com), the supply store for artists.

SPORTING GOODS

If you're going to recreate, you might need to gear up. One category of exercise is so simple and straightforward that all you'll need is a good pair of shoes—and the right duds. This would be the walking-hiking-jogging-running category.

You'll find everything from trail shoes to track spikes at **On the Run** (1310 9th Avenue, 415-665-5311). Don't be overwhelmed by the variety of choices. Remember, you can only wear one pair at a time.

THE CAMPER'S CORNER

"If shopping for a polar expedition, the following doesn't apply," advises veteran camper Kelli Elliott, "but most of the time, *Target* (5001 Junipero Serra Boulevard, Colma, 650-992-8433; 133 Serramonte Center, Daly City, 650-755-2393) is hard to beat for the basics. They usually have great prices and a good selection of inflatable mattresses, ice chests, tents, lanterns, folding chairs, camp grills, and insect repellant. I was surprised and impressed by their sleeping bag selection last season."

Seeking the requisite sunshower for your first Burning Man expedition? You can order one online at *shop-discount.com* or *campmor.com*, or check out a hard copy at *REI* (840 Brannan, 415-934-1938, rei.com), also good for backpacks, sleeping bags, and outerwear.

Lombardi's (1600 Jackson, 888-456-6223, lombardisports.com) is the favored choice for general sporting goods, with a strong selection of ski, snowboard, and all-around sports apparel. You'll pay full retail here, but they'll let you test drive a mountain bike by riding it around on their roof.

For discounted items and a good selection of athletic footwear, track down **The Sports Basement** (Mason Street, Building 610, the Presidio; 1415 16th St., 415-437-0100, sportsbasement.com), but do beware.

"If you haven't been to Sports Basement, you must check it out for yourself," says Kelli Elliott. "It's awesome!" But she adds, "Warning: do not visit unless you don't mind spending because they have such cool stuff, it's really hard to get in and out without lightening the wallet."

Kayaks probably don't top your "need to have" list, but if you're looking for a used one, try rummaging.com, which carries closeout, overstock, demo and liquidation kayaks at discounts up to 50%.

Roaring Mouse Cycles (1352 Irving, 415-753-6272, roaringmousecycles.com) comes highly recommended and sells road and mountain bikes, plus all the latest accessories. The spartan **Pedal Revolution** (3085 21st Street, 415-641-1264) peddles pedals and other parts that are both new and used, and offers a selection of new, custom-built and refurbished bicycles.

Out of the area sporting goods outlets include:

- *Any Mountain Outdoor Outlet, 2990 7th Street, Berkeley*
- *North Face Outlet, 1238 5th Street, Berkeley*
- *Ujena Swimwear, 1931A Old Middlefield Way, Mountain View*
- *Wildnerness Exchange, 1407 San Pablo Avenue, Berkeley*

chinatown: gifts for everyone!

Are there more Chinese-Americans in San Francisco than in China? There are certainly more t-shirts bearing likenesses of the Golden Gate Bridge. At five for $14, they make altogether appropriate gifts for your out-of-town friends. So do $2 slippers and $15 silk pyjamas.

Other treasures to be mined on the side streets: linen tablecloths, jade jewelry, plastic toys, herbal pharmaceuticals, paper lanterns, imported teas, and bargain-priced cookware.

LEISURE SHOPPING GRAND PRIZE

And the winner is... the Mission District! A stroll down Valencia Street alone will take you past at least a dozen leisure-friendly venues, such as:

 Abandoned Planet Bookstore *518 Valencia, 415-861-4695* Features two resident cats and comfy chairs and sofas, even a piano.

 Community Thrift *623 Valencia, 415-861-4910* CT donates part of your purchase price to whichever one of the 200 different charities on their list was designated by whomever donated your item.

 826 Valencia *826 Valencia, 415-642-5905, 826valencia.org/store* It's San Francisco's only independent pirate supply store!

Find tons of grocers on Mission Street itself, plus oodles of discount stores including the **99¢ & Over Discount Outlet** (2205 Mission, 415-647-9495), **Giant Value** (2558 Mission, 415-647-5382; formerly known as the "99 Cents Only Store" but not to be confused with the store above, trust us), and **One Dollar One Store** (1985 Mission, 415-626-1238), where everything really *is* just $1.

Wacky Mission District thrift stores include **Thrift Town** (2101 Mission, 415-861-1132), **Goodwill** (2279 Mission, 415-826-5759; Mission & South Van Ness, 415-575-2240), **Mission Thrift** (2330 Mission, 415-821-9560), and the **Salvation Army** (1500 Valencia, 415-643-8040).

PACK IT UP
As the typical unemployed budget would dictate, you're not likely to head home from these expeditions with bushels-full of bargains. That's okay, now's the time to travel light. Find out how to turn your sabbatical into time on the road in the next chapter.

CHAPTER 5
HIT THE ROAD

The world is a book,
and those who do not travel read only a page.

~ Saint Augustine

THERE'S no denying the genuine wonder and excitement of a jaunt overseas. If you're already a seasoned traveler with extra pages in your passport, this is hardly breaking news. Yet surprisingly few people take the opportunity, beyond a couple of weeks' vacation, to explore our world for an extended period.

Meaningful travel, in our opinion, educates you and expands your consciousness. It takes many forms, but two major factors unquestionably affect the depth of your trip: the duration of the journey, and how comfortable and familiar the surroundings are.

Here's a depressing statistic: numbers from the U.S. Department of State suggest that only about twenty percent of Americans have valid passports. Is it any wonder that we as a nation are sometimes baffled by other countries' views of the United States, when just one in five of us are crossing our borders to see what's out there? Our national ignorance of the world's affairs can have dangerous effects on international politics and policy. Consider this: the United States is routinely outvoted at the United Nations *one-hundred-forty* to *five*. And according to a University of Maryland poll in September 2004, thirty of our thirty-five closest allies oppose U.S. policies.

This leads us to our second premise: not only is travel extremely beneficial for your personal growth and exploration, but it also serves a higher purpose—increased cultural understanding, tolerance, and goodwill. As Mark Twain so keenly observed, "Travel is fatal to prejudice, bigotry, and narrow-mindedness, and many of our people need it sorely on these accounts. Broad, wholesome, charitable views of men and things cannot be acquired by vegetating in one little corner of the earth all one's lifetime." So think of travel as a significant responsibility—to yourself and those around you.

We strongly believe that travel can change your perspective on life, and many we spoke to agreed. Ariella Quatra, a film and television producer from San Francisco, shifted her outlook during her recent journey to Southeast Asia. "After eight months in Thailand, Laos and Cambodia, my perspective on what 'the good life' is has changed," she said. "I've learned that the value of mindful practice, everyday appreciation and gratitude is my personal key to leading a fulfilling and enriching life." Well said—we can only nod in universal agreement.

How long should your trip be? Only you can decide, but keep in mind that many before you have gone away a year or more and survived (and thrived) to tell the tale. Just take a look at the Aussies, known to go on walkabout for years at a time, if you need inspiration. Worried about marring your resume? Don't be. Savvy employers understand now more than ever that people need breaks from their day-to-day work. Think you're too old to travel, or have too many commitments at home? You're not, and you don't. Couples and families grow closer through their travel experiences. Homes can be sold or rented, bills can be paid in advance, pets cared for, children shipped off to boarding school (okay, we're kidding here). The point is, you'll always find excuses for not going, but how will these excuses sound ten or twenty years from now?

This chapter doesn't purport to be a comprehensive travel guide; we merely make some humble suggestions to get you started based on our own experiences and those of many other travelers. If none of them rev your engine, by all means—set your own itinerary. The important point is this: if you're fortunate enough to have the opportunity, take off and go!

DOMESTIC TRAVEL

As enticing as international travel may be, we often overlook great travel possibilities right in our own backyards. Considering that the United States is one of the top tourist destinations in the world, and that domestic travel is generally less expensive, you might try exploring down the street before you journey to the far side of the world.

Road Trips

Finally, you're free! And you have piles of time on your hands—but maybe not piles of loot. Enter the good old American road trip, an economical way to spark the wandering spirit. With the right car, it's a cheap alternative to air travel that can relieve stress, clear your head and rejuvenate your spirit.

Matt Green, a former software executive, found his post-work road trips to the desert rather soothing, to put it mildly. "Staying in a rat-shit hotel," he said, "I slept better than I did in those $350-a-night first-class hotels I stayed at when I was working."

America is one vast network of open roads, so the routes we suggest are only a starting point. And if your starting point isn't your hometown? Fly out to your ground zero and then buy or rent a car; invite friends who live near your launching point and use their car; or use a vehicle transportation company.

Wherever you begin and whatever method you choose to get there, don't forget to make a few wrong turns. You never know where they might lead you.

---

hoping to stretch your travel dollar?

Look up old friends. Surely they'll invite you to stay if you promise to do the dishes!

Consider bed & breakfasts. *BedandBreakfast.com* (bedandbreakfast.com) lists over 27,000 B&Bs; see also *Bed and Breakfast Inns of North America* (inntravels. com).

Arrange a homestay using *GlobalFreeloaders.com* (globalfreeloaders.com). The catch? You have to be willing to host from time to time as well.

Contemplate camping. There are more than 100,000 campsites in the U.S. alone. Bring a sun shower to freshen up in the morning, and you'll smell ahead of the game. See *Reserve America* for help (reserveamerica.com).

Load up the cooler! It'll shrink your food costs. Besides, where else are you going to keep your cold ones for the end of a long day's drive?

Sing songs in the car. Will it save you money? No, but everyone likes a sing-a-long, and it's one way to keep the driver awake!

IN SEARCH OF A HOMESTEAD

Think the days of homesteading in the Wild West are over? Think again. The stakes may have risen a bit, but the search continues, at least for those with an adventurous spirit.

Mike and Angela Sarmiento had always dreamed of building their own cabin in the woods, someplace "with a stream nearby filled with trout." They knew they'd have to raise some capital for their dream, so they bought an old home at below market price, restored it, then sold it when the market was hot. They squirreled away most of their profit for their dream property-to-be, but used a small portion to buy a sweet camper trailer that they could tow with their SUV.

Along with their beloved golden retriever, Kenzie, they spent several months driving through California, Nevada, Wyoming, Montana, Idaho, British Columbia, Washington and Oregon in search of the perfect homestead. Because the trailer was fully self-contained, they were able to prepare their own food and sleep in the trailer each night, regardless of where they went.

"The night we got engaged we were soaking in a tub, drawing out the plans for our cabin on a paper napkin," said Angela. "Two hours later the napkin was full of drawings and getting a little ragged from splashes of water…. Now we've been driving around looking for our homestead, but an architect friend of ours was kind enough to replace our tattered napkin with some real floor plans."

At last check, the couple was still merrily on the road in their quest. When they do find their dream property, they intend to sell the trailer and start building their cabin.

Of course, maybe they'll try to hang onto the trailer to keep the road close at hand

The West Coast Trail

Total Distance: *1,400 miles*
Drive Time: *3 days (one way)*
Start / End: *Vancouver / San Diego*

Pack up your vehicle and head out on the Pacific Coast Highway for a spectacular West Coast tour.

If you head south to San Diego from Seattle or even Vancouver, the climate will improve as you go. Take advantage of the many excellent coastal campsites along the way, and don't miss Mt. Rainier, Mt. St. Helens, Hood River, Humboldt, Santa Barbara, or La Jolla.

The Right Coast

Total Distance: *1,600 miles*
Drive Time: *3 days (one way)*
Start / End: *Portland, ME / Miami, FL*

Traipsing the eastern seaboard may seem at first glance to be a bland trip through miles and miles of urban wasteland. But look again, and you'll find a journey through American history, filled with quirky beach towns and fishing villages, and mixed with provincial charm and tradition. Beginning with some fresh Maine lobster, you can crawl your way down through the urban centers of Boston, Providence and New York, then ease your way into the quieter shores of Virginia, the Carolinas, and Georgia, and finish with a flourish in Florida.

Get Your Kicks...

Total Distance: *2,100 miles*
Drive Time: *4 days (one way)*
Start / End: *Los Angeles / Chicago*

Get hip to this timely tip: although it's no longer "The Mother Road" John

---

westys @ the wal-mart

Autumn and Joe Ervin drove from Northern Illinois to Key Largo (that's 1,600 miles!) in their trusty "Westy," a 1984 VW Vanagon Westfalia camper. They lived on $20 a day, plus whatever gas their economical ride consumed (19 mpg). Instead of burning their cash on hotels, they cooked and slept in the Westy each night (which comes complete with a fold-out queen-sized bed)—with a little twist.

On a tip from friends, they scouted out all the Wal-Mart Superstores along their route, and camped each night in the store parking lots. They weren't alone. Open 24x7, with clean bathrooms and supplies to end all supplies, Wal-Marts have become de facto pit stops for mobile campers. And if you wake up with a craving for a late-night snack, well, then, you're covered. No showers, so the Ervins "improvised."

"Owning a Westfalia means instant membership into the 'Westy Club,'" the couple told us. "In the mornings, we often found ourselves encompassed by other Westy travelers who would come and chat." The Ervins rewarded themselves with an $80 snorkeling trip when they arrived in Key Largo. We hope it doubled as a shower!

Steinbeck described in *The Grapes of Wrath*, Route 66 is still the iconic U.S. road trip, showcasing Americana at its finest. Immortalized in song and TV, "Historic Route 66" has connected Chicago to Los Angeles for almost 80 years. Put on some Nat King Cole and do what the man says—get your kicks.

You can travel this time warp in either direction. For the best views and the full historical experience, take a convertible—or even a motorcycle! To get yourself tuned up, motor on over to **Route66.com** (route66.com). To hook up with a phat Harley hog, see **Route 66 Riders** (route66riders.com).

The Coast-to-Coaster
Total Distance: *3,000 miles*
Drive Time: *4-6 days (one way)*
Start / End: *Newport, OR / Boston, MA (US-20);*
Oakland, CA / Ocean City, MD (US-50)

Everyone should drive across the U.S. at least once. Think of it as a rite of passage! For a speed run (set that radar detector), use the major interstates funded during the Eisenhower administration, such as I-70, I-80, or I-90. For a more leisurely trip, take the roads less traveled, such as "The Loneliest Road" (US-50) or "The Oregon Trail" (US-20). The Oregon Trail follows paths taken by early American settlers from the sandy, highly refined shores of Cape Cod to the rugged crunchiness of the Oregon coastline, with a little bit of everything in between. Don't rent any barrels at Niagara Falls but say hey to Yogi as you pass Wyoming's Yellowstone National Park. The two-lane US-50 is less dramatic, but will steer you through a fine and dandy sampling of small town America on your way from San Francisco to coastal Maryland.

Southern Man
Total Distance: *2,400 miles*
Drive Time: *4 days (one way)*
Start / End: *San Diego, CA / Tybee, GA*

The southern states boast some of America's most distinctive cultures, from Texan to Creole to Old South genteel. US-80 (not to be confused with the larger Interstate-80), stretches from southern California to Georgia, and passes through just about every southern state in between. You'll traverse the great plains of New Mexico and Texas, then find the true heart of

National Park Loop
Total Distance: *variable*
Drive Time: *10-28 days, depending on route and number of stops*

There's a reason people come from around the world to see our national parks—they're the best on the planet. Tour the parks of the west to finally understand the meaning of purple mountain majesties!

Kick off a giant loop along the north coast of California at Redwood National Park, home to some of the world's tallest trees. Continue along the Oregon coast and into Washington, where Mt. St. Helens (now a National Volcanic Monument), Mt. Rainier, Olympic, and North Cascades National Parks await you. Then cut across to Montana's Glacier National Park, and finally down to Wyoming for Jellystone—er, Yellowstone—the granddaddy of them all. The dazzling Grand Tetons beckon a short distance to the south.

When you reach southern Utah, break out the mountain bike and take your pick of parks, which include Arches, Canyonlands, Glen Canyon, Bryce Canyon, Capitol Reef, and Zion. The Grand Canyon lies across Arizona and it is, despite the crowds, undeniably spectacular.

If you're feeling lucky when you reach Vegas, slap your money on black. If not, avoid the magnetic pull and point yourself southwest to California's Death Valley, with its fantastic desert ecosystems. Continue north through Sequoia and Kings Canyon, and finish your journey in Yosemite, the crown jewel of the national park system.

parks prep

Can't wait to gas up the ol' family truckster? Make sure the time is right.

Professional tour director Tom Williams advises visiting in the fall. "The summer crowds are gone, the students are all back in school, and you get the great fall colors with cooler temperatures in the southwest." Avoid July and August, he says, unless you like it really hot.

Tom recommends a National Parks Pass ($50) with a Golden Eagle hologram ($15 extra) for entrance to any national park or land managed by U.S. government agencies.

To buy one or research your journey, see the *National Park Service ParkNet* (nps. gov).

PARK iT FOR AWHiLE

Steve Yung turned misfortune into opportunity when he was laid off. "Sometimes you just need to look for the opportunities when life hands you something unexpected," he told us. "When I was laid off, I was worried for a while, but then I saw it as a chance to do something that I had always thought about, but didn't think I would ever get the time to do—visit the National Parks." The road trip reinforced an old travel adage for Steve. "The journey was truly as important as the destination," he said. "To be able to not live by a schedule and literally stop off at the side of the road to smell the roses was a great feeling.... I came back refreshed and in the best shape of my life."

Dixie, from the Mississippi Delta through the Appalachian Mountains, finishing near Savannah, Georgia.

Hank, a California native, recalls fondly his detours in southern Texas, "floating down the Rio Grande on inner tubes, and sneaking across the border into Mexico to drink at local cantinas." Time your trip right, and you can swing through New Orleans for Mardi Gras, and help the local economy get back on its feet in the Crescent City.

Local Road Trips

If you don't have the time or the interest for a long road trip, you might enjoy a Sunday drive—or maybe even a *Monday* drive. You can make these road trip "quickies" in an afternoon or a weekend directly from San Francisco.

Santa Cruz

Drive time: 1-2 hours.

The drive from San Francisco to Santa Cruz along Highway One is curvy and coastal, and all the more exhilarating in a convertible or a Porsche (know anyone with a convertible Porsche?). You'll pass the scenic Pigeon Point lighthouse along the way, as well as the Año Nuevo nature reserve, home to California's largest population of elephant seals. The wonderful beach community of Santa Cruz boasts natural beauty and warmer weather than surrounding areas, plus an increasingly cosmopolitan nightlife.

Find out what to do in **Santa Cruz County** at santacruz.org.

Lake Tahoe

Drive time: 3-4 hours.

World class skiing and boarding in the wintertime; hiking, biking and camping in the summertime—Tahoe has it all, even ballooning! Stellar accommodations are available in all price ranges. Save money and increase fun by renting a cabin with a larger group. Any inch of the shore will do—the lake doesn't have a bad angle.

Explore virtually all that is Tahoe, including up-to-the-minute weather reports, at tahoe.com.

Point Reyes

Drive time: 1 hour.

Point Reyes National Seashore is a local treasure. Dozens of land and marine mammals and almost half of all North American bird species have been sighted within the boundaries of this biologically diverse coastal area. Hike, camp, or just crash out on the vast beaches, and be home in time for happy hour.

Find more information about Point Reyes on the **National Park Services** website: nps.gov/pore.

Wine Country

Drive time: 1 hour to Napa or Sonoma.

"Tempting beginning; full-bodied middle; long, strong finish," she purred with her eyes closed. A romance novel? Not quite. Just another connoisseur enjoying the sumptuous wines of Napa Valley. A single day spent visiting the wineries can improve your wine knowledge and have you expounding like the experts.

Be warned: most wineries charge for tasting these days, anywhere from $3–$10 for a flight of several wines. Tours, however, are generally free, and usually end with at least one healthy swig on the house.

For free tasting in Napa, try family-owned **Sullivan Vineyards** (1090 Galleron Road, Rutherford, 877-244-7337, sullivanwine.com). In Sonoma, swing by the **Benziger Family Winery** (707-935-3000, benziger. com) for their popular (and free) tram tour.

Plan your assault on either valley by typing its name into your browser: napavalley.com or sonomavalley.com.

leisure vineyards
star of leisure
1996
California Table Wine

49-Mile Scenic Drive

Drive time: 2 hours (without stopping).

San Francisco's 49-Mile Scenic Drive is one of those city-sponsored tourist routes that attempts to "help" you see all the sights. But what the heck, the sights in San Francisco are many, and this is one way to pack them all into one afternoon.

The original 49-Mile Drive, designed for the 1939 Golden Gate International Exposition, began at City Hall and finished at the then newly-opened Treasure Island. Today's revised route is a giant loop with no real beginning or end. The blue and white seagull signs help fly you along, but aren't always reliable—several areas are tricky to navigate, and the signs don't always match published maps. The route does hit pretty much all the major City tourist sites, if that's your speed.

For a fitness adventure, try tackling the route by bicycle! See **Chapter 7** under "Biking" for details.

General Tips for the Road

A little bit of planning will drive you a long way on the open highway. Tom Williams, professional tour guide and road trip expert, recommends cribbing from organized tour companies for free itinerary ideas. **TrekAmerica** 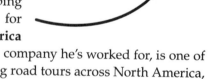 (800-221-0596, trekamerica.com), a company he's worked for, is one of his faves. After 30 years of running road tours across North America, they may have learned a thing or two.

Better yet, says Tom, consider going on one of the treks yourself. "They are hidden gems for people in the U.S. The company markets primarily to international tourists, but the trips are a great way for Americans to see their own country and to meet people from all over the world at the same time."

Tom also recommends the off-season to avoid crowds, save money and (sometimes) score better weather.

"Avoid hotels if at all possible," says U.S. tour guide Greg Blaug. "Beaches, campgrounds and hostels are always cheaper, and much more exciting."

Greg also strongly advises travelers keep an open mind. "No matter how well worked out your travel plans are, it's always nice to be able to change them when something else comes along."

the ultimate road trip

Bret Livingston and Patty Segar thought they'd unwind with a quick drive after they quit their jobs—across the North and South American continents. So they took a year, and hit the road.

The two outrigged their Toyota truck with a camper shell, complete with sleeping quarters, a propane stove, camping supplies, food, water, surfboards, snowboards and various other sundries they thought might come in handy on a leisurely one-year drive. They gassed up in northern Alaska and cruised the entire length of the Pacific coastline. Along the way, they encountered crazy bush pilots, plane crashes, gun-yielding banditos, over-sexed field workers, defective roof racks, extorting border agents, ornery customs officials, stomach-churning ferry rides and dubious characters of questionable legal standing.

Despite its challenges, the trip was the adventure of their lives and they wouldn't change it for anything. What's more, it didn't cost them a dime career-wise—they each went back to the same company that they'd worked for before they left. Let that be a lesson for the worrywart in us all!

"Travel and celebrate your free time while you got it," say Bret and Patty, who are proud new parents back in the States, "because it's sure to change when you have a kid!"

the green tortoise: an alternative to driving

The Green Tortoise has been running adventure travel buses since 1974, and "adventure" is truly the operative word. The trips are known for their communal atmosphere, with custom sleeper coaches, activities and group meals. "This is not gonna be one of those vacations where all you did was sit by the pool in the daytime and drink beer at night, only to forget all about it a few years later," says Greg "Bernie" Blaug. "If you're ready for fantastic scenery, beautiful people, quality homemade food and a memorable experience, we're ready for you." He should know—he became a driver and trip leader after falling in love with the trips as a passenger.

Based in San Francisco, where they also own and operate a youth hostel, the Green Tortoise steers regional, national, and international journeys. This ain't your average Greyhound, so be prepared to have some fun on "the only trip of its kind."

Green Tortoise Adventure Travel
800-867-8647
greentortoise.com

Road Trip Resources

Planning

The book *Road Trip USA* by Jamie Jensen can help drive your planning (check roadtripusa.com) but for more extensive resources and support, consider joining an auto club. You generally pay an annual fee, but will more than make it back with benefits such as maps, insurance, travel planning, and emergency roadside assistance for that inevitable breakdown on a lonesome highway.

AAA's local affiliate is the **California State Automobile Association** (150 Van Ness, 415-565-2141, csaa.com), the preeminent auto club in California. But there's a new kid on the engine block: **Better World Club** (betterworldclub. com). Better World prides itself on being the nation's first environmentally aware auto club, offering eco-friendly services such as hybrid car rentals, eco-travel, and an innovative bicycle roadside assistance program, in addition to benefits similar to AAA's.

Car Buying

Spare your own car the dings and dents by buying (and later selling) a used one. For deals on used cars, try **Autobytel** (autobytel.com), **Craigslist** (craigslist. org), **PoliceAuctions.com** (policeauctions.com), or the old-fashioned classified ads **San Francisco Chronicle Classifieds** (415-777-7777). The **Kelley Blue Book** (kbb.com) will tell you how much to pay—and it's free (the site, not the cars). Look for a reliable make such as a Toyota or Honda, or something easy to repair (anything old and American).

Driveaway Into The Wild Blue Yonder

If it was good enough for Jack Kerouac, it might work for you: drive someone else's car for a vehicle transportation company, sometimes referred to as a "driveaway."

It's pretty basic: you put down a security deposit (normally $300 cash) refundable upon "successful" arrival, and take one of their cars from point A to point B. They'll even pick up the first tank of gas. After that, you need only pay for gas and stick to a pre-determined time and mileage schedule, roughly 400 miles per day—which unfortunately won't get you to Mexico. Leisure local Tim drove from Denver to San Diego. "I scored a brand-new Mustang convertible," he said. "It was so sweet!"

Auto Driveaway Co. (800-346-2277, autodriveaway.com) is the biggest and best-known company, with offices throughout the U.S. and even a few in Canada.

Skipping The Road Altogether

Okay, so you can't drive forever. Eventually, you might tire of the wind in your hair, not to mention the bugs in your teeth. Time to spread your wings and fly!

Does a jumbo jet mean a jumbo fare? Not any more. In fact, you can proudly release your inner miser when it comes to airfares these days. Gregg Brockway, a co-founder of **Hotwire** (hotwire.com), says, "Americans are putting more of an emphasis on saving money. 'Cheap' isn't a dirty word anymore. These days, cheap is like a badge of honor—people will talk endlessly about how they saved twenty dollars on a hotel room or fifty dollars on airfare. They like to feel smart that they paid less than the next person." So go ahead, feel smart. Make our day!

Indeed, Hotwire is *the* central resource for finding deals on domestic airfare. As for the domestic airlines themselves, the smart money (not to mention the value) is on the young guns **Southwest Airlines** (southwest.com) and **JetBlue Airways** (jetblue.com). They've both managed to come up with a novel concept: flying people around the U.S. for cheap.

INTERNATIONAL TRAVEL

"Through travel I first became aware of the outside world; it was through travel that I found my own introspective way into becoming a part of it," wrote American author Eudora Welty. International travel can teach us as much about ourselves as it can the world around us. If you have the ways and means, the world is out there waiting for you. We highly encourage taking off for several months or longer if you can, but even a week abroad is better than none.

All of our travel ideas would fill another book; below are just a few uniquely suited for the leisure seeker or non-employed wanderer—inexpensive travel, a sophisticated travelers' infrastructure, or opportunities for volunteering, work or study.

As you travel, remember that you are both a pilgrim and an ambassador of leisure. Take some time to learn about your destination before you go. You can start your schooling on the **U.S. Department of State** website (state.gov, search for "Country Background Notes" under "Travel and Living Abroad").

And take some time, period. Most of the world doesn't operate at the pace of the American office drone. Everything takes longer, especially when you don't speak the language. You're on a journey, and you're on your own clock. Enjoy it.

Getting Started

A trip of a thousand miles begins with one step—to the library. Avoid the bookstores and the plethora of high-priced budget travel guides if you'd rather spend your hard-earned cash on that gilded Balinese headdress or another week at a hostel set in the rarified air of the Andes. Please, make your mother proud and return the books to the library when you're done.

The best book to start with, hands down, is *Consumer Reports Travel Well for Less*. With the objectivity they are famous for, Consumer Reports reviews and rates popular travel guides, websites, airlines, tour operators, rental car companies and the like. You can also check out the travel section of **ConsumerReports.org** (consumer reports.org) but note that subscriptions to the site currently run $4.95 per month or $26 per year.

Should you still have a hankering, after reading the book, to dog-ear your own travel guide, get one used at **Amazon.com** (amazon.com).

wORk iT

*Work your way around the world with
the following travel-friendly gigs:*

Scuba Instructor

Become a certified Scuba instructor or divemaster and work at the world's most beautiful tropical locations. Dive into your research at two watery sites: **PADI** *(padi.com, go to "PADI Pros")* and **NAUI Online** *(naui.com)*.

Club Med Staffer

You've seen it in the movies, now you can experience it for yourself. Get hired on as an infamous **Club Med** "G.O." (*Gentil Organisateur* in French), working in one of the many Club Med villages scattered throughout the world. Flexibility is key—you won't know where you'll be based until after you get hired but hey, that's part of the fun! Read up on all at *clubmedjobs.com*.

Cruise Ship Employee

Ahoy, all you Julie McCoy's! You social types can cruise your way around the globe. For general information to get started, sail on over to **Cruise Ship Jobs** *(shipjobs.com)*. Of course, if you want to get specifics, you'll have to purchase their book and CD for a couple dozen bucks or so. We know, we know—we'll take the matter up with Captain Stubing.

Deckhand

Thousands of boats out there await your sturdy seamanship as a deckhand on a private yacht. Surprisingly, experience is not always required, as many captains don't mind training young sailing protégés. Just make sure it's not Captain Ahab—a boat on the open seas becomes very small indeed (not to mention dangerous). Connect with boats through **Find a Crew Online** *(findacrew.com)*, where searching is free but contacting members directly will cost you a premium membership: currently $39 for sixty days.

An exemplary reference for seeing the world for the cost of sweat equity is now in its 11th edition: *Work Your Way Around the World* by Susan Griffith. Written from a British perspective, it is nonetheless thorough and informative for Americans. Consider yourself warned: this is one of those books that's liable to launch a thousand fantasies.

The Power of the Internet

There was a time when booking travel on the Internet promised huge savings over booking through the traditional travel agents or airline carriers. While deals do still exist online, a certain amount of price parity has emerged between traditional travel agents and online retailers and wholesalers.

The good news, however, is that the online travel world has quickly evolved into a virtual cornucopia of valuable info. "Sometimes you can save some money by booking with Orbitz or a Euro consolidator like Mobissimo, but I find the Net is much more useful for other benefits," says Michael Shapiro, travel writer and author of *Internet Travel Planner: How to Plan Trips and Save Money Online.* "I use online resources to discover and learn about destinations, to connect with people there before I go, and to learn about current political, economic and environmental conditions—by reading their local newspapers online, for example."

Lonely Planet (lonelyplanet.com) hosts a particularly good online travel forum called **The Thorn Tree** (see "Thorn Tree Forum" off their homepage), where thousands of travelers from around the world chime in on the latest and greatest destination in virtually every region of the world.

Travel For Free

If a lack of funds has held you back from journeying to exotic locales, think beyond cash. Believe it or not, there are ways to travel and stay for free, or at least at significantly reduced expense.

What's the catch? Well, for one, it may require some work on your part. But with a bit of ingenuity and a willingness to exchange some elbow grease, ultra-cheap travel is absolutely within reach. A word of caution: beware of unscrupulous websites that purport to find you, for a fee, free accommodations and travel deals. Trust your instincts— if the website doesn't disclose how many members they have or the frequency with which they post new listings—stay away! Also, do remember that "free" does not necessarily mean scot-free. Items may cost you zero in the dollar sense, but you very well might pay up in a different way, be it through barter or hosting or just plain inconvenience.

Your bible in the free department (which is itself not free, except at the library) is *Pay Nothing to Travel Anywhere You Like,* written by the king of freebies, Eric W. Gershman. Gershman breaks down all that is attainable for zero bucks in the travel biz. While some of the tips aren't for everyone (creating an "over 62" fake ID to get senior discounts, for example), it is nonetheless a helpful resource for all.

Stay, Sit and Swap

No, we're not talking about anything kinky (see **Chapter 6** for kink) but about alternative accommodation. Bypass cramped hostels and impersonal hotels by staying in someone else's digs.

Are you a born freeloader? It's not as bad as it sounds. Get free accommodation in exchange for your promise to host like-minded guests. **GlobalFreeloaders.com** (globalfreeloaders.com) happens to be loaded with good stuff on arranging homestays, both foreign and

BE A RUNNER

Air couriers are the insiders' source for remarkably cheap international flights, provided you have flexibility. These companies offer extreme discounts to someone (you, hopefully!) who will "courier" a shipment to its destination.

This isn't *Midnight Express*; passengers don't ever handle the shipment. They simply go through an extra administrative step with the air courier's agent upon departure and arrival. The courier must usually sacrifice any checked luggage and bring only a carry-on. Round-trip travel typically requires you to complete your trip within a given time period, ranging anywhere from seven days to six months.

In general, the closer to departure you purchase a courier flight ticket, the cheaper it is. According to travel experts, John F. Kennedy in New York is the best U.S. airport to launch from for trips to Europe, followed by San Francisco International for the Pacific Rim. One traveler we spoke with recently flew from San Francisco to Hong Kong round-trip for $150, and another made it to Sydney and back for $200!

Listings with the *International Association of Air Travel Couriers* (*courier.org*) require a $45-per-year membership for U.S. residents ($50 per year for non-U.S. residents) to peruse courier opportunities; browse the site first to decide if it suits your travel needs.

domestic. They charge no fees, serving only as a meeting ground for guests and hosts to make their own private arrangements for stays. Another good network to look into is **Hospitality Club** (hospitalityclub. org), which has a strong international focus.

Similarly, albeit more altruistically, **US Servas** (usservas.org) promotes cross-cultural understanding through cross-hosting. They enable people to host guests from all over the world in their homes, and provide listings for those looking for a hospitable place to stay. The fee is $85 per adult for unlimited home stays during a twelve-month period, plus a $25 deposit for host lists. For domestic travel, the fee is $50 for a twelve-month period plus a $15 deposit for host lists. Ask about their student and other discounted rates.

TRAVEL WON'T DETRACT FROM YOUR CAREER

Don't let your friends tell you that an extended hiatus will derail your career. Travel did exactly the opposite for Dennis, a financial services executive. His 14-month solo journey around the world enhanced his standing in the eyes of more than one potential employer, and ultimately helped him land a slot with a major bank.

"I was pretty concerned about [the gap] when I first got back," he told us. "I was making up all these excuses, trying to hide it on my resume. But it became apparent pretty quickly that the trip I took was perceived as an asset, not a liability. Employers kept wanting to talk to me about it!" Dennis was courted by several large financial firms before accepting an offer from his favorite. "Keep in mind that these were banks and investment houses," he added, "not exactly the most progressive firms in the world, so that says a lot."

A travel sabbatical worked for Dana Magenau, too. He scored a plum job as director of The GRAMMY Foundation in Los Angeles after more than a year spent climbing the world's biggest mountains. "I think they just figured if I could do something like that, then surely I could handle running a foundation," he joked.

Do you fancy someone else's castle? **The Caretaker Gazette** (care-taker.org) publishes a bi-monthly newsletter containing ads for home-owners near and far who require the services of a willing and respon-sible housesitter (hey, that's you!). The subscription costs $29.95 a year and includes email alerts for positions requiring an immediate filling.

If you own your own home, consider trading spac-es with other homeowners. Paul Heller, travel expert and founder of **The Big Blue Marble** (thebigbluemar-ble.com, a wonderful site full of tips on how to "travel like a local"), puts it bluntly: "It saves you a hell of a lot of money, and it's a lot more comfortable." You'll need to have a desirable home in order to attract a swap but if so, the benefits stand to be significant. "The quality of the accommodations can be amazing," Paul says. "I know people who've exchanged homes for multimillion-dollar mansions in Puerto Vallarta that overlooked the sea."

As with any situation involving strangers, use common sense and verify as much information as you can about your guests (or hosts) before they show up at your door. If you're the guest, choose reliable references such as former hosts, employers and persons who have ob-served you functioning in a position of trust. If you do arrange a stay at someone else's house, mind your manners—you were not raised in a barn so keep their home clean and follow their rules.

Transitions Abroad (transitionsabroad.com) maintains a compre-hensive listing of homestays, home exchanges, and plenty of other good stuff. Go to their "Family Travel" section linked from the homep-age. Homeowners can also check out **Global Home Exchange** (4ho-mex.com) for travel trades; annual membership costs $49 Canadian.

How to Save Money by Traveling Overseas

No place will deplete your savings faster than the good old U.S. of A. So it may seem a paradox, but you can actually *save* money by travel-ing. The dollar goes much farther in places like Southeast Asia, Latin America, or Eastern Europe. Says Paul Heller: "I often wonder why people retire in the U.S. at all. If you have a modest amount of money, I don't really know why people wouldn't go to Mexico or some other place where the cost of living is much lower."

If you're a renter, consider subletting your place while you're gone or giving up your lease and storing your furniture. If you own your home, think about renting it out. The money you save (or make) on rent could cover months of roaming abroad. You can also save significant money on the day-to-day expense of food and lodging in areas where the cost of living is low. Presumably, you won't be spending nearly as much money on items like clothing, gas and utilities—or burning through cash at fancy restaurants or bars—so even after subtracting the cost of getting there, you still come out ahead. Cha-ching!

INTERNATIONAL ITINERARIES

Although no corner of the planet should be considered out of the question, we hope the following ideas will set some wheels in motion.

Southeast Asia

Sample Budgets—

> **Vietnam:** *$1,000 per month*
>> **Laos:** *$500 per month (includes elephant rides)*
> **Malaysia:** *$750 per month (bicycle not included)*
> **Thailand:** *$750 - $1,000 per month (date with Leonardo DiCaprio costs extra)*

Major Access Points: Bangkok, Hong Kong, Jakarta, Manila, Singapore

Any seasoned traveler will tell you that Southeast Asia is one of the world's most fascinating and affordable destinations. Tom "Mr. Travel" Williams sums it up: "The variety in Southeast Asia is just incredible. I can hike a volcano in Indonesia, stay in a two dollar hut on the beach in southern Thailand, and eat extraordinary food in a Singapore street stall for one dollar. And as far as crowds go, there's always that next island out there that's still unspoiled."

Right now is a prime time to visit the region. Vast areas remain accessible, despite the damage and unfathomable loss of life caused by the Indian Ocean tsunami, and whatever you spend will help to soften the blow dealt to these tourist-dependent economies.

If you're used to the fast pace of Western life, it may take you a little while to slow things down in a region that's not in a hurry. "It actually took quite some time to learn to relax with a book in a hammock without feeling that nagging need to 'maximize productivity' or fill each moment with tourist activities," said traveler Ariella Quatra. "Eventually though, I was living like the local villagers in Laos—sleeping

SAN FRANCISCO SISTER CITIES

Abidjan, The Ivory Coast
Assisi, Italy
Caracas, Venezuela
Cork, Ireland
Esteli, Nicaragua
Haifa, Israel
Ho Chi Minh City, Vietnam
Manila, Philippines
Osaka, Japan
Paris, France
Seoul, Korea
Shanghai, China
Sydney, Australia
Taipei, Taiwan
Thessaloniki, Greece

Looking for a theme for your journey? Visit one of SF's 15 Sister Cities! Drop by their city hall and tell them you're from San Francisco. See if they'll roll out the red carpet for you!

when tired, only eating when hungry, and telling time by the sunlight."

Many parts of Southeast Asia, particularly Thailand and Malaysia, have an excellent travelers' infrastructure of inexpensive accommodations and transportation—perfect for stretching a non-working budget. Bangkok is a backpacker's haven for cheap plane tickets and other transport. It's also *the* place to connect with other like-minded travelers—it won't be difficult to find your non-working brethren here!

Sister Cities:
Ho Chi Minh City, Vietnam
Manila, Philippines

For more information:
Asia Holiday Travel, Inc.
(567 Pine #203, 415-421-6630)

•••••••

China

Sample Budgets—
  Western China: *$1,000 per month*
  Eastern China: *$2,000–3,000 per month*
Major Access Points: *Hong Kong, Shanghai, Taipei*

China demands its own mention, separate from the rest of Asia. More than just a country, it's an entire world in and of itself. From its urban industrial wastelands to its ancient imperial ruins, China is a land of contrasts. Beijing and Shanghai are fascinating cities, but let's not forget about Hong Kong, handed back to the Chinese in 1997, which still maintains the busiest port in the world. "Hong Kong sports the world's longest elevator," reports frequent flyer Chris O'Reilly. "And there's the ferry to the mainland. Does seventy-five cents fit a non-working budget?" Add to that the island of Taiwan and a country full of spectacular mountains, rivers and culture, and travel in China could fill up more than a year's itinerary (if you could manage to extend a visa for that long).

Sister Cities:
Shanghai, China · Taipei, Taiwan
Neighboring Sister Cities:
Osaka, Japan · Seoul, Korea

For more information:
China Travel Service
(930 Montgomery, 415-352-0388)
ChinaTravel.com
(chinatravel.com)

••••••••

India/Nepal/Tibet

Sample Budgets—
  Tibet: *$500 per month (prayer flags are free)*
  Nepal: *$500 per month (Everest will cost a bit more)*
  India: *$1,000 per month (includes all the naan you can eat)*
Major Access Points: *Mumbai (Bombay), Delhi, Kathmandu, Lhasa*

Of all the places in the universe to visit, this part of Central Asia may offer a Western traveler the most consciousness-altering experience. If exploring spirituality is one of your leisure goals, this region might reincarnate your spirit of self-discovery. Ross Taggart, now working for the U.S. Department of State on human rights issues, took a year off from teaching to live, study and teach at a Tibetan monastery in Dharmsala, a city in northern India. "The whole experience was very intense," he says. "It changed my view on life forever."

India won't be easy. The country has tested the mettle of even the most hardened travelers. But it has also provided rewarding revelations. The region's mix of Buddhist and Hindu religions adds to the rich experience.

The mountains of Nepal have long been a destination for international mountaineers and are home to some of the best trekking on the planet.

Tibet, for its part, has persisted in relative isolation. You'll need to secure a permit from China to visit this tiny country.

For more information:
India Tours & Travel (1533 Franklin, 415-673-2742)
Consulate General of India (540 Arguello, 415-668-0662)
VisitNepal.com (visitnepal.com)

Africa

Sample Budgets—
> *Tanzania: $1,000 per month; $3,000–$6,000 per month on safari*
> *South Africa: $500 per month (feral living)*
> *$1,000–$1,500 (standard)*

Major Access Points: Johannesburg, Nairobi, you name it

Africa is not a single destination but a giant continent of countries to explore. One would do best to focus on just a handful. South Africa's beautiful coastline and world-famous game parks summon the leisurely wanderer in the post-Apartheid era. Ted Witt, an operations director from California, spent one month in South Africa during a recent six-month journey. He tells us, "As long as all you're doing is surfing and hanging out, you can easily live like a king on a thousand bucks a month. You could pull it off even cheaper if you live more economically. Ostrich meat is really cheap, and low in fat!"

Tanzania and Kenya also offer adventure in abundance, be it surveying the Serengeti, climbing Kilimanjaro, or overlanding through some of the world's best game preserves. The exotic Zanzibar Archipelago, just 25 miles off the coast, offers pristine white sand beaches, and exceptional diving and snorkeling. Dana Magenau, who spent several months in Africa during a recent one-year sabbatical, says Tanzania was easily his favorite of the four African countries he visited. "The people, places and wildlife make Tanzania one of the most diverse countries I've ever visited. Where else could you safari in the Serengeti, climb one of the Seven Summits and dive in crystal clear waters near Zanzibar in just two weeks?" Other choice countries include mystic Morocco in the northwest; wildlife-rich Botswana in the south, or enigmatic Mozambique on the southeastern Indian coast. With so many choices, you may have to pick straws to make a final decision where to go (or where not to go)!

Sister City:
Abidjan, Côte D'Ivoire (Ivory Coast)

For more information:
Lonely Planet (lonelyplanet.com/worldguide/
destinations/africa)

South Pacific

Sample Budgets—

> **Tahiti:** *$3,000 per month (consider camping)*
> **Fiji:** *$1,000 – $2,000 per month (not including inter-island travel)*
> **Australia:** *$1,500 per month base ($3,000 per month including beer)*
> **New Zealand:** *$1,000 per month (bungee jumping, sky diving, rock climbing,*
> *life insurance, all extra)*

Major Access Points: *Auckland, Nadi, Pape'ete, Sydney*

Ay mate, is there anything more leisurely than island-hopping through the South Pacific? Well, if your name is Captain Cook, the answer is probably yes. Otherwise, the Society Islands (a.k.a. Tahiti), the Fijian island chain, the Cook Islands, and the islands in between all offer life at a most leisurely pace, with tall, swaying palms and gregarious, ultra-friendly locals. Dane Larson, a marketing consultant, surfed and lazed away several months in the Society Islands after a two-year stint of full-time work and says, "Life there was so slow, I almost got bored. *Almost.*"

Do yourself a favor while you're all the way down under, and continue to New Zealand, a land of vast, unspoiled nature. The country is an outdoor adventurer's dream. And, what the heck, since you already spent the 16 hours on a plane to get to the other side of the planet, you might as well throw in Australia as well, seeing as how it's one of the greatest destinations ever! You could spend a year there without skipping a beat. We wouldn't blame you if you up and emigrated!

In both Australia and New Zealand, the fully developed economy and English-speaking citizenry ease the task of securing an odd job, although acquiring a legal working visa is extremely difficult for Americans. Farming skills are particularly useful in New Zealand, where travelers can regularly trade farmhand chores for food and lodging.

Sister City:
Sydney, Australia

For more information:
South Pacific Express Travels
(1586 Bush, 415-775-8989)

Western Europe

Sample Budgets—

France: $2,500 per month (Champagne and Camembert extra)
Spain: $1,500 per month (includes flamenco lessons)
Sweden: $3,000 per month (consider camping for free in the woods)

Major Access Points: London, Paris, Stockholm, the list goes on and on...

Western Europe, while more conventional than the other destinations we list, still emanates an irresistible aura of history and culture. One can hardly deny the allure of sipping wine on a sunny afternoon at a sidewalk Parisian café or savoring the sumptuous cuisine of Sicily. The north offers the unflappable refinement of Scandinavia; the south, the hot, Latin rhythms of Spain and Portugal; and the middle, the canals and the seat of European government.

The budget can be tricky here, especially as the U.S. dollar slides further into an exchange rate abyss. In general, prices fall with latitude: Greece, Turkey, Italy, Spain, and Portugal are going to be your cheapest bets, while Scandinavia is one of the world's most expensive regions. Still, Western Europe's extensive hostel network and efficient train system have long made it a budget traveler's haven.

This may also be the region for you if you're interested in pursuing that studious sabbatical—say, in art, language, or cooking. The combination of English-speaking schools and "old world" expertise in certain specialty fields can make for a rewarding educational experience. For more information on European schools, see *The Back Door Guide to Short-Term Job Adventures* by Michael Landes, a book full of ideas for taking time off.

Sister Cities:
Assisi, Italy • Cork, Ireland
Paris, France • Thessaloniki, Greece

Neighboring Sister City:
Haifa, Israel

For more information:
Europe Travel
(447 Sutter, Suite 413, 415-395-9302)
Europe Vacations
(944 Market, 415-837-0218)

Eastern Europe

Sample Budgets—

Czech Republic: *$1,000 per month*
Croatia: *$1,000 per month*
Latvia: *$1,000 per month*

Major Access Points: Budapest, Prague, Warsaw, Zagreb, and so on

From the well-traveled Czech Republic, Poland, or Hungary, to the more obscure Slovakia, Serbia, or Croatia, Eastern European nations have plenty to offer the adventurous traveler. No one can deny the elegance and intrigue of such sophisticated cities as Prague or Budapest, but less-charted locales, like Slovenia, Albania, or the Baltic States of Estonia, Lithuania, and Latvia, all hide glorious treasures.

These days, the lines between Eastern Europe and Russia have blurred. Russia's still-volatile mix of the Old World, Eastern bloc-style culture combined with a deregulated economy can be both fascinating and dangerous—cultural treasures interspersed with crime and corruption. The Baltic States are a prime example, where Russian *mafiya* chat on cell phones in front of beautiful medieval churches.

Andis Blukis, an engineer and writer, lived overseas in Riga, Latvia. After jumping ship from a fast-sinking corporate vessel, he sought refuge in the small country of his ancestors. Originally planning a summer break, Andis remained in Riga a full year, working periodically as a software engineer for a Latvian phone company. "I worked with and learned from engineers who were rebuilding an unbelievably large and complex yet archaic phone call tracking system into Oracle as it simultaneously continued recording phone calls—the equivalent of rebuilding the engine of a 747 on the way across the Atlantic. Yet these same engineers also chose to haggle with an old bearded lady over the price of tomatoes, cream, and stinky cheese at the local medieval marketplace rather than go to a modern supermarket." He lived well in Latvia on approximately $1,000 per month.

For more information:
Consulate General of Russia
(2790 Green, 415-202-9800)
Russart Travel Service
(291 Geary, Suite 511, 415-781-6655,
russart4you.com)

Latin America

Sample Budgets—

Argentina: $1,500 per month (living well)
Costa Rica: $1,000 per month (even in the rain forest)
Mexico: $750 per month (sombreros extra)
Peru: $1,000 per month (including Machu Picchu)

Major Access Points: Mexico City, Guatemala City, Lima, Saõ Paulo, Santiago

"Latin America" is a broad term used to blanket a region of dozens of unique countries and cultures. From a travel standpoint, however, Latin America can be fairly divided into two primary areas: Mexico and Central America, for one, and South America, for the other.

The first region is almost as accessible by land as by air: Panama City is no farther from San Francisco than is New York, as the crow flies—or drives! Bring your water gear; two major oceans grace its shores and either side of the isthmus offers wonderful coastline to explore.

South America is more culturally diverse, with indigenous as well as European colonial influences on language, customs and architecture. From the sophistication of Buenos Aires to the raw, colorful communities of the Bolivian highlands, the continent begs to be explored. Bargains are not hard to find either. Argentina, with its economic woes, is particularly well-priced these days.

Sister Cities:
Caracas, Venezuela
Esteli, Nicaragua

For more information:
Buenaventura Travel
(800-836-8872, buenaventuratravel.com)
Exito Travel
(800-655-4053, exitotravel.com)
The South American Explorer's Club
(samexplo.org)

TRAVEL WITH A PURPOSE

Ever ponder how Sir Francis Drake was able to complete his miraculous voyage circumnavigating the globe? Looking for a way to immerse yourself into a foreign community and hold normal conversations with the locals?

Add some pizzazz to your travels by choosing a theme or a purpose for your journey. Theme-based travel gives you a vehicle for seeing the planet while granting you a fulfilling educational, cultural, physical (perhaps even metaphysical) experience. Your travels might revolve around a particular activity like mountaineering or surfing, or they could include studying language or history at a local university. You could even take a food or wine tour, and eat your way across Europe!

"Meaningful travel doesn't have to mean going to a developing country and doing backbreaking labor for weeks, or serving in the Peace Corps," says Michael Shapiro, author of *A Sense of Place* as well as the *Internet Travel Planner*. "All that is great, but you can do little things on routine trips that make travel meaningful. You can convey a package from someone in Cuba to a relative in the U.S. You can listen to someone's story. You can stay at a family-run guesthouse rather than in a chain hotel."

Study the Local Language

Nothing will ingratiate you to a foreign community like speaking the local language. The fastest way to ramp up your language skills is to immerse yourself in

language study in latin america? ¡que bueno!

Seeking to dramatically improve her Spanish, Heidi Wells went directly to the source. For three months, she lived in Xela (a.k.a. Quetzaltenango), Guatemala, where she enrolled in one-on-one Spanish classes, five hours per day, five days a week.

"My instructor, Victor, doubled as my local tour guide," Heidi told us. "We'd go anywhere I could think of, from grocery shopping to trips to the pig farm. Everywhere we went, Victor grilled me on my Spanish and taught me new words." Her Spanish went from basic to keen in a Latin heartbeat.

Back stateside, Heidi kept the lessons going by tapping into the Guatemalan community in her hometown—over *cervezas* at the neighborhood cantina.

¿Porqué no?

ENSURE YOU'RE INSURED

Chances are that your current health plan doesn't cover you on foreign soil. If you're leaving the country, you'll likely need a policy tailored specifically to traveling or living abroad. One broker specializing in travel-related insurance, **InsureMyTrip.com** *(insuremytrip.com)*, provides exactly that.

Peter Evans, their executive vice president, recommends figuring out your needs before evaluating plans. "People need to realize that travel medical plans are not major medical policies, but are designed more for emergencies," he says. "The more expensive programs, 'travel major medicals,' are designed more for expats."

Some plans cover accidental death (just in case), medical evacuations (just in case), and travel baggage, which is insurance for (no, not your spouse!) that iPod and other stuff.

Find useful tools to compare different plans on the InsureMyTrip site.

the dialect with in-country study. The learning process itself will be a terrific way to get to know people, and a heck of a lot of fun.

Some areas, such as Paris or Shanghai, are known for their language schools, but you should be able to find some form of instruction virtually anywhere you look—including truly virtual instruction online.

Start your research with **GoAbroad.com** (goabroad.com), which covers everything from learning languages overseas, to teaching English, to interning and volunteering abroad. **Languages Abroad** (800-219-9924, languagesabroad.com) is another useful resource that focuses exclusively on language immersion.

For information on specific foreign language classes, try language stalwart **Berlitz** (in the U.S. berlitz.us) and their Berlitz Study Abroad programs. They also offer plenty of courses in the U.S. as well as online.

Learning Vacations

Language may be an obvious study, but you can take it a step further and study some local flavor as well. Dance, cook, sing, or paint your way through a unique in-country learning experience. Heck, you could even improve your snowboarding form. Almost any learning endeavor that you tie into your travels will have you looking forward to examinations.

"I spent a month in Buenos Aires studying Tango—it was a great, great month, and very cheap," says Paul Heller. "When you're going to school every day, you really feel like you're part of the community. You're taking classes from a local, you're living with a local, you're meeting other foreigners and locals who are interested in a subject."

The 411 on learning vacations tends to be spread amongst several resources. **Transitions Abroad** (transitionsabroad.com) touts a keen "Adult Education" section linked from their home-page that's sure to tickle your fancy, if not your tootsies.

GREAT MOMENTS IN UNEMPLOYMENT

John Steinbeck
(1902–1968)
Not only did the Salinas-born writer John Steinbeck spend years of his life unemployed, partially-employed, or points in between, but woven throughout his most famous novels are persistent themes of unemployment, struggling workers, and the common man. *The Grapes of Wrath*, probably his most famous novel about labor, profiled the plight of dispossessed farmers during the Great Depression. • • • Steinbeck knew when to take a break. Fresh on the heels of *Grapes'* successful release in the spring of 1940, he sought refuge in Baja with close friend and marine biologist Ed Ricketts. The pair chronicled their adventures on the wild peninsula in *Sea of Cortez*, a literary voyage of natural beauty, exploration, and science.

TRAVEL RESOURCES

BEFORE YOU GO
for research, maps, books, foreign-language dictionaries and more
- **your local public library** *(publiclibraries.com)*
- **Hostelling International USA** *(hiayh.org)*
- **GORP** *(gorp.com)*
- **Rand McNally** *(randmcnally.com)*
- **Get Lost Travel Books** *(1825 Market, 415-437-0529)*

GUIDEBOOKS
- *Lonely Planet (lonelyplanet.com)*
- *Rough Guides (U.K.-based, roughguides.com)*
- *Time Out (timeout.com)*
- *Internet Travel Planner* by Michael Shapiro

BOOKING YOUR TRIP
- **Airtreks** *(877-247-8735, airtreks.com)*—an airline consolidator specializing in multi-stop, round-the-world tickets. Check out their online TripPlanner application for travel planning and pricing.
- **Air Brokers International** *(800-883-3273, airbrokers.com)*—an airline consolidator for cheap wholesale airline tickets.
- **Adventure Center** *(800-228-8747, adventurecenter.com)*—a wholesaler for international adventures. Good for group travel and ideas.
- **AAA Travel Agency** *(150 Van Ness, 415-565-2141)*
- **Southwest Airlines** *(800-435-9792, southwest.com)*
- **JetBlue Airways** *(800-538-2583, jetblue.com)*
- **International Association of Air Travel Couriers** *(courier.org)*
- **SmarterTravel.com** *(smartertravel.com)*
- **CheapTickets** *(cheaptickets.com)*
- **SideStep** *(sidestep.com)*
- **Orbitz** *(orbitz.com)*
- **Priceline** *(priceline.com)*
- **TripAdvisor, Inc.** *(tripadvisor.com)*

ROAD TRIPS
- **AAA** *(aaa.com)*
- **Auto Driveaway Co.** *(autodriveaway.com)*
- **Better World Club** *(866-238-1137, betterworldclub.com)*

OVERLAND TOUR COMPANIES
- **TrekAmerica** *(800-221-0596, trekamerica.com)*
- **Green Tortoise Adventure Travel** *(800-867-8647, greentortoise.com)*l

INTERNATIONAL JOBS
- **JobMonkey.com** *(jobmonkey.com)*

- **International Academy** (*international-academy.com*)
- **PADI** (*padi.com*)
- **NAUI Online** (*naui.com*)
- **Club Med** (*clubmedjobs.com*)
- **Cruise Ship Jobs** (*shipjobs.com*)
- **Find a Crew Online** (*findacrew.com*)
- *Work Your Way Around the World* by Susan Griffith

ACCOMODATIONS & CAMPING
- **BedandBreakfast.com** (*bedandbreakfast.com*)
- **Bed and Breakfast Inns of North America** (*inntravels.com*)
- **ReserveAmerica** (*reserveamerica.com*)
- **National Park Service ParkNet** (*nps.gov*)
- **American Youth Hostels** (*425 Divisadero, Ste. 307. 415-863-1444, norcalhostels.org*)

HOUSE SITTING, HOMESTAYS, & HOME EXCHANGES
- **GlobalFreeloaders.com** (*globalfreeloaders.com*)
- **Hospitality Club** (*hospitalityclub.org*)
- **US Servas** (*usservas.org*)
- **The Caretaker Gazette** (*caretaker.org*)
- **The Big Blue Marble** (*thebigbluemarble.com*)
- **Transitions Abroad** (*transitionsabroad.com*)
- **Global Home Exchange** (*4homex.com*)

LANGUAGE STUDY & TEACHING
- **GoAbroad.com** (*goabroad.com*)
- **Languages Abroad** (*800-219-9924, languagesabroad.com*)
- **Berlitz** (*berlitz.us*)
- **The Chronicle of Higher Education** (*chronicle.com*)
- **Dave's ESL Cafe** (*eslcafe.com*)

INTERNATIONAL VOLUNTEERING
- **Peace Corps** (*800-424-8580, peacecorps.gov*)
- **I-to-I** (*800-985-4864, i-to-i.com*)
- **Sierra Club** (*sierraclub.org/outings*)
- **Cross-Cultural Solutions** (*800-380-4777, crossculturalsolutions.org*)
- **The Center for INTERIM Programs** (*interimprograms.com*)
- **World-Wide Opportunities on Organic Farms** (*wwoof.org*)

MISCELLANEOUS
- **InsureMyTrip.com** (*insuremytrip.com*)
- *Pay Nothing to Travel Anywhere You Like* by Eric W. Gershman
- **South American Explorers** (*saexplorers.org*)
- **U.S. Department of State** (*state.gov*)
- **World Affairs Councils of America** (*worldaffairscouncils.org*)

Teach English Overseas

Teaching English can be a groovy way to both make money while you travel and interact with locals. Raquel Rodriguez, a teacher from New York, is a self-described serial ESL (English as a Second Language) teacher abroad. "I love to learn languages and experience new cultures," she says. "The job market for college level ESL instructors is also pretty dismal in the States. Back home, I always get by with piecing together several adjunct positions. Abroad, I can always find good full-time work." Indeed, Raquel is currently overseas on assignment in the United Arab Emirates.

Raquel advises lining up gigs prior to landing in the destination country, for potentially better wages and benefits. For jobs at the university level, she highly recommends **The Chronicle of Higher Education** (chronicle.com), the definitive job resource for work at universities around the world.

There are a plethora of sources and schools dedicated exclusively to ESL or EFL (English as a Foreign Language). In addition to GoAbroad. com and Berlitz, peruse the informative, home-grown website **Dave's ESL Cafe** (eslcafe.com). The coffee may be lacking, but the information certainly percolates and you can connect with ESL teachers from around the world.

Sports, Music, and Other Hobbies

If you're a rock climbing or river kayaking fanatic, you probably don't need much persuading to pack your gear and seek out foreign climbs and rivers. But even if you're not an expert, choosing an activity outside of your own country will show you altogether different sights and experiences.

Music, for example, is a fabulous way to bridge cultural chasms. If you play an instrument, strap it to the pack for jam sessions with local musicians.

"When I travel I always bring my half-sized travel guitar," says veteran wanderer Ted Witt. "Music is a universal language, and musicians are part of a tribe that spans the globe—so anywhere around the world you can communicate on a very direct level with the locals through music. I can think of some real breakthrough cultural exchanges—an all night bossa nova jam session in Brazil, a campfire

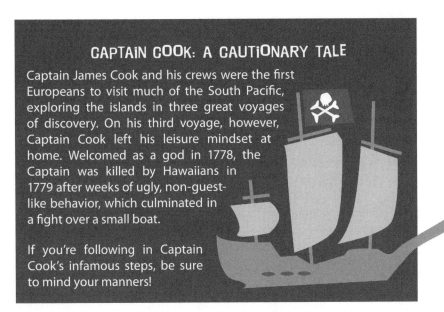

CAPTAIN COOK: A CAUTIONARY TALE

Captain James Cook and his crews were the first Europeans to visit much of the South Pacific, exploring the islands in three great voyages of discovery. On his third voyage, however, Captain Cook left his leisure mindset at home. Welcomed as a god in 1778, the Captain was killed by Hawaiians in 1779 after weeks of ugly, non-guest-like behavior, which culminated in a fight over a small boat.

If you're following in Captain Cook's infamous steps, be sure to mind your manners!

drum circle in Madagascar, a Guinness-soaked jig in Belfast—all spontaneous moments where I became an active participant in the community, rather than just a passive observer touring a foreign land."

We spoke with several people who toted their bikes along and cycled across countries as diverse as Europe, Cuba, and New Zealand. Breathing in the culture, meeting residents, and even sharing portions of the trip with local cyclists more than made up for the challenges (harsh weather, breakdowns, and accidents, to name a few) they reported. "New Zealand was a great place to bike," said Travis, an IT manager from Portland. "The roads were good, without much car traffic, and the scenery was amazing. And if I ever got tired of biking in the rain, I would just pull off and stay at one of the thousands of guesthouses."

Volunteer Vacations

"Volunteer vacations" are quickly rising in popularity, and organizations now specialize in arranging them. Programs run the gamut from remote environmental projects to inner-city teaching, and can range from two weeks to a year or more. The good news is there are a surprising number of ways to incorporate work and volunteering into your travels. "It's a wonderful way to meet people, learn about other cultures, and it's a great way to feel like you've had an opportunity to make a difference in someone's life," says travel guru Paul Heller.

The granddaddy of all volunteer vacations is the **Peace Corps** (800-424-8580, peacecorps.gov). One need not sacrifice two full years, however, to do some good whilst traveling. Numerous organizations offer shorter stints, some as brief as a week or less. U.K.-based **I-to-I** (800-985-4864, i-to-i.com) caters to the more adventurous volunteer, offering "meaningful travel" ventures, from teaching computer skills to youth in Tanzania, to assisting with shark research in South Africa.

For the environmentally conscious, the **Sierra Club** (sierraclub.org/outings) offers what they call "service trips" in the U.S. and U.S. territories. The trips focus on outdoor volunteering (no surprise) and can range from maintaining turtle nesting grounds on the island of Culebra, Puerto Rico, to tracking mountain lions in western Arizona.

Cross-Cultural Solutions (800-380-4777, crossculturalsolutions.org) offers what they call Intern Abroad, a two- to twelve-week program immersing volunteers into a variety of local cultures within the fields of education, healthcare, or social services. The **Center for INTERIM Programs** (interimprograms.com) seems to have been created for the specific purpose of helping people do something cool with their time off, or their "time on" as they like to call it. Their tagline ("If you could wave a magic wand, what would you do?") sums up their philosophy quite nicely, and their wish list (possibly yours, as well) includes programs as varied as surfing and studying Spanish in Central America to conducting whale research off the coast of Hawaii. Cool? You bet.

For more on Volunteer Vacations, see **Chapter 9** under "Volunteer Abroad."

go organic, dude

A network of organic farms around the world awaits the manual labor of those who like a more organic approach to volunteer travel. In exchange for work on their farms, many growers will offer up free room and board.

World-Wide Opportunities on Organic Farms, or ***WWOOF*** *(wwoof.org)* maintains a list of international organic farms that accept volunteer labor. The farm stays can be a rewarding way to tap into the local culture, as well as an opportunity to see some beautiful, rural areas.

Create Your Own Theme

If a pre-fabricated program is too confining for you, get creative and devise your own premise for a journey. Browse the annals of history for a topic that interests you, and design an itinerary around it. Your trip through Latin America could trace the conquests of Hernán Cortés, for example, or your South Pacific voyage could follow Captain Cook's—but be more courteous than he was! We heard of one couple who quit their jobs, flew to Italy, bought a Volvo and drove all over the Mediterranean following a map of the ancient Roman conquest. "We could always tell the Romans had been there," they said, "because the first thing they always did was build baths and roads."

PEACE

Long before volunteer travel programs became hip and trendy, the Peace Corps was doling out serious doses of life-changing experiences through two-year placements in developing nations around the world. Formed in 1961 under the leadership of President John F. Kennedy, the Peace Corps was founded as a way for Americans to serve their country in the interest of world peace. Volunteers get paid a local living allowance plus funds at the end of their service to help with the transition back to life in the U.S.

Another tried and true source of inspiration is literature: let Michener, Hemingway or Theroux steer you through new and exotic lands. Hemingway fans beware—more than a few have already made the pilgrimage to Pamplona.

Travel Without Leaving

Perhaps you don't have the budget for a big trip overseas, yet still would like to explore a new area or culture. Not to worry. With the level of ethnic and cultural diversity found in the United States, you are sure to find a palette of exotic colors and flavors right here at home.

Language, for example, doesn't need to be studied in a foreign country. You can do it right in your own hometown, and it's a great way to introduce yourself to a new region. Shake your international booty to some world music, and learn a thing or two about a regional dance in the process. Globally orient yourself with seminars, events, and talks on a topic or region of interest; they take place all the time in urban centers throughout the country.

A healthy starting point would be the **World Affairs Councils of America** (worldaffairscouncils.org). Reach out and connect with a council near you; they are sprinkled throughout the U.S. A journey of the mind can help satisfy and whet your appetite for travel at the same time—minus the jetlag and Aztec two-step of course.

- *World Affairs Council of Northern California*
  312 Sutter, Suite 200, 415-293-4600, *itsyourworld.org*

- *Abadá Capoeira San Francisco (Brazilian Cultural Center)*
  3221 22nd Street, 415-206-0650, *abada.org*

- *Instituto Italiano di Cultura San Francisco*
  425 Washington, Suite 200, 415-788-7142, *sfiic.org*

- *Russian Center of San Francisco*
  2450 Sutter, 415-921-7631, *russiancentersf.com*

- *Alliance Francaise de San Francisco*
  1345 Bush, 415-775-7755, *afsf.com*

- *United Irish Cultural Center*
  2700 45th Avenue, 415-661-2700

- *Chinese Cultural Center of San Francisco*
  750 Kearny, 3rd Floor, 415-986-1822, *c-c-c.org*

- *Japanese Cultural and Community Center*
  1840 Sutter, 415-567-5505, *jcccnc.org*

- *Mission Cultural Center for Latino Arts*
  2868 Mission, 415-821-1155, *missionculturalcenter.org*

A FINAL NOTE

Travel can be enormously fulfilling, even life-changing. Unfortunately, in this modern era it also can be hazardous, particularly for Americans. The status and safety of different international regions is constantly changing. Use your best judgment when choosing a destination and take appropriate precautions when traveling to "hot spots." Be sure to consult the latest travel advisories from the **U.S. Department of State** (state.gov) when considering international travel.

CHAPTER 6
UNEMPLOYMENT ON THE EDGE

Temptation rarely comes in working hours.
It is in their leisure time that men are made or marred.

~W.N. Taylor

TRAVEL can open your eyes, and introspection the windows to your soul, but nothing takes you farther from the office than living day-to-day with pure abandon. Wanna rock and roll all night? Run amok with the spring break crowds in Florida or Mexico? Go ahead, toss out your alarm clock. Let your hair down and dye it purple. Take a walk on the wild side. You're free at last!

A caveat—this chapter includes some anecdotes about illegal activities. Our aim is neither to promote nor condemn breaking the law, but merely to explore the full spectrum of leisure culture. Gambling, drugs, and other illegal activities are as real a part of San Francisco life as cafés and museums. Life on the edge can be as innocent as nude sunbathing or as risqué as watching a peep show—or starring in one. One thing's for sure: if you open yourself to new experiences, you'll find doors opening for you in return.

Just make sure the doors are ones you want to go through. Getting arrested, blowing your budget or losing the respect of friends or family would be anything but liberating. Remember that freedom is as much about charting new ground as it is about learning your limits. If you don't know your limits, take this opportunity to find out. Only you know how far you can safely push the envelope.

liquid innovation

The fame of the City's watering holes dates back to Barbary Coast days. The martini, a drinker's drink if there ever was one, was reputedly born at the Occidental Hotel back in the 1860s, where a bartender made it for a patron who wanted something strong enough to last the ferry ride from San Francisco to "Martinez" (get it?). Today's *Occidental Cigar Club* in the Financial District (471 Pine, 415-834-0485), has inherited both the name and the art of martini making, and is one of those "owner occupied" establishments that allow you to puff away to your heart's content.

Other drinks attributed to San Francisco include the Irish Coffee brewed at the notorious *Buena Vista Café* (2765 Hyde, 415-474-5044), and the Mimosa, supposedly invented at the now closed Jack's Restaurant by none other than director Alfred Hitchcock and financier Louis Lurie.

TIME TO PARTY

If you're thinking about conducting some personal chemistry experiments, history is on your side. San Francisco's "drug-friendly" culture has earned the city notoriety since the opium dens of the 19th century. Beatniks read their poetry through a haze of marijuana smoke; students manufactured LSD in their bathtubs in the 1960s; Ecstasy fueled all-night club dances in the 1990s. As for drinking—let's just say the City's relationship with booze has lubricated the town ever since its origins as the village of Yerba Buena.

A Night on the Drink

With plenty of time to ride out a morning-after hangover, you'll find unemployment offers an ideal time to tie one on. Not that you necessarily need any guidance in this area, but a few basics will surely enhance any fun night of drinking.

One, don't drink alone—get yourself some "drinking buddies." Girls or guys, it doesn't matter, but no one should be drinking solo.

Two, don't drive—take cabs or get a designated driver, no exceptions. There's absolutely no reason to get behind the wheel after a night of drinking in a city with as much transportation assistance as San Francisco.

Three, expand your horizons. Try some new and different places. There are thousands of bars within the city limits that have a heck of a lot more character than your run-of-the-mill yuppie bar (see **Dining & Nightlife** for inspiration).

Think there's no place like home? Save some money and host your own cocktail party. Stock up with proper cocktail gear: low and high-ball glasses, martini glasses, essential mixers, garnishes, a good bartending book (our personal favorite is *The Bartender's Bible*, by Gary Regan), and ice—always plenty of ice! Ask friends to bring over their booze of choice and voila! The party is on.

Whatever your choice, remember to drink plenty of water and take some aspirin before bed to help ease that morning pain.

A Day on the "Green"

No, it's not legal, but you'd be hard-pressed to find a major U.S. city that is more tolerant of marijuana use and cultivation. SF was among the first to allow the medical use of marijuana, passing Proposition 215 in 1996. Although at odds with federal lawmakers ever since, San Francisco has declared itself a sanctuary for the use, cultivation and distribution of medical marijuana.

So what does this mean to you, the edgy leisure seeker? Well for one

seeking fun?

True masters of fun can take merriment to a whole new level by perusing a copy of *The Fun Seeker's North America* by Alan Davis. This travel tome is painstakingly researched, and takes its fun quite seriously.

"I went to the Running of the Bulls in Pamplona, Spain," says Alan on how he came up with the idea for the book series. "I couldn't find any useful resources for the trip. By luck, I caught the most thrilling moment—the opening of the Fiesta. The whole event was the greatest party I'd ever seen. I decided to find all of the other great events and produce a guidebook that would be about being in the right place at the right time."

In addition to profiling and ranking events throughout North America, Fun Seeker's includes a Gold List of the best parties and party cities in the world. Las Vegas and New Orleans top the elite five-star city list (no surprise), while Burning Man and Mardi Gras nab top entertainment honors. Looking to hook up? Scan the "Mating Rating" in the back, which categorizes fiestas by level of nookie potential: "Viagra" (*there's hope*), "Prozac" (*slight chance*) and "Hemlock" (*no chance*).

DR. ECSTASY

As a pioneering pharmacologist, Alexander "Sasha" Shulgin maintains cult status both within and outside of drug circles. Born and raised in Berkeley (surprise), Shulgin has discovered and synthesized over two hundred psychoactive compounds during his 50-year career.

Yet what he's most widely known for is the popularization of MDMA, or what's known as Ecstasy, a drug he had no part in developing. Drug giant Merck took care of that back in 1914 when they patented it as a byproduct of another chemical synthesis, and promptly forgot about it. At the suggestion of a former student, Shulgin resynthesized MDMA in 1976 and documented its effects on humans.

While he himself didn't find the drug particularly transformative, once calling it a "low-calorie martini," he nonetheless thought it might be well-suited for psychotherapy. It was used by thousands of therapists until 1986, when the DEA placed it on the illegal list. And that, of course, is when it became "a hit" on college campuses throughout the U.S.

California maintains a more lenient legal policy on marijuana than most other states, calling it a "non-arrestable misdemeanor" (akin to a traffic ticket) for personal possession under 28.5 grams (roughly an ounce). It also means you will not have a difficult time locating high-quality pot from some reasonably reputable sources in and around San Francisco.

As local Ross Denny (name definitely changed) quips, "Weed will get you through times of no money better than money will get you through times of no weed." Well said! If you're experimenting for the first time, we're sure you can find friends for advice, support, and, er, collaboration.

You didn't hear it from us, but if you are so inclined, you may also be able to obtain your very own medical marijuana prescription for that which ails you. This is where those "doctor friends" can really come in handy. For more information and to learn about the risks involved, contact **California National Organization for the Reform of Marijuana Laws** (CA NORML, 2215-R Market #278, 415-563-5858, ca-norml.org).

Cannabis clubs in San Francisco are frequently changing locations. Try the **Vapor Room** (609A Haight, vaporroom.com), known for its high-quality product and extra friendly service.

Rave Away

San Francisco hosts a thriving DJ scene, some of which (but not all) is tied closely to Ecstasy, as well as other so-called "club drugs." The merits and safety of "E" are debatable, but one thing is rarely disputed—paired with good dance music, the Ecstasy-taker will likely want to dance all night long. Make sure you stay hydrated!

For hip club and DJ music scenes, try **Mighty** (119 Utah, 415-762-0151, mighty119.com, see **Dining & Nightlife** under "Staying Out Really Late"), a late-night club that attracts an alternative crowd; **Mezzanine** (444 Jessie, 415-625-8880, mezzaninesf.com), a multi-use venue that hosts a diverse assortment of events including top DJs, or **Shine** (1337 Mission, 415-252-1423), an intimate dance locale that gets good and funky.

SPIRITUALITY

Any situation that exposes one's core beliefs, material values, or immortal soul is an extreme activity indeed. If the Leisure Commandments don't move you, use your flexible schedule to explore your own personal spirituality. Don't go join a cult or anything, just investigate any longings for "The Infinite" you may have been suppressing. And remember: spirituality is found not necessarily within a group, but within an individual.

One-Time Dose of Church

Maybe you want to attend a single church service for a dose of religious culture or spiritual cleansing—or maybe you just need someplace to hang out on a Sunday morning! Whatever your motives, many local places of worship, even the famous ones, welcome "drop-ins."

Glide Memorial United Methodist Church

(330 Ellis, 415-674-6000, glide.org)
As those who've been there already know, Glide is more than going to church—it's a full-body experience. Every Sunday at 9am (and again at 11am), Glide rocks, breathes, and reverberates. For 40 years, Reverend Cecil Williams, who has "retired" but still manages to deliver plenty of sermons, has built and presided over one of the most recognized congregations in the U.S., whose parishioners include such notables as Oprah Winfrey. On any given Sunday you'll see yuppies jigging

alongside the homeless, in what is best described as an "only in San Francisco" event. Religion aside, Glide also provides countless social services to the city of San Francisco, from hot meals for the homeless to high-tech job skills training.

Grace Cathedral
(1100 California, 415-749-6300, gracecathedral.org)
Grace is the Episcopalian center of San Francisco. It offers concerts and open services for anyone who "seeks God and is drawn to Christ." It's a hip church, as indicated by its website (recent excerpts include a Burning Man photo feature and an eclectic music series). A choral service is performed within the cathedral's beautiful walls every Sunday at 11am, and their classical concert series is extremely popular.

FROM FLOWER POWER TO CULTS

San Francisco and the Bay Area have long been magnets for anyone seeking spirituality, self-help, or self-actualization—which means they've also been magnets for cults.

During the "Flower Power" era of the 1960s, impressionable youth flooded the Bay Area, living commune-style around Haight-Ashbury and Berkeley. Ten years later, the infamous Jim Jones led his People's Temple congregation on that fatal pilgrimage from San Francisco to Georgetown, Guyana (see **Chapter 4** for the whole story).

Even today, you won't have to look far for a wide selection of cults in the Bay Area. One organization recently under scrutiny was the **San Francisco Church of Christ**, affiliated with the industrious International Churches of Christ—but not to be confused with the mainstream Protestant "Church of Christ." The SFCOC reportedly had a habit of luring unsuspecting college students and young professionals, then using high-pressure tactics to convert them into "disciples." Former church members have in turn started their own non-profit organization: **Reveal** (*reveal.org*), chartered to disseminate truthful information about the church and help members leave if they want to.

Organized Religion

We're not going to begin to try and broach this topic here, just provide with you with a few local resources on the majors to get you started.

- **Catholicism**
  St. Mary's Cathedral (HQ of the Archdiocese of San Francisco, 1111 Gough, 415-567-2020, stmarycathedralsf.org)
  St. Ignatius Church (650 Parker, 415-422-2188, stignatiussf.org)

- **Hinduism**
  Vedanta Society (2323 Vallejo, 415-922-2323, sfvedanta.org)
  Chinmaya Mission (1050 Park Avenue, San Jose, 408-998-2793, chinmaya-sanjose.org)

- **Islam**
  Islamic Society of San Francisco (20 Jones, 415-863-7997)
  Islamic Center of San Francisco (400 Crescent, 415-641-9596)

- **Judaism**
  Jewish Community Center of San Francisco (3200 California, 415-292-1200, jccsf.org)
  Beyt Tikkun Synagogue (510-528-6250, beyttikkun.org)
  Chochmat HaLev (2215 Prince Street, Berkeley, 510-704-9687, chochmat.org)

---

retreats

The beautiful wilderness settings of the **Green Gulch Farm** and **Tassajara Zen Mountain Center** (see main text) are especially conducive to meditation.

Green Gulch Farm offers a public program every Sunday that includes meditation instruction, a lecture, tea and lunch, all for a small requested "donation" of $8 for the lunch (participants are also asked to donate something to the temple).

Tassajara, a full-fledged Buddhist monastery, is closed to the public for much of the year but open to guests from May through August (reservations absolutely required). Inner-peace comes at a price if you stay on the premises. A cheaper alternative—for a limited number of day guests—is the $25 day pass ($12 for children), a real bargain when you consider it buys you full access to their excellent facilities, which include hot springs, steam rooms, sun decks, hot plunges, jacuzzis and showers.

BURNING MAN: A RELIGIOUS EXPERIENCE?

What began in 1986 as a small Summer Solstice celebration on Baker Beach has become a worldwide movement: **Burning Man** (*burningman. com*), an annual event that welcomed more than 40,000 participants in 2006.

Every year during the week prior to and including Labor Day weekend, attendees (many of them from San Francisco) make the annual pilgrimage to Black Rock Desert in Nevada. What transpires can be adequately understood only by those who experience the phenomenon in person. Suffice it to say, the event could qualify in any number of categories within this very chapter: drugs, sex, extreme activities, and, yes, even religion.

At its core, Burning Man is simply a pure celebration of creativity, community, and self-expression. There's only one rule: participate, don't spectate. If you go, strap on your safety helmet—you're in for a wild ride!

Buddhism and Zen Centers

We bow to the late, great leisure master Bruce Lee: "The less effort, the faster and more powerful you will be." Heeding Bruce's wise advice (and San Francisco's Asian influences), a variety of local Zen and Buddhist centers are seeking to lead you to enlightenment.

The **San Francisco Zen Center** (sfzc.com) is one of the foremost Buddhist sanghas outside of Asia. You'll find classes, retreats and workshops at any of its three practice centers: the **Beginner's Mind Temple**, also known as **City Center** (300 Page, 415-863-3136); **Green Dragon Temple**, or **Green Gulch Farm** (Muir Beach, 1601 Shoreline Highway, Sausalito, 415-383-3134); or **Tassajara Zen Mountain Center**, also known as **Zen Mind Temple** (39171 Tassajara Mountain Road, Carmel Valley, 831-659-2229). Beginners can start with the Saturday 8:45am introductory session at City Center.

The Mission District's **San Francisco Buddhist Center** (37 Bartlett, 415-282-2018, sfbuddhistcenter.org) is an almost entirely volunteer-run organization that manages to put on an impressive number of classes, events, and retreats. Don't be discouraged if it takes them a few days to return your messages or e-mails; patience and kindness are essential to your Buddha nature.

Personal Growth

There may come a time in your life when it's time to hand over the keys to someone else, and let them take you for a little ride. With luck, you won't end up in a long Kool-Aid line in the middle of the jungle, or in a deep slumber in a San Diego bunk bed sporting a pair of Nikes! Despite the sensational press over these horrible aberrations, there are some very positive and effective self-help programs out there—just find the one that's right for you.

In the Bay Area, try the **Gestalt Institute** (163 East Blithedale, Mill Valley, 415-383-3756, gestaltinstitute.com). It has a legitimate reputation for helping both academics and working (and non-working!) professionals. Another option might be **Sedona Training Associates** (928-282-3522, sedona.com), which is good enough for Joan Collins as well as for many psychologists. Although it's headquartered in Arizona, it holds frequent seminars in San Francisco.

Many local psychologists also specialize in personal growth services, so if one-on-one therapy is more appealing to you, try starting with the **San Francisco Psychological Association** (415-681-3063, sfpa.net) for a local referral.

If you find yourself suddenly in the "wrong" organization, there are groups that can help. Research the **American Family Foundation** (AFF, csj.org), whose mission is to study, educate, and assist people with relation to cults. Also see **CultsOnCampus.com** (cultsoncampus.com) for general information and resources on cults.

GETTING EXTREME

If you prefer the natural high of an adrenalin rush, try extreme sports. San Francisco often hosts ESPN's "X-Games" and is home to almost every imaginable risk-taking activity. If you're feeling extra edgy, do it all without health insurance! (Otherwise see **Chapter 3** for insurance resources).

Bungee Jumping

If jumping from a bridge, out of a hot air balloon, or off a giant crane attached to nothing but a giant rubber band appeals to you, then bungee jumping is for you. At a cost as low as $50 per jump, it makes for a relatively cheap thrill. For jumps in and around Northern California, contact **Bungee Experience** (209-295-6123, californiabungeee.com). Have a nice fall…

Hang Gliding

Ever wanted to fling yourself off a cliff and fly like a bird? **Fort Funston** (Highway 35 near John Muir Drive) is your place, where hang gliders and paragliders congregate and launch themselves over the edge of the Pacific Ocean. Another popular launching point, north of the City, is **Mount Tamalpais** in Marin County, where you can soar over Stinson Beach. **San Francisco Hang Gliding Center** (510-528-2300, sfhanggliding.com) provides lessons, rental equipment, and other hang gliding resources.

Skydiving

There's no rush like falling out of an airplane, whether it's a one-time tandem jump or the first of many solos. **Skydive San Francisco** (707-894-9241, skydivesf. com) can serve your needs. Just remember, when "push" comes to "shove," you have to jump out of a plane strapped to a sack of silk. Bon voyage!

Auto Racing

You may always have dreamed of screaming around a racetrack at top speed. Or perhaps you want to test the limits of your own car. Okay, maybe you're just bored and need to get out of the house. It may be time to get behind the wheel!

Start out on cruise control for the three-hour drive to the race track at **Thunderhill Park** (in Willows, north of Sacramento, 530-934-5588, thunderhill. com). Then rev up your engine with their popular high performance driving school. You'll need your own street-legal car (we highly recommend a Porsche

---

bridge to bridge

Law-abiding citizens, avert your eyes now. We've heard a rumor that some drivers use local bridges at off hours to "determine" how far the needle spins on their speedometer.

The Bay Bridge *was* the bridge of choice, with its split upper and lower one-way levels, until the non-stop construction began. But there's an even bigger obstacle: the highway patrol is on the case. Patrollers often lurk at the Treasure Island on-ramp late at night, waiting to nab speedy drivers.

Westward to 280, perhaps?

911, but that's just us), a three-point belt-harness for both front seats (i.e., the standard shoulder and lap strap), a Snell-rated helmet, and a cool leather jacket. Okay, the jacket's optional. For $225, you get an all-day training class on the track, lunch, and a much-coveted Thunderhill t-shirt. Plus, you get to brag about the day's events over beers afterwards with your new driving comrades.

Shark Diving

Northern California coastal waters are home to *carcharodon carcharias*, a.k.a. the great white shark. One of the most densely populated great white habitats happens to be just off the coast of San Francisco, in the Farallon Islands. Spend the day on a Sanctuary Adventure with the **Farallones Marine Sanctuary Association** (farallones.org); kayak and boat tours offer close encounters with sharks, whales, elephant seals and sea lions, as well as many species of birds. To get even more edgy, don a wetsuit and jump into a shark cage for an up-close-and-personal glimpse of a great white. It's an experience you won't soon forget.

For info on whale watching trips (sans shark diving) to the Farallones, contact the **Oceanic Society** (415-474-3385, oceanic-society.org, then "Whale Watch"). Day trips cost $75 per person Fridays and Mondays, and $78 per person on weekends. Several companies operate shark diving expeditions to the Farallones—curiously, all seem to be affiliated and use the same divemasters. Try **Incredible Adventures** (800-644-7382, incredible-adventures.com/shark_encounter.html). Save your pennies for this one, as the trips are not cheap, running $700–$1,000 per person!

SEX IN THE TIME OF UNEMPLOYMENT

Sexuality and unemployment go together like—well, let's just say they go together. Sex and sexual pursuits take time, energy, and often a certain degree of (pardon the pun) flexibility. For this reason, time off offers the perfect opportunity to put some zest back into your sex life, be it within an existing relationship, or out in the risqué world of the San Francisco underbelly.

Ross Denny (name still changed), our resident green expert, agrees. "One of the nice side benefits to being unemployed and having carnal relations is that you can have a relatively sleepless night, see your lover off to their job in the morning, then go back to bed and catch 40 more winks." He's also a fan of the dual leisure model. "If you find a partner who's also unemployed, then *every* night is a Friday night!"

If it's sex you're looking for, San Francisco is a fruitful place. The City deserves its reputation as one of the most sexually liberated urban centers in the country. There are numerous sexual pursuits to be found in the area, both above and below board. From gay to heterosexual to every combination in between, chances are there are venues and opportunities to meet your needs.

THE MARINA SAFEWAY: FACT OR FICTION?

Ever since Armistead Maupin's popular 1970s serial *Tales of the City* hailed it as *the* pick-up spot in the City, the **Marina Safeway** has held legendary status as a place to hook up. But is this "meat market" reputation still justified?

Many of its frequent patrons say the Marina Safeway's standing is more folklore than reality. Several San Franciscans, in fact, let slip that either location of **Trader Joe's** (3 Masonic, 415-346-9964, or 555 9th Street, 415-863-1292) is the preferred new spot for those looking to get their melons squeezed.

Hooking Up

Is it an intense, immediate connection without emotional commitment, or a simple hit-and-run? No matter the vocab, the one-night stand is a time-honored tradition that fits right into a noncommittal phase of life. If the briefest of flings are your style, be safe and responsible—and then have a go at it! You're going to need to pick a few places to go, and we feel obliged to throw out some suggestions.

Restaurants are becoming the new singles bars, or so it seems in San Francisco. In keeping with this theme, **Solstice** (2801 California, 415-359-1222) in Pacific Heights dishes up sunny cuisine along with unattached minglers (and the lighting seems to make everyone look that much better). **Mamacita** (2317 Chestnut, 415-346-8494) in the Marina is spicy in more ways than one. As for bars, in Russian Hill, try the **Royal Oak** (2201 Polk, 415-928-2303) or **Tonic** (2360 Polk, 415-771-5535) for fraternity-like mingling. Speaking of fraternities, **R Bar** (1176 Sutter, 415-567-7441) is a fun Nob Hill haunt where the focus seems to be on drinking and connecting up. North Beach has plenty of options, but **Tony Nik's** (1534 Stockton, 415-693-0990) is a great place to meet your neighbor, good for singles and couples alike. In the Mission you can take your pick, but you might buzz by **Medjool** (2522 Mission, 415-550-9055) and if the downstairs is too slick for you, head to the rooftop deck; or try **Pink** (2925 16th Street, 415-431-8889) to find yourself a (dance) partner. SOMA's **111 Minna** (you guessed it, 111 Minna, 415-974-1719) is a hip locale where a lot of connections are made nightly.

SAN FRANCISCO'S WILD CHARACTERS ★ Carol Doda ★

In the mid-'60s, San Francisco's reputation as a center for the bawdy and naughty was thrust into the modern era, in large part (and we do mean large) thanks to a then-little-known waitress named Carol Doda. Performing at the Condor Club in North Beach and donning what was dubbed a "topless" bathing suit, she danced her way into titillating infamy.

Doda was an early experimenter with silicone as a body enhancer, and the bathing suit showcased what would soon become her world famous breasts, which went from size 34B to 44DD. Her act included a dramatic entrance whereby she would be lowered from the ceiling dancing on top of a grand piano. Her stirring performances would spark the launch of the modern-day topless dance club. In the late '60s and early '70s she also worked as a spokesmodel for local television station KICU Channel 36, or "The Perfect 36."

Her film credits include several vintage X-rated flicks as well as a role in the 1968 psychedelic romp, *Head*, which starred The Monkees. Doda retired from the entertainment industry in the '80s, and currently is proprietor of Carol Doda's ***Champaign and Lace Lingerie Boutique*** (1850 Union #1, 415-776-6900).

For same-sex hook-ups, the popular **Martuni's** (4 Valencia, 415-241-0205) is a warm and friendly piano lounge where patrons often sing along with the music. Women will have better luck at the **Lexington Club** (3464 19th Street, 415-863-2052, lexingtonclub.com) for female-to-female mingling.

Bars not your scene? Try your local café, laundromat, or grocery store. People are generally much more approachable there than in the average bar. Try this as an opening: "Hi. I'm not working and having fun during my time off. Care to have fun with me?" Okay, so maybe save that line for the EDD office.

Enjoy a different kind of "suds" between wash cycles at **Brain Wash** (1122 Folsom, 415-861-3663), where you can even catch the occasional live band. Care for some appetizers, too? The **Marina Safeway** (350 Bay, 415-781-4374), has long been hailed as San Francisco's meat-market of choice (and we don't mean ground chuck!), yet its reputation appears to be waning (see box above). The **Castro Safeway** (2020 Market, 415-861-7660) is the shopper's choice for same-sex connections.

For café society, mingle with the beautiful people at **The Grove** (2250 Chestnut, 415-474-4843), or hang with young freelancers and med students at **The Canvas** (1200 9th Avenue, 415-504-0070, thecanvasgallery.com).

special performances

Once home to porn queen and sex educator Annie Sprinkle's provocative sex shows, *848 Community Space* (848 Divisadero, 415-922-2385, *848.com*) shows it all—and we *do* mean all. "We have done and will continue to do almost anything!" they say. It's not an understatement. Host to anything from yoga to literary smut to pagan rituals, 848 provides the most open of open forums. Check their calendar for a performance to match your taste.

Strip Clubs

Strip clubs can be fun for boys and girls alike. Ironically, although the modern topless dance club was born in North Beach in the 1960s, San Francisco is now noticeably light on quality strip clubs ("quality" being a relative term here). Striptease connoisseurs need not despair; there are still a few nuggets around.

The **Gold Club** (650 Howard, 415-536-0300) is probably the best option for food, drink and bare breasts. Bargain hunters note—the daily happy hour is from 3pm-7pm, with free admission.

For a strip club of a more, shall we say, "advanced" nature, the **Lusty Lady Theatre** (1033 Kearny, 415-391-3991) is the best value in town. Admission is always free, and private viewing rooms start as low as a quarter. It happens to be the first strip club in the country where all the employees, including the dancers, are unionized. You just can't beat union labor!

Massage Parlors

This section speaks mainly (though not exclusively) to our male readers, so you men out there, listen up: San Francisco is home to one of the most extensive networks of Oriental massage parlors outside of Asia, serving a wide range of tastes and budgets. Keep in mind that these "parlors" aren't always operating above board and that unfortunately, the women aren't always working of their own volition.

That being said, one that our "experts" highly recommend is the **Empire Health Club** (428 O'Farrell, 415-441-4133). Prices begin in the $50-60 range for a half-hour "house massage," rise to $100-150 for a massage with a "happy ending," and swell further from there. And if you have to ask what a happy ending is, might we suggest you skip the massage parlor altogether?

Erotica

Modern porn—at least the film variety—grew up in San Francisco (ah, the memories). The Mitchell Brothers founded their porn empire

GOOD VIBES AT GOOD VIBRATIONS

Back in 1977, sex therapist Joani Blank noticed a lack of resources for women seeking quality sexual information and products, so she created her own store to provide a pleasant, clean, and safe shopping experience for women as well as men. From this humble beginning, *Good Vibrations* (603 Valencia, 415-522-5460; 1620 Polk, 415-345-0400; 2504 San Pablo Avenue, Berkeley, 510-841-8987, *goodvibes. com*) grew into what is now not only a San Francisco institution, but a nationally recognized resource for sexual education and merchandise. Sex-goody connoisseurs will delight in the Valencia Street location's Vibrator Museum, which takes visitors on a historical journey through the evolution of vibrators, as well as the store's infamous "Wall O'Dildos," which is, we trust, self-explanatory.

in the 1960s, making the City a hub for the X-rated film industry until everyone moved south to Los Angeles in the 1980s. You'll still find plenty of good "research" material (film and otherwise) for your sex-capades, but it varies widely in atmosphere and quality.

For some down-n-dirty porn emporiums, flip through **Frenchy's** in the Tenderloin (1020 Geary, 415-776-5940), or the venerable **Big Al's** in North Beach (556 Broadway, 415-391-8510), which claims to have the "best selection of DVDs in the City." For a brighter, more "couples friendly" atmosphere, the place to go is **Good Vibrations** (see box below).

For good old-fashioned film, try the landmark **Mitchell Brothers' O'Farrell Theatre** (895 O'Farrell, 415-776-6686) or any of the much cheaper but dicier adult theaters along Market Street near the Tenderloin.

art of the pole dance

Tired of going to parties and being too embarrassed to pole dance in front of your friends? Okay, so maybe you'd just like to check it out in a safe, private environment. *S Factor* (2159 Filbert, 415-440-6420, *sfactor.com/sf*) exercise studio is all the rage in the City, and striptease and pole dancing classes are their specialty. Spin and shimmy to your heart's content in one of their eight-week courses. Do the clothes come off? Find out for yourself...

Sex Education

If you're serious about getting educated, you're in the right place, as it just so happens that the City is home to the **Institute for the Advanced Study of Human Sexuality** (1523 Franklin, 415-928-1133, iashs. edu). Harboring the largest collection of sexual materials in the world, the institute offers advanced degrees in sexology, including masters and doctorate programs. For more relaxed tutelage, try **Good Vibrations** (see "Good Vibes" previous page). They teach a range of evening classes, from safe sex workshops to BDSM role playing, which—the authors can attest—are both informative and fun.

If you're the shy type, bone up online with **San Francisco Sex Information** (877-472-7374, sfsi.org). Their well-maintained site and hotline is a non-judgmental, one-stop information clearinghouse on sex, and their volunteers are extensively trained. Finally, you can enroll in "adult" education courses at **UC Berkeley Extension** (unex.berkeley. edu) or **City College of San Francisco** (ccsf.edu).

Sex Clubs

If you're really looking to stretch your sexual boundaries, you might consider going to a sex club. San Francisco has several, all legally owned and operated. The only catch—alcohol and other drugs are strictly prohibited. God forbid people mix their alcohol with their orgasms!

Probably the best and most popular is the **Power Exchange** (74 Otis, 415-487-9944, powerexchange.com), which caters to just about every imaginable taste and gender. The venue is divided into two separate clubs: one exclusively for gay and bisexual men, and the other for couples and just about everybody else.

Both clubs used to operate seven days a week, but have recently curtailed to 4-5 nights per week (it seems times are tough, even for sex clubs). If a standard night is not wild enough for you, you can sample one of their special events such as the Fetish Ball & Slave Auction. Crack that whip!

PLACES

Everybody has a favorite outdoor romping ground (don't they?). If you don't, maybe it's time to get one. This list comes from our friends at the **Bay Guardian** (415-255-3100, *sfbg.com*), who have bravely done some research in the noble interests of journalism and public service. Some people return to these sites year after year—or, in some cases, night after night.

• **Red Rocks** (16th Street @ Roosevelt, near the Randall Museum). A little rock enclave above the Castro that's popular with hikers during the day; after dark, it becomes a slice of lurid heaven.

• **Buena Vista Park** (Haight @ Lyon). A popular spot at night for anonymous encounters, mainly of the male variety.

• **Windmills at Golden Gate Park** (West end of Golden Gate Park). For years known as a gay cruising area for anonymous sex, this spot gets downright seedy.

• **Angel Island** (415-435-1915, *angelisland.org*). Plan a date with your partner to this state park, and combine fabulous views with plenty of nooks and crannies. Weekdays are best, when it can be almost deserted.

Gay and bisexual men might also check out **Eros** (2051 Market, 415-864-3767, erossf.com), which emphasizes safe sex, or the overtly-named **Blow Buddies** (933 Harrison, 415-777-4323, blowbuddies.com), a private club that caters to a variety of fetishes. Lastly, insiders recommend **Mack Folsom Prison** (1285 Folsom, 415-252-7127, mackfolsomprison.com) as a quality men's-only membership club—just look for the "Mack" on the door.

MORE FUN WITH YOUR BODY

Many forms of cosmetic self-expression simply won't fly in an office environment, even if that office *does* have a ping-pong table. But if you're no longer reporting to The Man, it might be time for you to dye your hair a crazy color, stick a big ring in your nose, or get that cool snake tattoo you've been eyeing at the local ink parlor. Lower Haight and the Mission are your neighborhoods of choice in this department. A mid-week field trip can help you research these various body alterations.

Tattoos

Tatt' calling your name? You're in luck—San Francisco's tattoo artists are world-famous. One of the best parlors in town is **Sacred Rose Tattoo** in the Mission (491-A Guerrero, 415-552-5778, sacredrosetattoo.com). Just remember—tattoo removal is painful and expensive; anything inked into your skin at 25 should look just as good on you at 50.

Body Piercing

Conveniently located just around the corner from Sacred Rose Tattoo is **Body Manipulations** (3234 16th Street, 415-621-0408, bodym.com), where you can obtain any type of body piercing, branding, or "scarification" under the sun, some of which may make you squirm. Body Manipulations merits the distinction of being the oldest piercing studio in San Francisco, and also maintains the best reputation.

Hair

Nothing signifies a break from conventionality quite like fluorescent spiky hair. To get some groove back into your own, try **Edo Salon** in the Lower Haight (601 Haight, 415-861-0131), or **Glama-Rama** in the Mission (417 South Van Ness, 415-861-4526). Keep in mind when you're done with all that crazy hair, it was your idea, not ours!

 **Leisure Liz**

You like going out with your friends.

You wake up next to a stranger and say, "This could be the start of a beautiful friendship."

You usually have enough money to be able to pay for your entertainment of choice.

You enjoy telling your friends stories about what you did last night or last week.

Sleazure Larry

You no longer have any friends.

You wake up next to a stranger and say, "Who the !$#@ are you, and what are you doing in my bed? Oh—we're not *in* my bed?"

You constantly scrounge for jack to support your activities and owe several people money.

You're ashamed to tell your friends what you did last night or last week—assuming you remember it.

WHEN LEISURE BECOMES SLEAZE-URE

What if you find yourself not only on the edge, but over it? Pay attention to your quality of life; these edgy adventures are supposed to improve your life, not detract from it. If you're concerned about whether you're overindulging in drink, drugs, alcohol, sex, gambling or any other vice, get some help.

Time to Go on the Wagon?

It's amazing how fast an open tab can drain the budget—especially a leisure budget. For now, consider a sojourn to sobriety. Amy O'Reilly (name changed) gave up drinking after her high-tech employer laid her off, so she "could keep a clear head, and not get too depressed."

Same goes for other drugs. Dr. Anthony Liguori, assistant professor working in Human Behavioral Pharmacology at Wake Forest Medical Center, has given his monkeys large daily doses of THC (no, you can't get the monkey job). Guess what—it turns out that the constantly stoned really *are* less motivated. If "wake and bake" has become your non-working motto, it might be a good time to give your liver, lungs and mind a break.

Addictions

A pleasure becomes an addiction when you can't stop, even though you know you should and you aren't even enjoying it anymore. Almost any behavior can become addictive if you're vulnerable, especially if you're depressed.

Here are a few of the organizations that want to help you when you can't help yourself.

- *Freedom from Smoking*
  800-LUNG-USA, *californialung.org*
- *Nicotine Anonymous*
  415-995-1938, *nica-norcal.org*
- *Gamblers Anonymous*
  800-287-8670, *gamblersanonymous.com*
- *Overeaters Anonymous*
  St. Francis Hospital, 900 Hyde @ Pine, 2nd Floor
  415-436-0651, *oasf.org*
- *San Francisco Alcoholics Anonymous*
  415-674-1821, *alcoholics-anonymous.org*
- *Haight Ashbury Free Clinics*
  Alcohol Treatment Services: 558 Clayton, 415-487-5624, *hafci.org*
  Substance Abuse Treatment Center: 529 Clayton, 415-565-1908, *hafci.org*
- *Narconon*
  atop Mt. Madonna near Watsonville, CA, 800-772-5570
  california-drug-rehab.com

EXERCISE THE POWER OF CHOICE

Whoa, some sobering thoughts to end on. But time off is all about choice, edgy or otherwise. Time off can—and should—give you a level of control over your life you've never had before. It's the time to take charge, whether that's through experimentation or by setting new goals. If your new personal power includes the physical, read on for a guide to fitness and recreation in the City by the Bay.

CHAPTER 7
FITNESS & RECREATION

Leave all the afternoon for exercise and recreation, which are as necessary as reading. I will rather say more necessary because health is worth more than learning.

~Thomas Jefferson

ET'S face it, getting in shape doesn't happen overnight. Fitness takes time and dedication. But what better challenge to tackle in order to add some "life" to your work-life balance? Recreational pursuits help refresh the spirit, and can deliver a new perspective.

Physical activity helps keep you out of the doctor's office, a boon if you're underinsured. It makes you look good. More important, it makes you feel good, and it's the perfect way to maintain a sense of achievement if by chance you don't have a regular employer to reward your accomplishments.

In fact, staying fit will be more important than ever if you suddenly have fewer commitments. Exercise keeps you moving. Consider it a crucial obligation—to yourself. Others might come to the rescue if you blow your sabbatical budget, but no one else can work out for you.

Set modest goals if you're just starting—lose 10 pounds, run a 12K race—or simply look better naked. If you're already reasonably fit, choose something more aggressive like competing in a marathon or triathlon. Or, if you just want to get out of the house more, perhaps walking, hiking or biking is enough. Regardless, shoot for a pattern that you can stick with whether your schedule is rigid or flexible. Maintaining a healthy mind and body is yet another key to the lifestyle of leisure.

THE GYM WORKOUT

Once you've committed to fitness, the next choice is where to work out. Gyms are a reliable option. "I got up at 5am every single day and went to the gym," Marsha Converse told us. "It was one of the best things I did for myself after I got laid off."

Private health clubs abound in San Francisco. Their luxury touches vary from the ear-splitting rhythms of **24-Hour Fitness** (eight San Francisco locations, 24hourfitness.com) to an onsite spa and butternut squash risotto (zero calories, honest!) at the posh **Bay Club** (150 Greenwich, 415-433-2200, sfbayclub.com), but even the sparsest weight room will pump you up. Monthly dues vary accordingly.

LOCAL CLUBS	
Club One seven SF locations clubone.com	**Sports Club/LA** 747 Market, 415-633-3900 thesportsclubla.com
Gold's Gym 2301 Market, 415-626-4488 1001 Brannan, 415-552-4653 goldsgym.com	**Crunch Fitness** six SF locations crunch.com

The deal at the **Embarcadero YMCA** (169 Steuart, 415-957-9622, ymcasf.org/embarcadero) may have the most muscle, with no upfront membership fee, no minimum time commitment and moderate monthly dues. The Y's four floors of fitness include a rooftop track, an indoor Olympic-sized pool and classrooms for cardio-kickboxing and tae kwon do.

If you get your kicks from Pilates, try a small neighborhood health center such as **Elevation Pilates** (3425 Balboa, 415-386-9008, elevationpilates.com), or **The Center Studio** (2168 Market, 415-861-3932, thecenterstudio.com).

The university gyms also make good neighbors. Residents within a certain radius are eligible for annual membership at the first-rate **Koret Health & Recreation Center** (at USF, Turk & Parker, 415-422-6821, usfca.edu/koret). Koret's got it all: an Olympic-sized pool (see "Swimming" later in chapter), three basketball courts, five racquetball courts, a weight room, two aerobics studios and one sun deck—for tanning the old-fashioned way. Neighbors who live within the bounds of 3rd Avenue, Lyon, California & Haight can join for $600 per year. Others can pay a drop-in day pass for $15, or a fifteen-use pass for $78, good anytime except Monday through Thursday after 2pm.

There's a new health center that's rivaling Koret's status as top dog in the City: UCSF's recently-finished **Bakar Fitness & Recreation Center** (1675 Owens, 415-514-4545, mbfitness.ucsf.edu), located on their new campus at Mission Bay. The facility is open to the public (availability permitting), and among other fitness goodies features a dramatic outdoor pool with a view of downtown, and a wide variety of the very latest exercise equipment.

UCSF's other workout facility, **Millberry Center** (at UCSF, 500 Parnassus, 415-476-1115, cas.ucsf.edu), is open to neighbors and the general public during liberal off-peak hours. Millberry and Bakar members receive discounts not only on athletic classes and training, but across a whole spectrum of recreation, from concerts and movies to equipment rentals and outings from **UCSF's Outdoors Unlimited** (500 Parnassus, 415-476-2078, outdoors.ucsf.edu, and see the **Leisure Shopping Guide**).

GYM SLUTTING

Can't decide where to work up a sweat? Try "gym slutting:" going from one free trial membership to another. Most chains offer two weeks gratis to first-time local guests. Hit up five of the franchises in the City, and that's 2+ months of gym membership—for free!

Dana Magenau did just that when he first came to San Francisco. "I felt it was in my best interest to thoroughly investigate the pros and cons of each and every gym out there," he told us with a wink.

The best introductory rates come from yoga and Pilates studios. If the first class isn't free, it's sure to be cheap, as low as a dollar a day on the "90 days for $90" plan at *Sacred Space Healing Center* (776 Haight, 415-431-0878, *sacredspace-sf.com*). By the time you're done making the rounds to other yoga open houses, you'll probably be done with your sabbatical. At least with all that stretching, you won't be a corporate stiff.

MiND & BODY

Rough and tumble contact sports not your style? Then peace out through Tai Chi or yoga.

Tai Chi

The **Golden Gate Park Tai Chi Class** (Spreckels Lake, 36th Avenue & Fulton) schools students on weekends, no charge. The experts rise, shine, and salute at 6:30am, and beginners join in a couple of hours later. This group also teaches at **City College of San Francisco** (John Adams Campus, Masonic & Hayes), **AP Giannini Middle School** (3151 Ortega, 415-759-2770), and cable Channel 29.

During the week, the faithful practice at Golden Gate Park's 6th Avenue cul-de-sac (a.k.a. **Roller Village**) and in its **Music Concourse** (surrounded by the Academy of Sciences, the closed de Young Museum and the former Asian Art Museum). Tai Chi'ers also favor **Washington Square Park** (Columbus & Union) in the wee hours of the morning.

Yoga

Strike a pose with yoga, another way to ease into exercise. **Yoga Tree** (780 Stanyan, 415-

---

burn, baby, burn

You might anticipate getting in the best shape of your life with all this time to pump iron. The funny thing is, you'd burn calories just reading, or sunbathing in the park—even rolling a joint! Your basal metabolic rate (BMR) measures how many calories you burn to maintain normal body functions like breathing, heartbeat, and staying warm, and it accounts for 60-70% of the calories you fire through each day.

So if you're firmly planted on the couch watching Oprah, why bother with exercise?

Here's why. Even at rest, a pound of muscle burns more calories than a pound of fat—*twenty-five times* more. True, you'd have to do some serious strength training to add more than five or ten pounds of muscle, but increasing your BMR by building muscle will still give you that extra edge in keeping in shape even when you're sitting on a chair behind a desk.

Calculate your BMR online at *Global Health & Fitness* (*global-fitness.com*, "Free Tools & Content").

Their "BMR Calculator" will tell you how many calories you can consume without gaining weight. It takes into account the burn from key leisure activities such as Strolling (210 calories/hour), Golfing with a Pull Cart (300 calories/hour), and Square Dancing (350 calories/hour—yee haw!).

387-4707, yogatreesf.com) is a popular studio these days, and it has new locations sprouting up all over the City, including sites in the Mission, Hayes Valley, and the Castro. **The Mindful Body** (2876 California, 415-931-2639, themindfulbody.com) will indeed be mindful of your body as you partake in their large selection of Hatha and Ashtanga yoga classes.

Don't let them call it Hot Yoga, though, unless they're paying dues to Bikram Choudhury. He founded *and copyrighted* the routine of 26 Hatha yoga poses performed in a very warm room and known as Bikram Yoga. Bikram is not always a battle—many instructors tailor their sessions to newbies and pregnant women—but advanced practitioners revel in the more competitive environment.

particularly hot studios

Funky Door Yoga
1749 Waller, 415-668-2227
1364 Polk, 415-673-8659
186 2nd Street, 415-957-1088
2567 Shattuck Avenue, Berkeley, 510-204-9642
funkydooryoga.com

Global Yoga
2425 Chestnut, 415-292-9774
6300 California, 415-751-6908

Bikram's Yoga College of India
455 Judah, 415-753-8694

THE GREAT OUTDOORS

How about those outdoor workouts? Shuffle along amidst redwood, fir and eucalyptus trees, or whack tennis or croquet balls at **Sigmund Stern Grove** (19th Avenue & Sloat). The adjoining **Larsen Park** has both tennis and basketball courts, plus an indoor swimming pool (see **Sava Pool** in "Swimming" later in chapter), although classes soak up most of the pool schedule. **Parkside Square**, also next door, adds a baseball diamond and a court apiece to the tennis and basketball rosters.

The **Presidio** is another free public "gym" available around the clock (see **Bay Area Ridge Trail** under "Biking" and "Hiking"), but for sheer variety and expanse, no City land tops the green acres of **Golden Gate Park**.

GOLDEN GATE PARK

Golden Gate Park (415-831-2700) is a one-stop workout shop! The wild and wooly park contains more than 1000 acres of athletic wonderland, compared to 25,000 square feet for a typical San Francisco health club (never mind that 74,999 other "members" will be working out with you on any given weekend). Here's the whole circuit:

• Smash and volley on the 21 recently resurfaced courts in the **Golden Gate Park Tennis Complex** (across JFK Drive from the Conservatory of Flowers, 415-753-7001). Reservations are required for weekends and holidays only; call on Wednesdays between 4-6pm. Get the scoop on rates, free youth tennis and the **Adult Beginning Drop-In Tennis Program** on Saturdays from the clubhouse (415-831-6302). • Would you rather two-wheel it? Rent a **mountain bike** or **beach cruiser** from **Wheel Fun Rentals** (next to Stow Lake Boat House, 415-668-6699, wheelfunrentals.com) and cycle from the top of the Panhandle down to Ocean Beach. Middle Drive is closed to cars on Saturdays. • Inline skaters should turn out on Sundays and holidays, when JFK Drive is closed to cars between Kezar & Transverse Drives. The **Golden Gate Park Skate Patrol** (volunteers trained in First Aid and CPR) services this emissions-free zone. Sundays attract roller skaters, too (takes you back, doesn't it?). DJ David G. Miles, Jr., a.k.a. the Mayor of Golden Gate Park and the founder of Skate Patrol, starts pumping the jams around noon at **Roller Village**, the park's freshly paved and expanded roller disco (Fulton & 6th Avenue, near the Rose Garden). • Reel down the tempo at the **flycasting ponds** (near JFK Drive & 36th Avenue and the Bison Paddock, 415-386-2630). You'll have to bring your own equipment, but the ponds require no reservation and are considered some of the best in the country. The nearby **Angler's Lodge** is free on Tuesdays, Thursdays, Saturdays and Sundays. • We could get into this no-reservations agenda. Are you with us? Walk right up to the publicly-priced nine-hole **Golden Gate Golf Course** (47th Avenue & Fulton, behind the Beach Chalet, 415-751-8987).

Bikers and bladers will like the smooth race track at the **Polo Field** (opposite 35th Avenue), also known as Golden Gate Park Stadium and familiar to many as the Bay to Breakers after-party site (see **Fairs & Fests**). The Polo Field hosts soccer games and a parcourse, too.

Ditto for the two indoor and two outdoor handball courts (on Middle Drive East between Martin Luther King Jr. & Bowling Green Drives, opposite 7th Avenue and north of the Big Rec baseball field). • The **Archery Field** (47th Avenue just off Fulton) provides bales of hay, but your real target is up to you. Rent equipment at the nearby **San Francisco Archery Pro-Shop** (3795 Balboa, 415-751-2776, bysel.com). • Rent a **boat**—row, pedal, or motor—and float around Strawberry Hill and past Huntington Falls in **Stow Lake** (Boathouse near JFK & Cross Over Drives, 415-752-0347). • Horseback riders have been out of their saddles since 2001, when the 130-year-old **stables** closed for renovation. Chaps your hide, does it? Then support the **San Francisco Stables Foundation** (155 17th Avenue, 415-255-2003) in lobbying for new non-profit stables, which would be unique in the City and would offer guided rides along the park's 12 miles of bridle trails. • Or use those trails for hiking. Both bridle and walking trails stretch to almost every corner of the park, including the **Senior Citizens' Exercise Course** (Fulton & 36th Avenue, behind the Senior Center). • Alterna-sportsters play Ultimate Frisbee at the **Kezar Triangle** (just west of Kezar Stadium) and also at **Sunbather Meadow** (across from the handball courts). •

KEZAR STADIUM

Although the site dates back to 1922, the City rebuilt the original *Kezar Stadium* (on Frederick, near the Haight) after the 1989 Loma Prieta earthquake. And what a fine job they did! This former home of the San Francisco 49ers now seats 10,000 and houses all-weather track and field facilities for high school football games and other team sports, including *rugby*.

• Want to join a team that's more conventional? (Hint: it's *not* the Leisure Team.) • • Play baseball on the two diamonds at **Big Rec Ball Field** (north of 7th Avenue), softball in **Mother's Meadow** (at Waller & Kezar) or at **Speedway Meadow** (JFK Drive south of 24th Avenue), or soccer at the **Beach Chalet Soccer Complex** (just east of the windmill behind the Beach Chalet). The **Athletic Fields Reservation Office** is in **Pioneer Log Cabin** (near Stow Lake, 415-831-5510). • • Find feisty pickup basketball in the **Panhandle** (Masonic between Fell & Oak)—no reservations required, just "game." •

public pools

Balboa Pool
San Jose & Havelock
415-337-4701

Coffman Pool
Visitacion & Hahn
415-337-4702

Garfield Pool
Harrison & 26th Street
415-695-5001
water aerobics

Hamilton Pool
Geary & Steiner
415-292-2001
masters workouts
water aerobics

King Pool
Carroll & 3rd Avenue
415-822-2807
75' x 42' & kid's pools

Mission Pool
Linda & 19th Street
415-695-5002
outdoor, summer only

North Beach
Lombard & Mason
415-391-0407
two 90' x 25' pools
water aerobics

Rossi Pool
Arguello & Anza
415-666-7014
water aerobics

Sava Pool
Wawona & 19th Avenue
415-753-7000
masters workouts
water aerobics

WATER SPORTS

Swimming

Hazel Langenour became the first woman to swim across the Golden Gate channel on August 11, 1911 (the same year Californian women won the right to vote). Enquiring minds want to know: did she train at a public pool?

The **Recreation & Park Department** (501 Stanyan, 415-831-2747 for the Aquatic Office, sfgov.org, search for "rec park") maintains plenty of heated and affordable public pools: only a dollar a swim for those in "economic need" and just one quid more for a lesson. Recreational swim hours vary by season and are limited at times to an hour a day, but most pools are indoor and 40' x 100' unless otherwise noted. Facilities include showers, changing areas and bring-your-own-lock lockers.

The functional but sparse city pools, however, pale in comparison to the City's best pool: at the **Koret Center** (see "The Gym Workout"). Koret features an Olympic-sized indoor pool (that's 50 meters, in case it's been a while since you've seen the summer Olympics), a competitive masters swim team, even certified lifeguards. A close second is the outdoor pool at **Bakar Fitness & Recreation Center** (see "The Gym Workout"). With a sweeping view of downtown to your north, you can work on your breast stroke and your tan at the same time.

The **Dolphin Swimming & Boating Club** (502 Jefferson, Aquatic Park, 415-441-9329, dolphinclub.org) has been a

San Francisco institution since 1877. Even local health guru Jack LaLanne is an honorary lifetime member. Dolphins swim at Aquatic Park and escape from Alcatraz (see following page). They pay a fair price

GREAT MOMENTS IN UNEMPLOYMENT

Fitness maverick *Jack LaLanne* is world-famous for his tireless work ethic, even though he's never clocked in with an "employer" in his life. Instead, he chose a path of entrepreneurship at an early age. As a teen, he was inspired by a crusading nutritionist speaking in Oakland, and discovered the Berkeley YMCA soon after. At age 21—about 40 years ahead of his time—LaLanne opened an Oakland gym, the nation's first modern health club. ••• LaLanne came up with early designs for many of today's weight and exercise machines, and spread the gospel of fitness through a variety of products and media, including a television show that aired daily for an incredible 34 years. At 89, he's still going strong, threatening to celebrate his 90th birthday by swimming—handcuffed and shackled—from Alcatraz to Fisherman's Wharf, a feat he performed at age 60 while towing a 1000-pound boat. In fact, nutty local stunts have always been a staple with LaLanne: at age 40, he swam the length of the Golden Gate Bridge, underwater, with air tanks and 140 pounds of equipment; at age 44 he paddled 30 miles from the Farallon Islands to the San Francisco shore; and he's swum to shore from Alcatraz several times, typically with his limbs bound and thousands of pounds of cargo in tow. Why? To add to the challenge, of course. As LaLanne has shown over and over, *"If your mind can conceive, your body can achieve."*

to do so, but it's worth every penny and jar of petroleum jelly to Dolphin Club Polar Bears—swimmers who log in 40 miles or more during winter. Brrrrr!

Triathlon Clubs

The in-house masters swim team of the **Golden Gate Triathlon Club** (ggtc.org) takes care of its water workouts at **Herbst Natatorium** (2001 37th Avenue). The first session is free, then it will run you $6 to drop in and $45 to swim all month. Individual membership in U.S. Masters Swimming is required, at $25 a year.

But why not go the whole nine yards? (Actually, it's a little longer than nine.) Triathlon training is all the rage in San Francisco, especially with women. **Beyond Limits Women's Sports** (415-533-3095, beyond-limits.com/triclub) invites athletes of any level to introduce themselves to the club with a free swim or running workout. The **San Francisco Triathlon Club** (sftriclub.org) doesn't dangle a freebie to newbies, but a $65 payment to this non-profit will get you 12 months

THE ESCAPE FROM ALCATRAZ TRIATHLONS

With all the ways to escape from Alcatraz these days, it's a good thing there's no longer a prison out there. Aside from various swim-only events, no less than three triathlons kick off at the Rock: (1) the *"New Balance Escape from Alcatraz" Triathlon* (in June, *tricalifornia.com*, 831-373-0678); (2) Envirosport's *"Alcatraz Escape from the Rock" Triathlon* (in June, *envirosports.com*, 415-868-1829); and (3) the private *"Escape from Alcatraz"* co-sponsored by the Dolphin Club and its neighbor, the **South End Rowing Club** (in October, *dolphinclub.org*).

Although each is intense, it's the Dolphin's self-proclaimed "granddaddy of escapes" that's got us thinking. Thinking things like, "Who in their right mind would swim 1.25 miles in the Bay—without a wetsuit or fins—then bike 14 miles over the bridge to Mill Valley, and then run 13 miles over Mount Tam's Dipsea Trail to Stinson Beach and back?"

Dolphins, that's who. These urban polar bears have braved the 50°F-61°F Bay water since 1877, well before Aquatic Park opened to the public in 1939. Cold water swimming generates the development of white blood cells, which fight off disease. Polar Bear Peter Drino claims that no one gets sick at the Dolphin Club. What's another 27 miles of biking and running when you've got health like that?

What would *you* be thinking during the 35 to 100 minutes it takes to swim to shore from the Rock—worrying about sharks? No need. No one's been attacked inside the Golden Gate for over 130 years. Not that we're due or anything...

of membership—and a water bottle! Pay $50 to the Golden Gate Triathlon Club (see above) to participate in running and biking workouts, as well as swimming, for a year from the day you sign up.

Rowing & Kayaking

Try the venerable **South End Rowing Club** (500 Jefferson, 415-776-7372) for rowing and swimming, or handball when you're in landlubbing mode. Like the **Dolphin Club** (see "Swimming" above), South End charges non-members $6.50 a day. The Dolphin Club itself has 16 rowboats and several open-water shells, as well as kayaks and a second rowing facility at Lake Merced. **UCSF RecSports** (recsports.ucsf.edu) also has a rowing club at Lake Merced, where it rents its rowing equipment to the public for $230 per year.

For more sea kayaking, talk to UCSF's **Outdoors Unlimited** (see "The Gym Workout")—they offer Ocean Beach outings and moonlight paddles to Angel Island. **Sea Trek** (415-488-1000) rents kayaks on Angel Island itself to those who have experience and a reservation.

---

skating on thin ice

Okay, so it's frozen, but ice is still H2O, which makes ice skating *sort of* a water sport. Figure your eights or skid to a hockey stop at the only outdoor rink in San Francisco: the **Kristi Yamaguchi Holiday Ice Rink** (Justin Herman Plaza, 415-956-2688), open in winter. (We're talking January here, not June!)

If you'd rather remain indoors, glide over to the **Yerba Buena Ice Skating Center** (above the Moscone Center, 750 Folsom, 415-820-3532, *skatebowl.com*).

TENNIS

San Franciscans can play the budget-friendly sport of tennis year-round. You might even make a friend or two while you're at it. In fact, the three courts at **JP Murphy Playground** (1960 9th Avenue @ Ortega) boast the best "pick up" tennis in the Bay Area.

If you're just starting out, then you're in luck, as the City's Recreation & Park Department (sfgov.org/site/recpark_index.asp) offers free lessons at courts across

town. You just have to show up with a racquet and a can of tennis balls to donate. Go to their website and search "tennis" for more details.

The pristine courts of the City's private tennis clubs are for members only. Not only do you have to be a member to use the 12 indoor or 12 rooftop courts of the **SF Tennis Club** (645 5th Street, 415-777-9000, sftennis.com), but you have to wrangle an invite from another member just to join. The club does offer *something* for nothing—the excellent pointers on their website!

HOLDING COURT

| *Rossi Playground* Arguello & Anza 415-666-7011 (restored surfaces, new fencing and new benches) | *Mission Dolores Park* Dolores & 19th Street 415-554-9529 (6 courts) | *McLaren Park* Mansell & Visitacion 415-337-4700 (8 courts) | *Hamilton Rec Center* 1900 Geary @ Steiner 415-292-2008 (a pool to splash around in after your match; table tennis, too) |
| | *Moscone Rec Center* Chestnut & Buchanan 415-292-2006 (4 courts) | *Mountain Lake Park* Lake & 12th Avenue 415-666-7005 (ducks and geese) | |

GOLF

You might assume that green fees would blow a leisure budget. Guess again. For only $40/year, SF residents can buy a Golf Resident card and get significant discounts at five of the six city-owned golf courses. Pick one up at City Hall (Treasurer's Office, Room 140, 1 Dr. Carlton B. Goodlett Place).

Then tee off for nine holes at the par 27 **Golden Gate Park Golf Course** (see "Ultimate Gym" earlier in chapter) or for a full 18 at the par 68 **Lincoln Park Golf Course** (34th Avenue @ Clement, 415-221-9911). Admire the flora and fauna from the 18 holes of par 72 **Sharp Park** (at the foot of Sharp Park Road off of I-280, Pacifica, 650-359-3380) or turn 9 holes into 18 by teeing off from different pins the second time around at **Gleneagles Golf Course** (in McLaren Park, 2100 Sunnydale, 415-587-2425). Since Gleneagles is leased to a private management company, your resident card won't work here.

The 18 holes at the newly renovated **Harding Park Golf Course** (99 Harding Road @ Skyline, near Lake Merced, 415-661-1865) are the crown jewel in the City's golf program. It has developed a reputation as one of the best municipal courses in the country, good enough to attract the PGA and a big pro tourney every three years. The City has also renovated the 9-hole Fleming Park (adjacent to Harding Park).

BIKING

Swimming? Tennis? Golf? Enough already with the country club sports. It's time to change gears—into biking gear, that is.

If you don't own a bike, a rental will run you about $5/ hour or $25/day. Shops providing sales, repairs, parts, and rentals are located throughout the city, but are concentrated around Golden Gate Park and around Fisherman's Wharf. The following stores rent bikes; some rent skates and blades, too.

Fisherman's Wharf Area

Bay City Bike Rentals & Tours
(2261 Taylor @ Beach, 415-346-2453, *baycitybike.com*)

Bike and Roll Adventure Bicycle Co.
(899 Columbus, 415-229-2000, *bikeandroll.com*)

Blazing Saddles
(1095 Columbus; 2715 Hyde @ Aquatic Park; Piers 41 & 43; 415-202-8888, *blazingsaddles.com*)

Golden Gate Park Area

Golden Gate Park Bike and Skate
(3038 Fulton, 415-668-1117)

Surrey Bikes & Blades
(50 Stow Lake Drive, 415-668-6699)

Avenue Cyclery
(756 Stanyan, 415-387-3155)

critical mass

Despite a bit of road rage from gridlocked drivers and over-zealous cyclists, the "unorganized coincidence" known as *Critical Mass* (*critical-mass.org*) still rolls through town each month, reclaiming public streets for bicycles with the rallying cry, "We're not blocking traffic, we *are* traffic!"

This two-hour holiday from cars starts from *Justin Herman Plaza* (foot of Market @ Embarcadero) at 6pm on the last working Friday of each month. Most participants cheer and holler through the Broadway Tunnel (or wherever else they roll that night) while most onlookers smile and wave them on.

From its humble beginnings with 48 riders in year one, Mass has spread to 300+ cities around the world. In its heyday, you could trace the route by watching where the TV choppers flew. More than 10,000 cyclists turned out to celebrate its tenth anniversary on September 27, 2002.

Find out more in *Critical Mass: Bicycling's Defiant Celebration*, an anthology edited by Chris Carlsson, one of the original riders.

The **San Francisco Bicycle Coalition** (415-431-2453, sfbike.org) offers general information on biking in the City, and cooperates with the **Department of Parking and Traffic** and the **Bicycle Advisory Committee** to provide the *San Francisco Bike Map & Walking Guide*. The Bike Map shows street grades, bike lanes, bike paths and three official bike routes—the "Waterfront" (15 miles), the "Tour of Parks" (25 miles) and the "City Loop" (30 miles).

Biking in San Francisco is so good that Henry Kingman wrote a whole book about it: *Short Bike Rides In and Around San Francisco*. Find history, pictures, detailed routing and mileage for rides like the "Sneaky Crosstown Route" and the "Midtown Mosey."

Mountain Biking

You're not obligated to mountain bike just because you live 20 miles from the sport's birthplace, but how can you not? "Downhill runs [are] the ultimate test of handling," according to Joe Breeze of **Breezer Bikes** (P.O. Box 717, Sausalito, breezerbikes.com). Them there are fightin' words!

The dirt and rocks of **Mount Tamalpais** in Marin County prompted custom bike-manufacturer Gary Fisher and his friends to deck out their rides, which led to the first formal, timed downhill race and eventually seeded the growth of the whole industry (see box next page). Mount Tam remains one of the country's most visited mountain biking spots. Whether you're heading all the way up or only as far as the Headlands, find downloadable maps and recommended single track, advanced, and winter rides at marintrails.com/biking.

GO TELL iT ON THE MOUNTAIN

Otis Guy, Gary Fisher, Tom Ritchey, Joe Breeze and friends could hardly have predicted that their enthusiasm for chugging up Mount Tam's steep slopes (on one-speed bikes!) and barreling back down again would earn them a place in local lore. After all, they weren't the first ones to do it.

A group of cyclists known as the Canyon Gang held their earliest races on Mount Tam in 1971, aided by the "balloon tire:" a tire phat and knobby enough to handle the punishment of rapid off-road descents. Five years passed before the first official race on October 21, 1976, down the east face of Pine Mountain just north of Mount Tam. The blistering speeds so hammered the riders' coaster brakes that they had to re-pack their hubs with new grease in order to make the ride again. The trail itself became known as Repack, still a popular and intense 2-mile, 1300-foot downhill bomb for the fearless.

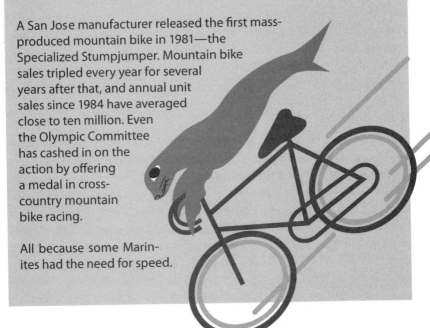

A San Jose manufacturer released the first mass-produced mountain bike in 1981—the Specialized Stumpjumper. Mountain bike sales tripled every year for several years after that, and annual unit sales since 1984 have averaged close to ten million. Even the Olympic Committee has cashed in on the action by offering a medal in cross-country mountain bike racing.

All because some Marin-ites had the need for speed.

touring

While they're nowhere near as ubiquitous as mountain bikers (or bike messengers, for that matter), long-distance riders do have a place in the City. Those who want the challenge can spin along the local segment of the *Pacific Coast Bicycle Route* (adv-cycling.org, under "Routes & Maps" then "Pacific Coast"). Route 95 stretches a full 1,830 miles from Oregon to Mexico, rolling through San Francisco along the way.

If you go off road (as you should) in Golden Gate Park, hit it on a weekday so you don't run into (or over!) pedestrians. Most of the trails are bike-legal, although you'll see tell-tale treads on a few no-bike zones anyway.

The Presidio, on the other hand, closes most trails to mountain bikes. The bike-able portion of the **Bay Area Ridge Trail** (415-561-2595, ridgetrail.org) in the Presidio runs a puny 2.5 miles. Yet, as **San Francisco Mountain Biking** (sfmtb.com) envisions it, an official Presidio Loop could be so much more—10.1 miles and an 1140-foot elevation gain. Download the *San Francisco Mountain Biking Map* from their site, plus see maps of challenging routes such as The San Francisco Epic (24.62 miles, 1661-foot elevation gain) and the Mount Davidson There-And-Back (over 18 miles and 1146 feet up).

What, you want *more*? Then snag a copy of *Mountain Bike! Northern California* by Linda Austin, which details 100 rides. If you'd like some in-person advice, chat with the nice folks at **Valencia Cyclery** (1077 Valencia, 415-550-6601, good for beginners to intermediates) or **American Cyclery** (858 Stanyan, 415-876-4545; 510 Frederick, 415-664-4545, americancyclery.com), which specializes in advanced bikes as well as riding gear.

Excursions

Some cyclists simply seek leisure. (Say *that* ten times fast!) For those who favor fun over fitness, we highlight three sightseeing rides.

The first is **49-Mile Scenic Drive**—map available online (onlyinsanfrancisco.com, click on "Maps" then "Citywide Map") or in hard copy at the **San Francisco Visitor Information Center** (Hallidie Plaza, 900 Market @ Powell, 415-391-2000). It could take a while to bike this baby (4-6 hours of riding time, plus frequent beer, snack, and photo-op stops) so bring a lock. You'll want to replace the freeway stretches with some alternate streets so consult the map on that one. Beware of a few ambitious hills, including Twin Peaks, Land's End, and California Street on Nob Hill. Take your time, please, and if it suits you, don't hesitate to stretch the trek out over several days, as any *leisure connoisseur* would.

Make the much shorter jaunt across the Golden Gate Bridge any time of day or night. No schedule, that's leisurely too! The bridge ride covers only 1.7 miles, unless you tack on the climb to the Marin Headlands. You are required to ride on the east side path on weekdays between 6:30am and 3:30pm, and on the west side path at any other time. No pedestrians are allowed on the west side, not ever, so if you're prone to collisions, that's the path for you.

Pedal from there to **Sam's Anchor Café** (27 Main Street, Tiburon, 415-435-4527, samscafe.com). The ride from the City is only half the fun! Follow the old Southern Pacific Railroad tracks (which used to connect to a ferry station in Sausalito) and then the scent of Eggs Benedict and Bloody Marys. Afraid you'll get a little tipsy while you're there? By all means, take the ferry back!

FITNESS HOBBIES

Workouts don't all need to be about pain and suffering. Fitness hobbies offer numerous benefits—they focus your mind, they give you a sense of accomplishment, and they improve your physical conditioning at the same time. All that, and they're a heck of a lot of fun!

Walking

Healthy feet can hear the very heart of Mother Earth—or so said that Sioux sage, Sitting Bull. We couldn't agree more. Walking is a great way to kickstart a lapsed cardio program. Take a walk in the park—any park—or, for a more urban adventure, stroll along the Embarcadero

parcourses

With a name as dated as "Jazzercise," parcourses are indeed a throwback, but we'll bet you didn't know that they arrived in the U.S. via San Francisco. Back in 1973, a Bay Area real estate developer named Peter Stocker, after seeing outdoor courses of exercise stations over in Europe, assembled the very first parcourse in *Mountain Lake Park* (the Presidio, near Park Presidio @ Lake) using handmade wooden signs.

Amazingly, a few remain around San Francisco (unlike Ripley's Museum, believe it or not!). Instructions on exercises like the Achilles stretch, log hop, vault-bar and up to two dozen others are evenly spaced throughout courses on *Marina Boulevard*, in *Golden Gate Park* (around the Polo Field), and around *Lake Merced*. For a quicker workout, ride your bike between stations. Or, roll your own parcourse: do calisthenics at regular intervals during a run.

adjacent to the Financial District. What was once an industrial wasteland is now a delightful waterfront promenade, seven miles from end to end.

Another visually appealing and easy waterfront walk is the Golden Gate Promenade, four miles from Aquatic Park past the Marina Green to Fort Point. Stock up on supplies at the (oh my gawd!) **Marina Safeway** (15 Marina @ Laguna). Perambulate past the kite-flyers on the **Marina Green** (Marina Boulevard between Scott & Webster), pass the volleyball players near the **St. Francis Yacht Club,** and sail on into **Crissy Field** (see **Chapter 4**). If you're feeling ambitious, continue an extra 1.7 miles across the Golden Gate Bridge. Only the east side is open to pedestrians, but that's okay—you'll enjoy unobstructed views of the famous skyline.

Oh, did we forget to mention that hill? The foot of the bridge looms a couple hundred feet above Fort Point. Alex, a financial analyst, knows the route well. "I was on a serious walking regime after having a quintuple bypass," he told us, "but the hills were really killing me." Oh, the irony! Alex complained to his doctor. The prescription? More hills! "When I'm not trudging up to the bridge, I walk the crooked part of **Lombard Street** (between Hyde & Leavenworth)—backwards." See "Running Stairs" later in the chapter if you're inclined to find more inclines.

SUDS IN THE WOODS

Deep in the heart of Muir Woods up in Marin lies what could easily be mistaken for a mirage: a Swiss-style alpine chalet at the end of a hiking trail... serving cold beer. Is it real? We'll let you discover for yourself. *The Tourist Club* is run by Naturfreunde (Nature Friend), a members-only group originally based out of Vienna, Austria. The club is open on weekends from May-September, save the second Sunday of the month when it's closed for work parties. On the third Sunday of May, July and September, the lederhosen and musical instruments come out for some oom-pa-pa fun.

And where is this so-called "club" located? That we'll leave up to the true leisure seekers among us. Suffice it to say, seek and ye' shall find.

LOCAL CAMPING

While Northern California is chock full of great camping options, there are a few within easy striking distance of the City that you could just as easily hit up on a weeknight as you could a full weekend.

Angel Island is the largest island in the bay, making **Angel Island State Park** (415-435-1915, *angelisland.org*) quite popular in summer for hiking, biking and camping. Its fire roads and foot trails include 8 miles of steep roadway and the 5-mile mostly-flat Perimeter Trail. If you're up for a little altitude adjustment, take the short but angular Northridge/Sunset loop trail to the Mount Livermore summit—the 360-degree view is fantastic.

You'll have to pack your gear up the same steep slope to reach the island's nine campsites, each equipped with a picnic table, food locker, running water, pit toilet, and BBQ (no wood fires allowed), but having the park to yourself after the last ferry leaves and being able to see the night lights of San Francisco and the Golden Gate Bridge right from your sleeping bag will more than make up for the cold, wind, and fog. Or so says Tom Stienstra, author of not only *California Hiking* but also *California Camping*. Call **ParkNet** (800-444-7275) for reservations. Unless you're up for a frigid swim through a major shipping channel filled with sweeping currents, the way to get there is on the **Blue & Gold Fleet** (Pier 41, Fisherman's Wharf, 415-705-8200, *blueandgoldfleet. com*). It takes 40 minutes each way and costs $10.50 round trip, which covers the park entry fee.

Kirby Cove (Marin Headlands, 800-365-2267, *nps.gov/goga/camping/ kirby.htm*) is a magical retreat that's just a stone's throw from the hustle and bustle of the Golden Gate Bridge. Managed by the National Park Service as part of the Golden Gate National Recreation Area (GGNRA), the cove and surrounding grove offers day use facilities in addition to four overnight campsites.

Go to sleep to the sound of foghorns echoing into the night, and awake to a prime view of the Golden Gate Bridge. Even the name "Kirby Cove" sounds peaceful. For weekend camping, plan on making reservations four months ahead, but consider that the site also makes a perfect midweek getaway—after your night in the woods, you can get up early and still make it to work on time... or not! The season runs April 1 through October 31.

Head back to the flatlands along the **Great Highway**. You'll have to share the trail with bicyclists and joggers, but the smell of the salt air will make any congestion worth braving. Starting at the south end (Great Highway @ Sloat) and walking north will eventually lead you to the **Cliff House** (1090 Point Lobos, 415-386-3330, cliffhouse.com) and the **Camera Obscura** (a giant antique camera that produces 360-degree views of the Seal Rocks area, giantcamera.com). If you've practiced on any of San Francisco's other steep streets, the ramp up from sea level to the landing above Seal Rocks will be a breeze.

an urban workout: running stairs

For a really intense workout, hustle up and down any of the City's more than 350 stairways.

At the pinnacle of difficulty is the set in the 'Set, a.k.a. the *Temple of Doom* (between 16th Avenue & Funston; Moraga & Pacheco), which features a series of steep stairs, ratcheting ever-skyward (they don't call it the "Temple of Doom" for nothing!). The Temple is frequented by runners and surfers, and includes a natural (unnatural?) chin-up bar over the first set of stairs for interval training.

No less difficult are the *Lyon Street Stairs* (ascending from Green to Broadway), which Marina-types ascend to stick closer to home. Should you miss the tourists on your way up the *Coit Tower Stairs* (Filbert @ Telegraph Hill Way) from North Beach, look for them as you trot back down the hillside via the *Filbert Street Steps* (from Sansome to Coit Tower) to the landscaped Levi Plaza.

Thank you sir, may I have another? Yes, you may. Locate all the stairs your heart (pumping, undoubtedly) desires in *Stairway Walks in San Francisco* by Adah Bakalinsky.

Hiking

What mountain biking is to touring, hiking is to walking. The same dirt trails allow for similar off-road adventure—just at a slower pace.

More than 50 miles of trails weave through the 6300 acres of redwood groves and oak woodlands in the **Marin Headlands** (just north of the Golden Gate Bridge). Those who conquer the climb to the 2571-foot peak of **Mount Tamalpais** (801 Panoramic Highway, Mill Valley, 415-388-2070) will be rewarded with amazing views and maybe even refreshments—the stand is open daily during summer and on weekends the rest of the year. The picnic tables stay put year-round.

Back in San Francisco proper, **Land's End** trails run from Seacliff to the former site of the **Sutro Baths** (near Point Lobos @ 48th Avenue). The trailhead for the Presidio's 2.5 mile stretch of the **Bay Area Ridge Trail** (see "Biking" above) is near Arguello Gate and the Presidio Golf Course Clubhouse.

For more hiking routes, see the comprehensive alphabetical trail index posted on **San Francisco Bay Area Hiker** (bahiker.com), or find a copy of *California Hiking* by Tom Stienstra & Ann Marie Brown.

Jogging (Or Is It Running?)

Even though you can jog just about anywhere you can walk or hike, certain spots attract more joggers than others. The trail around **Lake Merced** (Harding Road off Skyline) is one of them, as is Ocean Beach at low tides when the sand is hard and flat. The Embarcadero is popular with the corporate set at lunchtime or after work.

Want a lane of your own? Circle a track at a high school or at **Kezar Stadium** (see "Golden Gate Park, The Ultimate Gym" earlier in chapter). If you trot out to **Fort Point**, find the painted handprints (and doggie paw prints!) on the wall and give 'em ten. They're there to give you a sense of completion.

non-race footraces

Although it's not competitive for the vast majority of participants, San Francisco's *Bay to Breakers* (see Fairs & Fests) is the largest footrace in the world. In fact, the crowd is so dense for the first mile or two, you couldn't run it if you tried.

"Drinkfest" would be a better word than "footrace" to describe the **Urban Iditarod** (urbaniditarod.com). Still, this trek around the City by humans imitating canines does involve sneakers, a stop watch and a winner's stand. Throw in a few shopping carts and you've got yourself a race. Woof!

If you're old enough to remember Wayne Walker, you are way overdue for a sabbatical. This former 49er and local sportscaster threw down the gauntlet to Race the Cable Cars up Hyde Street. Beaten badly, Wayne was, back in the day when this kind of promo (for Rice-a-Roni?) was still original. Wait, it still is!

Join the members of the **San Francisco Road Runners Club** (415-273-5731, sfrrc.org) on Tuesday nights or Saturday mornings, year-round. Although SFRRC's annual membership is not cheap, the first gallop is always free and drop-ins cost just $5—plus the ubiquitous liability-waiver form. Who needs rights when you can run with the fast crowd?

The **MetroSport San Francisco Run Club** (415-923-6453, e-metro-sport.com) welcomes runners of all levels, even those who merely jog. Meet them on Wednesdays at the corner of Filbert & Fillmore for six to eight miles, no charge (just don't bogart the refreshments, they're for members only). World class athletes occasionally join similar Wednesday freebies of about five miles, no set route (but lots of hills), sponsored by the **Niketown San Francisco Running Club** (278 Post @ Stockton, 415-392-6453). Niketown's refreshments are free for everyone, plus they throw a monthly raffle and occasional seminars into the mix.

Running & Racing

Any doubts about when you graduate from jogging to running? A ticking clock and a number safety-pinned to your shirt will dispel them. It's a race. You paid money. You'd *better* be running!

Racing is a great way to measure progress, as well as augment your wardrobe. (Another t-shirt? At least this one doesn't scream "dot-com victim!") The challenges, which range from short course to long, start with the 5K run/walk and 10K **Run to the Far Side** (Golden Gate Park, produced by RhodyCo Productions: 415-759-2690, rhodyco.com). Contestants, who are both in costume and out, race through scenic Golden Gate Park in November. All racers also gain free admission to the California Academy of Sciences.

Will you run faster in June when you **See Alice Run** (Golden Gate Park, produced by RhodyCo Productions: 415-759-2690, rhodyco.com)? Maybe the concerts and giant post-race party will sustain you through the 5 mile (8K) run and walk through Golden Gate Park. You'll

a drinking club with a running problem

The Hash House Harriers was formed in 1938 by a British expat living in Malaysia, and has grown into a global organization with more than 1,500 chapters in nearly every major city in the world.

Based on the original concept of hare-and-hounds style chases, hash trails are set up by "hares" who set clues for the following pack of "hounds," who run from clue to clue, with everyone finishing at what's called the "On-In" or finishing point. A variety of social tomfoolery ensues there, including ample drink and song.

In San Francisco, stay fit and meet people all for the low, low price of $0 with the local chapter of *Hash House Harriers* (415-566-4274, *sfh3.com*). If you're a neophyte, beware of the "Down-Down."

have to push a little harder for the **Bridge to Bridge Run** (Bay Bridge to Golden Gate Bridge, 415-995-6899, bridgetobridge.com), a 12K sanctioned race (or 7K run and 5K walk). Everyone starts together in front of the Ferry Building.

The **San Francisco Half-Marathon & 5K** in January (415-333-4780, pamakids.org) is one of the nicest half marathons around, starting and ending in Golden Gate Park with a romp alongside the Pacific Ocean en route. If you're prepared to go the full distance, enter the **San Francisco Marathon** (415-284-9653, chroniclemarathon.com), the last Sunday in July.

TEAM SPORTS

Few endeavors fire up the competitive engines faster than team sports, where winning's not everything, it's the only thing—besides the beer and pizza after the game, that is.

Working out with others will keep you enthused about sports and focused on a group goal. You'll keep those sports metaphors current, too, in case you head back to a workplace where phrases like "dropping the ball" and "hitting a home run" are common parlance (see also "Bullshit Bingo" in **Chapter 12**).

Rec Leagues

League play in the City ranges from mainstream, at the **Golden Gate Sport and Social Club** (ggsportandsocialclub.com), to pickup soccer to Ultimate Frisbee. Organized street and roller hockey leagues compete at school playgrounds in the Marina (try **Bladium In-Line Hockey League**, 510-814-4999, bladium.com).

If the words "full contact" excite you, play with the **San Francisco Fog** (sffog.org), a men's and women's rugby club whose goal is the inclusion of gays and people of color. And **Team SF** (teamsf.org) invites everyone under the sun (and the rainbow) to organize and/or participate in just about any sport imaginable (table tennis, anyone?). None of these catch your fancy? Then start a league of your own! If Madonna and Geena Davis can do it, you can too.

Pickup or Drop In

Can't handle the obligation of an organized league? That's perfectly natural. It's a symptom of *job churn*—a condition brought on by a little too much structure. Play pickup or drop in instead. The eligibility rules for the **UCSF Drop In Leagues** (recsports.ucsf.edu) couldn't be simpler: just show up and pay! Women's basketball runs $20 per quarter, and volleyball and badminton are each $18 for 5 drop-ins. The tennis club charges $20 per person per quarter to cover the cost of reserving the courts.

For pickup basketball—if you've got game—travel to the courts in the **Panhandle** (between Fell & Oak near Masonic), at **Duboce Park** (Scott & Duboce), or on many other playgrounds. **Potrero Hill Recreation Center** (801 Arkansas, 415-695-5009) also sports courts, as well as a gymnasium, a baseball diamond, tennis courts, and a playground, plus an O.J. Simpson mural (which you can revere or throw tomatoes at, depending on your perspective).

Jackson Playground (17th Street between Carolina & Arkansas, 415-554-9528) fields baseball, a playground, and yet more basketball, both indoor and outdoor. Soccer is a little harder to find, but try the new fields at **Dolores Park** (Church/Dolores & 18th/20th Streets).

EXTREME SPORTS

Most extreme sports require extreme money. Take hanggliding, for example. Even if you're dead set on careening off the edge of a cliff with synthetic wings strapped to your back, think about spectating at **Fort Funston** (Highway 35 near John Muir Drive) before you drop roughly $300 per tandem flight (or more for lessons).

Same goes for kiteboarding: **Crissy Field** is the center here, but observe the experts before you dive in. Crissy Field is also the City's sailboarding hub, although with heavy winds, strong currents and shipping lanes, it's definitely for experts only. You'll have to travel across the Bay to find equipment, rentals, and lessons for both sports at **Berkeley Boardsports** (1607 University, Berkeley, 510-843-9283, boardsports.com).

Surfing

Want an experience that's as leisurely as it is extreme? Go surfing. "Surfing was made for time off, and it's no coincidence that the two go hand in hand," says local surfer Ted Witt. "You can cruise up and

MAKE THE MOUNTAIN COME TO YOU

Rockclimbing at *Yosemite* (see *Chapter 5*) is a world-class pursuit that you can practice far closer to home, at *Mission Cliffs* (2295 Harrison, 415-550-0515, *touchstoneclimbing.com*). By local climbers' accounts, Mission Cliffs rocks. "It's a great place to connect with other climbers and plan outdoor excursions, as well as learn the basics if you're new to the sport," says climber Heather Emigh.

Mission Cliffs boasts a 50-foot lead wall and a bouldering cave, as well as a fully-equipped weight room, locker room, and sauna. Day passes run $10 on weekdays before 3pm, $18 at other times. The $90 you drop on a one-month pass (or the $160 for ten visits) can be applied toward the initiation fee if you later decide to join.

down the coast endlessly looking for the best possible spot, wait out the swell or tide, and stay out as long as you want."

Surfing **Ocean Beach** (Great Highway from Balboa to Sloat) could be considered a pretty good workout, but for experts only. For the best selection of boards and wetsuits, drop into **Wise Surfboards** (800 Great Highway, 415-750-9473, wisesurfboards. com); for cool clothes to go with, hit **Aqua Surf Shop** (2830 Sloat, 415-242-9283; 1742 Haight, 415-876-2782, aquasurfshop.com); and for the underground connection, slide into **SF Surf Shop** (3809 Noriega, 415-661-7873). Finally, for a retro ride combining surfing and art, take off to **Mollusk Surf Shop** (4500 Irving, 415-564-6300, mollusksurfshop.com)

Skateboarding

"Skating is not a crime!" so goes the rally-cry. In SF, how-ever, many sidewalk areas remain "legally" off limits to skat-ers. That doesn't seem to quell the City's strong skate culture. Bullet down **Fell Street** for an adrenalin-pumping downhill run (if you can time the lights, that is). For street skating, cruise along the **Embarcadero** or in and around **Kezar Stadium**. To get more space, local downhill carver Chris Flesher prefers the Sunset slopes out towards the beach. "I like to come down Ortega when the sun is out because you get a good look at the ocean with the afternoon sun shining on it." Watch out for those stop signs!

Skates on Haight (1818 Haight, 415-752-8375, skatesonhaight.com; 1219 Polk, 415-447-1800, skates.com) is *the* preeminent skate shop in town. The Haight Street location can outfit all of your skateboarding needs and provide in-line rentals, while the Polk Street virtual store (internet orders only) will roll you through the in-line world.

Adventure Clubs

The list of extreme adventures is extremely long. Sample them all—bungee jumping, skydiving, cave crawling, snowboarding, rafting—with an adventure club:

- *Bay Area Outdoor Adventure Club*
  415-954-7190, *outdooradventureclub.com*

- *Adventurous Woman Sports*
  Pier 38, Suite 1, 415-397-7678, *adventurous.com*

- *Outdoor Action Fitness*
  415-289-1367, *outdoorfitness.com*

- *Absolute Adventures*
  415-505-5964, *absoluteadv.com*

- *girlsAdventureOUT*
  800-509-3954, *girlsadventureout.com*

friday night skate

So you're groovin' out at the *Bus Stop*, imbibing a fine malt liquor and admiring your own hip-hugging boot-cut jeans. You sense a growing buzz, vaguely '70s and strangely familiar. The Bay City Rollers? (S, A, T-U-R, D-A-Y, *night!*)

But wait, this is *Friday* night, and the hum you hear is from the spinning wheels of the *Midnight Rollers*, San Francisco's own neo-retro skate group.

Participating in a ten-year-old tradition, inliners and rollers alike gather from all over the Bay Area to make this crazy circuit-skate. The pre-skate dance commences at 8pm in *Justin Herman Plaza*, rolls all around the City—even through the Broadway Tunnel—and ends up back where it began.

For more info on this and other City skating, contact David Miles (415-752-1967, *cora.org*).

GET OUT THERE

As the Bay Area Outdoor Adventure Club says—try new sports, meet new people! Mine the next chapter for even more ideas on how to add a little pizzazz to your social calendar.

CHAPTER 8
FAMILY & SOCIAL LIFE

*There was a definite process by which one made
people into friends, and it involved talking to them
and listening to them for hours at a time.*

~ Rebecca West

FULL-TIME work and a healthy social life can be frustratingly at odds for many of us. Long hours, the daily pressures of demanding jobs, and business travel conspire to sap our energy for relationships.

Time off, on the other hand, presents a chance to revitalize your social life, whether you're married or single, young or old. Now is the time to turn favorite acquaintances into friends, and favorite friends into even better friends. It's time to go out on that date, cook for your spouse, or host that long-awaited dinner party. And if you're a busy parent, you already know how precious extra hours with your kids can be.

Reconnect with loved ones and make new friends during your work hiatus. Or, if you're in full-time work mode, make an effort to carve out some extra time for your relationships. After all, our social connections truly are the zest of life!

*San Francisco is
a mad city—inhabited
for the most part by
perfectly insane people
whose women are of a
remarkable beauty.*

~Rudyard Kipling

FOOTLOOSE AND FANCY FREE

Flirting Before 5pm

People are surprisingly more approachable during the day. If you're single and looking to make friends, instead of going to the typical night spots (i.e., bars and nightclubs), try cafés, retail shops, or galleries during daytime hours.

"Finding somebody new who's also free during the day is always a treat," says Joani Blank, author and founder of **Good Vibrations** (goodvibes.com). "It's important for people to find lovers who likewise don't have to get up early in the morning!"

Chapter 4 lists our favorite "hanging out" cafés, but not the **San Francisco Museum of Modern Art** (151 3rd Street, 415-357-4000, sf-moma.org), a great place to meet other art aficionados. The affiliated **Cafe Museo** (415-357-4500) right next door provides an easy transition step for that chance encounter. Try the first Tuesday of every month, when admission is free.

Union Square is an untapped wellspring for new acquaintances or a worldly romance. Thousands of shoppers, both international and local, descend upon this downtown area daily. Should you make a connection while trying on that coat at Macy's, amble over to **Café Claude** (7 Claude Lane @ Bush, 415-392-3505), a hip joint just off Union Square. For a more swanky atmosphere, try afternoon tea or a cocktail at the **Onyx Lobby Lounge** in the lobby of the **Westin Saint Francis Hotel** (335 Powell, 415-397-7000).

Enroll in Activities

That old adage is trite but true: you'll meet people who share your interests when you go do things you like to do. So sign up for a class, join a group, or take up a new sport.

Marina Sarmiento, a single attorney in San Francisco, touts organized dancing as a no-hassle way to make new friends. She swings into action at something called **Lindy in the Park** (lindyinthepark. com), a swing dance group that meets every Sunday from 11am–2pm (temporarily meeting on JFK Drive near the de Young Museum). "It's a great way to meet people, and you don't have to worry about getting turned down to dance," Marina tells us. "There's a swing dancing etiquette, so you don't get that meat market feel."

Straight male leisure seekers take note: yoga classes have great gender ratios, primarily filled with women! Plus, the atmosphere is soothing and relaxed. Just don't intrude on others' space during their practice. Particularly social studios include the Stanyan Street location of **Yoga Tree** (780 Stanyan, 415-387-4707, yogatreesf.com), and **Global Yoga** (2425 Chestnut, 415-292-9774; 6300 California, 415-751-6908), which specializes in Bikram Method Yoga. Both are top studios in the fitness sense as well (see **Chapter 7** under "Yoga").

Single women, don't despair; team sports tilt the odds back in your favor, whether you're watching or playing. Sports bars during football season are packed on Saturday and Sunday afternoons; tackle them all, and then bring your own game to a local sports league. **Golden Gate Sport and Social Club** (415-921-1161, ggsportandsocialclub. com) is the premier organization for adult sports leagues in San Francisco, and offers everything from softball to street hockey. Coed football teams match five men with three women—see, your odds are already improving!

scrumming

If the words "tight scrum" are enough to get you sweaty, take the word of same-sex seekers who tell us that rugby is a fruitful way to "interact" with other gays. The *San Francisco Fog* (415-267-6100, *sffog.org*) is a club that, in their own words, "pursues the participation of people of color, gay men, women, and other groups traditionally underrepresented in rugby."

Women wanting to run and scrum can also look into the *San Francisco Golden Gate Women's Rugby Club* (*geocities.com/sfwomenrugby*).

Artsy types looking for a queer connection may prefer the **Queer Cultural Center** (queerculturalcenter.org), a virtual organization that showcases and promotes queer artists' work. Its site lists local gay art events, among other information.

Host Parties

Now's the perfect time to throw that dinner or cocktail party. Ask your friends to invite some new people, and you can do the same. Small gatherings are a great way to make new acquaintances. The more ambitious can host an "unemployed" theme party: have everyone bring their best (and worst) unemployed stories, and play games such as Layoff Lamenting (or the "How I Got Laid Off" one-upping game), or Travel Challenge—whoever has the best travel story wins.

Marina Sarmiento, our resident swing dancer, became legendary among friends for her enticing singles parties. "I got the idea from 'Sex and the City.' They had a 'recycling' party, but I didn't want to call mine that. So I named it 'The Single, Mingle, Tingle, Wine Soirée.' Everyone was required to bring a single friend and a bottle of wine, or they weren't allowed through the door." The parties are on hiatus now: Marina's first four were so successful, she's had a boyfriend for more than a year.

Dating Services & Social Clubs

We know, we know—modern dating services and social clubs aren't for everyone. But several of you have claimed success, or at least positive experiences, so we're going to pass along a few recommendations.

Not surprisingly, tech-savvy San Francisco is very open to the whole online dating phenomenon. The pre-eminent service is **Match.com** (match.com), where users can search through thousands of potential "matches." This includes any combination of gender matches—boy meets girl, girl meets boy, girl meets girl, boy meets boy (but not anything in between!). It takes a while to go through all the postings but hey, time is (hopefully) what you got.

Be warned: the City is a small community, and your anonymity isn't assured. Make sure you're comfortable with others knowing you're using the service. Just ask Kurt Fenton (name changed), a technology strategist in San Francisco, whose degree of separation from a woman he met on Match.com was just one: "I couldn't believe it—I had just started using the service. I went out on one date, and it turns out the girl was my friend's roommate!" He still recommends the service, though.

A singles group exclusively for the Bay Area is **Table for Six** (888-640-4646, tableforsix.com). Members dine with others of like interests in groups of six at restaurants throughout the Bay Area. Everyone pays for their own dinner, avoiding any awkwardness surrounding the bill. Check, please?

Urban Diversion (1329 Columbus, Suite B, 415-776-7455) is a social adventure club that aims to divert from the norm by throwing folks together through skydiving, river rafting, and other pulse-quickening activities. Member Marcus Ronaldi likes the departure. "Urban Diversion puts the emphasis on fun, not on treating dates like job interviews." The coolest part? They have their own clubhouse hideaway for members, complete with a tiki bar!

Single women can look into **Spinsters of San Francisco** (sfspinsters.com), an all-women's philanthropic group that isn't a singles group *per se* (or so they say), but one that definitely has a strong social emphasis. The sorority-averse need not apply.

The **Bachelors of San Francisco**, dubbed the oldest social club in the City, is also mixing and mingling—often with the Spinsters. Send them a

the need for speed

Speed dating is a new idea that might be zooming to a bar near you. An LA rabbi invented the concept in 1999 to help connect Jewish singles, and it's now blossomed into a full-fledged industry.

Single men and women of pre-determined age ranges go to a bar and meet each other through a series of rapid "dates," usually ten minutes or less. After the meetings, potential matches indicate whether they'd like to contact the other person; if both parties agree, they share contact information.

San Francisco bachelor J.J. Dillon recently experienced this social phenomenon. "Any woman who asked me what I did outside of work stayed on my list," he told us, "and any woman who asked what kind of car I drove did not."

Believe it or not, dozens of companies would like to whisk you around the dating block. One of the biggest and best-run is *8minute-Dating* (8minutedating. com), which boasts five event organizers in SF alone. Another homegrown escort is *Impact Date* (impactdate. com), which floats among the swankiest joints in town.

postcard if you want to hang out... or not. Adventurous gay men and women can give **San Francisco Gay Singles** (sanfranciscogaysingles. com) a whirl.

josh finds his muse

"As a writer, you always need fresh ideas to play with," says San Franciscan Josh McHugh. "The ideas that come to you via media, whether TV, print, or even the Web, are, by definition, processed and, as a result, a bit stale. The good stuff comes from live conversations."

Josh recently spent the better part of a Friday tooling around Fillmore Street in Pacific Heights, with *Tully's* (2455 Fillmore, 415-929-8808), a hub of community activity, serving as ground zero. Among those he met were a construction foreman, a professional musician, a dot-com-forced-retiree-turned-coffeehouse-manager, and a baby-toting mom doubling as a caterer and taking her own baby steps—as a home IT network administrator.

"Talking with humans, face to face, is by far the best way to get brand-new ideas bouncing around," Josh reports. "Plus, shooting the shit with people in a coffee shop is a lot more fun than squinting at a screen."

Volunteer

That's right, volunteer; the hidden perk is social interaction. Work at an event you couldn't otherwise afford, such as the Cystic Fibrosis Foundation's Great Strides event, or one of the American Cancer Society's evening galas. You'll meet a ton of new people, usually in a relaxed setting. Plus, you get the bonus of knowing you're helping a cause.

Be Open at All Times

A horse with blinders only sees the racetrack; an overemployed San Franciscan only sees the job. Downtime rips those blinders off, leaving us open to new encounters. Once you're open, you might be overwhelmed with opportunities.

The anonymous J.D., an attorney in San Francisco, finally had the energy to meet new people during a recent period between law firms. He chose to focus on dating, so much so that he found himself dating two women at the same time—something he doesn't necessarily recommend!

You might be surprised at how many new people you can meet on any given day and how little you know about the people you've already come across. Try this exercise: during your daily routine, whatever it may be, introduce yourself to each and every person you interact with and spend a moment to learn something about them. Start at the coffee shop in

GET ON THE A-LIST

Valerie Britt created **The A-List** (415-567-3165, *thealist.org*) in 1998 to provide a select list of the best parties, charity galas, and special events in and around the San Francisco Bay Area—and to support local non-profit and arts communities in the process.

Today, with over 20,000 subscribers and more than a million page hits per month on her website, it's safe to say she's succeeded. From four-star galas to festivals to fundraisers, The A-List has it covered.

Sign up for her e-mails if you want to stay in the know, just don't complain if you find yourself going out every night of the week!

the morning; include the bus driver if you take public transportation, the gas station attendant, the florist, the bartender, and so on. Josh McHugh, a San Francisco-based writer, took the opportunity to do just that during a recent break between assignments and found it refreshing—and a good muse! (See previous page.)

RECHARGING YOUR RELATIONSHIPS

How many times have you heard your significant other tell you, "I never see you anymore?" Have you forgotten your dog's name? If you're like most of us, juggling full-time work and relationships is a challenge. Whether you're married, just beginning to date someone, or somewhere in between, take this opportunity to recharge your relationship. Here are some ideas to get you started.

Cook For Your Partner
Cooking for someone (assuming that you enjoy it) is a wonderful way to show them you care. Use extra time in the early evening to prepare a scrumptious meal, so when your significant other is done with work, you can enjoy dinner together. You'll save money, spend quality time in the privacy of your own home, even be able to choose your own music! For some altogether luscious

ideas about cooking and romance, check out **Sex and the Kitchen** (sex andthekitchen.com), a web site dedicated to culinary and romantic delights.

Plan a Weekend Getaway

Choose a place you've both wanted to go: the mountains, the coast, or maybe wine country? Make it a surprise and you'll be a star in your partner's eyes for sure. You have literally thousands of choices, particularly if you're willing to spend some cash. If you're not, some less expensive—albeit alternative—escapes are within striking distance of San Francisco.

Coast south along Highway One to two of our favorites that won't drain the budget. **Pigeon Point Lighthouse Hostel** (210 Pigeon Point Road/Highway One, Pescadero, 650-879-0633, norcalhostels.org) is spectacularly stationed along the San Mateo coastline, about an hour's drive south of San Francisco. It has both shared and private rooms, and a hot tub cradled in the cliffs above the Pacific Ocean. **Point Montara Lighthouse Hostel** (16th Street at California Highway One, Montara, 650-728-7177, norcalhostels.org), is only thirty minutes from the City, and is also perched atop cliffs along the water. Private rooms (with shared bath) at both hostels ranged from $50–$60 per night for two in 2003, and reservations are mandatory, best made well in advance. Because these are run as hostels, they do come with their share of rules—such as curfews—so be sure to check those out ahead of time.

Twenty minutes north of San Francisco, nestled on Mount Tamalpais, lies another alternative getaway: **The West Point Inn** (Mount Tamalpais, Marin, 415-388-9955, 415-646-0702 for reservations). This rus-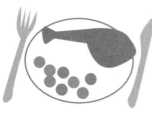tic mountain cabin is hike-in only, and what it lacks in refinement it more than makes up for in character and breathtaking vistas. Guests pack in their own food and bedding, and have a choice between stand-alone cabins or rooms inside the inn itself. The cost in 2003 was $30 per person for either type of accommodation.

For a more upscale weekend, you might consider staying at a bed & breakfast. Although not always cheap, they usually offer better value than your average hotel. Good sources for finding B&Bs in Northern

California include the book *Absolutely Every Bed & Breakfast: Northern California*, by Carl Hanson, and the excellent web resource **Bed & Breakfasts Online** (bbonline.com).

Out to Lunch

Stop by your partner's workplace (if there is one!) for an impromptu lunch date. Eating lunch together is an unusual event for most couples so it makes for a nice treat. You'll score major brownie points, maybe even impress the co-workers. Add to that the possibility of additional networking opportunities, and you might make this a regular occurrence!

Think Romance

Love is eternal, but romance takes time. With some extra hours you can plan all sorts of little surprises. Surprise your loved one by decorating the house with candles, preparing a fragrant bubble bath, or offering your services as a masseur or masseuse. Or take your partner

UNEMPLOYMENT AND POPPING THE QUESTION

Ted Witt credits a stint between jobs with taking his relationship to the next level. He fell in love with Shauna while they were working for the same company. After both were laid off, Shauna found another job relatively quickly but Ted decided to enjoy a full year off. Rather than strain their relationship, Ted's unemployment energized it.

He didn't wait for *Re-Employment* before asking Shauna to marry him. Though concerned about how his jobless status would look to his in-laws to-be, Ted did secure the blessing of Shauna's father first (okay, so he fibbed a little about some "consulting" projects) and then had plenty of time to plan the engagement, before and after he popped the question.

Shauna and Ted are now married and living happily ever after.

somewhere special in nature, perhaps to the beach to watch the sunset, or on a picnic in the woods (Golden Gate Park has plenty of great picnic grounds). As cliché as it may sound, the simplest efforts are often the most romantic.

LOVE IN THE TIME OF UNEMPLOYMENT

What's that you say? No time for love? If you're not working, you no longer have that excuse. And if you are working, then you'll just have to make the time, because love requires it. Think about the last time you fell in love with someone. Somehow you found the time to dream, plan, hope, and strategize about your blossoming relationship. You

DATING AS A FULL-TIME JOB?

No one ever said that dating couldn't be a full-time job. After getting laid off from her job as a staff writer for *Red Herring* magazine, Ann Marsh decided the time had come for her to have a serious relationship. Tired of not meeting the right men, Ann took to the task at hand. Using an ambitious, systematic dating strategy, she went about the process of finding the right man with all the zeal of an industrious entrepreneur. Six months later, she claimed to have gone on dates with no fewer than one hundred men! The work paid off: Ann met Johanne, and they've been married now for several years. No one ever said that dating couldn't be a full-time job!

might not have even realized it at the time, but you probably dropped many other things in order to focus on the new person in your life.

In researching an article on unemployment and relationships, Ann Marsh, a freelance writer from Los Angeles, found several young career-driven individuals who had either put off serious relationships or neglected them altogether. It was only after they became disillusioned with their jobs or got laid off (or both) that they finally got involved in a serious relationship. Considering her own status, Marsh took these words to heart (see "Dating as a Full-Time Job" above).

Erik Wohlgemuth, an environmental consultant in San Francisco, was working a flexible twenty hours a week when he first met his girlfriend Arah, who in turn had recently left her job at Booz Allen.

He says they probably wouldn't have ended up together if they hadn't had that free time. "We both had recently gotten out of serious relationships, and were enjoying our new-found freedom," Erik told us. "Arah and I were also able to take off on more spontaneous dates, such as a last-minute visit to New York over the holidays, and a romantic road trip to Bend, Oregon."

RECONNECTING WITH FRIENDS

Like all relationships, good friendships require time, energy, and nurturing, yet we too often neglect them when we're busy with work. We might want our platonic relationships to be like they are on the TV show, *Friends*—jovial camaraderie, back-slapping good times, everyone always there for each other—but good friendships take a lot of work.

Your friendships may take on new dynamics. If your friends traditionally identified you with your work or career, they may now rediscover you in a different light. This can have a snowball effect, teaching you more about your friends outside their own work environments.

Organize rallying events for yourself and your companions: a weekly "friends dinner," for example, or a movie night, or simply a trip to the local café. Consider a leisure retreat with other friends who also have flexible schedules, letting you and your cohorts get to know each other in a different environment. Road trips allow ample bonding time (see **Chapter 5**). Backpacking, spas, sporting events, camping—all are great ways to rally a small group and spend dedicated time together.

all together now

SF was made for the friendly, so gather yours together for some good clean fun.

Relax and rejuvenate midweek at The City's favorite spa, *Kabuki Springs & Spa* (Japan Center, 1750 Geary, 415-922-6000, *kabukisprings. com*). The communal baths are reasonably priced at $20 Monday through Friday, before 5pm; $25 evenings and weekends. Tuesday is the only coed day, clothing required (bummer!); otherwise, the baths are gender-divided by day of the week.

Or, rally the troops for bowling night at *Presidio Bowling Center* (in the Presidio, corner of Moraga & Montgomery, Building 93, 415-561-2695), an old military bowling alley that is now open to the public. Heck, join a league! "We got our favorite bar to sponsor us," says J.J. Dillon, "and beers were on the house every night we won a game."

Rob Darren (name changed) organized a weekly guys movie night with his friends, many of whom weren't working, choosing a different theme each week. "It was a great way to get everyone together," he told us, "although you could definitely tell who was working and who wasn't. We'd host it on a weeknight, and the employed guys wouldn't drink much and would slip out relatively early. But those of us who weren't working, we'd sometimes tear it up into the wee hours, and we definitely bonded around that."

THE TAO OF BOJON

"What's better than your dream job?" asks the King of Bojon. "No job!" The **Bojon** site (*bojon.com*), created and maintained by San Franciscan Tom Haan, has created a community and local buzz among laid-off high tech workers.

Brian Cox, Tom's friend's little brother, coined the term "bojon" in the early 1990s. A sophomore in college in Wrightsville Beach, NC, surrounded by upperclassmen boasting about the great gigs they had lined up for after graduation, Brian wanted to sound equally sophisticated. He told his brother's friends he was going to work for Bojon. "It's a French company," he claimed. And it's also "no job"— spelled backwards!

Tom is quick to set his site apart from those that express bitterness about being laid off. Bojon is not an ephemeral concept. "Somebody who is uptight about not having a job and who is running around pressing resumes is not truly bojon," Tom explains. "Conversely, somebody who loves his profession and is passionate about his work can be bojon." Tom quotes the Chinese philosopher Chang Ch'ao: "Only those who take leisurely what the people of the world are busy about can be busy about what the people of the world take leisurely."

The Buddha couldn't have said it better himself.

CREATIVELY ODD

GREAT MOMENTS IN UNEMPLOYMENT

What to do when you've been laid off, have no real work or social life to speak of, and sit around and watch television all day? No problem: take your creative energy, combine it with some minimal Flash development skills and a wicked sense of humor, and create the most popular Internet cartoon series ever. Set up a tip jar on the site, and sit back and watch the money roll in, along with book and other development deals.

Odd Todd (oddtodd.com) did just that, and may be the one having the last laugh. His site has received more than one million hits from over 40 different countries, and Todd Rosenberg has become a media darling, appearing on CNN and the *Today* show, among others. His new book, *The Odd Todd Handbook: Hard Times, Soft Couch* may further solidify his position as a true leisure legend.

SF's Unemployed Communities

Speaking of unemployed bonding, the Bay Area's economic climate has created a new category of social events that revolve around unemployment. Not only are these great ways to share experiences with your fellow unemployed, but they're also excellent opportunities to meet new people.

Several of these groups have either evolved into job search services (e.g., the pink slip parties) or waned away, but a few remain. **Bojon** (bojon.com) is one such survivor, throwing quarterly parties to celebrate the "Kingdom of Bojon." Signing up for the Bojon mailing list will score you invitations to join other leisure seekers at official Bojon festivities. **Craigslist** (craigslist.org) serves as a *de facto* community for the unemployed. In particular, check out the sections on "jobs" and "community," as well as the "personals" section (if you're so inclined). **Oddtodd.com** (oddtodd.com, see **above**) of Internet layoff fame is a place to connect digitally with like-minded leisurely folks (or at least watch some funny cartoons!). Check out **Laid Off Land**, a Yahoo

kids

One could hardly argue against spending more time with your kids. Of course, some of you with little terrors may be looking for just the opposite: reprieve! Kidding aside, it's been a delight and inspiration to hear of so many people who've taken sabbaticals to get closer to their little ones.

Steve Wozniak of Apple Computer fame has long preached the virtues of society's paying more attention to children. After taking a rather extended period "off" from Apple (way back in 1985!), Woz actively helped found several local organizations supporting children and education, including The Tech Museum and the Children's Discovery Museum of San Jose.

Stacie Parker, an entrepreneur who owned two shops on Union Street, sold both to focus on raising her children. "Retail is no life for a parent," she said. "I had a 24-hour-on-call schedule. And I poured myself wholly into the daily grind, traveling to tradeshows and working late nights and weekends in the stores. But at 35, I had waited a long time to be a mom. So at that point I felt no guilt in giving up my business."

discussion group linked from the Odd Todd home page.

UNEMPLOYMENT & FAMILY

We have some idea of who *you* are—unemployed or *aspiring unemployed*—but little knowledge of your family. You all had parents, of course (and some of them were even human!). Perhaps you're from a family of six with lots of aunts and uncles and several sets of grandparents. Think of all the leisure loan potential!

Your family can be a tremendous source of support during time off, be it weeks, months, or even years of unconventional living. But keeping up the role you filled when you had a job can be trying. Your spouse, parents, or even kids may have certain expectations of you, and taking time off doesn't always fit neatly within those parameters. Maybe you never want to go back to work. What would your family think about that?

It could be time for you (like Chevy Chase) to load up the "family truckster" and hit the road on the way to Wally World (but please, leave your crazy aunt at home). Or, if you're still unattached, perhaps you'd prefer to drift in your parents' pool, contemplating your future (á la Dustin Hoffman).

Whatever avenue you choose to get some quality time with your family—kids, spouse, parents, siblings or others—make sure you get it while you can, understanding that it might take an extra effort to adjust. Below are some suggestions on how to relate, where to take your children in San Francisco, how to organize family activities, or how to take a family vacation, Griswold-style!

Husbands and Wives

Is life different for married couples when one or both aren't working? Remember *Ozzie and Harriet*? *Leave it to Beaver*? Dad earned the dough and Mom spent it—on the family and the home, of course! While that may now seem archaic, it did give couples the luxury of more free time, or at least the appearance of it. We can debate gender roles and family values, but the bottom line is that the spouse who is not working will have more time and energy to focus on the family.

Scott Philips, who negotiated a partially paid sabbatical with his employer, Accenture, was able to spend valuable time with his Czech-born wife in her home country, much of it at her family's home in the woods of Bohemia, such an appropriate place for leisure! According to Scott, "We got to know each other pretty well over the last year, without all of the job-related stress in the way. I think it's made us a stronger couple. In terms of shared experiences, it was like having five years of American time together."

Adjusting

As beneficial as it can be, being out of work can also cause domestic turmoil. The myth that equates unemployment with laziness or underachievement can strain a couple, creating a lack of respect and understanding, and ultimately animosity. Ironically, according to career counselor Rochelle Teising, dual-income couples are likely to feel this tension the most: the partner that's still working full-time perceives the other to be loafing at home. It's hard for anyone living with a partner who is enjoying time off not to be jealous, Teising says.

Matt Green experienced this firsthand, admitting it was tricky to be around his family all the time after he quit his job. "Now that I'm not working, my wife Val's life hasn't changed," Matt says, "but I'm out riding my motorcycle, meeting my friend for a beer, and that's something I have to be sensitive to. Jealousy's too strong a word, but she's thinking, 'I still have to do what I do and you get to go play.'"

Matt's wife eventually asked him to take on more of the household responsibilities. The transition was difficult, as Matt didn't feel he was skilled at anything around the house. Take doing laundry, for example. "During this motorcycle trip I was just on, I thought about going to a laundromat, and I said, nah, I'm going to wear what I have on for three days and then go back to Vegas and just buy new clothes. And that's what I did."

Once Matt was able to relax and show more patience, the family slipped into a comfortable routine, and he was able to spend more quality time with his wife and kids—which was his ultimate goal.

Family Activities

Now that you've made the effort to take more time for your family, what're you going to do with them? Sitting around the house watching *Oprah!* is hardly quality time. Even a city as cosmopolitan as San Francisco has better kid-friendly activities.

For outdoor adventures during the daytime, one option is to take the kids to Crissy Field. **Parks as Classrooms** is a joint program of the National Park Service and Golden Gate National Recreation Area, and **Crissy Field Center** (Building 603, Mason & Halleck in the Presidio, 415-561-7690, crissyfield.org) is its local education center. Enroll your children in one of their excellent programs, or simply take the family to the park and enjoy the beautiful setting.

Another outdoor option is a kid-friendly hike. Your sprites will enjoy Mount Tamalpais in Marin or Tilden Park in the East Bay as much as you do. For thorough information on hiking with children in the Bay Area, including tips and recommendations, visit **Bay Area Hiker** (bahiker.com, link to "hiking with kids").

Yerba Buena Gardens in San Francisco's SOMA district (899 Howard, yerbabuena.org) have just about everything you could possibly imagine to occupy

tykes & travelin'

California teachers Karin & Joe Dixon didn't let parenthood slow them down. Karin pursued a Fulbright scholarship in Stockholm and Joe came along for the ride to take care of their infant son, Amos, who was eleven months old at the time. They traveled through parts of Norway and Germany in addition to living in Stockholm, all the while toting Amos along in the Baby Björn.

For preparation, Karin and Joe recommend *Lonely Planet's Travel With Children* by Cathy Lanigan. Karin also recommends taking a high-quality stroller, a good plastic pouch bib, backpacks instead of suitcases, and plenty of emergency snacks. She says breastfeeding, for those still nursing, can make traveling more leisurely for parent and child.

the little rascals' short attention spans (or just get them out of your hair for a few minutes!). One part of Yerba Buena called **The Rooftop**, located on the City block bordered by Mission, Howard, 3rd & 4th Streets, is a mecca for kids. Start with **Zeum** (4th Street & Howard, 415-820-3320, zeum.org), a wonderful art and technology center for children of all ages. The Children's Garden is also a small tyke's dream come true, with ladders, slides, a sandbox, a maze, and all sorts of other fun "stuff." Exhausted chasing the little ones around? Hit the **Yerba Buena Child Development Center** (790 Folsom @ 4th Street, 415-820-3500, southofmarketchildcare.org) when your patience has worn thin and you're ready to let someone else take care of the kids for awhile. Actually, it's a diverse children's center that offers a variety of programs, but unfortunately you'll have to enroll ahead of time.

The **Metreon** (101 4th Street @ Mission, 415-369-6000, metreon.com) entertains children well into their teen years. The more cultured (and ambitious) can try the **San Francisco Museum of Modern Art** (see "Flirting Before 5pm" earlier in chapter). Last but not least is the **Exploratorium** (3601 Lyon, 415-561-0360, exploratorium.edu), an SF treasure that will delight both adults and kids from grade school on up.

A notable online resource for San Francisco family outing ideas is **GoKid.org** (gokid.org), a nonprofit online guide dedicated to kid-friendly stuff in the City.

Family Vacations

If life's a journey you take with your family, why not get out there and hit the road for real? Although traveling with your family can be trying, it can be extremely rewarding too. We subscribe to the Nike school of thought in this department: "Just do it."

Travel for Kids (travelforkids.com) is a helpful website for kid-friendly travel preparation as well as ideas for international and local destinations. Their San Francisco section includes a thorough list of local ideas, too.

GREAT MOMENTS IN UNEMPLOYMENT

12

My Pretty Po-Knee

Stay-at-home dad Robert Klick was bouncing daughter Maddi on his knee when he had a vision: an adorable stuffed pony he could attach to his leg, letting her ride in style. The Po-Knee was born, was featured on Oprah and sold 2,500 units during its first three minutes on QVC. The Po-Knee has given Klick more time to indulge in his favorite activity of all: playing with daughter Maddi and son Cameron.

CONGRATULATIONS ON THE BABY!
(NOW WE HAVE TO LET YOU GO)

Micki Karrer's maternity leave had a rude beginning. Then-head of marketing for telecom startup Sigma Networks, Micki got laid off two weeks before she was to go on leave—right before her due date! Because the company shut down soon thereafter, she lost her health insurance as well.

Luckily for the whole family, Micki's husband's insurance kicked in to cover most of the maternity expenses and, much to her credit, she was able to adapt quickly. In retrospect, she sees the sudden time off as a blessing. "The timing worked out great," she told us, "as I was able to take about nine months off, which was perfect. Also, with a baby on the way, I had more perspective than many of my colleagues did, and could just focus on being a mother."

Not all new mothers will be so lucky, of course. Don't count on your employer to create quality time for you and your family. It's still up to you to strike the balance, which means being prepared to leave work behind when you have to.

From Here to Maternity

Being a new parent is no vacation, but parental leave is at least somewhat institutionalized, which makes it pretty much the only type of time off that's legitimate in the eyes of the mainstream. So do what you can to take advantage of time allowed.

The process of maternity and paternity leave has evolved over the years. The federal Family and Medical Leave Act (FMLA) of 1993 stipulates that certain employers (generally, public agencies and businesses with fifty or more employees) must grant eligible employees up to twelve weeks unpaid leave for the birth and care of an employee's newborn child. For more information on the FMLA, check with the **Department of Labor** (dol.gov).

Some larger employers do offer paid maternity-leave benefits, but sadly these perks aren't universal. If your employer is more family-neutral than family-friendly, think about staggering your leave: Mom takes four months off, then, as she transitions back to work, Dad takes six weeks. Most mothers use some combination of short-term disability, vacation, sick leave, and unpaid leave at the birth of a child. Short-term disability covers all or a portion of your salary during times when you are unable to perform your job due to a disability (like giving birth), and is offered by some companies, unions, and certain states, such as California and New York.

Andrea Ghez, a professor and scientist at UCLA, took advantage of the university's flexible maternity-leave benefits, and used a combination of time off and flex-time during her baby's first six months. "There wasn't much precedent for me to follow. If you can believe it, I was only the second woman in my department to take maternity leave as an active, full-time professor."

Unfortunately for everyone, this type of benefit is usually available only to mothers. Some companies, however, do offer personal leave above and beyond the federal law. Maureen Feeney works at Avago Technologies (formerly Agilent/Hewlett-Packard), one of the more progressive employers in the country; she recommends negotiating for your leave. She did just that, received ten weeks of paid maternity leave, and was able to tack on another six months of unpaid leave, for a total of nearly nine months. Her husband Jeff, however, who also works for Avago, wasn't so lucky; at the time he had to use vacation days in order to get paid time off. Unfair!

The good news for Jeff and other Californians is that the recently-passed **Paid Family Leave** law (paidfamilyleave.org) extends partially-paid paternity leave to fathers through the State Disability Insurance Program. We can only hope other states will follow.

Regardless, we encourage all mothers and fathers to ask for extended leave during their newborn's first year and beyond. Look at it this way: you're not just asking for yourself, you're setting a precedent for all your future-parent colleagues. Your employer may surprise you; many are, if not sympathetic, at least open to negotiation.

Some terrific sources on the subject delve into much greater detail. *Everything a Working Mother Needs to Know About Pregnancy Rights, Maternity Leave and Making Her Career Work for Her* by Anne C. Weisberg and Carol A. Buckler has been the babymaker's bible for years. Also cherished is *Life After Baby: From Professional Woman to Beginner Parent* by Wynn McClenahan Burkett, which focuses on professional women entering parenthood. Web-savvy moms can study up at **BabyCenter** (babycenter.com, search "maternity leave") for a good rundown on the basics.

Single Parents

A single parent might not have much wiggle room when it comes to taking time off, but that doesn't mean it can't be done. Careful planning and a strong support network of friends and family will help.

Adrianna Moore (name changed) spent many months taking involuntary time off in 2002. As a single mother of two, she didn't enjoy her time off so much as survived it, but she did feel it was important to present her situation positively to her children. "I didn't feel guilty, but I was worried about finances—and my kids noticed I was sad." She managed to maintain a positive outlook during a challenging time, in part by working out "a ton." Go Adrianna!

Marsha Converse, also a single mother, lost her job with Northpoint Communications during company-wide layoffs. Despite serious financial and personal turmoil, her son says she emerged from the experience "less stressed and more level-headed." She says, wisely, "I feel like getting laid off made me a human being again. I feel like I now know what's important."

LASTING CONNECTIONS

Heavy stuff, to be sure, but time off, whether forced or voluntary, gives countless people new perspective on their relationships, with universally positive results. If you care to share that positive impact, take the next chapter to heart, and get out there and volunteer. It's only right for you to start sharing the leisure!

CHAPTER 9
SHARING THE LEISURE

Never doubt that a small group of thoughtful,
committed citizens can change the world;
indeed it is the only thing that ever has.

~ Margaret Mead

IF you've hopped off the job train and spent time at the leisure station, chances are you've been focusing on you, and "getting" a whole lot of good stuff in the process. There comes a time, however, when most of us yearn to spread that good fortune around, like peanut butter on a slice of Wonder Bread. As Winston Churchill famously said, "We make a living by what we get, we make a life by what we give."

Giving to a worthy cause creates an upward spiral of swirling dividends that enrich the community at large. If you feel frustrated, anxious, angry, or just fed up with the world's problems, there's no better antidote than to get off your keister and do something to help. Volunteer for a cause you believe in and you'll know that you've moved from the ranks of the rankled to the echelon of the engaged. It's a sure-fire way to get those warm fuzzies that your old cubicle could never provide.

Volunteering then triggers one of the great paradoxes of the universe: the more you give, the more you get. We're not talking just the personal satisfaction of knowing you've made a difference, here. We're talking perks. Bennies. Righteous reimbursement. Donate your time and you could learn new skills, make influential contacts, score free food and drink, augment your T-shirt collection with the customary freebies (and let's face it, who actually goes out and buys T-shirts anymore?) and get a desk, a phone, even a new title of your choosing.

Give, to get, to give more, to get more...good gravy! It's a wonder we're not volunteering all the time.

Volunteering is a San Francisco tradition. Each generation leaves its own legacy of giving, like the Jewish immigrants who founded the Eureka Benevolent Society in the mid-1800s to feed and shelter widows and children. San Franciscans were also at the forefront of AIDS fundraising before the epidemic was even in the news (see below).

Now is the time to carry that tradition forward. "We've gotten a lot of great volunteers who are temporarily unemployed," says Natasha Glushkoff, who runs the volunteer program for **San Francisco Architectural Heritage** (2007 Franklin, 415-441-3000, sfheritage.org). "A few have always wanted to volunteer but have 'always been so busy.' So far, all have stayed active or at least connected with us even if they found jobs again."

GETTING STARTED

With all the worthy causes in San Francisco, it's a challenge just deciding which ones to support. Fortunately, some centralized resources can help you choose.

HISTORY OF THE AIDS QUILT

In 1987, a small group of activists and citizens met in a San Francisco storefront with the goal of creating a lasting memorial for those who had died of AIDS. The meeting served as the genesis and foundation of both the NAMES Project and The AIDS Memorial Quilt.

The quilt is now housed in Atlanta when it's not touring the rest of the country, and it serves as a powerful reminder of the enormity of the AIDS epidemic. It's composed of approximately 48,000 panels commemorating over 88,000 individuals, weighs close to 54 tons, and has been put to good use by the *NAMES Project Foundation* (404-688-5500, *aidsquilt.org*), whose mission is "to preserve, care for, and use The AIDS Memorial Quilt to foster healing, heighten awareness and inspire action in the struggle against HIV and AIDS." NAMES has raised more than $3 million for AIDS service organizations throughout North America.

A good starting point is **The Volunteer Center of San Francisco** (1675 California, 415-982-8999, thevolunteercenter.net). The Center's website includes information on group volunteering, special events and other one-day opportunities. The center will even help you form your own nonprofit.

The **Bay Area Volunteer Information Center** (volunteerinfo.org) is a more grassroots clearinghouse. Their "Volunteer Opportunities Hotlist" helps fill jobs from repairing computers to picking fruit to making sandwiches.

Do you have a particular date or a certain skill in mind? The web engine at **SF Bay Area Volunteer Solutions** (volunteersolutions.org/sfbay), sponsored by the United Way, lets you search by your skills, interests and availability.

If you want to volunteer but aren't sure how much time you'll have, reach out to **Hands on San Francisco** (330 Townsend, Suite 16, 415-541-9616, hosf.org). They publish a monthly calendar of projects that don't call for any minimum commitment. Their nights and weekends projects accommodate even those with a day job.

EVERY VOLUNTEER OPP UNDER THE SUN

VolunteerMatch (www.volunteermatch.org) is a highly-touted online resource founded in 1998 by Jay Backstrand, a one-time marketing manager at computer giant Sun Microsystems. He witnessed firsthand the power of the Internet in coordinating Sun's corporate volunteer efforts. "Before VolunteerMatch," Jay told us, "it was often very challenging to translate volunteer inspiration into volunteer action. With the service, it has become much, much easier to simply get involved."

VolunteerMatch has generated nearly two million referrals to tens of thousands of non-profits nationwide since its founding. "It's incredible to see that the organization is having a positive impact and making such a tremendous difference," Jay says. "Because of our service, more and more people are choosing to volunteer, and to me, that's extremely rewarding."

volunteer etiquette

True, volunteer jobs don't pay and you can't really get fired. That doesn't mean the normal rules of courtesy don't apply. People are counting on you! Call if you're going to be late or have to cancel. If you have to bow out of an ongoing commitment, try to find a replacement. It's only right, plus the MC at that fundraiser dinner you just flaked on might reappear across the table—at your next job interview!

BUILDING SKILLS

Do you want to get into event planning but need more experience? Would you like to improve your salesmanship? Use volunteering to build your resume. Team up with a non-profit and help them raise money, or volunteer to organize a special event for a philanthropic organization. Countless non-profits will provide you with skills training in return for your time and effort—and that's a win-win as far as we're concerned

Take, for example, the below invitation to potential volunteers from the **San Francisco Choral Society** (236 West Portal #775, 415-566-8425, sfchoral.org):

Admit it—at some point you've thought about making a few fundraising calls but then it dawned on you, "I can't even ask for extra ketchup; how could I ask for a donation?" Guess what? You don't actually have to know how. We'll train you. This free training will be conducted by a professional development consultant. You gain marketable skills, the chorus gains donations and everybody is happy.

We couldn't have said it better ourselves! This pitch is certainly more persuasive than being begged and cajoled.

SFCS is not the only nonprofit that dangles the training carrot to attract quality volunteers. Natasha Glushkoff reports that docents of the Haas-Lilienthal House tours enjoy "all sorts of fabulous lecturers" in a "really awesome" nine- or ten-week class. Other volunteers receive free **Heritage** membership.

Dane Larson volunteered at the **Cystic Fibrosis Foundation** (415-331-0650, cff.org) and was surprised to find it helped build his sales skills. "They had me on the phone every day, asking companies to donate prizes for their auctions and special events. It got to the point where I wouldn't take no for an answer. Of course, it helped that it was for a charity because I could really lay on the guilt trip." For more on (leisurely) skill-building, jump ahead to **Chapter 11**, where you'll find all sorts of unorthodox job hunting ideas.

GET OUT OF THIS HOUSE

Environmental groups have long made San Francisco their home, including the venerable **Sierra Club** (85 2nd Street, 2nd Floor, 415-977-5500, sierraclub.org). Naturalist John Muir and others founded the Sierra Club in 1892, and in 1893 they set up their first office at the California Academy of Sciences in Golden Gate Park. The headquarters has remained in the City ever since.

> *Everybody needs beauty as well as bread,*
> *places to play in and pray in, where nature may*
> *heal and give strength to body and soul alike.*
> ~John Muir, *The Yosemite* (1912)

Go out and celebrate San Francisco's environmental heritage. Enjoy the great outdoors and spruce up its appearance at the same time. Here are some links to organizations with regular volunteer days:

Volunteers in Parks Program
parks.ca.gov
click on "Volunteers in Parks"

Trail Center
trailcenter.org
click on "Volunteer!"

Greenbelt Alliance
greenbelt.org
choose "Get Involved" then "Volunteer/Intern Opps"

Several organizations sponsor beach cleanups at Ocean Beach, including the **Surfrider Foundation** (sfsurfrider.org), and the **California Coastal Commission** (coastal.ca.gov, search "coastal cleanup").

Golden Gate National Parks Conservancy (415-561-3034, parksconservancy.org) wants *you* to steward some parks. Get involved with the Presidio through **Presidio Park Restoration** (Park Stewards Volunteer Hotline, 415-561-3034, ext. 3445). More than 2,000 volunteers help restore the Presidio's open spaces each year. Call for information on upcoming workdays.

Perhaps you revel in napping under big shady trees? Enjoy the crunch-crunch of pine needles and branches under your feet? If so, **Friends of the Urban Forest** (Presidio, Building #1007, 415-561-6890, fuf.net) would like to speak with you. FUF is a community-based group that works to expand and protect San Francisco's urban forests, also known as "trees." Join FUF for a one-day planting binge—they'll even provide lunch! If rescuing our ailing leafy friends is more your speed, join their "treeage" program (get it?) and cruise the streets of San Francisco looking for TIT's (Trees In Trouble). They need your help!

Be a park hero by donating some time to the **Golden Gate National Recreation Area** (Volunteer Coordinator, Fort Mason, Building 201, 415-561-4755, nps.gov). Not only is the GGNRA the largest urban park in the world, but it's home to some of the most spectacular open space in the country. Get the insider scoop on this tremendous resource by collecting data on wildlife, growing native plants, or protecting endangered species. Volunteers receive free orientation and training.

ACTING LOCALLY

Helping your neighbors might not have the glam appeal of a volunteer vacation or a stint monitoring an overseas election, but it sure can put your own problems in perspective.

Reading Aloud

If you've gotten this far, we know you can read. Help others learn to read too, through **Project Read** (San Francisco Public Library, 100 Larkin, 415-557-4388, projectreadsf.org), the adult literacy program of the San Francisco Public Library. Volunteer tutors attend an orientation and twelve hours of tutor training—not a bad perk if you're also looking for paid tutoring work. This project requires a commitment to tutor the same person for one year, once or twice a week. In return, you'll receive up to six ongoing tutor trainings.

Are you good at reading out loud? Here's your chance to speak out—on air. The **Rose Resnick Lighthouse for the Blind** (Volunteer Coordinator, 214 Van Ness, 415-431-1481, lighthouse-sf.org) needs volunteers to read the daily news to their blind or visually impaired radio audience. The Lighthouse could use your practical services as well, helping campers enjoy summer swimming, hiking, and horse-

FORCED VOLUNTEERING

Sometimes, volunteering just makes common sense. The inconvenient times when you're facing a jail sentence, for example. Be sure your lawyer is familiar with the **San Francisco Pretrial Diversion Project** (SFPDP, 567 7th Street, 415-626-4995, *sfpretrial.com*), a program formed to provide first-time non-violent misdemeanor offenders the opportunity to perform community service in lieu of prosecution (sorry, repeat offenders are out of luck). Volunteering might never look so appealing!

Project 20 (as it's otherwise known) was formed in 1976 by socially conscious lawyers, judges, and citizens, and is now one of the most infamous programs offered by SFPDP. Under Project 20, beleaguered parking and traffic offenders work off their tickets by performing visible Department of Public Works projects such as painting over graffiti, cleaning streets, or sweeping sidewalks. Like most things related to parking and traffic in the City, the program has a lot of rules. Read up on them at *sfpretrial.com/project20.html*. Happy cleaning!

back riding at Enchanted Hills Camp in wine country. You receive training, room and board, and campers gain independence and confidence in their abilities.

Nurture Your Neighbors

Consider yourself fortunate if you are not suffering from abuse or AIDS, and doubly fortunate if you can help those who are.

Join forces with the respected **Riley Center** (415-552-2943, rileycenter.org) to help abused women get out of a bad situation. Volunteer roles include Crisis Line Advocate, Children's Activities Volunteer, and language translation.

Get involved with local healing by assisting the **UCSF AIDS Health Project** (415-476-3890, ucsf-ahp.org). Help people reduce the risk of HIV transmission, cope with emotional challenges of HIV infection, or support friends and family. AHP offers not only volunteer opportunities, but also a formal post-baccalaureate internship program for the truly inspired.

Teach tech to Tenderloin residents at the Computer Training Center of the **San Francisco Network Ministries** (559 Ellis, 415-928-6209, sfnetworkministries.org). The Reverend Cecil Williams would also

weekday specials

Feel like riding a bike? Join *Trips for Kids of Marin* (415-458-2986) on a Wednesday or Thursday for a mountain bike trip through the Marin Headlands with inner-city youths. You'll need your own gear and a sack lunch. Riders meet at *Re-Cyclery* (610 4th Street, San Rafael, 415-458-2986).

Project Open Hand (730 Polk, 415-447-2300, *openhand.org*) provides meals to impoverished HIV/AIDS sufferers and seeks volunteers seven days a week who can "slice and dice," are "good with a shopping cart," or can take "meals with love out on the road and deliver."

Environmentalists can contact the *Rainforest Action Network* (221 Pine, Suite 500, 415-398-4404, *ran.org*), who, in their own words, are "not your typical tree-huggers." Volunteers are needed in RAN's SF office Monday-Friday, 9am-5pm, for general office work, data entry, mailings, and banner- and sign-making. Every Thursday from 6pm-10pm you can mail your way to pizza bliss with their Bulk Mail Pizza Parties! RAN also offers a variety of internships, from media outreach to research.

like your help at **Glide Memorial Church** (330 Ellis, 415-674-6000, glide.org) and one of its many volunteer service programs, from meals to health to education. **Dolores Street Community Services** (938 Valencia, 415-282-6209, dscs.org) is another grassroots group founded to help working immigrants and AIDS sufferers.

If you prefer to dress down while socializing, try a one-time group project, like building a house with **Habitat for Humanity** (78 Ocean, 415-406-1555, habitatsf.org).

Still thinking globally? Whet your international appetite by helping **Global Exchange** (2017 Mission, Suite 203, 415-255-7296, globalexchange.org) with international human rights issues and policies. Their programs include study tours, retail stores promoting alternative trade, educational development, media outreach, and human rights campaigns.

WORKING WITH KIDS

Perhaps no one deserves your charitable attention more than children in need. If teaching is your bag, help the kids through **San Francisco School Volunteers** (601 McAllister, 415-749-3700, sfsv.org), who will set you up to tutor students, read to children or chaperone field trips. Volunteers can tutor math and reading through community organizations too, such as the **Hunter's Point Boy's and Girl's Club** (729 Kirkwood, 415-822-7140).

Bond more deeply with children (and make more of a commitment) at **Big**

Brothers Big Sisters of San Francisco & The Peninsula (731 Market, 6th Floor, bbbsa.org), and the Columbia Park Boys and Girls Clubs (nine locations including 450 Guerrero, 415-864-2724; 163 London, 415-334-2582). They provide clubhouses around the City where kids learn arts and crafts, sports and health, character, leadership and other good citizenship skills.

If you seek a rewarding challenge, contact SFCASA (100 Bush, Ste. 650, 415-398-8001, sfcasa.org), an organization that pairs up volunteers one-on-one with children living in foster care. "CASA" stands for Court Appointed Special Advocate. Each volunteer advocate becomes a sworn court officer who works to understand the interests and legal needs of the child they represent, and to make sure that lawyers, the courts and social services agencies are protecting them. Becoming a CASA advocate is an intense but important commitment. If you are going to stick around San Francisco, now might be a good time to get the 36 required hours of training under your belt.

WORKING WITH SENIORS

The elderly have made their contributions to the community, so why not give them something in return? Benefit from the wisdom of experience by befriending a senior through Little Brothers—Friends of the Elderly San Francisco (909 Hyde, Suite 628, 415-771-7957, little-brothers.org/sanfrancisco). They organize programs ranging from

COMMUNAL GIVING

Volunteering was more than a temporary diversion for Dave Casuto. He burned up his volunteer hours at the *Burning Man* office (see "Participate" at *burningman.com*) in 2001 and enjoyed it so much that he continued volunteering on weekends even after he found a full-time job. "It was a great way to connect to an amazing community," Dave told us.

Apparently the experience was inspirational. Several years later, Dave and some colleagues founded *Senior Surf* (415-509-3725, *senior-surf.org*), a nonprofit dedicated to computer education for seniors. With their Mobile Computer Initiative, the organization is delivering high-quality computer courses to retirement communities throughout the Bay Area.

volunteer visits to special events and parties. And get this, they offer skill-building internships, in areas such as database management, non-profit management, and event planning.

To help deliver the basic necessities of life to the elderly, hop on board with **Meals on Wheels** (1375 Fairfax Avenue, 415-920-1111, mowsf.org), one of the most successful charities around. Donate a lot or a little, and see clear, immediate results. The "How to Help" section of their website lists opportunities such as grocery shopper, meal server, even lunchtime performer! What better opportunity for budding musicians to gain a dedicated audience and strut their stuff? (Word to the wise: go easy on the speed metal or punk rock lyrics.)

WORKING WITH ANIMALS

Today's urban dogs and other animals have it tough. For one, they can no longer feast on plump peacocks in Golden Gate Park! (See the story of Connemara, **Chapter 4**.) For another, their numbers continue to grow without a corresponding increase in homes or services.

Plenty of wayward pets and animals need your assistance. First stop should be the **San Francisco SPCA** (2500 16th Street, 415-554-3000, sfspca.org), a group focused on saving our homeless canine and feline friends, and providing them with care and treatment. Search the SPCA website under "Help Us" for details on cat socializing, dog walking, or adoption counseling.

San Francisco Animal Care and Control (1200 15th Street, 415-554-6364, sfgov.org/site/acc_index.asp) is the official city agency charged with assisting our animal companions—several other non-profits partner with them. City agencies need friends, too, so the SFACC has enlisted the **Friends of San Francisco Animal Care and Control** (1200 15ᵗʰ Street, 415-822-5566, fsfacc.org), who invite you to join them in supporting the goals of the SFACC.

WORKING THE ROOM

Want to meet and greet while you're volunteering? No problem. The concept of "social volunteering" is popular and highly refined in San Francisco.

One Brick (onebrick.org) was founded with this exact premise in mind: to create a friendly and social atmosphere around volunteering. The organization supports other local non-profits, and its so-called "commitment-free volunteering" is designed to make it easy and more flexible for volunteers to donate their time.

It's no coincidence that Dave Shefferman, co-founder and executive director, helped create the group during a break between jobs. "After the dot-com bust many of us were unemployed and looking for things to do that were inexpensive and could make us feel better about how crappy life seemed at the moment," he says. "Volunteering was perfect. We turned it into something social, fun and a great networking opportunity."

Other particularly social groups include the **Commonwealth Club's IN-FORUM** (595 Market, 415-597-6700, commonwealthclub.org) and the **World Affairs Council's Young Professionals International Forum** (312 Sutter, Suite 200, 415-293-4600, itsyourworld.org). Both openly discuss the sometimes-controversial issues relevant to the 21- to

swanky parties

Day-of assistance with special events is fun, on site, and very social. It often helps to raise boatloads of money. Sound like your scene? Then don your tux or evening gown, and help the rich and notable loosen their grip on their wallets. Start with:

• the *San Francisco Volunteer Center* (thevolunteercenter.net), which lists one-day events under "Special Event Volunteering"

• the swanky events of the *American Cancer Society* (201 Mission, Suite 720, 415-394-7100, cancer.org), which can double as great networking opportunities

• the *Cystic Fibrosis Foundation* (415-331-0650, cff.org) , which uses special events as one of its primary fundraising vehicles, and is always looking for volunteers

40-year-old set, and offer opportunities to organize events that benefit their parent organization. As an added bonus, get elected to chair the Council's International Forum and you'll sit on the board—alongside well-connected San Franciscans.

Want to support the arts instead? Check out the **San Francisco Opera's Bravo! Club** (301 Van Ness, 415-861-4008, sfopera.com), dedicated to building a young audience for the opera. Young singles support dance too, through the **San Francisco Ballet's ENCORE!** (455 Franklin, 415-553-4634, encoresf.org).

VOLUNTEERING ABROAD

A volunteer stint abroad can find you tutoring kids in a rural village, helping to preserve the rain forest, or rebuilding houses after a disaster. Those are but a few possible endeavors; the options are as varied as volunteering in your own community, with the added benefit of immersion in another culture. For more on volunteering abroad, see "volunteer vacations" in **Chapter 5**.

Work Camps and Placements

Overseas volunteer options fall generally into one of two categories: "work camps," which are bare-bones volunteer groups that usually have projects ranging from one week to one month and are relatively inexpensive; and volunteer placement organizations, which are more costly but also provide extensive support and amenities. Some organizations charge fees that can really stretch a leisure budget, so this is one crusade you definitely want to do your homework on.

Below are a couple of homework assignments, after you finish the required reading: *How to Live Your Dream of Volunteering Overseas* by Joseph Collins, Stefano DeZerega, and Zahara Heckscher.

Work Camps:
Volunteers For Peace (vpf.org)
Service Civil International (sci-ivs.org)

Placement Organizations:
Global Volunteers (globalvolunteers.org)
Amizade (amizade.org)

Elective Elections

Want to promote freedom and democracy around the world without donning battle fatigues or toting a weapon? Volunteer to monitor an overseas election. The need is out there (just like the truth), and you'll play a critical role in helping ensure elections are both free and fair.

Jason Julian, an attorney in California, has made monitoring elections a habit over the last decade, venturing overseas six times to regions of emerging democracy such as Bosnia, Liberia and Ukraine. It has been a reality check.

"As United Nations Volunteers, we had to do a lot of organizational and logistical support work relevant to the election, as opposed to just watching for fraud or other irregularities," Jason told us. "My most memorable experience was in Liberia in 1997 just after the end of the civil war there. The whole country had a post-apocalyptic 'Mad Max' feel and landscape to it. One day I saw two young girls fist-fighting in the street and one picked up a large gray object to hit the other. When I got a bit closer I could see (to my shock and surprise) that she was wielding a human skull. I asked a Liberian mechanic in our post where she got the skull and he nonchalantly replied, 'Oh, they are all around.'"

If this has you scratching your head, take it as a sobering reminder that people still sacrifice their lives in other regions of the world to fight for basic freedoms that many of us take for granted.

> **Monitoring Elections:**
>
> *United Nations Volunteers (unv.org)*
> *The Carter Center (cartercenter.org)*
> *PAE React (pae-react.com)*
> *Organization for Security and*
> *Co-operation in Europe (osce.org)*

GIVING AND LIVING LEISURE

That's a lot of giving going on! But as the cliché goes, you get what you give. The more good vibes you share through volunteering, the safer the world becomes for leisure.

Keep that "Share the Leisure" feeling in mind as you transition out of pure recreational mode into your next big life endeavor, be it heading for the halls of academia or (ack!) going back to work.

PART THREE

RE-ENTRY

CHAPTER 10
BACK TO SCHOOL

*"Woo-hoo! I'm a college man! I won't need my high
school diploma any more! I am so smart! I am so
smart...S-M-R-T! I mean, S-M-A-R-T..."*

~ Homer Simpson, Homer Goes Back to College

YOU might be wondering what to do *after* your Leisure Odyssey.
Hopefully you'll score some stress-free fun before facing this decision, but what if you're still not ready to go back to work? What if you
loathe your career and aren't sure what you want to do next? Don't
panic. There *is* a solution. It's time to go to school.

Going back to school is a major undertaking, especially if it means
foregoing a high-paying job. The possibility of debt and career derail-
ment can loom large. You might wonder if it's worth the investment.
But think about it this way: you have the rest of your working life to
earn dollars, but you may never have a better chance to further your
education. Most fellow earthlings are lucky to get a high school degree, much less finish college or go to grad school. From that perspective, consider any type of schooling a privilege.

Higher education can serve as a panacea for that which ails the leisure seeker. You get to ditch the pressures and responsibilities of a
job (temporarily) while working toward a worthy goal: greater knowledge. But being job-free is not the only benefit—if you've longed to
study the classics like history, art or literature, the books are waiting
for you. Looking to change careers? A new degree can open doors as
well as your mind. Maybe it's a trade that appeals to you. Become a
certified bartender. Go to beer school!

You can never learn too much. If you can fund more school, get thee
to thy registrar and get those neurons firing.

GRADUATE SCHOOL

Lisa Turner decided to apply to a graduate journalism program after getting laid off from her dot-com job. "The prospect of giving up a big salary to go back to school was daunting," she told us. "But coming from a position of unemployment or self-employment, it was more realistic."

Robert L. Peters' book *Getting What You Came for: The Smart Student's Guide to Earning a M.A or a Ph.D.* can help you weigh the pros and cons of becoming a student again. But don't limit your calculus to the practical; some of life's most enriching experiences result from factoring in the whimsical, too.

leisure studies

The scholastic study of leisure is multi-disciplinary, drawing from fields such as history, sociology, economics and politics to describe how people spend their free time. Many reputable universities have Leisure Studies departments, including **San Francisco State** (Department of Recreation and Leisure Studies, 1600 Holloway, Gym Building, Room 207, 415-338-2030). The department offers bachelor's degrees in Recreation and master's degrees in Recreation Administration. You can even specialize in "therapeutic recreation" to become nationally certified as a recreation therapist.

Now *that's* a program we can get behind!

more leisure...

Gena Bilden, assistant dean of student services for the graduate programs at **Saint Mary's University of Minnesota** (smumn.edu), realizes that most students go to grad school to advance their careers and increase their salaries, but cautions applicants against going to grad school for the wrong reasons. "I've sat in class with individuals who proclaim that all they want is a piece of paper," she told us. "If they don't come away with the knowledge, they have only wasted their time and money."

Research

You'll find comprehensive information on programs in the U.S. and abroad at sites like **GradSchools.com** (gradschools.com). The site is funded by sponsoring universities, which means the information is free but might be skewed in favor of those sponsors. **Peterson's** (petersons.com) produces another free education portal with a good search engine; just be prepared for them to hard-sell you one of their many books. A more neutral source of U.S.

graduate program rankings is *U.S. News & World Report* (usnews.com, "Rankings & Guides," then "America's Best Graduate Schools").

The Admissions Process

Applying to grad school and getting accepted are two entirely different steps. The admissions requirements and application process will be much more stringent than the hoops you jumped through for your undergraduate study. Don't be intimidated—you won't be the first or the last to go through the rigors. In fact, guiding applicants through the admissions maze has become its own thriving industry.

> **...more leisure**
>
> If you think leisure might be the field for you, try your hand at an actual course. Heidi Wells took one as an undergrad at San Francisco State. "I got a 'C' on my first paper," she told us. "A 'C' in leisure? I couldn't let that happen. It was odd taking leisure so seriously, but I ended up with an 'A' in the class." Heidi graduated at the top of her leisure class, recently completing her third extended trip abroad.

If you have your eye on the business world and making tons of money, for example, you can buy the book by Matt Symonds and Alan Mendonca, *ABC of Getting the MBA Admissions Edge*. If you aspire to heal others, check out Andrew Goliszek's straightforward *The Complete Medical School Preparation and Admissions Guide*. And if you advocate justice for all, pony up for *Law School Admissions Adviser* by Ruth Lammert-Reeves.

Entrance Exams

No institutional process would be complete without good old-fashioned standardized tests. Welcome to the wonderful world of acronyms: GRE, GMAT, LSAT, MCAT, TOEFL...YIKES! Those who dwell in the neo-acronym world of high-tech will feel right at home.

As with research, there are companies that can help—for a not-so-nominal fee. **Kaplan** (800-527-8378, kaplan.com) and **The Princeton Review** (800-273-8439, princetonreview.com), two preeminent test preparation companies, offer live and online courses for all common standardized tests. Live course fees start at a whopping $800. Even the more economical online courses with self-study materials will soak up anywhere from $100 to $500 of your freedom funds. If you're the self-disciplined type, practice some frugality and go with materials from the bookstore.

Are the pricey courses worth the money? Ted Witt bumped up his GMAT score a modest 30 points after taking a live course. He admits, though, that he might have been a little preoccupied—his second try was only six days before his wedding!

"I decided to take the test again four weeks later with no studying," he told us. "One hundred and ten points higher that time." Guess it took a while for the course info to sink in, or maybe the test is just that random. Ted's final answer? "Prepare with books or a class, and if you aren't happy with your score, take the test again."

WHO'S GONNA PAY?

Most university programs require serious cash. Never fear. An intrepid trailblazer like you should be able to mine at least one of the following sources.

Scholarships

Parental sponsorship not an option? Then think "scholarship." Scholarships are fantastic, untapped resources, many of which garner little competition. These treasures won't stay hidden for much longer, though. The Web makes it infinitely easier to ferret them out.

Folks we know rave about the **Catalog of Federal Domestic Assistance** (cfda.gov) as a starting point. One of the least commercial online sources is **Scholarships.com** (scholarships.com), whose sophisticated search engine helps you manage their extensive database. **Broke-Scholar** (brokescholar.com) boasts a database of more than 650,000 scholarships worth over $2.5 billion. And **FastWeb** (fastweb.com), owned by the career website Monster, lets you search for colleges as well as scholarships, for free.

For information on general financial aid within the state of California, see the website of the **California Student Aid Commission** (csac.ca.gov), which focuses primarily on grants and loans. Many of their programs are geared towards low-income students and families.

Student Loans

If you've squeezed out whatever scholarship money is available and you are still short on tuition, consider a student loan. Most are offered at exceptionally low interest rates, many are subsidized by the federal government, and repayment schedules are usually flexible.

A loan is still a loan, however, no matter how attractive the terms. Do the math and make sure you're comfortable with how much you'll owe once you've earned your degree. Consult the **U.S. Department of Education** (ed.gov under "Financial Aid") for information on grants and direct loans from the federal government.

Other Federal Government Aid

Get back some of your hard-earned tax dollars by taking advantage of other forms of government aid. The National Science Foundation has developed a program called the **Integrative Graduate Education and Research Traineeship** (igert.org), designed to improve the graduate school experience by providing interdisciplinary training in the sciences, mathematics, engineering and technology. Students accepted into the program receive (gulp hard) $30,000 per year, plus tuition and fees! And of course, veterans should definitely look into the **GI Bill** (gibill.va.gov)

Employer's Tuition Reimbursement

Think of it as the GI Bill for the private sector: some companies will pay for or reimburse your tuition to attend graduate school (with a promise of you returning to your job for a certain time period), so make sure not to pass up this employment perk. Not all companies have formal programs, particularly smaller firms, but that doesn't mean you shouldn't ask. Be sure to highlight how it will help you be a better employee.

the scholarly bay

The Bay Area's university scene doesn't match Boston's in terms of density, but it does in terms of prestige and variety. The graduate schools at Berkeley and Stanford consistently rank among the best in the country. Together, researchers at local universities have garnered 54 Nobel Prizes, including three in 2006. That's no shortage of brain power! (How many Nobel laureates *does* it take to change a light bulb?) Venture capitalists credit this environment with creating a fertile nesting ground for technology and innovation.

Universities within the city limits include San Francisco State University (SFSU), University of San Francisco (USF), University of California San Francisco (UCSF), Golden Gate University, and the Academy of Art College. Berkeley, Stanford, San Jose State, and Santa Clara Universities loom within striking distance.

loans that can bring you to tears

About six months after joining her first-choice law firm in San Francisco, Erica Madison (name changed) found herself crying in her office one night. "Practicing law was nothing like studying it," she told us, "and I realized I was handcuffed to working at this place I didn't like, in order to pay off the huge private loans I took, in order to get the education I got, in order to get this job—that I didn't like!"

All's well that ends well, though: Erica devoted a huge portion of her salary to paying off those loans as fast as she could, knocking off almost *a hundred thousand dollars* in less than three years.

Two years later, she changed careers and has now happily returned to academia, working for a university while earning her Masters in Education.

The Source of Last Resort

That's right, the parents. Paying tuition is a legitimate use of their money, right? Wrangling financial aid from your folks might take some fancy persuasion, however.

Mary Mangold's father was skeptical when she asked for a loan to go to film school, so she got creative. "I brought Dad to an open house at the college for extended learning downtown," Mary said. "My future film teacher was so inspiring that my dad agreed to support me."

When you're making your pitch, highlight the ways that the university experience will make you a better person and increase your earning power in the long run. Don't forget to mention how it could boost your ability to care for your elders in their retirement: a little leisure for you now means greater leisure for them later. Isn't it nice how that works?

GOING TO SCHOOL OVERSEAS

Did you miss out on that undergraduate semester abroad? Go now! You'll reap the benefits of travel and education in one neat package.

Brian Pollack went on exchange to Madrid for six months during his MBA program at the University of Washington. "It was one of the best times of my life," he says. "Madrid is an amazing city, and the Spanish culture suited me perfectly." Most universities offer overseas exchange options to their graduate students in addition to their undergrads.

Not matriculated in a degree program? Don't despair. Any number of fields offer stand-alone international programs. An exceptional starting point for research is the **Bechtel International Center**

(422 Lagunita Drive, Stanford, 650-723-1831, stanford.edu/dept/icenter) at Stanford University. Here you'll find information on all things international, from overseas education to global employment opportunities. Online, check out **Studyabroad.com** (studyabroad.com) for a comprehensive directory of programs abroad.

PROFESSIONAL PROGRAMS

Not everyone aspires to become a doctor, lawyer, or business executive, but few can deny the broad-reaching benefits of a professional degree. Counting Berkeley, Stanford, UCSF, and Hastings, there's no shortage of top programs here in the Bay Area, along with stiff competition. Win entrance to any of these local programs and make mom and dad proud.

Business School

Future titans of industry can earn an MBA just about anywhere, but they won't be alone. The good news is that applications for full-time programs have trended down the last few years, according to the Graduate Management Admission Council. The bad news is that the decrease is mostly just a fallback from a record spike of applicants in 2002. The bottom line: you'll have some company applying to business school.

For overall quality of program, the **Haas School of Business at UC Berkeley** (510-642-1405 for full-time program, haas.berkeley.edu) and the **Stanford Graduate School of Business** (650-723-2146, gsb.stanford.edu) stand well above the rest of the pack. The 2003 *US News & World Report* survey ranked Stanford number one in the nation for full-time MBA programs, and Haas number ten.

Medical School

Despite insurance companies' continued squeeze on the entire medical profession, becoming a doctor remains a noble calling. Acquire the power to heal at the world-class **UCSF School of Medicine** (415-476-4044, ucsf.edu), where you can study alongside Nobel Prize winners. The **Stanford School of Medicine** (650-723-6861, med.stanford.edu) ain't half bad, either. The two schools excel in both research and medical practice, and have joined forces in many endeavors.

Law School

Maybe you've always dreamt of arguing your case in front of a jury or suing the pants off of your neighbor. Consider getting a law degree first.

Hang out at San Francisco's other "beach"—the concrete deck at **Hastings College of the Law** (200 McAllister, 415-565-4623, uchastings.edu). **Stanford Law School** (650-723-2465, law.stanford.edu) and **UC Berkeley's Boalt Hall** (510-642-1741, law.berkeley.edu) will also wise you up to the ways of the law, albeit in a less urban environment. All three are highly regarded programs, with Stanford and Berkeley again ranking near the top.

NIGHT SCHOOL AND CONTINUING EDUCATION

If a full-time program doesn't fit the bill, maybe a part-time program will. We're biased towards full-time programs (no work!), but if you absolutely must, consider night school or continuing education. You can customize most programs to accommodate your (pending?) work schedule.

Executive/Part-Time MBA Programs

Executive MBA programs, which allow a student to earn an MBA without quitting the day job, are increasing in popularity. Just think, you get to work full-time *and* go to school—double the fun! A word of caution: most executive programs charge as if an employer were footing the bill.

East Coast tradition embraced West Coast innovation in 2001, when the University of Pennsylvania's highly regarded Wharton School opened **Wharton West** in San Francisco (101 Howard, Suite 500, 415-777-1000, west.wharton.upenn.edu). Early enrollees have given high marks to both its executive MBA program and its open enrollment executive education courses at the historic Folger Building. Now *that's* good coffee!

The Professional MBA for Executives program at **USF School of Business and Management** (2130 Fulton, 415-422-2221, usfca.edu/sobam) offers a solid curriculum to support those with regional business aspirations. **SF State College of Business** (1600 Holloway, 415-338-1276, cob.sfsu.edu), the local workhorse university, presents its version as an Accelerated MBA. Finally, **Golden Gate University**

LOVING THE STUDENT LIFE

Working in an unstructured atmosphere, on your own time schedule, in a creative learning environment—it sounds terrible, doesn't it? Jay Drake worked for six years before returning to law school, where he reveled in the student lifestyle. He found the youthful, academic environment energizing. "I was always amazed at how some law students cried about how hard it was being in school," Jay told us. "Having been in the working world for a number of years I would laugh, remind them that being a student has many advantages, and that if they think school is hard to wait until they start the daily grind of the working life with all of its stresses and frustrations." Jay is now an attorney in San Francisco, with fond memories of his student hiatus.

(415-442-6500, ggu.edu) offers a Strategic Executive MBA (SEMBA—sounds like a Latin dance!) program.

Outside the City, the **Haas School** (510-642-0292 for part-time programs) offers both weekend and evening MBA programs. Both are excellent values, and thus are highly competitive. *US News and World Report* consistently ranks the part-time program as one of the best in the country. In a strategic alliance designed to maximize synergies (that's biz school speak!), Haas has combined forces with **Columbia Business School** to offer an executive MBA program on the Berkeley campus (510-643-1046, berkeley.columbia.edu), which also ranks well nationally. Down in San Jose (do you know the way?), **San Jose State University's College of Business** (cob.sjsu.edu) offers two evening MBA options, with the added advantage of strong ties to the Silicon Valley business network.

Law School at Night

Not everyone who wants to study law can afford to study in a full-time program. If you can't seem to break away during the day, it *is* possible get your law degree in the evenings. Thank goodness there's still a way to get more attorneys out there!

The part-time evening program at **Golden Gate University School of Law** (415-442-6630, ggu.edu/school_of_law) is the most flexible, and can arrange for you to attend day classes part-time after you're

student discount, please!

You didn't hear it from us, but City College will issue you a student ID on the spot when you register for a class. If you later cancel your registration, you'll still have your ID. What you do with that ID is up to you, but you might consider getting a few discounts on movies, museums, and the like. No one ever said a student had to be under 25....

admitted to the night program. The **USF School of Law** (415-422-6586, usfca.edu/law) has a part-time, mostly evening, JD program. Unfortunately, neither Stanford nor Hastings nor Boalt offers a part-time program.

Continuing Education

Continuing ed can spark your intellect and open up new cerebral worlds—or it can teach you how to taste wine, repair your car, or do your taxes. Either way, it expands your horizons, and that's a big part of the practice of leisure.

Almost all of the local universities offer some form of continuing adult education. **UC Berkeley Extension** (510-642-4111, unex.berkeley.edu) has three campuses in San Francisco (425 Market, 8th Floor, 415-284-1060; 95 3rd Street, 415-284-1081; Jewish Community Center, 3200 California) in addition to locations in Berkeley, Oakland, and Redwood City. Their courses include certificate and special programs as well as a broad variety of general ed classes. Some of the spicier courses from their Spring 2003 catalog included "Love, American Style: A Cultural History of Sexuality in the United States" and "The Greatest Wines in the World."

SF State College of Extended Learning (1600 Holloway; 425 Market, 2nd Floor, 415-405-7700, cel.sfsu.edu) has a fine selection of continuing education courses, with an additional location in Oakland (2201 Broadway Street).

SFSU's pioneering **Multimedia Studies Program** (425 Market, 2nd Floor, 415-405-7700, msp.sfsu.edu/home.html) was at the forefront of the Internet boom and vaulted countless local students into the world of multimedia and the Web.

At just $20 per unit for residents, courses at **City College of San Francisco** (415-239-3000, ccsf.edu) might be the best bargain around. For-credit courses are available on just about any subject imaginable, and non-credit division courses are tuition free. That's right, FREE. Students need only show up on the first day of class and buy their own books and supplies.

Vocational Schools

If you want to acquire a set of skills quickly, vocational schools can get you where you want to go. They usually specialize in a focused trade, such as technology, design, or culinary studies.

The nationwide **University of Phoenix** (185 Berry, 800-448-6775, phoenix.edu) presents a variety of practical programs for working adults, including business, technology, healthcare and education. Another option is **Heald College** (350 Mission, 415-808-3000, heald.edu), which offers associate degrees and certificate training, primarily in technology.

If the above say nothing but "yawn" to you, jump to some more vivacious options, below.

ALTERNATIVE EDUCATION

"Alternative education" is a peculiar expression, really—sort of like "alternative rock." What exactly constitutes "alternative?" Who decides what is "alternative" versus "mainstream?" Damned if we know. In any event, we feel compelled to share some options you might not find in your average Ivy League course catalog.

Drop-In Schooling

The loosely-defined concept of auditing classes gained popularity in the '60s. Needless to say, it's a very cost-effective method of study, and one that's flexible. You can study what you want, decide when you want to go to class, and the admission requirements are quite lax—as in nonexistent!

Policies vary among universities and professors, so you might have to check around a bit before choosing your "major." Generally speaking, the larger the university and the bigger the class, the easier it will be to audit.

take two

Susan Logas, a 52-year-old mother who retired early from a career in telecommunications, returned to school at City College to study computer science. Several years later, she had completed certificate programs in Unix System Administration and Web Administration.

"I love going to City College," Susan told us. "I love being an adult student—it's a whole different perspective. I know how to study. I know how to listen. And I know how to support the teachers." Susan's now contemplating re-entering the workforce as a system or web administrator, thanks to her fine new education.

THE AUDIT ARENA

Not surprisingly, UC Berkeley tends to be lenient in the audit arena, although gone are the days when just about any inquisitive soul could sit in on their class of choice. Jeremy Cantor audits at least one class there a semester. Of course, it helps that he works for the university! Despite Jeremy's insider advantage, he trusts that most professors will be happy to accommodate an auditor if the class has space, and you approach them early, with a genuine interest in the subject.

Jeremy recently audited a graduate-level course in Public Health Policy with the professor's permission. "It's a great way to break up my week," he told us. "A good class is a stimulating, challenging environment and when you audit, there's no required work. I've been able to check out a number of career and grad school possibilities."

If you ask the professor up front if you can audit the class, you risk being asked for proof that you're enrolled in the university. This is where holding on to that old student ID card would come in handy!

Stealth mode might be an option for larger classes, but that means skipping exams and other graded assignments. Whether you have the professor's permission or not, one major drawback of auditing is that there's no chance for credit or to bring home an "A" on your report card. No extra allowance for you!

Mom, Dad—I Want to be a Chef

San Francisco is a culinary mecca and home to several internationally recognized culinary academies, a boon if soufflé is "ze way" you'd like to make your living.

The **California Culinary Academy** (625 Polk, 888-897-3222, baychef.com) offers not only instruction for students but gourmet dining for the public at very reasonable prices (see **Dining & Nightlife**). The world-renowned cooking school cranks out chefs who go on to cook at top venues around the globe. If you'd like to bake like the masters, perfect your (spring-) form at the **San Francisco Baking Institute** (480 Grandview Drive, South San Francisco, 650-589-5784, sfbi.com), "where better baking begins" (but where, pray tell, does it end?). The well-respected **Culinary Institute of America at Greystone** (2555 Main Street, St. Helena, 800-333-9242, ciachef.edu) is just a stone's throw away in nearby wine country, and well-worth the commute—chefs from here land sweet gigs at the most chic restaurants around.

Another Round?

Bartending can make for a lively career or merely a quick cash stop-gap. The evening hours assure plenty of lounge time during the day.

Higher education in the field is available at the **American Bartenders School** (800-532-9222, barschool.com), which offers degrees in the time-tested field of "mixology." It could be just the medicine that the doctor ordered.

But wait, there's competition in the world of cocktail education. The **National Bartenders School** (870 Market, Suite 828, 800-646-6499, nationalbartending.com) is home-grown and eager to train you. So, too, is the **San Francisco School of Bartending** (760 Market, Suite 833, 415-362-1116, sfbartending.com), which touts a classroom replica of a bar, "except for the hangover." Woo-hoo! Bartending courses at different schools cost from $500-$1,000 and will have you drink-ready in about two weeks.

KEEP THE MIND BREWING

Remember surveying the drunken crowd at an all-school kegger and thinking, "Man, if only I knew how to make my *own* beer... I could make a fortune!" Time to bring that fantasy to life—if not for the fortune, then at least for the beer. Beer making has graduated from backyard to big time. Want to go old-school? Hop in the footsteps of beer giant Dan Gordon (of Gordon Biersch) and head to the prestigious *Weihenstephan (wihenstephaner. de)*in the heart of Bavaria, the birthplace of brew. Take a more modern approach at *UC Davis (ucdavis.edu)*, where you can earn an undergraduate or master's degree in brewing science, or just enroll in an extension program. Total new-schoolers can follow virtual courses at *American Brewers Guild (abgbrew.com)*, which includes apprenticeships in brewpubs throughout the U.S.

A new concept has hit the City like a cool draft: beer school. Educate yourself in the art of brewing fine hops and malts at **21st Amendment** (563 2nd Street, 415-369-0900, 21st-amendment.com), a restaurant and brewery near AT&T Park. 21st-A co-owner "Professor Nico" Freccia will take you through the history and craft of different beer styles. "Beer is the oldest man-made beverage and the history of beer parallels the history of mankind," he says diligently. Each one-night course comes complete with a syllabus, appetizers, and (but of course) plenty of liquid samples. The whole keg and caboodle consists of five courses; tuition is usually $20 a night.

so you've always wanted to be a...

• *Mechanic* •
Break out the tools in the Automotive Technology program of **City College of San Francisco's Office of Vocational Education** (415-550-4440, *ccsf.edu/Services/Vocational_Education* [note the capital letters here], locations throughout San Francisco). Students can earn certificates in mechanics as well as body and fender repair.

• *Esthetician* •
Get the skinny on all kinds of beauty training at the **San Francisco Institute of Esthetics and Cosmetology** (1067 Folsom, Suite 200, 866-734-3244, *san franciscoinstitute.com*) in their programs for cosmetologists, estheticians, and nail technicians (hey, it's technical!).

more...

HOLISTIC SERVICES

Have you always dreamt of laying your hands on others? Poking needles through someone else's skin? (Minds out of the gutter, please.) You might be a born holistic healer with the untapped potential to treat your fellow human. The following dynamic programs can help you help others.

Massage Therapy

Who doesn't like a massage therapist? (Especially one you are dating!) They spread more joy than perhaps any other class of professionals, and feed off of that joy in return. Liz King, a massage therapist from Pacifica, says her career is very fulfilling. "I know that I am positively influencing people's lives, and helping them relax."

If you want to become this popular and get paid for it to boot, you'll need training. There are countless school listings to massage through, including the **San Francisco School of Massage** (1327 Chestnut, Suites A & B, 415-474-4600, sf-schoolofmassage.com).

Teaching Yoga

New yoga schools are popping up like flies in and around the City, and schools need teachers. Stretch your boundaries by teaching others to stretch theirs. You'll keep a fit mind and body while you're at it.

Barbara MacMillan, a self-proclaimed yoga fanatic, enrolled in an intensive four-week program at **Greenpath Yoga** (2242 Lombard, 415-775-7545, greenpathyoga.org) and now teaches at several studios in Mill Valley. She also offers private lessons at her home. "The best part of teaching yoga is that it provides the most fulfilling work atmosphere I've ever had," she says. "The energy is positive and everyone leaves the lesson feeling better than when they arrived." If that's not a glowing endorsement, we're not sure what is.

Other notable instructor schools include **It's Yoga** (848 Folsom, 415-543-1970, itsyoga.net), which specializes in Ashtanga, and **Yoga Center of Marin** (142 Redwood Avenue, Corte Madera, 415-927-1850, yogacenterofmarin.com), which bases its courses primarily on Iyengar. Some programs offer scholarships or tuition payments on a sliding scale.

...cont'd

• Pilot •
Take off into the wild blue yonder if you must, but please—take some lessons first! Crissy Airfield now harbors snowy egrets, not planes, so buzz on down to the San Carlos Airport and *Bel-Air International* (795 Sky Way, San Carlos, 650-596-9900, *belairintl.com*). There you can train for anything from piloting a private plane to commandeering a jumbo jet.

• Veterinarian's Assistant •
If you're not up for the commitment of a veterinary program like the one at UC Davis, then pony on up to *Santa Rosa Junior College* (1501 Mendocino Avenue, 800-564-7752, *santarosa.edu*) and enroll in their Animal Science Certificate Program. Their courses will prepare you to be a veterinarian's assistant (or ranch manager—giddyup!). Imagine the possibilities—you might win that coveted sheep scholarship after all.

Chinese Medicine & Acupuncture

Are you a stickler for acupuncture? Sorry, we're just poking fun. This and other alternative health practices have flourished in the U.S. during the last 20 years, as more and more people explore the healing power of ancient Chinese therapies.

In the Bay Area, the two most prominent acupuncture schools are the **American College of Traditional Chinese Medicine** in Potrero

citizen's academy

Do you aspire to be a better citizen and contribute more to your community? You can train in the fine practice of citizenship through the *City of Oakland's Citizens' Academy* (Office of the City Manager, Oakland, 510-238-3301). The purpose of the program is "to engage Oakland citizens with their City government by providing an interactive forum to learn first hand how the City of Oakland is structured and managed." You have to apply (and be accepted), and the weekly classes are held on weekday evenings and Saturdays.

Walk the beat with the SFPD through their *Citizens' Police Academy* (350 Amber, 415-401-4701, *ci.sf. ca.us/police*, "Citizen's Academy"). This program, predictably, focuses more on municipal policing, and aims to "develop a closer understanding and working relationship between the San Francisco Police Department and communities served." Classes meet on Monday nights for 13 weeks in a row, and participants are expected to attend all classes. Those with spotty criminal records need not apply.

Hill (455 Arkansas, 415-282-7600, actcm. edu) and, across the Bay, the **Academy of Chinese Culture and Health Sciences** (1601 Clay Street, Oakland, 510-763-7787, acchs.edu). Both are accredited by The Accreditation Commission for Acupuncture and Oriental Medicine (ACAOM).

San Francisco's own Chinese medicine guru is author and wellness pioneer **Doc Misha** (docmisha.com). Her site on Traditional Chinese Medicine features books, clinics and all sorts of other "wellness" goodies.

Chiropractic

Are chiropractors truly medical doctors? It's debatable. Go to school and then decide for yourself whether you've become a "real" doctor or not.

Cracking the code on chiropractic schools in the Bay Area is a bit of a challenge, with surprisingly few focused purely on SMT (that's Spinal Manipulation Therapy, for all you neophytes). Try **Palmer Chiropractic West** (90 East Tasman Drive, San Jose, 408-944-6000, palmer.edu), renowned for its focus on sports medicine and training, or **Life Chiropractic College West** in the East Bay (25001 Industrial Boulevard, Hayward, 800-788-4476, lifewest.edu). And remember—it's not "cracking" but "spinal manipulation."

Belly Dancing

Last but not least, we come to the study of belly dancing. What back-to-school discussion would be complete without touching on this incomparable art? And you thought all those dancers at Kan Zaman were *born* with rolling stomachs and gyrating hips. Au contraire, mon frère—those dancers trained for years in order to master their craft.

Belly dancing has its roots in Middle Eastern culture and the traditional dance is quite conservative. Practiced by women for other women only under the guise of a fertility ceremony, it was reputedly taught to young girls as a way to strengthen their abdominal muscles in preparation for childbirth.

Leave it to western culture to add the erotic touch. Apparently the hip and abdominal movements were too risqué for conservative western views at the end of the 19th century, so the dance was branded as immoral. This only piqued the public's interest. Hollywood latched onto the dance and contributed the seductive costumes and naval jewelry that prevail among belly dancers today.

Why the heck do we care about the history of belly dancing? We're not really sure. All we know is that we like it, and we're all for the modern sensual versions too. Further, we encourage the leisurely study and practice of the art.

Curious students can contact the preeminent school in San Francisco, if not the country: **Fat Chance Belly Dance** in the Mission (670 South Van Ness, 415-431-4322, fcbd.com), which specializes in American Tribal Style Bellydance.

Fabulous Fat Chance Founder Carolena Nericcio is also the author

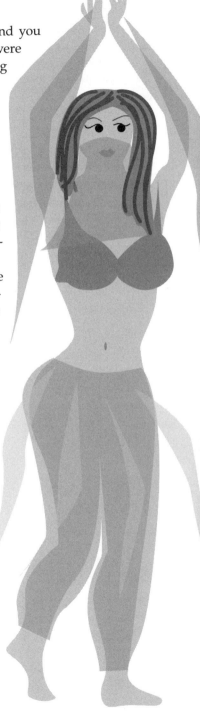

of *The Art of Belly Dance*, which covers the history of the dance as well as provides illustrated instructions for all the basic steps.

Liz King took regular lessons at **Downward Dog Yoga** in Pacifica (94 West Manor Drive, Pacifica, 650-355-9642, downwarddogyoga.com) and hopes to begin performing. "It's not just a workout," she says. "It's a reconnection to my femininity."

FINAL EXAM

Powerful stuff indeed. Whether reconnecting with your femininity or your ability to mix drinks, studying queuing theory or organic chemistry, you'll never go wrong furthering your education. However, if you must (and we do mean must) go out and get yourself a job, read on to learn how you can find fulfilling work without giving up your hard-earned sense of leisure.

"Find a job you like and you add five days to every week."

~H. Jackson Brown, Jr.
Author, *Life's Little Instruction Book*

WHY would a book about savoring time off focus several chapters on work? Talking about jobs in a book on leisure might seem ironic, but most people not only need to work, they *want* to work—as long as that work is something they feel good about.

True, looking for a job can be a major drag. But exploring career possibilities can also be exciting and cathartic, particularly if you're able to re-evaluate your skills and passions, and remove what we call *Work Inhibitions*. No, we're not talking about the corporate decorum that keeps you from photocopying your bare bottom after too much champagne at the office holiday party. We mean self-imposed restrictions based on those pesky little "S" words: salary and status.

Take this time to think, inhibition-free, about your ideal job. Do you want to work for yourself or someone else? A big organization or small? A business, a non-profit, or something altogether different? If you just want to fund more leisure, this meditation won't take long. But if you're ready for deeper career soul-searching, it deserves significant time—in fact, it's a lifelong pursuit.

So when you're good and ready to take the plunge back into the working world (or are just in dire need of a steady paycheck), turn to this chapter for some informal job search ideas that will stave off the *Post-Sabbatical Blues*.

Just make sure you look for work that will feed your spirit as well as pay the bills. Remember, nothing anchors a life of leisure more than a job you can't wait to get to each day!

CAREER = LIFESTYLE

Plenty of great resources expound on career transitions, career self-analysis and the like—including the venerable *What Color is Your Parachute* by Richard N. Bolles (jobhuntersbible.com) and *I Could Do Anything If I Only Knew What It Was: How to Discover What You Really Want and How to Get It* by Barbara Sher—but few address the importance of lifestyle in choosing your path. Separating work and play, vocation and vacation, can be a paramount mistake if your goal is to create a healthy work-life balance.

"All planning should begin with personal planning," says Gary Ryan Blair (goalsguy.com), a specialist in goal setting. "Any choice one makes regarding career will affect their quality of life. Therefore it is imperative to determine quality of life first and then create the opportunity that best supports your personal life agenda."

It's never too late to point your career in a new direction and do something that supports a more rewarding lifestyle.

ZEN AND THE ART OF JOB HUNTING

Like dating, job searches obey a natural rule: the harder you pursue, the more elusive your quarry. We've all experienced the phenomenon of being more attractive to others when we're already in a relationship. The same holds true in the work world: potential employers find us more attractive if we're already involved with another organization. Great, but what if you *don't* have a job? Remember that you don't have to *be* taken to *seem* taken—or at least desirable. By conveying that you're not desperate for a job, you'll come across as confident, secure and in demand, whether you really are or not. Easier said than done, but definitely worth a try.

Work is love made visible.
~Kahlil Gibran

Let the beauty of what you love be what you do.
~Rumi

Your work is to discover your work, and then with all your heart to give yourself to it.
~Buddha

leisurely work & the wisdom of the ages

Whatever your circumstance, keep reminding yourself that you are a valuable, unique asset—because you are! Your job search is simply a matter of figuring where your talents best fit within the work world, not about whether you will be hired by a particular industry or organization.

So don't look for a job, at least in the traditional sense. Let the job come to you, Zen master. Radiate the aura of a survivor. Even though you're searching for work, your world won't end if you don't land a given job.

Staying calm about your job search is not to say that you can sit and wait for the phone to ring; it just means that job searching is not a competition that you win or lose. You won't earn points for talking to the most HR people, scheduling the most interviews or garnering the most offers. You will score by landing a job that you love.

seek the zone

What do you do when you can do anything you want to? Can you translate that into a paying job? Maybe not, but then again— maybe you can. When time disappears and not a thought enters your mind but what you're doing at that moment, what is it that you're doing? Look for a job that includes those activities and skills.

"If you have to settle for less than your dream job in the short term, stay committed to what you ultimately want to create in this world," says Joel Garfinkle, founder of **Dream Job Coaching** (dreamjobcoaching.com). In other words, seek the zone.

"What Do You Do (For Fun)?"

Untraditional job hunting tactics range from going to parties to taking ski weekends to playing golf. Sound like fun? Sound leisurely? It can be. No one ever said searching for a job meant sending out hundreds of resumes, or spending long hours at home in front of the computer. Leave the career fairs to those who feel the need to don a business suit and stand in long lines with resume in hand.

Do you like parties? Find some! In fact, go out and have fun at whatever it is that you like to do. Depriving yourself of your favorite activities or interests in favor of an extra hour in front of the computer is hardly going to benefit your search. Indeed, driving yourself crazy with the job hunt is not only detrimental to your frame of mind, it can actually hinder your search.

"I firmly believe that looking for a job is *not* a full-time job. I don't think anyone can sustain that kind of pace," says Terry Karp, career counselor and co-founder of the **Bay Area Career Center** (57 Post, Ste. 804, 415-398-4881, bayareacareercenter.com). "If you sit at home in front of the computer all day you're going to burn out really quickly, and you're not going to have the stamina that you need to stay in it for the long haul—which you might need to do."

Career advisor Dr. Jan Cannon agrees. "Don't make yourself a slave to the job search. You need to change your scenery by going to a museum, taking a walk in the woods, spending time with friends in a social setting, even going to the movies. Balance is key." So if you like to snowboard, go snowboarding. If you like to golf, get a foursome together. Better yet, invite a friend to bring along an associate who might be a good contact. It's remarkable how many people find a job, or at least a job connection, by pursuing their natural ambitions.

FIND THE FUN
Socially speaking, the good gigs are found where the fun is. If the job hunt is getting you down, crib these hip tips.

Cafés. Where does the working set get their daily dose of caffeine? Find out, and schedule that half-caff, double-shot, soy latte accordingly.

Dog Parks. Whether in dating or in job hunting, trust man's best friend to break the ice. Dog parks, particularly ones strategically located near business offices, can get you talking "doggie snacks" with the vice president of marketing in no time.

House Parties. A pillar of the social job hunt strategy—get yourself on those invite lists, and go easy on the pesto dip.

Team Sports & Clubs. Time to join the local softball/soccer/volleyball team. Find one affiliated with a company you want to work for, and you're golden. Not athletically inclined? Then the local computer club, perhaps.

Golf. They say a significant portion of business deals get closed on the links, why not close on a job?

Homecoming. Employ your family and friends. They know you better than you think, and they have your best interests in mind. And you'll get a home-cooked meal out of it!

Skiing/Snowboarding. Plenty of quality time on the ski lifts interspersed with periodic adrenaline rushes make for ideal bonding conditions.

Reunions. Visit your alma mater to reconnect with your fellow alums. College, high school, fraternity, sorority—heck, even your Tuesday night poker buddies—bring people back together man. After all, most of them have jobs. You don't! And if a few beers happen to be involved....

Employment by Osmosis

Much like a groupie backstage at a rock concert, you too must be a "hanger-on" to the employed set. As much as we laud the cafés and other weekday hangout spots in the leisurely sense, you might want to curtail those three-hour coffee sessions now (we know, it seems like sacrilege!). When your goal is to find an employer, you need to share a table with someone who's working. Call it employment by osmosis.

Short of hanging out in your best friend's office all day, try timing your meals to catch the working set during morning coffee, lunchtime or happy hour. Find out if any of your friends need a date to a company cocktail party or holiday gathering and volunteer your services. If you can afford it, join a health or social club. Anything to get yourself out of the house and around those with jobs!

Mine Your Friends & Family

Surprisingly, a lot of people shy away from reaching out to friends and family while they're job hunting. Check this impulse in yourself, for this is a time when you could really use their help.

Don't be shy. Ask those closest to you to assist. You'll surely return the favor when the time comes. Get your friends and family working for you and follow up with them diligently. They are your emissaries as well as your support team and can make your search a lot easier. Who better to market your value than the people who know you best?

put on your party hat

Sitting at home watching *Desperate Housewives* is not going to broaden your network or expose you to new career possibilities (although it might expose you to something else). Get out and socialize, be it at a bar in the evening, a book club every Thursday night, or a fundraiser at your local museum. Iron your slacks and get yourself out!

House parties are a job-search gold mine, particularly those thrown by your friends. The guest list itself reflects a subtle screening process: you'll enjoy a built-in trust based on the fact that you're all friends of the host. Talk with people about their jobs and let it be known that you're looking for work yourself.

Don't walk around with your resume, but do ask questions, and be receptive when others offer information. They will probably help if they feel they're able. Remember, people want to work with other people they like. If they like you in a social context, they're more likely to support your working for their company.

You could be surprised to discover how many people they know in high places.

Adrianna, an attorney who was *Limbo-Employed* for six months, asked her friends and family for honest feedback on her strengths and weaknesses. "It got them involved without blatantly asking for their Rolodex," she said, "and it helped them to understand better to whom and to where they could recommend me."

Right Place, Right Time

Several job hunters we spoke with let slip that they strategically plan their morning coffee sessions—geographically, to be near companies they want to work for; and time-wise, when they know employees will be stopping in for their morning jolt. Perhaps you won't have to curtail those coffee sessions after all, although you may have to get up a bit earlier!

WINE, DON'T WHINE

Will Eagle's wage fell from $135 an hour for high-tech consulting to $8 an hour selling wine, but his passion for the grape kept him going. He rapidly earned buying power at **The Wine Club** (*thewineclub.com*), met more people in the industry, and expanded his already impressive knowledge of fine wines. Drank his fair share of them, too! Will eventually landed a job in wine public relations but The Wine Club lured him back with a management and in-house public relations position of their own.

"Sometimes you've just got to look around," Will says. "I was in The Wine Club making a purchase one day, and there was a 'help wanted, no experience necessary' sign on the back of the door. When the clerk asked if there was anything else he could get me, I responded, 'Not unless you want to get me an application.' I was working there within a week, and I considered it a tremendous education. The only bad thing is, now everyone hands me the wine list when we go out!"

Going to business conferences is another great way to get you in and around employers. You'll learn about the industry to boot. While their time may be limited, decision makers often float around the company booth, where you can chat them up. Your attending the conference in itself shows them your interest in the industry.

"I had a client who walked into the booth of a company she wanted to work for and sat there un-til someone would

talk to her," says Deborah Brown-Volkman (surpassyour
dreams.com), career coach and mentor. "She was very polite and
friendly with everyone. And it worked."

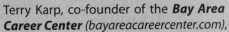

BARK, BUT DON'T BITE

Terry Karp, co-founder of the **Bay Area
Career Center** *(bayareacareercenter.com)*,
had one industrious client who used her cute and playful Jack Russell
Terrier to full advantage. She wrote up a target list of companies in
Silicon Valley, and "coincidentally" walked her dog past each company
building at lunchtime. Her adorable Terrier worked like a magnet. She
was inevitably approached by company employees wanting to play
with her dog, and eventually she networked her way right into a plum
job. So there you go—add "cute dog" to your list of jobhunt resources.
You might even consider renting one for the day!

NETWORKING

Every person and every book you turn to when you're looking for a
job will stress the value of "networking." You might get sick of hearing it. While we don't dispute its value—even "hyper-networking"
has its place—not all networking was created equal.

"Some networking is as useless as can be," says Dick Bolles, author
of perennial jobhunt bible *What Color is Your Parachute.* "Most people
understand networking to mean going to as many cocktail parties
as possible and collecting business cards from everyone they meet,
which is, of course, stupid." Bolles advises people use a more focused
approach instead, and build up their own "grapevine" to take advantage of the large proportion of open positions that never make it to the
job boards. "In seventy-five percent of all job vacancies, the employer
fills it by talking to his or her network," he says. "The resume just isn't
going to find those jobs."

Several of the networking tools that have emerged in recent years
are worth mentioning. **LinkedIn** (linkedin.com) is designed to connect people professionally. The way it works is fairly straightforward:
every person who signs up on the LinkedIn website puts together
a profile as well as a list of others they'd like to invite to join their

GET CREATIVE

According to a survey by **The Creative Group** of Menlo Park, California (*creativegroup.com*), job seekers use some downright wacky tactics to stand out in the crowd during a tight job market.

Advertising and marketing executives were asked the most unusual tactic they had seen. Among the responses: singing telegrams, resumes written on softballs, and lottery tickets included in place of cover letters. One eager interviewee even followed up by sending a pair of socks to the hiring manager. Their lucky interview socks, perhaps? We just hope they were washed!

network. The "network effect" essentially takes over and people connect up with colleagues of colleagues in a variety of professional interests, including job hunting and hiring. **Friendster** (friendster.com) is focused more on the social and less on the professional, but operates to similar effect.

A GUIDE TO LOCAL NETWORKING

Here's the local spin on where to meet and greet people in the best position to help you.

Bars & Restaurants

Many a professional connection has been made over an adult beverage at the corner tavern. Of course, we would *never* endorse drinking just to get drunk (would we?) but alcohol does serve as a so-called social lubricant… so when it's time to find a job, you need to graduate from the coffee house to the bar.

For "Financial D" networking (investment bankers, legal eagles and the like), **The Royal Exchange** (301 Sacramento, 415-956-1710, royalexchange.com) is an institution. Here you'll find suits mixing with khakis, lawyers mixing with bankers, and the occasional miscreant mixing with—the stir stick? The crowd tends to be on the younger side, but the place does see its share of "suit" veterans. Right next door is **Harrington's Bar & Grill** (245 Front, 415-392-7595), a good place for a boozy lunch during the week. You'll see button-up business types coexisting with mechanics and construction workers.

For an old school, cigar-smoking crowd, try lunch or cocktails around the corner at **Tadich Grill** (240 California, 415-391-1849), which also happens to be the oldest restaurant in California, dating back to 1849 (note the phone number). Moving to the Embarcadero, the much newer **Americano Restaurant & Bar** (8 Mission, 415-278-3777) in the Hotel Vitale is definitely a place to connect up—and it's not bad for business networking too!

For a completely different scene, **111 Minna** (111 Minna, 415-974-1719, 111minnagallery.com) hosts a raucous happy hour that attracts tech folks and creative hipsters alike. While some decent new-economy banter flies around there, the techies network best at **Café Mars** (798 Brannan, 415-621-6277), given that several software companies, including Adobe Systems, are just down the street.

Lalita Distinctive Thai (96 McAllister, 415-552-5744) is a drinking hangout for Hastings law students and practicing litigators alike. Criminal trial attorneys, however, frequent the **Absinthe Brasserie and Bar** (398 Hayes, 415-551-1590) near City Hall.

Literary and creative types seek like-minded souls at **Vesuvio** in North Beach (255 Columbus, 415-362-3370), or across the alley at the famed **City Lights Books** (261 Columbus, 415-362-8193). If politics and city government are your thing and you can afford an $8 cocktail, try **Jardinière** (300 Grove, 415-861-5555) where mayoral types and other city big-wigs hang out.

membership groups

You need not belong to the highly exclusive and secretive **Bohemian Club** (415-885-2440) to network through social organizations (although you're welcome to give it a go—good luck!).

Consider other less "gentried" groups, such as the **Commonwealth Club** (see **Chapter 9** under "Working the Room"), which bills itself as the "nation's oldest and largest public affairs forum." Over the years, it has hosted such luminaries as Teddy Roosevelt, Bill Clinton, and Bill Gates. The $110 annual membership could be well worth the investment.

The **World Affairs Council** (also from **Chapter 9**, "Working the Room"), another member organization, hosts over 200 events a year on international politics, business, education, and art. An individual membership will set you back $85.

These orgs might cost ya' but remember—membership does have its privileges.

if *i* won the lottery...

What would you do if you won the lottery? Would you follow Steve Martin's lead in *The Jerk* and get a house with a bathtub shaped like a clam, a solid red billiard room with a giant stuffed camel, and a disco room complete with its own disco dancers? Would you donate money to Mexico to stop the spread of the ugly sport of cat juggling? Okay, so maybe you'd do something a little more productive (not that there's anything wrong with a clam shell bathtub, mind you).

As goofy as it sounds, contemplating an unexpected financial windfall can give you insight into where to steer your career. If money were suddenly not a concern, what *would* you want to do for work?

Of course, money *is* a reality that factors into the final equation. But removing it initially, and then working backward to solve the financial piece of the puzzle, can help free you to follow your passions.

Networking Organizations

On the more formal side, organizations exist for the sole mission of bringing people together for professional purposes. The **Churchill Club** (churchillclub. org) touts itself as Silicon Valley's premier business and technology forum. A $125 annual membership fee entitles you to program discounts, but you don't have to be a member to attend events. The **San Francisco Chamber of Commerce** (235 Montgomery, 12th Floor, 415-392-4520, sfchamber.com) has all kinds of good stuff designed to connect you up, from international mixers to Business After Hours, a monthly networking forum. See their website under "Programs & Events" for the full scoop.

ELIMINATE EXPECTATIONS

As we mentioned at the beginning of the chapter, dealing with expectations poses a real challenge in any employment re-immersion process. If you have a strong idea of what you want to do next, set yourself free to pursue your goals. Let go of your salary expectations. Be ready to sacrifice responsibility or stature in return for greater personal fulfillment. As career coach Joel Garfinkle reminds us, "Finding your dream job brings you fulfillment. It allows you to feel lighter about your life and what you want to give to the world."

Erik Olsen, a producer in New York, left a television job at ABC so he could further pursue his passion to write. The change cut his income significantly. "You only go around in life once, so you better choose carefully what you're going to do with

GREAT MOMENTS IN UNEMPLOYMENT

Richard Bolles, author of **What Color Is Your Parachute**, wrote his best-selling treatise on job hunting after a budget crunch cost him his own job as canon pastor at Grace Cathedral in San Francisco. No sooner did he find another position than did he recognize the same career anxiety among the campus ministers he was now supervising. To help them with job switching and procurement, Bolles self-published 100 copies of his 168-page job hunter's "bible" in 1970 and handed them out for free.

Over 30 years later, *Parachute* sells 15,000 to 20,000 copies each month and, in 1995, made the Library of Congress's Center for the Book's list of "25 Books That Have Shaped Readers' Lives." Bolles pioneered the concept that the best way to find a job is to focus on the skills and talents you want to use and then find an organization that needs them. An ordained Episcopalian priest, Bolles is considered the father of career soul-searching.

your time here," says Erik. "Some people see money as the goal, but it's always seemed to me that unless you actually enjoy what you're doing, unless you actually create something cool, you've wasted your time."

Erik is now working purely as a freelance producer and writer, a tough profession he says, but something he loves to do. "Sadly, lots of jobs that are enjoyable don't pay well. That's just the nature of supply and demand. So often, to do what you want to do, you have to forgo big money and prestige. At times, that can suck—being poor is often a drag—but in the end, you'll be happier."

Victims of the technology crash in 2000 and 2001 had to take several steps backwards before moving forward. Tim was the co-founder of an Internet startup and worked as head of operations for nearly four years. Despite this experience, he had a difficult time transitioning to a different industry.

i *think* i can, i *think* i can

Scot Montagnino had worked for years as a chef in catering companies and restaurant kitchens. He had fine wine training and French service finesse. His dream job? Private chef. But he couldn't muster the pluck to translate his skills into a resume. "Although he actually had all the experience and skills he needed for the job, they weren't 'traditional' in the sense that we could list them from A to Z," his friend Dylan de Thomas told us.

So Dylan helped his nervous friend with a re-write. "I had watched his career progress and I knew he had what it took," Dylan said. "It took hours but I finally convinced him that he was as good as I knew him to be."

After enhancing his resume, and writing a sincere and honest cover letter, Scot landed that dream job. He's now a private chef to a big city bigwig.

"People looked at being at a dot-com as a joke," he told us. "As far as potential employers were concerned, it was as if those years didn't even exist." But once Ted released the memory of his old salary and status, he landed a gig in organic produce, an industry that has always interested him.

STAYING MOTIVATED

Keeping your spirits and motivation up during the job hunt can be extremely challenging, particularly in an employment market where job searches can take six months or more. Maintaining a positive attitude, in addition to keeping you healthy and sane, is critical to presenting your very best self to prospective employers.

Dr. Jan Cannon agrees. "Staying 'up' during a job search of any length is important, but especially when the search is extended. If you find yourself slipping into despair, take a break and do something totally different for a day or so. Clear your head. Renew your spirit. And then get back to work."

She recommends several techniques to keep yourself motivated, including joining other job seekers for support, setting up a formal schedule to achieve a sense of accomplishment and control, and maintaining a healthy body. "As clichéd as it might sound, get enough sleep, eat properly and get daily exercise. Keeping your body in its best condition goes a long way to keeping your mind and spirit in good shape, too."

Your personal support team, whether friends, family or other job hunters, will be paramount. Peter Hannah, a former technology worker who went back to school to become a career counselor, speaks from both personal and professional experience. "I cannot emphasize strongly enough the importance of a support network. And be honest with these people. If you're feeling down, or stuck, or apathetic, you can be sure that they all have at one point too."

LOST TIME ON THE RESUME

Are you worried about gaps in your resume? Don't be overly concerned. **Monster** (monster.com) reminds us that one in every five workers is unemployed at some point each year. Odds are, that crowd includes some of your potential employers. If that doesn't make them sympathetic to your situation—we forbid you to work for them!

But back on this planet, the sad truth is that not everyone who receives your resume will see your time off as the major accomplishment that it is. *We* know that you weren't just on vacation, you were building leadership skills through travel and outdoor adventures, presentation skills through karaoke… but it might take some ingenuity to convey the extent of your dedication to your future employer.

Dick Bolles has long opposed the use of resumes to begin with, and argues that you should always handle the gap issue face-to-face. "I would always explain it in person, and not try to explain it on a resume," he says. "It's important to tell employers what the results were [of taking time off]. Just saying 'I took time off and thought about what I wanted to do with my life' is universally perceived as a pretty lame excuse. They know the person really wanted to see Yosemite and Hong Kong and other things like that. But if the job hunter says 'I took it off for this purpose and here are the results' and they've done the self-inventory before they put themselves out there in the job market, then that is a reason I think everyone understands and would applaud."

Deborah Brown-Volkman agrees that it isn't the time that matters, it's what you did. "You're making a case for yourself to the employer," she says. "It always matters, they will always ask, sometimes just out of curiosity—but again, it depends on what you did. It can feel like an interrogation, but just make your case."

When you look back at how you've spent your time, get creative when filling in those resume gaps. *How* creative is up to you, but the

i'm paying you for what, exactly?

Back in high school, Mary Mangold sought advice on how to make use of her talents. "I always knew I was creative but I never knew how to get there," she said. "I talked to my high-school career counselor about all the things I wanted to do. When I stopped talking, he looked at me—stared at me—and said, 'You have just got the longest eyelashes I've ever seen.'"

Thank goodness, most of today's career counselors are more professional. If you're having a difficult time charting a new career path or finding the right job, consider hiring one. They're not recruiters or "headhunters" but trained professionals who focus on counseling and coaching. Services range from low- or no-cost job placement assistance to in-depth life coaching that requires a significant financial commitment.

Choose your guidance wisely, as there's a range of advice available, not all of it useful.

tongue-in-cheek suggestions on the facing page should help get your hamster wheel spinning.

GETTING SOME COACHING

Dick Bolles puts it bluntly when it comes to career counselors. "Some of them are wonderful, others should be shot at sunrise," he says. "Everything depends on who the counselor is."

"A career counselor will never tell a person anything that they don't know about themselves already," says Terry Karp. "But all the information gets tangled up in the brain, and people don't have perspective on it. A counselor can help the client gain access to that information and relate it to the world of work."

The greater the transition you're attempting to make, the more likely some type of coaching is going to be helpful. "Retooling yourself can be a daunting task," says Dr. Jan Cannon. "You might have the feeling that you're starting over from scratch, but that's not true. You do have experience that will be valuable in your new job—things like knowing how businesses work, getting along with co-workers, work habits, etcetera. They'll give you an advantage over workers with no experience."

Bolles strongly advises people to shop around—especially considering what counseling costs. "If they charge you a huge fee up front, I run for the door and I advise everyone who appreciates my counsel to do the same," he says. Bolles does acknowledge that the right advisor is worth every cent.

Leisure Leo
1392 La Playa
San Francisco, CA 94122
leo@leisureteam.com

Key Qualification: Master of Leisure
Objective: To marry my passions with my work.

PROFESSIONAL EXPERIENCE

Dec 2005   **Marine Biology Researcher**
              [*Translation:* sat on the beach]

Nov 2005   **Public Speaker**
              [*Translation:* karaoke bar junkie]

Oct 2005   **Restaurant Management Intern**
              [*Translation:* sat at the bar]

Sep 2005   **Construction General Contractor**
              [*Translation:* built a rolling bar for Mardi Gras parade]

Aug 2005   **Volunteer Worker**
              [*Translation:* constructed papier mâché palm trees for Burning
              Man theme camp]

Jul 2005   **Change Management Consultant**
              [*Translation:* helped best friend get over breakup]

Jun 2005   **Subject of Monitored Health Study**
              [*Translation:* friends watched me drink too much and then fall
              down]

May 2005   **Employed by the State**
              [*Translation:* collected Unemployment Insurance]

April 2005   **Employed by the State**
              [*Translation:* incarcerated]

Mar 2005   **Freelancer**
              [*Translation:* "freelancer"]

Feb 2005   **Healthcare Consultant, Financial Counselor, Expert
              Time Manager and Personal Assistant to Busy
              Executives**
              [*Translation:* raised a family]

Jan 2005   **Teacher**
              [*Translation:* taught little brother to snowboard]

EDUCATION
Training [surfed the Net]
Continuing Education [surfed the Net]
Executive Education [surfed the Net]
Adult Education [slept around]
Cultural Exchange Student [ordered margaritas in Cabo]

Do yourself a favor before shelling out big bucks for a full-blown analysis from a Ph.D., and consult the **National Career Development Association** (866-FOR-NCDA, ncda.org). Their "Need a Career Counselor?" section recommends ways to choose the right counselor, and their search engine catalogs individual professionals by state. The site also lists a wealth of Internet resources for career planning, most of them free.

FREE HELP

Chances are that you're in cash conservation mode if you're looking for work, making free resources attractive. Your quest for more free help should begin with **The Riley Guide** (rileyguide.com). This stellar, well-organized site is compiled by career consultant Margaret F. Dikel, and provides, to her credit, largely unbiased job search information. Its sections such as "Prepare to Search," "Execute a Campaign," and "Target & Research" can add structure to your task, if nothing else. Oh yeah, they also have links to hundreds of thousands of jobs.

If you're the testing type, a good self-analysis site for career and beyond is **QueenDom.com** (queendom.com), which offers "an interactive avenue for self-exploration with a healthy dose of fun." Works for us! Their career section includes book recommendations, counseling referrals, discussion boards, and more tests than you can shake a number-two pencil at. The site includes both free and pay-for content, but the pay-for material is good and relatively inexpensive.

Locally, free help is available through **Experience Unlimited** (745 Franklin, 415-771-1776, edd.ca.gov/jsrep/jseuloc.htm), funded by the California Employment Development Department. It's right next door to the **San Francisco EDD** (801 Turk, 415 749-7503)—in fact, you might feel like you're *at* the EDD. You become a "member" by volunteering 16 hours per month, and attending two general meetings and one department meeting per month.

Sponsored by the SF Chamber of Commerce, **The Job Forum** (235 Montgomery, 12th Floor, 415.392.4520, thejobforum.org) has a mission to "provide ideas, advice, counsel and encouragement to job seekers (and career changers) in the San Francisco Bay Area." It's not an employment agency, but a forum to support the job search process through weekly evening meetings. The **Private Industry Council of**

San Francisco (745 Franklin, 2nd Floor, 415-923-4003, picsf.org) is a local nonprofit that provides employment and training services. They operate several One Stop Career Link Centers in the City which offer a variety of free services.

Another option to consider is your old alma mater. Leverage their career resources and extensive alumni network for your personal analysis and search. Although they may gear their services toward graduating students, universities are normally more than happy to help cheery—and potentially money-donating—alumni.

SELF-EMPLOYMENT

Even when you're not working, you probably come up with countless ideas on how you would do things better than your old boss. Here's your chance! Time off can spur you to start your own venture and see where it leads.

One outstanding perk is that even though no one else reports to you, you're still your *own* boss. Self-employment is often a one-way street for that very reason. "I don't think I'll ever work for someone else again," said Lisa Turner, who broke free from corporate life to become an independent marketing and public relations consultant. "I finally came to terms with the fact that it never was my style and likely never will be."

Starting Your Own Business

If you want some help to get started on your way to cutting your own paycheck, turn to **Nolo** (800-728-3555, nolo.com), with their great selection of "how to" books for the blossoming entrepreneur, and the **Small Business Administration** (455 Market, 6th Floor, 415-744-6820, sba.gov/ca/sf), which can assist with loan guarantees and advice. To get yourself in a risk-taking, entrepreneurial frame of mind, nothing beats the inspiring guide, *Making a Living Without a Job: Winning Ways For Creating Work That You Love* by Barbara Winter.

If you're just starting out, rest assured that you won't necessarily need a huge bankroll or a loan. You will have to make some sacrifices. "You can start a business on peanuts," says Joe Gilmartin, original owner of the **Black Horse London Pub** (1514 Union, 415-928-2414) and now proprietor of the White Horse Trading Company, a small pub in Seattle. "My beer license was only $450. I sold my motorcycle for $500 and slept on a friend's couch for a year."

THE PANTS HEARD 'ROUND THE WORLD

In what began in part as a mockery of the fashion industry, San Franciscan Chris Lindland has created nothing less than a cultural phenomenon: Cordarounds—the world's first horizontal corduroy pants, skirts and jackets.

Utilizing creative marketing, a savvy PR campaign and a wry sense of humor, Chris, along with business partner Enrique Landa, have quite literally turned apparel on end. The clothes are only available online through their highly entertaining website, and they operate the business out of a ramshackle basement in Fort Mason, San Francisco.

Has Chris created the world's most irreverent clothing company? Perhaps. But he also keenly recognizes the role leisure plays in spawning inspiration. "Time away from work opens your mind to creative thoughts and careers," he says. "While I had the idea for Cordarounds years ago, I never was able to consider it as a business until I had the time off to do so."

Since then, his horizontal corduroy pants have found their way into the pages of the *New York Times*, *Newsweek*, on NPR, and dozens of other media outlets. They ship to all points of the globe, including Greenland. David Letterman even ordered a pair!

Check out the horizontal phenomenon at ***Cordarounds.com.****

*Mention Time Off! The Leisure Guide to San Francisco *or* Leisure Team *when ordering, and Cordarounds will take $10 off any pair of pants (good through December 2007).*

WORK AS LEISURE

Is it worth it to go to work for yourself or to continually search for more meaningful employment? Joe Gilmartin thinks so. "The bottom line is, I have job security," he says. "I can control how long I'm going to have a job."

The professionals echo the sentiment. "Finding work that aligns to you will make work feel more like leisure, because you'll be doing what you do naturally and effortlessly," says career coach Joel Garfinkle. "It brings you fulfillment, and allows you to feel lighter about your life and what you want to give to this world."

How very leisurely!

CHAPTER 12
LEISURE BACK TO WORK

Oh, you hate your job? Why didn't you say so? There's
a support group for that. It's called everybody,
and they meet at the bar.

~ Drew Carey

YOU'RE not sure what it is, but a distant rhythm is beating ever louder in the back of your head: thump-bump…thump-bump…thump-bump. Is it the latest over-hyped, over-marketed single from U2? The pounding of an aboriginal drum from the deserts of Australia? No. The far-off thumping you hear is the alien call of employment, creeping slowly back into your psyche.

Of course, if you've gotten close to the bottom of your freedom funds, the noise could be merely the resounding clank delivered from the hollow depths of a depleted bank account, in which case the thought of a regular paycheck would be a welcome relief.

But while work might relieve one type of anxiety, it could very well cause another—the fear that your days of leisure are gone for good. After all, even the most fulfilling work is still work.

Ultimately, though, we are no more slaves to our work than we allow ourselves to be. The key is to bring a relaxed mindset into the workplace, and to keep it there. Setting proper boundaries creates a more tranquil—and in turn enjoyable—work atmosphere, which keeps the pressures of the job manageable. You *can* foster a culture of leisure at work, and you can band with your employer and colleagues to do so—but it all begins with you.

BE EFFECTIVE, NOT AFFECTED

One of the toughest aspects of shifting from full-time leisure to full-time work is the feeling that you've lost control of your agenda. Being constantly in reaction mode is quite un-leisurely. Lend more order and sanity to your day with the following "work smart" tactics.

Start Work Before Work

There's no need to start your day with an emergency. Yet, in many jobs, if you arrive at the official beginning of office hours, the red light on your voicemail box will already be lit and people may even be lined up at your door. Try getting in fifteen or thirty minutes early, and don't answer the phone or take any appointments before 9am (or whenever your shift starts). Maybe you'll be able to return one of those voicemails with a message saying, "Thanks for calling about that project. It's done."

Even better, start tomorrow's work yesterday—take fifteen minutes at the end of each workday to set six goals for the next day, so that you won't get sidetracked fighting fires when you come in. Prioritize. Stick to your plan. You'll sleep better for it.

GREAT MOMENT IN RE-EMPLOYMENT

The World's Shortest Retirement?

In 1963, Mary Kay Ash was looking forward to retirement after a long career in the male-dominated world of direct sales. Bored one night, she sat down at her kitchen table. She made two lists. The first list contained the positive qualities of the companies she had worked for. The second list was of the qualities that could be improved. Looking at the lists made her realize (with apologies to Mark Twain) that reports of her retirement had been greatly exaggerated. She launched Mary Kay Cosmetics on Friday, September 13, 1963.

Time After Time

While it may not be possible all of the, er, time—leave at a reasonable hour each day. Leaving on time will do a couple of things. First, you'll get a reputation. Your co-workers and colleagues will learn not to task you with projects right before you leave; they'll come to you sooner in the day with their requests, which will make it less likely that you'll be stuck working late on a deadline.

Second, being more disciplined with your time can help you to become better focused. How many times have you frittered away large chunks of the clock because you assumed you would have to work late anyway? Leaving on time forces you to be more efficient. You'll also be more likely to ask others for help when you need it.

Your exact hour of departure will depend on your situation, but there's nothing wrong with leaving a 9-to-5 job at 5pm. There, we said it—and we'll be happy to write your employer a note.

TALK ABOUT RECOMPRESSION

A high-level executive client of career coach Dr. Dory Hollander's increased her productivity—and in turn, her performance—by reducing her work hours in order to spend more time volunteering outside of work.

"She had to discreetly time-compress whole chunks of her job, doing in a day what used to take three," says Dr. Hollander. "She had to position her successes so everyone would see that she was a contributor to corporate success. While she spent more and more time fighting for the community causes she believed in, she became more sought after and valued at work. Paradoxically, by compressing her job in order to free up time for her causes, she became *more* work-focused when she was there, not less."

See if you too can compress your work, and utilize the time saved not to do more work, but to stow away precious free time for yourself. Most people don't realize how much time they actually waste until they take close inventory of how they spend their work day. And if too much compression gets your spine and nerves (not to mention your undies) all in a bunch, remember to use relaxing activities, both physical and otherwise, as a way to decompress.

Stay Late

Leave work on time, but stay late. Come again? It might sound contradictory, but spending the occasional evening at work (assuming that you work standard daytime hours) can allow you to catch up without constant interruption—no colleagues to distract you and no phones ringing off the hook. You can concentrate on more proactive projects that would otherwise be difficult to focus on if your day-to-day job involves putting out a lot of fires.

Daniel, an architect working in Chicago, occasionally stays late on Friday nights to catch up on work, as well as to unwind from a long week. "It's not like I do it all the time," he says, "but sometimes when everyone is rushing out for the weekend, I just like to stay and chill for a while. It relaxes me, and it's one of the few times I can clear my head."

Finishing your work week at your own pace can allow you to enjoy the weekend to its fullest. Unfinished tasks won't nag at your conscience all weekend. You won't be harried and rushing out to a Friday night dinner with friends who are probably just as tired as you are. Wouldn't it be more relaxing to get together on a Saturday night instead?

You can even take some time for yourself: pay bills, answer some personal email, read a magazine. We're not suggesting spending every night at the office, just consider it once in a while. It could be the most peaceful time you'll spend at work, even if it means missing happy hour every now and then.

Beware of False Deadlines

Jane once stayed in her office literally all night finishing a project for some dud who'd put her on a deadline, only to admit later that he'd just wanted her to work on his project first. He went on to boast that he ended up not needing her work at all. Jane then lost even more precious hours plotting her revenge!

Don't be a Jane. If your co-workers are well-intentioned but prone to panic, ask what will happen if the task is not done by tomorrow. Take a moment, light a candle and chant this mantra: "There is nothing, and I mean nothing, that cannot wait until tomorrow." Surely you can work together to set a more reasonable deadline. And if your colleagues really *are* that devious? Consider keeping a copy of Sun Tzu's *Art of War* on hand.

Delegate

If you want something done right, do you really have to do it yourself?

Mastering control over your working hours means regularly asking yourself, "How important is right versus done?" If you're facing a task that only you are genuinely qualified to do, so be it. If you're keeping work to yourself out of expedience, turn the project over to a colleague and act as their coach. Taking those few extra minutes now will save you time in the long run, especially for recurring tasks.

Not incidentally, delegating will help you move up the ranks more quickly by multiplying your productivity and freeing up your time to learn new skills. This concept is nothing new, but it's key to creating a leisurely workday.

anti-deadline mantras

There's nothing that can't wait until tomorrow.

I can help you later, but not right now.

I'm afraid I can't meet that deadline.

There might be someone else who can do this sooner.

Schedule Downtime

Working smart and not long includes scheduling breaks. "Taking breaks allows you to get the perspective to make decisions that support and honor you," says career coach Joel Garfinkle, founder of **Dream Job Coaching** (dreamjobcoaching.com). Psychologist Dr. Joyce Brothers says the same thing: "No matter how much pressure you feel at work, if you could find ways to relax for at least five minutes every hour, you'd be more productive." A well-timed break will keep you from sitting there, stalled, trying to force inspiration on yourself.

Instead of frittering away work hours on procrastination, use that time to do something more satisfying. See a matinée, go home an hour early and garden, or take a class. Jeremy Cantor, an employee at UC Berkeley, has a friend who schedules at least two hours into her Palm Pilot each week for pure downtime. "Now I do it too," Jeremy says. "It's great. I take it as seriously as any other appointment."

You can schedule breaks inside the office as well as out. If you have a desk job, set aside thirty minutes a day to answer personal email or surf the Net. You're going to do it anyway. This way, you'll know

don't let this happen to you!

A business executive in England was spotted on the freeway one night, drifting from lane to lane at 70mph, and driving with his interior light on. Why? Because he was reading a book propped up on his steering wheel—to catch up on work! This stunt got him reported, and then convicted of dangerous driving, for which he temporarily lost his license.

Is any work that important? We don't think so. If you have a choice (and you always do), leave it at the office.

it's coming up. You'll be less distracted thinking about personal tasks or entertainment when you could be getting work done. Whatever you do during a break, plan your day to include plenty of them.

Mix It Up

Can't decide if you're a morning or a night person? You don't have to. If you have enough flexibility to alter your hours during the day, trade off between being an early bird and a latecomer. Varying your schedule will keep things fresh. Vince, a financial services director, does this to relaxing effect; take a page from his day planner.

"You can come in early and leave early—maybe go for a swim, a hike in the foothills, or maybe a relaxing drive," Vince suggests. "Or pick a morning to hang out: read the paper, go for a run, make a breakfast burrito, whatever. Leave late if you need to, but mix up the routine. It gives you something to look forward to, especially if you don't do any travel for work."

Catch a Leisure Nap

What do you miss most about your work-free days? For Andrew Riley, a high-tech worker who recently started a new job after a layoff, that would be naps. "I miss my naps even more than my previously inflated salary," he says.

So why not nap at work? Fewer than one percent of American employers promote it, yet 36 percent of Americans say they do it, according to a recent human resources management study. We endorse each one of these sleepy rebellions. If the stars of ER can hide in the back office of the emergency room and catch some short-term winks, why not the rest of us?

Several government agencies use nap programs for employees who work in high-risk environments. Naps can increase alertness, reduce errors and absenteeism, improve effectiveness and generally keep a smile on your face. "Workplace napping is a natural, no-cost way to increase worker productivity," say Dr. William Anthony and Camille Anthony, the authors of *The Art of Napping at Work*.

A nap can be as simple as a 15-20 minute siesta in your office, or a few minutes of zoning out while appearing to study your email. Naps can be taken while you're "on the phone" too.

Find more tips on how to nap and how to lobby management in favor of napping from **The Napping Company, Inc.** (napping.com). And on the first Monday after we spring forward into daylight-savings time, don't forget to celebrate National Workplace Napping Day!

Care For Your Mental Health

Remember all those personal chores you took care of during the day when you weren't working? There is no reason to give them up when you're back at the job. Translate "doctor's appointment" into "mental health break" and take a few hours off. Savor a late breakfast, catch a baseball day game or relax at the beach if you live near the coast. Go ahead, play hooky now and then.

In fact, take a whole weekday off. Don't go anywhere. Just hang out. Or, if you want to take a day trip—say to a popular weekend spot—you can avoid the crowds. If your company allows for telecommuting, take two weekdays and work remotely yet close by, just as if you were working from home.

Not all of this has to be off the record. Wouldn't your boss allow you a short respite after an exceptionally hard stint of work? You never know until you ask.

Keep your breaks clean in this sense though: don't squander your leisure. If you already take lengthy lunches or fritter away hours at the water cooler,

bosses need naps too

Howard, a mid-level manager, wasn't a big fan of annual reviews, but who is?

He had accomplished a few things that year, so he wrote himself some notes, entered the boss's chambers and began to recite. It got quiet. He looked up and saw his boss's head nodding—further, further—until he was out!

Howard waited quietly for a full fifteen minutes, just about the perfect length for a refreshing snooze. Then his boss woke up. "Anything more?" his boss asked. "Nope," Howard said.

Howard left his "review" and got a raise two weeks later.

If you're a manager who wants to protect your budget, stay sharp. Take naps!

realize that you're just extending the overall amount of time you spend at the workplace. The more you focus on work while you're at work, the more you can get away from it entirely and enjoy the rest of your life.

LEAVE WORK AT WORK

Let Your Brain Work Without You

You can go one better than finishing the day's work on Friday—try planning ahead for the next week, too. It takes only minutes to make a list of things to do first thing Monday. The act of writing a list can plant ideas in your subconscious that will stir around even after you've left the office, and you won't even feel it! This is the magic of the subconscious mind. Come Monday, you'll somehow be full of creative solutions to problems that seemed insurmountable the week before. While you're at it, make a list of your key accomplishments during the week. A little pride never hurts.

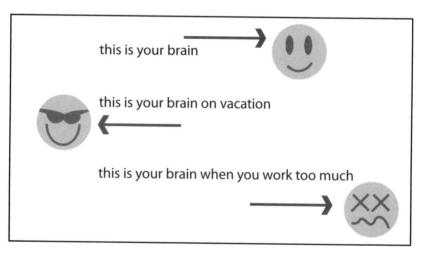

Keep 'Em To Yourself

Speaking of weekends (or whatever your regular days off are), we suggest you keep them to yourself. A normal full-time schedule is not supposed to encompass a full seven-day week. Whenever you're tempted to go into the office on a Saturday or a Sunday or, even worse, you think about taking work home, repeat the anti-deadline mantra: "There is nothing, and I mean nothing, that can't wait until Monday."

Really think about it. How many times have you panicked over some fire at work and realized later that, with a little reflection, you could have come up with a more efficient solution?

If a short-term deadline makes it imperative that you work on a weekend, trade out that weekend day for a weekday off. If your corporate culture doesn't support that, rally your colleagues together and see if you can't change the tide.

Use All Your Vacation Days

Tragically, Americans on average squander a total of 20-30% of their vacation time per year, and about a quarter of them take no vacations at all. Vacation days should be enjoyed, not stockpiled or wasted. If you're fortunate, your manager will feel the same way.

"One owes it to themselves, their family and their company to plan—and take—their vacation," says Bill Coleman, co-founder of BEA Systems, Inc., a large California-based software company. "While I was CEO of BEA, I encouraged my staff to take a two-week or longer break at least every other year, during which their business voicemail and email were turned off. Vacation time for me is where I can get perspective. In fact, my best epiphanies came when I was off for at least two weeks." BEA's use-it-or-lose-it vacation policy backs this up: employees cannot accrue more than 150% of their allotted annual vacation. Once they hit that ceiling, they don't earn more days until they stop and take a break.

Although there are plenty of trips you can't take while fully employed, you can still cover some ground in the typical two weeks off. Whether or not you have a trip planned, spend some weekdays out of the office. Better yet, tell everyone you're taking a trip but then stay

ask for unpaid leave

Many companies will be amenable to granting you extra vacation days—if they're unpaid. One single mother we know has negotiated an extra week's leave into every job offer she's ever had, and she spends it with her kids during their summer vacation.

If you didn't negotiate time off up front, ask for it now. Propose a couple of unpaid weeks off at a time when your department is trimming its budget. What boss could say no to that?

Keep your ears open for sabbatical packages, too. Scott Phillips accepted his company's offer of a twelve-month leave at 20% pay. During his break, he finished writing a novel while living with his wife in her native city of Prague, where 20% of a U.S. salary goes a fair distance.

at home. You'll enjoy completely unscheduled time to yourself, and you'll be able to relax and enjoy your own city for a change. "Commit to your vacation days at the beginning of the year," Coach Garfinkle advises. "Make them as important as you would the birth of a child."

FOSTER A CULTURE OF LEISURE

All these suggestions sound great in theory, but could be hard to implement if you can't get others around you (your boss, maybe?) to buy into the concept. Peace of mind starts with you, to be sure, but to change more than yourself, you'll have to win over others to the cause. Don't be shy about sharing your philosophy with your friends, your co-workers and even your boss. Big changes can happen when people band together. Here are a few ideas to inspire your colleagues to adopt the leisurely 'tude at work.

TOTE YOUR LEISURE GEAR

Relaxation is infectious, so dress for the part. Keep a scrapbook open to the best photo from your last trip. Surround yourself with symbols of leisure and your hobbies. Co-workers are bound to wonder why you always seem so relaxed. At a minimum, it will give pause to those who constantly feel the need to escalate a crisis.

"Scuba didn't make the work go away," says Marlo Sarmiento about his job overseas near the dive-haven of Palau, "but it sure did make me happy." That showed in the underwater photos he displayed in his office. Licensing attorney Karen burned scented candles while she worked. "I got some grief from the salespeople for it," she said, "but it sure kept the room from getting too gamey during those marathon contract negotiations."

Build Your Own "Leisure Team"

Hoard your techniques, and you'll be a leisure team of one. Share your leisure insights! Although company perks like in-house massage therapy and pool tables might be part of a bygone era, creating an atmosphere of camaraderie will always be in vogue. "Workers who care about each other want to support each other," says Coach Garfinkle, "which creates an atmosphere of, 'I want to be here.'"

John Greene, a software support engineer and rock keyboardist, was recruited on his first day of work by his company band, the Low Hanging Fruit. "We played several company parties including a couple of cruises on the Bay," John recalls. "While the management-promised soundproof room never materialized, we do still have a piano and a drum kit in the rec area. LHF got the crowd dancin' and the bodies shakin'."

Socializing with people you like to work with (and can get things done with) will only bring more leisure to your day. Friday afternoon Happy Hours aren't too hard to pull off—rotate sponsorship of them through different departments to foster some friendly competition.

In fact, choose any activity or topic of conversation that takes you away from work for a moment. "I keep a lot of toys in my office," says Jeremy Cantor. "Balls, hacky-sacks, other things to toss around. People play with them when they come in to visit." Needless to say, Jeremy's got a lot of companionship at work.

This kind of grassroots effort is bound to be more effective than any top-down, contrived team building exercise—plus, it's free. What manager could say no to that? On that note, make sure your team includes your boss. If your boss isn't an ally, try to get one who is.

office exercise

You want to keep your blood pumping at work, not raise your blood pressure. Stretch in the doorway. Dance around. Stand up (sit down, fight fight fight!).

Does your company have a gym? Use it in the morning to get your energy up and your endorphins going, and invite others to join you. No gym? Never fear.

"I used to lie on my back and do stretches while talking on the phone," says Dane Larson, an avid surfer. "It helped a lot when my back hurt, and often sparked some good conversation."

Office Yoga by Darrin Zeer seeks to "inspire you to take good care of yourself at the office and throughout the day" with all kinds of tips on how to relax and keep breathing at work. May all its readers reach the promised Office Nirvana!

LINGO BINGO
**and other
reindeer games**

The heyday of office pinball machines, pool tables, and aromatherapy might have passed...

...but that doesn't mean there aren't still games to be played.

If you can't convince your boss to officially endorse games at work, how about a rousing round of Lingo Bingo—a sure way to pass the time in a boring meeting. Players stay tuned for meaningless blather like "stakeholder," "think out of the box," and "step up to the plate." As soon as you hear five in a row—BINGO!!!

Find four pre-printed gamecards at the colorful website, **Working Wounded** (workingwounded.com). See also the **Web Economy Bullshit Generator** (dack.com, click "web" then "web economy bullshit generator"), where users can combine any number of verbs, adjectives, and nouns to create true "bullshit." What's really frightening is how many of the phrases actually sound familiar—like maybe you've hear them in the office before?

Unfortunately for many of us, it's because we probably have—over and over again. Hey... that's bullshit!

Petition Management

You can change your own workstyle and you can speak out individually or in a group, but systemic change has to come from the top. If you're not a decision maker yourself, press your case with those who are. Did you know that MRI scans of fatigued brains look exactly like ones that are sound asleep? Slip that factoid into your next conversation with your boss, then make a request for a leisure-friendly policy like company-wide meeting-free hours.

Find more ammunition in *Work to Live* by Joe Robinson, founder of the Work to Live campaign (worktolive.info).

LEISURE TEAM'S COMPANY HALL OF FAME

Fortune magazine ranks their best every year. So do numerous other publications. But based on what measure—how good the coffee tastes? Many companies' generous benefit plans are designed primarily to keep you working there longer and harder. We say the number one benefit is time, whether in the form of reasonable work hours, ample vacation, or a formal sabbatical policy.

U.S. Companies That Consistently DELIVER THE LEISURE

Patagonia *(Ventura, California; patagonia.com)*
Patagonia epitomizes cool. Offices near the beach and a flex-time work policy allow workers the ability to surf during daytime hours. Paid environmental sabbaticals and on-site yoga keep employees coming back for more.

FedEx *(Memphis, Tennessee; fedex.com)*
Forget about the image of Tom Hanks' character as a workaholic FedEx employee in the 2000 film *Cast Away*. In real life, FedEx employees have plenty of reasons to smile; overwork isn't one of their ills. Free plane rides on its U.S. flights keep workers travel-happy and in 2003, the company spent $17 million on tuition reimbursement—meaning employees are definitely getting "schooled" on FedEx's dime.

American Express *(New York, New York; americanexpress.com)*
In the financial services sector, perks don't get much better than at AMEX. They offer paid six-month overseas rotations and sabbaticals that benefit local communities, and are famous for their generous tuition reimbursement program.

SAS *(Cary, North Carolina; sas.com)*
Talk about leisure: employees get to set their own hours! In addition, on their corporate campus is a self-contained recreation center with a ten-lane swimming pool, volleyball courts, tennis courts (lessons included)—even a putting green.

Google *(Mountain View, California; google.com)*
Sure, it helps that a substantial portion of the company's employees are millionaires, some of them hundreds, even thousands, of times over. That extra spring in everyone's step isn't just because the company cafeteria's blueberry muffins are so good. But Google is a survivor from the dot-com go-go days, and has been providing serious recreation at its world-famous Googleplex even before its bally-hoo'ed IPO, providing bicycles, musical instruments, pool tables, foosball tables, on-site massage and roller hockey (twice a week), among other perks.

[and the winner is...]

Your Own Company, Inc.

Okay, so maybe this is cheating, but we contend that the most leisurely organization (in a fulfillment sense) to work for is your own. Remember—that includes being an independent contractor or consultant, too. The upside? You like your boss (you), you report to yourself, and you set your own hours. The downside? Although you might be doing something you love, entrepreneurs consistently work longer hours than full-time employees, which can significantly impinge on your time off. So be fair to yourself. Make sure you give yourself time off!

LEISURE EVERYWHERE

We'll consider this chapter a success if any of its ammunition helps you make the case for more leisure at work. Speak up and speak often: leisure belongs everywhere, even in the office.

leaving
LEISURE CITY

i♥leisure

CONCLUSION

*To be for one day entirely at leisure
is to be for one day an immortal.*

~Chinese proverb

WE'RE *almost* ready to rest our case for leisure. Have we inspired you to take a break? If you've been plotting your getaway from the confines of your cubicle during your lunch hour, we have succeeded. We've done our job too if your layoff was easier to handle or your sabbatical a little jazzier. If you've discovered something new about yourself or San Francisco, all the better.

We hope you'll practice the *art of leisure* both at work and at play. Plan vacations with your friends and take them. Host leisure parties. Share this book!

Are you still not persuaded to lose a job at least once in your life? To take a step back from your day-to-day work and gain some perspective? Or perhaps just add more leisure into a working world? Then we'll leave you with some words of inspiration from our friends. Instead of overworking, you could be reaping all sorts of benefits from leisure—like they and countless others have.

RETREAT, REFRESH AND REJUVENATE
like Matt Vitamante

"I did so many great things during my break. I went surfing, visited family, went backpacking in Yosemite—I even went to Burning Man for the first time. For me, taking time between jobs opens the mind, strengthens the body, and nourishes the soul."

FIND FOCUS
like Mary Mangold

"Sometimes it will seem like your unemployment is not temporary but it is. I'm glad I got laid off, in the end. If I didn't, I'd still be working on junk mail for E*TRADE."

VOLUNTEER
like Dave Shefferman

"With One Brick we turned volunteering into something social, fun and a great networking opportunity. Not only are we having a huge impact on the community, but we're getting something out of it for ourselves as well. Countless friendships, relationships and careers have flourished as a result."

START A BUSINESS
like Chris Lindland

"Time away from work opens your mind to creative thoughts and careers that wouldn't otherwise come along. While I had the idea for my clothing company [Cordarounds] years ago, I never was able to consider it as a business until I had the time off to do so. Now my horizontal corduroy pants have found their way into the New York Times, Newsweek, NPR, and 50 other publications that don't start with N."

CREATE YOUR OWN JOB
like Eddie Foronda

"It doesn't look like there's a whole lot happening, initially, but you have to tap into what you can do and your interests and just do it. Craigslist charges you nothing to start a business."

SURPRISE YOURSELF
like Maureen Brown
"The biggest surprise was how un-bored I am. I thought I'd go crazy with nothing to do. Now I'm wondering how I'll ever have time to work again."

FALL IN LOVE
like Ann Marsh
"We have an over-employed society in general. People who work too much don't have the time to be good significant others. When that changes, people have time to fall in love, like I did!"

TIE THE KNOT
like Lynn Yuen
"When I first got laid off, I was a wreck. So sad, depressed and the world was one black cloud. After a year-and-a-half of travel, surfing, going to the gym, lounging, seeing friends and a therapist, reading, having time to date—and now with Mr. Right who just went ring shopping last night—well, it all worked out."

IMPROVE YOUR HEALTH
like Alison Madden
"I cut out alcohol and ramped up my hot yoga practice. It led to better health and balance by lessening stress, and helped me drink more water and get more sleep."

TAP INTO YOUR CREATIVITY
like Rachel Karagounis
"You become more creative when you're not working. Your thoughts change, your routines change, you figure out ways to make your money last longer. You find things that cost less. You become a temporary artist until you go back into a schedule."

HAVE SEX
like Joani Blank
"It's free and it's not fattening."

LEARN TO RELAX
like Jamie Alfaro

"Work has been my primary focus my entire adult life. All of my enjoyment was centered around work. I want to learn about what relaxing actually is."

LIVE ON LESS
like Dave Scheff

"If I were a millionaire, I wouldn't be living any better—except maybe I'd have a pool."

TRAVEL, REFLECT AND DISCOVER
like Michael Shapiro

"We can lose our direction when we don't take time off. I've gained clarity and perspective in my life during what some call 'downtime.' But for me it's 'up time'—I feel most alive when traveling; I feel I'm learning, connecting, growing, exploring myself, exploring the world. I don't see any substitute. As wonderful as armchair travel is, there's no replacement for getting out of that comfortable chair and hitting the road."

INSPIRE OTHERS
like Tess Roering

"Last night, I spoke with a really good friend who'd been talking for months and months about starting her own business, but was afraid to take the risk. She said it wasn't until I called her to tell her I quit my job that she was like, 'What am I waiting for?' She quit her corporate job and started her own company, working out of her home. Life's about liking what you do and how you spend your time and who you spend it with. That's what makes it good and that's what makes you successful, in my mind."

SHARE THE LEISURE
like the Leisure Team!

ACKNOWLEDGEMENTS

THANKS to the Leisure Team players! This book would not be here were it not for your help, and it's better thanks to all of your efforts.

Our All-Star "Staff"

★ Moira Bartel, writing, editing, research ★ Jennifer Birch, editing, proofing ★ Sara Irvin, illustration ★ Nalani Jay, proofing ★ Ellen Clair Lamb, first edition editing ★ Sue LaTourrette, proofing ★ Jamie Leap, book design, web design, illustration ★ Christie Miller, layout, coaching ★ Kathryn Otoshi, design ★ Kate Williamson, editing, proofreading, research

Most Valuable Players
Thanks for your valuable expertise, keen insights, and in-depth local knowledge:

Cecile Andrews • Dick Bolles • Alayne Brand • Po Bronson • Neil Brown • Gretchen Burger • Dr. Jan Cannon • Dave Casuto • Ann Crittenden • John de Graaf • Rob DeWaters • J.J. Dillon • Karin Dixon • Hope Dlugozima • Hank "Mister SF" Donat • John Drake • Jason Enea • Joel Garfinkle • Tracy Geraghty • Joe Gilmartin • Tom Haan • Charles "Burrito Master" Hodgkins • Dr. Dory Hollander • Carl Honoré • Deirdre Hussey • Jason Julian • Terry Karp • Chris Lindland • Dana Magenau • Odd Todd • Chris O'Reilly • Erik Rauch • Peter Reich • Joe Robinson • Marcus "Mr. Happy Hour" Ronaldi • Marlo Sarmiento • Conrad Schmidt • Lesley Schwartz • Matt Seliga • Dave Shefferman • Rochelle Teising • Chet Van Duzer • Matt Vitamante • Jeanette Watkins • Ethan Watters • Ted Witt • Lynn Yuen • Steve Yung

The Dedicated Fans
Sue & Peter LaTourrette • significant others for their eternal patience • our loyal friends

The Coaches
Tracy Fortini and the crew at PGW

The Rooting Section
Thanks to everyone we interviewed; to all the survey participants; to our friends and families for their title votes, wicked write-ins and keen feedback. Thanks especially to Bill Ralph and Jeff Stamper at Malloy.

Our "Landlords"
Thanks for the Internet access, eternal patience and tasty java!
• Bazaar Café • The Canvas Gallery • Java Beach Café • Velo Rouge Café

GLOSSARY OF
LEISURE LINGO

WHAT *is* Leisure Lingo, exactly? It's an attempt to remedy the serious lack of on-the-mark definitions for many of the concepts described in this book. Clearly, time off—whether planned, forced or otherwise—is a poorly defined notion in our work-centric culture. Leisure Lingo adds some clarity and fun to those non-working times.

ACCIDENTAL SABBATICAL

(mainstream)	*(Leisure Team)*	*(example)*
A break taken by accident, or not by choice.	A gift of time away from work that, given the right frame of mind, can be a wonderful and fulfilling period in a person's life.	When layoffs were rumored to be coming on Friday, Jerry began plotting his *accidental sabbatical* from the confines of his cubicle. First stop? Southeast Asia...

ART OF LEISURE

(mainstream)	*(Leisure Team)*	*(example)*
None. Leisure is not an art.	The skill, craft or phenomenon of creating a fulfilling life of leisure; making the easy way appear even easier.	Although it took a lot of hard non-work for him to master it, Alex felt he was well-schooled in the *art of leisure* after traveling the world for a year.

ASPIRING RETIRED

(mainstream)	*(Leisure Team)*	*(example)*
None.	Someone who's waiting for their options to vest or has saved up money and when the time is ripe, will jet off the job for good.	The company committee on Functionally Allocated Business Processes was chock-full of *aspiring retireds*.

ASPIRING UNEMPLOYED

(mainstream)	*(Leisure Team)*	*(example)*
None.	Someone who's working way too much, observing their unemployed friends and thinking the grass seems a whole lot greener on the other side.	Mary, an *aspiring unemployed*, spent long afternoons staring out of her downtown office window at the sailboats drifting by on the Bay.

CASUAL EMPLOYMENT

(mainstream)	*(Leisure Team)*	*(example)*
Employment that is not permanent but not necessarily temporary. Exempt from sick leave, holiday leave, parental leave and unfair dismissal provisions.	The best kind!	Because Ken was on good terms with his former employer, he was allowed to maintain his prior health insurance coverage, yet pursue the *casual employment* that he found so much more fulfilling.

COASTER

(mainstream)	*(Leisure Team)*	*(example)*
A round object, preferably composed of semi-porous stone, upon which to set a cold drink to keep it from sweating into the table.	Someone who has enough money to sustain a healthy period of time off but not enough to retire, so is mastering the art of leisure before returning to a paying job.	Karen and Isidro had so many *coaster* friends, they decided to get married in Hawaii. The reception lasted three weeks.

CONSULTING

(mainstream)	*(Leisure Team)*	*(example)*
Offering your expert opinion or advice in exchange for pay.	A loosely conceived term used to describe a multitude of activities including volunteering, networking, traveling, meeting with friends to drink coffee and discuss new business ideas, and meeting with friends to drink beer and pontificate on the lagging economy.	Six months after getting laid off, Tara had accumulated so much *consulting* work that the local brew pub started charging her rent for her barstool.

FLUIDLY EMPLOYED

(mainstream)	*(Leisure Team)*	*(example)*
None.	A nebulous state whereby the distinction between work and non-work is blurred, usually applying to individuals who work for themselves or within the creative arts.	On any given weekday morning in Hollywood, most cafés are packed full of entertainment types. Are they working? Are they taking the day off? It's hard to tell, as most are *fluidly employed*.

FRICTIONAL UNEMPLOYMENT

(mainstream)	*(Leisure Team)*	*(example)*
Short-term joblessness associated with mobility. A person who leaves a job to find something better is considered frictionally unemployed. This type of unemployment also characterizes workers in industries subject to seasonal fluctuations, e.g., construction, agriculture or winter recreation.	Unemployment that causes unnecessary friction within one's family or oneself. Common among Type A personalities and those who don't plan ahead. Can be increased by pressures imposed by others.	Jerry realized how *frictionally unemployed* he was when his father asked him repeatedly at Thanksgiving, "So what *are* you going to do with your life, son?"

JOB CHURN

(mainstream)	*(Leisure Team)*	*(example)*
Jobs are created and destroyed all the time. If more jobs are being created than destroyed, the unemployment rate goes down and we feel good because it looks like our economy is growing. If fewer jobs are being created than destroyed, we head to the unemployment office.	The feeling you get in the pit of your stomach when you think about going back to work. Can be cured with heavy and continuous doses of leisure.	When he thought about how close to the end of his sabbatical he was, Scott got a serious case of *job churn*. Fortunately, bringing leisure back to work with him kept his *job churn* in check.

LAYOFF BLUES

(mainstream)	(Leisure Team)	(example)
None.	When you play them backwards, you get your job back.	Janice used to croon the *layoff blues* but she changed her tune once she started practicing leisure.

LEISURE CONNOISSEUR

(mainstream)	(Leisure Team)	(example)
None.	One who's gained wide experience in the various classes of leisure, including world travel, creative self-employment, music and athletic challenge. Most comfortable on sabbatical, in the company of other ladies or gentlemen of leisure, or spreading the word on the art of leisure.	Sam knew he'd become a true *leisure connoisseur* when he could no longer remember what day of the week it was.

LEISURE PATRON

(mainstream)	(Leisure Team)	(example)
None.	A patron of the art of leisure. Can come in the form of a rich uncle, a government grant or a corporate sponsor.	Sarah was able to extend her on-location study of fine Bavarian beers when her German uncle donated to the cause, becoming her *leisure patron*—and new favorite uncle!

LEISURE SEEKER

(mainstream)	(Leisure Team)	(example)
None.	One who pursues a life of relaxation and personal fulfillment. An enlightened one!	Bill knew he'd become an advanced *leisure seeker* when he chose to take a year off to travel instead of accepting a promotion.

LIMBO-EMPLOYED

(mainstream)	(Leisure Team)	(example)
None.	Not quite working on a career but stymied in the full-time practice of leisure by the need to pay bills. Related terms: underemployed, misemployed.	Tom's on-again, off-again consulting gigs left him stuck in the mire of *limbo-employment*.

McJOB

(mainstream)	(Leisure Team)	(example)
None.	What a writer, actor, or musician has to finance a creative career.	Until Caleb's band gets a record deal, he's keeping his *McJob* at Starbucks.

MISEMPLOYMENT

(mainstream)	(Leisure Team)	(example)
Forced career change or temporary work taken just to pay the bills.	Settling for work that is unsatisfying and unfulfilling.	An artist at heart, Sheara was suffering from a horrible bout of *misemployment*— working long hours at a law firm with no time to spend the beaucoup bucks she was making.

NON-EMPLOYED

(mainstream)	(Leisure Team)	(example)
A non-factor or non-contributor to the gross national product.	Unemployed and loving it!	Jason began competing in triathlons and got in the best shape of his life while *non-employed*.

ORGANIZATIONALLY AVERSE

(mainstream)	(Leisure Team)	(example)
Maladjusted; malfunctioning within group structure; not a "team player."	Prone to independent thought and an entrepreneurial spirit. A person whose creativity feels stifled in a highly structured environment.	Ernie was a serious job hopper, but discovered he was just *organizationally averse*. Now he works for himself as a consultant.

OVERWORK OGRE

(mainstream)	*(Leisure Team)*	*(example)*
None.	The boss who won't let you take a vacation even after a long stint of long hours, or claims offense anytime real life interferes with your job.	Rachel found herself offering her *overwork ogre* an apology that her grandmother's sudden illness had not come at a more opportune time.

POST-SABBATICAL BLUES

(mainstream)	*(Leisure Team)*	*(example)*
None.	A type of dirge, commonly performed on a 12-string guitar and most emotionally played when dealing with the harsh reality of going back to full-time work.	Working with headphones on at his new desk job, Carter suddenly realized he'd been singing the *post-sabbatical blues* out loud while his co-workers listened in.

PRE-RE-EMPLOYED

(mainstream)	*(Leisure Team)*	*(example)*
None.	Not looking for a job right now but expecting to do so in the near future.	Rob frequented Baker Beach more and more as he entered his *pre-re-employment* stage, bagging rays and thinking deep thoughts about leisure.

PRESENTEEISM

(mainstream)	*(Leisure Team)*	*(example)*
A word used by human resources professionals to describe employees who are putting in a lot of hours but not being very productive.	A big bummer, not to mention wasteful, as extra hours of unproductive face time at work could be better spent increasing leisure time.	*Presenteeism* was rampant in Jackie's office, with co-workers blabbing all day on the phone but then staying late as a false display of dedication. She preferred to go in, get her work done, and get out of there.

PROTESTANT LEISURE ETHIC

(mainstream)	(Leisure Team)	(example)
A moral mandate to avoid idleness and convert all downtime into so-called productive leisure, such as a hobby.	A well-intentioned but incomplete ethic that reflects an American obsession with output and success.	The *Protestant Leisure Ethic* drove Amy to squander her European sabbatical marching diligently through museum after museum taking copious notes.

PROTESTANT WORK ETHIC

(mainstream)	(Leisure Team)	(example)
A term coined by Max Weber to describe the productivity-oriented culture giving rise to capitalism in Western Europe and later the United States. The ethic that spawned what Weber called the "spirit of capitalism."	Does not compute.	Leisure connoisseur Carey stared blankly from the bow of the boat as her friend, Blythe, recited the history of the *Protestant Work Ethic.* "Huh?"

PURITAN SOCIAL ETHIC

(mainstream)	(Leisure Team)	(example)
An ethic prevalent in the Massachusetts Bay Colony, which dictated that wasting time was evil. Its more benign tenets include living simply and being thrifty.	Say again?	Not applicable. Incorrect when used in writing or speaking, according to the grammar of Leisure Lingo.

REAL JOB

(mainstream)	(Leisure Team)	(example)
A job with regular, daytime hours where you work for someone else and no one questions your job title.	A job you can get fired from.	Rex was tired of worrying about layoffs so he quit his *real job* and went into business for himself.

RE-EMPLOYED

(mainstream)	(Leisure Team)	(example)
Would you believe it? This word is not in the dictionary yet. We'll take a leap of faith that it would be defined as "employed again."	Entering back into the workforce, and dealing with the "culture" shock that comes with it. Not unlike a spacecraft re-entering the earth's atmosphere and heating up from the friction and stress.	Jeri was having trouble getting to household chores like laundry now that she was *re-employed*, so she stocked up on a lot of new underwear and socks.

RETIRED

(mainstream)	(Leisure Team)	(example)
Withdrawn from one's occupation, business, or office; having finished one's active working life.	Happy! Leisurely! Free! Hallelujah!	Jamie threw a hearty fiesta in celebration of his newly *retired* status after his technology startup went public. Unfortunately, he quickly had to become *re-employed* six months later when his stock dove underwater.

SABBATICAL

(mainstream)	(Leisure Team)	(example)
A leave usually taken every seventh year. In Jewish antiquity, it refers to the sabbatical year in which the Israelites were commanded to suffer their fields and vineyards to rest or lie without tillage.	A godsend!	Sharon awarded herself a masters degree in Leisure after her long-awaited *sabbatical* studying at a culinary school in Tuscany—and threw some stellar dinner parties for her friends, too.

SELF-EMPLOYED

(mainstream)	(Leisure Team)	(example)
Earning a livelihood directly from one's own trade rather than as an employee of another.	Fulfilled! Self-actualized! Free! (But possibly working too much.)	Darryl was *self-employed* as a landscape architect, working hard but with lots of flexibility.

SELF-UNEMPLOYED

(mainstream)	(Leisure Team)	(example)
None.	Refers primarily to someone who has started a business but is not making any money yet.	So Neil, howz work these days? Oh, well I don't do it any more, I am *self-unemployed*. Neil, did you get laid off? No, I made a choice, I am *self-unemployed*. How are you paying the bills without a job? Well, *self-unemployment* brings a whole new perspective to bills.

SIT

(mainstream)	(Leisure Team)	(example)
To rest with the torso vertical and the body supported on the buttocks.	A verb describing the placid state of someone who's "between jobs." A primary pastime of a leisure connoisseur.	LC: "Yo, whassup?" Slave: "I'm workin'. You?" LC: "I *sit*." Slave: "True."

SLAVE

(mainstream)	(Leisure Team)	(example)
Unpaid and involuntary worker. One who works extremely hard. One bound in servitude as the property of a person or household.	Paid yet reluctant worker. Someone who works for The Man. In Leisure Lingo, to "slave" is to work extremely hard at a job that you don't like.	Alyssa tried to convince herself that her new software job would look good on her resume but deep down, she knew she was just a *slave*.

THE GRIND

(mainstream)	(Leisure Team)	(example)
A crunching or pulverizing action, often used in reference to the fineness of coffee grounds, or to the clenching and gnashing of one's teeth.	The endless churn of the industrial machine, which sucks in and consumes all that crosses its path, including well-intentioned but unsuspecting workers.	Sophia couldn't take one more day of *The Grind*, so she summarily quit her job and took the summer off to practice yoga and learn how to play the guitar.

THE MAN

(mainstream)	*(Leisure Team)*	*(example)*
The "it" person, the master. To be "The Man" is to be a person who's hip, happenin' and in charge.	The Orwellian presence of the powers that be in a structured employment environment, which inhibits its workers' freedoms in order to achieve its objectives. To be working for "The Man" is to be restricted to doing only what someone else wants you to do. See *Slave*.	Alejandro realized that unless he took a chance and started his own graphic design business, he'd probably be working for *The Man* the rest of his life.

UMU

(mainstream)	*(Leisure Team)*	*(example)*
Misspelling of the word for the large, flightless Australian bird related to and resembling the ostrich.	Urban, middle-aged and unemployed.	Harrison was pleasantly surprised to meet so many other *UMUs* in the brownstone where he lived, so he formed a Thursday night club where they would all go out together.

UNDER-EMPLOYED

(mainstream)	*(Leisure Team)*	*(example)*
Someone who wants to work but has stopped looking, or is employed part-time but wants full-time work.	A term that reflects the misconception that everyone should work full-time; a malaprop brought on by peer pressure or financial constraints.	Michael thought he was grossly *underemployed* until he learned to stop overspending; then he realized that his salary paid more than enough to finance his leisure, and then some.

UNEMPLOYED

(mainstream)	*(Leisure Team)*	*(example)*
Out of work, especially involuntarily. Jobless. Not being used. Idle.	Blissful! At ease! Emancipated! (But maybe a little worried about money.)	Leo was *unemployed*. Leo was happy.

UNEMPLOYED HONEYMOON

(mainstream)	(Leisure Team)	(example)
None.	The euphoric period immediately after leaving a job when the world is new again, every sight and sound speaks to you and the leisure possibilities are boundless.	Liam and Marissa left their jobs at the same time and shared substantial bliss during their *unemployed honeymoon*. Unfortunately, once the honeymoon ended, so did their relationship.

LEISURE ODYSSEY

(mainstream)	(Leisure Team)	(example)
None.	The quest one embarks on after leaving full-time work, whether by choice or circumstance. A journey to the promised land.	Trevor took off from work for several "mental health" days so he could plot his upcoming *leisure odyssey*.

WASTED LEISURE TIME SYNDROME

(mainstream)	(Leisure Team)	(example)
A particular kind of work spillover in which exhausted and drained workers can do little more with leisure time than engage in undemanding, unfulfilling and empty activities, as coined in 1973 by the late Swedish Professor Bertil Gardell.	*Wasted* leisure time?!	Join Leisure Team to help eradicate *wasted leisure time syndrome* from every city and town on the planet!

WORK INHIBITIONS

(mainstream)	(Leisure Team)	(example)
Social norms, specific to formal working environments, that keep workers from doing anything unconventional.	Career planning blinders, usually in the form of the ill-conceived pursuit of salary or status.	Once Jenny shook her *work inhibitions*, she more easily mustered the courage to leave her finance job and follow her dream of becoming an interior designer.

THE LEISURE LIBRARY
SELECTED SOURCES & FURTHER READING

21st Century Leisure: Current Issues by John R. Kelly and Valeria Freysinger (Allyn and Bacon, 2000).

ABC of Getting the MBA Admissions Edge by Matt Symonds and Alan Mendonca (The MBA Site Ltd., 2001).

The Art of Napping by William Anthony (Larson Publications, 1998).

The Art of Napping at Work by Camille and William Anthony (Larson Publications, 1999).

The Art of War by Sun Tzu (Clearbridge Publishing, 1999).

A Sense of Place: Great Travel Writers Talk About Their Craft, Lives, and Inspiration by Michael Shapiro (Travelers' Tales, 2004).

The Back Door Guide to Short-Term Job Adventures: Internships, Extraordinary Experiences, Seasonal Jobs, Volunteering, Work Abroad (4th Edition) by Michael Landes (Ten Speed Press, 2005).

Bargain Hunting in the Bay Area (13th edition) by Sally Socolich (Chronicle Books, 2000).

The Bartender's Bible: 1001 Mixed Drinks and Everything You Need to Know to Set Up Your Bar by Gary Regan (HarperTorch, 1993).

Beating the Success Trap: Negotiating for the Life You Really Want and the Rewards You Deserve by Ed Brodow (HarperCollins, 2003).

Bed & Breakfasts and Country Inns (16th Edition) by Deborah Edwards Sakach (American Historic Inns, 2004).

Blindsided: Financial Advice for the Suddenly Unemployed by Edie Milligan (Alpha Books, 2001).

¡Burritos! Hot on the Trail of the Little Burro by David Thomsen and Derek Wilson (Gibbs Smith Publishers, 1998).

The Cafés of San Francisco (3rd edition) by S. Green, R. Green, and A.K. Crump (TCB-Café Publishing, 2006)

California Camping: The Complete Guide to More Than 1,500 Tent and RV Campgrounds (14th edition) by Tom Stienstra (Foghorn Press, 2005).

California Hiking: The Complete Guide to More Than 1,000 of the Best Hikes (7th edition) by Tom Stienstra & Ann Marie Brown (Foghorn Press, 2005).

The Complete Idiot's Guide to World Religions (3rd Edition) by Brandon Toropov and Luke Buckles (Alpha, 2004).

The Complete Medical School Preparation and Admissions Guide (3rd Edition) by Andrew Goliszek (Healthnet Press, 2000).

Consumer Reports Travel Well for Less, ed. Consumer Reports (Consumer Reports, 2003).

Critical Mass: Bicycling's Defiant Celebration, ed. Chris Carlsson (AK Press, 2002).

Downshifting: How to Work Less and Enjoy Life More by John D. Drake (Berrett-Koehler Publishers, 2001).

Educational Travel on a Shoestring: Frugal Family Fun and Learning Away from Home by Judith Waite Allee and Melissa L. Morgan (Shaw, 2002).

Everything a Working Mother Needs to Know About Pregnancy Rights, Maternity Leave and Making Her Career Work for Her by Anne C. Weisberg and Carol A. Buckler (Main Street Books, 1994).

Find a Job: 7 Steps to Success by Dr. Jan Cannon (Cannon Career Development, 2004).

Finding Funding: The Comprehensive Guide to Grant Writing by Daniel M. Barber (Daniel M. Barber, 2002).

F'd Companies: Spectacular Dot-Com Flameouts by Philip Kaplan (Simon & Schuster, 2002).

The Fun Seeker's North America: The Ultimate Travel Guide to the Most Fun Events and Destinations (2nd Edition) by Alan Davis (Greenline Publications, 2003).

Go Away: Just for the Health of It by Mel Borins, M.D. (Wholistic Press, 2000).

Histories of Leisure: Leisure, Consumption & Culture, ed. Rudy Koshar (Berg Publishers, 2002).

Hobbies: Leisure and the Culture of Work in America by Steven M. Gelber (Columbia University Press, 1999).

How to Live Your Dream of Volunteering Overseas by Joseph Collins, Stefano DeZerega, and Zahara Heckscher (Penguin Books, 2002).

How to Retire Happy, Wild, and Free by Ernie J. Zelinski (Ten Speed Press, 2004).

I Could Do Anything If I Only Knew What It Was: How to Discover What You Really Want and How to Get It by Barbara Sher (Dell, 1995).

I'll Grant You That: A Step-by-Step Guide to Finding Funds, Designing Winning Projects, and Writing Powerful Grant Proposals by Jim Burke and Carol Ann Prater (Heinemann, 2000).

In Praise of Idleness: And Other Essays by Bertrand Russell (Routledge, 2004).

In Praise of Slowness: How a Worldwide Movement is Challenging the Cult of Speed by Carl Honoré (HarperSanFrancisco, 2004).

Internet Travel Planner: How to Plan Trips and Save Money Online (2nd Edition) by Michael Shapiro (Globe Pequot, 2002).

The Joy of Not Working: A Book for the Retired, Unemployed, and Overworked (21st Century Edition) by Ernie J. Zelinski (Ten Speed Press, 2003).

Kellogg's Six-Hour Day by Benjamin Kline Hunnicutt (Temple University Press, 1996).

Law School Admissions Adviser (2000 Edition) by Ruth Lammert-Reeves (Kaplan, 1999).

The Lazy Person's Guide to Happiness: Shortcuts to a Happy and Fulfilling Life by Ernie J. Zelinski (Thomas More Publishing, 2001).

The Lazy Woman's Guide to Just About Everything by Judie O'Neill and Bridget Fonger (Elephant Eye Press, 2001).

Life After Baby: From Professional Woman to Beginner Parent by Wynn McClenahan Burkett (Wildcat Canyon Press, 2000).

Life or Debt: A One-Week Plan for a Lifetime of Financial Freedom by Stacy Johnson (Ballantine Books, 2001).

Living Well On Practically Nothing by Edward Romney (Paladin Press, 2001).

Lonely Planet China (9th Edition) ed. Damian Harper, et al. (Lonely Planet Publications, 2005).

Lonely Planet Eastern Europe (8th Edition) by Tom Masters, Lisa Dunford, and Mark Elliott (Lonely Planet Publications, 2005).

Lonely Planet San Francisco (5th Edition), by Tom Downs (Lonely Planet, 2006).

Lonely Planet Southeast Asia on a Shoestring (13th Edition) by Kristin Kimball, China Williams, Marie Cambon, and Mat Oakley (Lonely Planet Publications, 2006).

Lonely Planet Travel With Children (4th Edition) by Cathy Lanigan (Lonely Planet Publications, 2002).

Making a Living Without a Job: Winning Ways for Creating Work That You Love by Barbara Winter (Bantam, 1993).

Moon Handbooks South Pacific (8th Edition) by David Stanley (Avalon Travel Publishing, 2004).

Money Troubles: Legal Strategies to Cope With Your Debts (9th Edition) by Robin Leonard (Nolo, 2003).

Mountain Bike! Northern California by Linda Austin (Menasha Ridge Press, 2000).

The Odd Todd Handbook: Hard Times, Soft Couch by Todd Rosenberg (Warner Books, 2003).

Office Yoga: Simple Stretches for Busy People by Darrin Zeer (Chronicle Books, 2000).

The Overworked American: The Unexpected Decline of Leisure by Juliet B. Schor (Basic Books, 1992).

Pay Nothing to Travel Anywhere You Like by Eric W. Gershman (Great Pines Publishing, 1999).

The Price of Motherhood: Why the Most Important Job in the World is Still the Least Valued (2nd Edition) by Ann Crittenden (Owl Books, 2002).

Rick Steves' Europe Through the Back Door 2006 by Rick Steves (Avalon Travel Publishing, 2005).

Road Trip USA: Cross-Country Adventures on America's Two-Lane Highways (4th edition) by Jamie Jensen (Avalon Travel Publishing, 2006).

Rough Guide to Europe 2006 by Rough Guides (Rough Guides, 2005).

San Francisco Bike Map & Walking Guide (Rufus Graphics, 2001).

San Francisco Bizarro, by Jack Boulware (St. Martin's Press, 2000).

San Francisco Secrets, by John Snyder (Chronicle Books, 1999).

Scenarios for Success: Directing Your Own Career by Rochelle Teising and Catherine Joseph (Rudi Publishing, 1998).

Secret San Francisco, by David Armstrong (ECW Press, 2001).

Six Months Off: How to Plan, Negotiate, and Take the Break You Need Without Burning Bridges or Going Broke by Hope Dlugozima, James Scott, and David Sharp (Henry Holt, 1996).

Small Business Taxes Made Easy: How to Increase Your Deductions, Reduce What You Owe, and Boost Your Profits by Eva Rosenberg (McGraw-Hill, 2004).

Stairway Walks in San Francisco (6th edition) by Adah Bakalinksy (Wilderness Press, 2006).

The Story of Leisure: Context, Concepts, and Current Controversy by Jay S. Shivers and Lee J. deLisle (Human Kinetics Publishers, 1997).

Take Back Your Time: Fighting Overwork and Time Poverty in America, ed. John de Graaf (Berrett-Koehler, 2003).

The Theory of the Leisure Class by Thorstein Veblen (Dover Publications, 1994, originally published by Macmillan, 1899).

Time Off From Work: Using Sabbaticals to Enhance Your Life While Keeping Your Career on Track by Lisa Angowski Rogak (John Wiley & Sons, 1994).

Time Out San Francisco (4th edition) by Penguin Books (Penguin USA, 2002).

Vagabonding: An Uncommon Guide to the Art of Long-Term World Travel by Rolf Potts (Villard, 2002).

What Color Is Your Parachute? A Practical Manual for Job-Hunters and Career-Changers (2006 Edition) by Richard Nelson Bolles (Ten Speed Press, 2005).

Work to Live by Joe Robinson (Perigree, 2003).

Work Your Way Around the World (12th Edition) by Susan Griffith (Vacation Work Publications, 2005).

Your Rights in the Workplace by Barbara Kate Repa (Nolo, 2002).

iNDEX

JOIN THE LEISURE TEAM!

GREAT MOMENTS iN UNEMPLOYMENT

12
LEISURE TEAM FOUNDED!

Leisure Team Productions produces books, events and other media to promote the art of leisure.

Leisure Team came to life in 2002, founded by two unemployed former classmates over several rounds of cask-conditioned ale at the Black Horse London Pub (coincidentally, the site of their original corporate headquarters). Tired of misguided perceptions of unemployment and the national obsession with work, Leisure Team decided to join hands with other organizations and individuals who have found more balance in life, to feature them in a deservedly flattering light, and to throw some raucous fiestas in the process.

Time Off! The Leisure Guide to San Francisco is now in its second edition, and is the original title in the *Time Off!* book series.

Do you want to join the Leisure Team? You can! All it takes is an email address. Sign up now at *leisureteam.com*. To give feedback or to talk about working together, contact us at:

Leisure Team Productions
1392 La Playa
San Francisco, California 94122
info@leisureteam.com

ABOUT THE AUTHORS

The founders of leisure itself? Well, not quite. Kristine Enea and Dean LaTourrette attended K-12 together and have lived in San Francisco since finishing college—Dean in points West and Kristine in points East. They rode the dot-com wave (both up and down) and have been successfully non-employed since 2001, pursuing creative interests and attempting to perfect the leisure lifestyle. Leisure Team Productions and the *Time Off!* book series were born during this time.

Kristine Enea

Kristine used to negotiate deals for a large software company but she saw the light and decided to take off and travel. Her subsequent trek to Panama City, Panama, and back—by car—led to the expansion of her family in the amount of one dog and several cats. She is a film-fest junkie who has been known to deplete her bank account to make it to Telluride around Labor Day. In addition to co-authoring the *Time Off!* books, Kristine also works as a business and legal consultant for technology companies, allowing her to maintain the flexibility necessary for spontaneous leisure.

Dean LaTourrette

Dean has worked in marketing on and off for the past 15 years—"on" during periods of full-time employment with a variety of companies, and "off" during extended hiatuses to travel, surf and write. He has written for numerous publications, including *Men's Journal*, *San Francisco Magazine*, and *The Surfer's Journal*. Dean swears that the idea for this book came to him while he was sneaking a nap at work, which only reinforced his desire to quit his job and write it. In addition to creating and co-authoring the *Time Off!* series, Dean directs all publishing efforts for Leisure Team Productions.

ORDERING INFORMATION

Books by Leisure Team Productions:

* TIME OFF! THE LEISURE GUIDE TO SAN FRANCISCO
* TIME OFF! THE UPSIDE TO DOWNTIME

Look for Leisure Team books at your leading bookseller, or to order directly online visit *leisureteam.com.*

For distributor inquiries or bulk orders, please email us at: *orders@leisureteam.com.*

leisure team productions

share the leisure!